McGraw-Hill | **Reading**

Wonders

WITHDRAWN

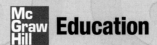

McGraw-Hill **Education**

Bothell, WA • Chicago, IL • Columbus, OH • New York, NY

 TextEvaluator

ETS and the ETS logo are registered trademarks of Educational Testing Service (ETS).
TextEvaluator is a trademark of Educational Testing Service.

Cover and Title Pages: **Nathan Love**

www.mheonline.com/readingwonders

C

The *McGraw·Hill* Companies

 Education

Send all inquiries to:
McGraw-Hill Education
Two Penn Plaza
New York, New York 10121

Printed in China.

7 8 9 DSS 17 16 15 14

McGraw-Hill Reading Wonders

CCSS Reading/Language Arts Program

Program Authors

Dr. Diane August
Managing Director,
American Institutes
for Research
Washington, D.C.

Dr. Donald Bear
Iowa State University
Ames, Iowa

Dr. Janice A. Dole
University of Utah
Salt Lake City, Utah

Dr. Jana Echevarria
California State University, Long Beach
Long Beach, California

Dr. Douglas Fisher
San Diego State University
San Diego, California

Dr. David J. Francis
University of Houston
Houston, Texas

Dr. Vicki Gibson
Educational Consultant
Gibson Hasbrouck and Associates
Wellesley, Massachusetts

Dr. Jan Hasbrouck
Educational Consultant
and Researcher
J.H. Consulting
Vancouver, Washington
Gibson Hasbrouck and Associates
Wellesley, Massachusetts

Margaret Kilgo
Educational Consultant
Kilgo Consulting, Inc.
Austin, Texas

Dr. Jay McTighe
Educational Consultant
Jay McTighe and Associates
Columbia, Maryland

Dr. Scott G. Paris
Vice President, Research
Educational Testing Service
Princeton, New Jersey

Dr. Timothy Shanahan
University of Illinois at Chicago
Chicago, Illinois

Dr. Josefina V. Tinajero
University of Texas at El Paso
El Paso, Texas

 Education

Bothell, WA • Chicago, IL • Columbus, OH • New York, NY

PROGRAM AUTHORS

Dr. Diane August

American Institutes for Research, Washington, D.C.

Managing Director focused on literacy and science for ELLs for the Education, Human Development and the Workforce Division

Dr. Donald R. Bear

Iowa State University

Professor, Iowa State University

Author of *Words Their Way, Words Their Way with English Learners, Vocabulary Their Way*, and *Words Their Way with Struggling Readers, 4–12*

Dr. Janice A. Dole

University of Utah

Professor, University of Utah

Director, Utah Center for Reading and Literacy

Content Facilitator, National Assessment of Educational Progress (NAEP)

CCSS Consultant to Literacy Coaches, Salt Lake City School District, Utah

Dr. Jana Echevarria

California State University, Long Beach

Professor Emerita of Education, California State University

Author of *Making Content Comprehensible for English Learners: The SIOP Model*

Dr. Douglas Fisher

San Diego State University

Co-Director, Center for the Advancement of Reading, California State University

Author of *Language Arts Workshop: Purposeful Reading and Writing Instruction* and *Reading for Information in Elementary School*

Dr. David J. Francis

University of Houston

Director of the Center for Research on Educational Achievement and Teaching of English Language Learners (CREATE)

Dr. Vicki Gibson

Educational Consultant Gibson Hasbrouck and Associates

Author of *Differentiated Instruction: Grouping for Success, Differentiated Instruction: Guidelines for Implementation*, and *Managing Behaviors to Support Differentiated Instruction*

Dr. Jan Hasbrouck

J.H. Consulting Gibson Hasbrouck and Associates

Developed Oral Reading Fluency Norms for Grades 1–8

Author of *The Reading Coach: A How-to Manual for Success* and *Educators as Physicians: Using RTI Assessments for Effective Decision-Making*

Margaret Kilgo

Educational Consultant Kilgo Consulting, Inc., Austin, TX

Developed Data-Driven Decisions process for evaluating student performance by standard

Member of Common Core State Standards Anchor Standards Committee for Reading and Writing

Dr. Scott G. Paris

Educational Testing Service,
Vice President, Research

Professor, Nanyang Technological
University, Singapore, 2008–2011

Professor of Education and Psychology,
University of Michigan, 1978–2008

Dr. Timothy Shanahan

University of Illinois at Chicago

Distinguished Professor, Urban Education

Director, UIC Center for Literacy

Chair, Department of Curriculum &
Instruction

Member, English Language Arts Work
Team and Writer of the Common Core
State Standards

President, International Reading
Association, 2006

Dr. Josefina V. Tinajero

University of Texas at El Paso

Dean of College of Education

President of TABE

Board of Directors for the American
Association of Colleges for Teacher
Education (AACTE)

Governing Board of the National Network
for Educational Renewal (NNER)

Consulting Authors

Kathy R. Bumgardner

National Literacy Consultant

Strategies Unlimited, Inc.
Gastonia, NC

Jay McTighe

Jay McTighe and Associates

Author of *The Understanding by Design
Guide to Creating High Quality Units* with
G. Wiggins; *Schooling by Design: Mission,
Action, Achievement* with G. Wiggins;
and *Differentiated Instruction and
Understanding By Design* with C. Tomlinson

Dr. Doris Walker-Dalhouse

Marquette University

Associate Professor, Department
of Educational Policy & Leadership

Author of articles on multicultural
literature, struggling readers, and
reading instruction in urban schools

Dinah Zike

Educational Consultant

Dinah-Might Activities, Inc.
San Antonio, TX

FOLDABLES

Program Reviewers

TEACHING WITH

INTRODUCE

Weekly Concept
Grade Appropriate
Topics, including Science
and Social Studies

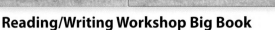

• Videos
• Photographs

Reading/Writing Workshop Big Book

TEACH AND APPLY

**Listening
Comprehension**
Complex Text

**Shared Reading
Minilessons**

Comprehension
Skills and Strategies,
Genre, Phonics,
High-Frequency
Words, Writing,
Grammar

Interactive Read-Aloud Cards

• Visual Glossary
• eBooks
• Interactive Texts
• Listening Library
• English/Spanish
  Summaries

**Literature
Big Books**

Can I pat it?   I like to pat it.

**Reading/Writing Workshop
Big Book and Little Book**

Master the Common Core State Standards!

DIFFERENTIATE

Leveled Readers
Small Group Instruction
with Differentiated Texts

- eBooks
- Interactive Texts
- Level Reader Search
- Listening Library
- Interactive Activities

Leveled Readers

INTEGRATE

Research and Inquiry
Research Projects

Text Connections
Reading Across Texts

Talk About Reading
Analytical Discussion

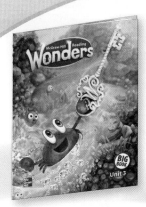

- Online Research
- Interactive Group
  Projects

Collection of Texts

ASSESS

Unit Assessment

Benchmark Assessment

- Online Assessment
- Test Generator
- Reports

**Unit
Assessment**

**Benchmark
Assessment**

PROGRAM COMPONENTS

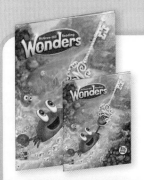

Big Book and Little Book of Reading/Writing Workshop

Literature Big Books

Interactive Read-Aloud Cards

Teacher Editions

Teaching Posters

Puppet

Leveled Readers

Your Turn Practice Book

Visual Vocabulary Cards

Leveled Workstation Activity Cards

CCSS Assessing the Common Core State Standards

Retelling Cards

Photo Cards

High-Frequency Word Cards

Sound-Spelling Cards

Response Board

Unit Assessment

Benchmark Assessment

Go Digital

For the Teacher

For the Students

Plan
Customizable Lesson Plans

Assess
Online Assessments Reports and Scoring

Professional Development
Lesson and CCSS Videos

My To Do List
Assignments Assessment

Words to Know
Build Vocabulary

Teach
Classroom Presentation Tools Instructional Lessons

Collaborate
Online Class Conversations Interactive Group Projects

Additional Online Resources
ELL Activities
Tier 2 Intervention
Interactive Games and Activities
Word-Building Cards
Sound-Spelling Songs
Sound Pronunciation Audio

Read
eBooks
Interactive Texts

Play
Interactive Games

Manage and Assign
Student Grouping and Assignments

School to Home
Digital Open House Activities and Messages

Write
Interactive Writing

School to Home
Activities for Home
Messages from the Teacher
Class Wall of Student Work

www.connected.mcgraw-hill.com

UNIT 4 CONTENTS

Unit Planning

Weekly Lessons

Program Information

Nathan Love

Week 1

TIME FOR WORK

READING

Oral Language
ESSENTIAL QUESTION
What do people use to do their jobs?
Build Background
CCSS **Oral Vocabulary Words**
L.K.5c *equipment, uniform, expect, remained, utensils*
CCSS Category Words: Job Words
L.K.5.a
Comprehension
Genre: Informational Text
Strategy: Ask and Answer Questions
CCSS **Skill**
RI.K.7 Key Details

Word Work
CCSS **Phonemic Awareness**
RF.K.2d Phoneme Isolation
Phoneme Blending
Phoneme Categorization
CCSS **Phonics** Short o ♪
RF.K.3b **Handwriting:** Oo
CCSS **High-Frequency Words:** *you*
RF.K.3c
Fluency
Letter and Word Automaticity
Model Fluency

Week 2

MEET YOUR NEIGHBORS

Oral Language
ESSENTIAL QUESTION
Who are your neighbors?
Build Background
CCSS **Oral Vocabulary Words**
SL.K.4 *appreciate, cultures, prefer, proud, tradition*
CCSS Category Words: Food Words
L.K.5.a
Comprehension
Genre: Fiction
Strategy: Ask and Answer Questions
CCSS **Skill**
RL.K.3 Character, Setting, Events

Word Work
CCSS **Phonemic Awareness**
RF.K.2d Phoneme Isolation
Phoneme Blending
Phoneme Segmentation
CCSS **Phonics** /d/d ♪
RF.K.3a **Handwriting:** Dd
CCSS **High-Frequency Words:** *do*
RF.K.3c
Fluency
Letter and Word Automaticity
Model Fluency

LANGUAGE ARTS

Writing
Trait: Ideas
Group Related Ideas
CCSS Shared Writing
L.K.1f Descriptive Sentence
Interactive Writing
Descriptive Sentence
Independent Writing
Descriptive Sentence
CCSS **Grammar**
L.K.1f Adjectives

Writing
Trait: Word Choice
Use Words to Describe Things
CCSS Shared Writing
W.K.8 Menu
Interactive Writing
Menu
Independent Writing
Menu
CCSS **Grammar**
L.K.1f Adjectives

Week 3
PITCH IN

Oral Language
ESSENTIAL QUESTION
How can people help to make your community better?

Build Background

CCSS L.K.4.a **Oral Vocabulary Words**
community, improve, confused, harvest, quarrel

CCSS L.K.1.e Category Words: Position Words

Comprehension
Genre: Informational Text

Strategy: Ask and Answer Questions

CCSS RI.K.1 **Skill**
Key Details

Word Work
CCSS RF.K.2d **Phonemic Awareness**
Phoneme Identity
Phoneme Blending
Phoneme Segmentation

CCSS RF.K.3a **Phonics** Review ♪

Handwriting: Ii, Nn, Cc, Oo, Dd

CCSS RF.K.3c **High-Frequency Words:** *to, and, go, you, do*

Fluency
Letter and Word Automaticity
Model Fluency

Unit 4 Assessment
Unit Assessment Book
pages 43–56

Writing
Trait: Word Choice
Use Words to Describe People

CCSS W.K.8 Shared Writing
Expository Sentence

Interactive Writing
Expository Sentence

Independent Writing
Expository Sentence

CCSS L.K.1f **Grammar**
Adjectives

Half Day Kindergarten

Use the chart below to help you plan your kindergarten schedule to focus on key instructional objectives for the week. Choose Small Group and Workstation Activities as your time allows during the day.

Oral Language
- **Essential Questions**
- **Build Background**
- **Oral Vocabulary**
- **Category Words**

Word Work
- **Phonemic Awareness**
- **Phonics** /o/o, /d/d ♪
- **High-Frequency Words:** *you, do*
- **Letter and Word Automaticity**

Reading/Comprehension
- **Reading/Writing Workshop**
  Tom on Top!; Sid; I Can, You Can!
- **Big Books:**
  Whose Shoes? A Shoe for Every Job; What Can You Do with a Paleta?; Roadwork
- **Interactive Read-Aloud Cards**
  "Little Juan and the Cooking Pot"; "Cultural Festivals"; "The Bundle of Sticks"

Language Arts
- **Shared Writing**
- **Interactive Writing**
- **Independent Writing**

Independent Practice
- **Practice Book pages**
- **Workstation Activity Cards**

www.connected.mcgraw-hill.com
Interactive Games and Activities

Reading/Writing Workshop Big Book

Unit 4
Around the Neighborhood

The Big Idea
What do you know about the people and places in your neighborhood?

Come on Through, Miss Sally

This the way we pull away,
pull away, pull away,
This the way we pull away,
all day long.

Come on through, Miss Sally,
Miss Sally, Miss Sally;
Come on through Miss Sally,
all day long.

READING/WRITING WORKSHOP BIG BOOK, pp. 4–5

The Big Idea *What do you know about the people and places in your neighborhood?*

Talk About It

Ask children to think of all the places they go in and around their neighborhood. These places could include school, the grocery store, the post office, and places of worship, among others. Have children discuss the people that have jobs in these places and the kinds of work they do. Ask children to describe places in their neighborhood where people volunteer. Such places could be permanent, such as hospitals, or temporary events, such as festivals. As children engage in the discussion, encourage them to take turns talking. Remind them to speak clearly and loud enough for others to hear when it is their turn to talk. Also model discussion skills by helping them ask one another to share ideas and opinions.

Sing the Song

Introduce the unit song: "Come on Through, Miss Sally." Read the lyrics of the song. Ask children:

→ *Where are some places you could take a walk to in your neighborhood?*

→ *Are the places where other people live near you close together or far apart?*

→ Tell about any neighbors you might see on a neighborhood walk.

Play the song "Come on Through, Miss Sally." After listening to the song a few times, ask children to join in. Audio files of the song can be found in the Teacher Resources on www.connected.mcgraw-hill.com.

Research and Inquiry

Weekly Projects Each week children will be asked to find out more about the topic they are reading about. Children will be asked to work in pairs or small groups to complete their work. Children use what they learn from their reading and discussions as well as other sources to find additional information.

Shared Research Board You may wish to set up a Shared Research Board in the classroom. You can post illustrations and other information that children gather as they do their research.

> **WEEKLY PROJECTS**
> Students work in pairs or small groups.
> **Week 1** Jobs Board
> **Week 2** Our Neighbors Display
> **Week 3** Community Plan

Writing

Write about Reading Throughout the unit children will write in a variety of ways. Each week, writing is focused on a specific writing trait. Scaffolded instruction is provided through Shared Writing and Interactive Writing. Children review a student writing sample together and then write independently, practicing the trait.

> **WEEKLY WRITING**
> **Week 1** Group Related Ideas
> **Week 2** Use Describing Words
> **Week 3** Use Describing Words

Music Links

www.connected.mcgraw-hill.com Integrate music into your classroom using the downloadable audio files in the Teacher's Resources online. Songs for this unit include:

> **WEEKLY SONGS**
> → La Piñata
> → I've Been Working on the Railroad
> → If You Take an Octopus to Dinner
> → Did You See a Dolphin?
>
> **HOLIDAY SONGS**
> → O Hanukkah
> → We Wish You a Merry Christmas
> → All Who Born in January; Jolly Old Saint Nicholas
> → The More We Get Together; Turn Me 'Round
> → Bonhomme! Bonhomme!
> → The Year-Naming Race (story)

Celebration Posters

Celebrate Display the Winter Celebrations poster. Use it to remind students of important holidays during the season. Commemorate the holidays by selecting from the activity suggestions provided in the Teacher Resources found at www.connected.mcgraw-hill.com.
Teaching Posters are available for Fall, Winter, Spring, and Summer.

Teaching Posters, pp. 1–4

WEEKLY OVERVIEW

Literature Big Book

Listening Comprehension

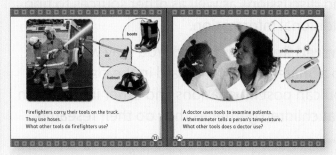

Whose Shoes? A Shoe for Every Job, 5–31
Genre Informational Text

"Workers and Their Tools," 32–36
Genre Informational Text

Interactive Read-Aloud Cards

"Little Juan and the Cooking Pot"
Genre Tale

Oral Vocabulary

equipment   expect
uniform   remained
utensils

Minilessons   ✔TESTED SKILLS CCSS

✔**Comprehension Strategy** .... Ask and Answer
Questions, T13

✔**Comprehension Skill** .... Key Details, T22

👉 **Go
Digital**

www.connected.mcgraw-hill.com

TIME FOR WORK

Essential Question
What do people use to do their jobs?

WEEK 1 →

Big Book and Little Book
Reading/Writing Workshop

Shared Reading

Can **you** see a 🔲 firehouse? 9

"Tom On Top!" 8–15
Genre Informational Text

High-Frequency Word you, T17

Minilessons ✔TESTED SKILLS CCSS

✔**Phonics** .... o (initial/medial), T15
Writing Traits....................... Ideas, T18
Grammar .... Adjectives, T19

Differentiated Text

Approaching   **On Level**   **Beyond**   **ELL**

TEACH AND MANAGE

What You Do

INTRODUCE

Weekly Concept

Time for Work

Reading/Writing Workshop
Big Book 6–7

Go Digital

Interactive Whiteboard

TEACH AND APPLY

Listening Comprehension

Big Book
Whose Shoes? A Shoe for Every Job
Genre Informational Text
Paired Read "Workers and Their
Tools"
Genre Informational Text

Minilessons
Strategy: Ask and Answer Questions
Skill: Key Details

Interactive Whiteboard

Shared Reading

Reading/Writing Workshop
"Tom on Top!"

Minilessons
/o/o, High-Frequency Word: *you*
Writing, Grammar

Mobile

What Your Students Do

WEEKLY CONTRACT

PDF Online

Go Digital

**Online
To-Do List**

PRACTICE AND ONLINE ACTIVITIES

Your Turn Practice Book, pp. 101–108

**Online
Activities**

Leveled Readers

Mobile

Go Digital! www.connected.mcgraw-hill.com

DIFFERENTIATE

Small Group Instruction
Leveled Readers

Mobile

INTEGRATE

Research and Inquiry
Jobs Board, pp. T52–T53

Text Connections
Compare Workers and
Equipment, p. T54

Talk About Reading
Becoming Readers, p. T55

**Online
Research**

WORKSTATION CARDS

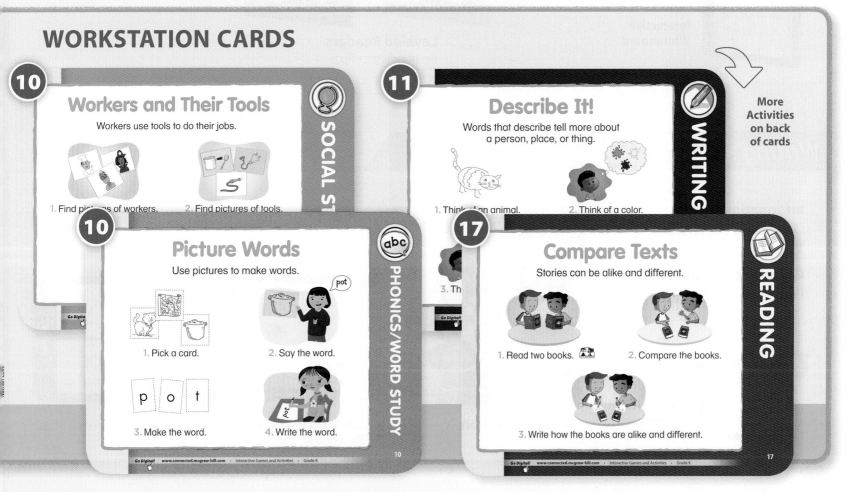

10
Workers and Their Tools
Workers use tools to do their jobs.

1. Find pictures of workers.   2. Find pictures of tools.

SOCIAL STUDIES

11
Describe It!
Words that describe tell more about
a person, place, or thing.

1. Think of an animal.   2. Think of a color.
3. Th...

WRITING

**More
Activities
on back
of cards**

10
Picture Words
Use pictures to make words.

pot

1. Pick a card.   2. Say the word.

p o t

3. Make the word.   4. Write the word.

PHONICS/WORD STUDY

10

17
Compare Texts
Stories can be alike and different.

1. Read two books.   2. Compare the books.

3. Write how the books are alike and different.

READING

17

Go Digital! www.connected.mcgraw-hill.com • Interactive Games and Activities • Grade K

DEVELOPING READERS AND WRITERS

Write About Reading • Analytical Writing

Write to Sources and Research

Respond to Reading, T13, T61, T69, T75, T79

Connect to Essential Question, T13, T45

Key Details, 22

Research and Inquiry, T52

Teacher's Edition

Literature Big Book
Whose Shoes?
Paired Read: *"Workers and Their Tools"*

Interactive Whiteboard

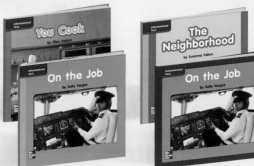

Leveled Readers
Responding to Texts

Writing Process • Independent Writing

Informational Text
Descriptive Sentences, T40–T41, T50, T58

Conferencing Routines
Peer Conferences, T50

Interactive Whiteboard

Teacher's Edition

Leveled Workstation Card
Describe It!, Card 11

Writing Traits • Shared and Interactive Writing

Writing Trait:
Ideas
Descriptive Sentences, T18, T32

Teacher's Edition

Ideas,
p. 18

Adjectives,
p. 19

Reading/Writing Workshop

Go Digital

Interactive Whiteboard

Leveled Workstation Card
Describe It!, Card 11

Grammar and Spelling/Dictation

Grammar
Describing Words
(Adjectives), T19

Spelling/Dictation
Words with Short *o, a,* and *c, m, p, t,* T47, T57

Go Digital

Interactive Whiteboard

Teacher's Edition

Go Digital

Online Grammar Games

Handwriting

SUGGESTED LESSON PLAN

	DAY 1	DAY 2

READING — Whole Group

Teach and Model

Wonders
Whose Shoes?

Literature Big Book

Reading/ Writing Workshop

DAY 1

Build Background Time for Work, T10
Oral Vocabulary equipment, uniform, T10
✔ **Listening Comprehension**
• Genre: Informational Text
• Strategy: Ask and Answer Questions, T13
Big Book *Whose Shoes?*
✔ **Word Work**
Phonemic Awareness:
• Phoneme Isolation, T14
Phonics:
• Introduce /o/o, T15
Handwriting Oo, T16
High-Frequency Word you, T17

Practice *Your Turn* 101–102

DAY 2

Oral Language Time for Work, T20
✔ **Category Words** Job Words, T21
✔ **Listening Comprehension**
• Genre: Informational Text
• Strategy: Ask and Answer Questions, T22
• Skill: Key Details
• Guided Retelling
• Model Fluency, T27
Big Book *Whose Shoes?*
✔ **Word Work**
Phonemic Awareness:
• Phoneme Isolation, T28
Phonics:
• Blend Words with /o/o, T29
High-Frequency Word you, T29
Shared Reading "Tom on Top," T30–T31

Practice *Your Turn* 103

DIFFERENTIATED INSTRUCTION — Small Group
Choose across the week to meet your student's needs.

Approaching Level

DAY 1

Leveled Reader *You Cook,* T60–T61
Phonological Awareness Onset and Rime Segmentation, T62 (TIER 2)
Phonics Sound-Spelling Review, T64 (TIER 2)
High-Frequency Words Reteach Words, T66 (TIER 2)

DAY 2

Leveled Reader *You Cook,* T60–T61
Phonemic Awareness Phoneme Isolation, T62 (TIER 2)
Phonics Connect to /o/o, T64 (TIER 2)
High-Frequency Words Cumulative Review, T66

On Level

DAY 1

Leveled Reader *On the Job,* T68–T69
Phonemic Awareness Phoneme Isolation, T70

DAY 2

Leveled Reader *On the Job,* T68–T69
Phonemic Awareness Phoneme Blending, T70
Phonics Review Phonics, T71
High-Frequency Words Review Words, T73

Beyond Level

DAY 1

Leveled Reader *The Neighborhood,* T74–T75
Phonics Review, T76

DAY 2

Leveled Reader *The Neighborhood,* T74–T75
High-Frequency Words Review, T76

English Language Learners

DAY 1

Leveled Reader *On the Job,* T78–T79
Phonological Awareness Onset and Rime Segmentation, T62 (TIER 2)
Phonics Sound-Spelling Review, T64 (TIER 2)
Vocabulary Preteach Oral Vocabulary, T80
Writing Shared Writing, T82

DAY 2

Leveled Reader *On the Job,* T78–T79
Phonemic Awareness Phoneme Isolation, T62 (TIER 2)
Phonics Connect o to /o/, T64 (TIER 2)
Vocabulary Preteach ELL Vocabulary, T80

LANGUAGE ARTS — Whole Group

Writing and Grammar

DAY 1

Shared Writing
Writing Trait: Ideas, T18
Write a Descriptive Sentence, T18
Grammar Adjectives, T19

DAY 2

Interactive Writing
Writing Trait: Ideas, T32
Write a Descriptive Sentence, T32
Grammar Adjectives, T33

DAY 3	DAY 4	DAY 5 Review and Assess

READING

Oral Language Time for Work, T34 **Oral Vocabulary** expect, remained, utensils, T34 ✓ **Listening Comprehension** • Genre: Tale • Strategy: Ask and Answer Questions, T35 • Make Connections, T35 **Interactive Read Aloud** "Little Juan and the Cooking Pot," T35 ✓ **Word Work** **Phonemic Awareness** • Phoneme Blending, T36 **Phonics** • Blend Words with Short *o*, and *n, p, t, c, m*, T37 • Picture Sort, T38 **High-Frequency Word** you, T39 **Practice** *Your Turn* 104–106	**Oral Language** Time for Work, T42 ✓ **Category Words** Job Words, T43 ✓ **Listening Comprehension** • Genre: Informational Text • Strategy: Ask and Answer Questions, T44 • Text Features: Labels • Make Connections, T45 **Big Book** Paired Read: "Workers and Their Tools," T44 ✓ **Word Work** **Phonemic Awareness** • Phoneme Blending, T46 **Phonics** • Blend Words with Short *o, a*, and *m, p, t*, T46 **High-Frequency Word** you, T47 **Shared Reading** "Tom on Top!" T48–T49 **Integrate Ideas** Research and Inquiry, T52–T53 **Practice** *Your Turn* 107	**Integrate Ideas** • Text Connections, T54 • Talk About Reading, T55 • Research and Inquiry, T55 ✓ **Word Work** **Phonemic Awareness** • Phoneme Categorization, T56 **Phonics** • Read Words with Short *o, a*, and *c, m, p, t*, T56 **High-Frequency Word** like, T57 **Practice** *Your Turn* 108

DIFFERENTIATED INSTRUCTION

Leveled Reader *You Cook*, T60–T61 **Phonemic Awareness** Phoneme Blending, T63 **Phonics** Reteach, T64 **High-Frequency Words** Reteach Words, T66	**Leveled Reader** *You Cook*, T60–T61 **Phonemic Awareness** Phoneme Categorization, T63 **Phonics** Blend Words with /o/o, T65 **Oral Vocabulary** Review Words, T67	**Leveled Reader** Literacy Activities, T61 **Phonemic Awareness** Phoneme Categorization, T63 **Phonics** Reread for Fluency, T65 Build Fluency with Phonics, T65 **Comprehension** Self-Selected Reading, T67
Leveled Reader *On the Job*, T68–T69 **Phonemic Awareness** Phoneme Categorization, T70 **Phonics** Picture Sort, T71	**Leveled Reader** *On the Job*, T68–T69 **Phonics** Blend Words with Short *o*, T72 Reread for Fluency, T72	**Leveled Reader** Literacy Activities, T69 **Comprehension** Self-Selected Reading, T73
Leveled Reader *The Neighborhood*, T74–T75 **Vocabulary** Oral Vocabulary: Synonyms, T77 *Gifted and Talented*	**Leveled Reader** *The Neighborhood*, T74–T75 **Phonics** Innovate, T77	**Leveled Reader** Literacy Activities, T75 **Comprehension** Self-Selected Reading, T77 *Gifted and Talented*
Leveled Reader *On the Job*, T78–T79 **Phonemic Awareness** Phoneme Blending, T63 **Phonics** Reteach, T64 **High-Frequency Words** Review Words, T81 **Writing** Writing Trait: Ideas, T82	**Leveled Reader** *On the Job*, T78–T79 **Phonemic Awareness** Phoneme Categorization, T63 **Phonics** Blend Words with /o/o, T65 **High-Frequency Words** Review Category Words, T81 **Grammar** Adjectives, T83	**Leveled Reader** Literacy Activities, T79 **Phonemic Awareness** Phoneme Categorization, T63 **Phonics** Reread for Fluency, T65 Build Fluency with Phonics, T65

LANGUAGE ARTS

Independent Writing Writing Trait: Ideas, T40 Write a Descriptive Sentence Prewrite/Draft, T40–T41 **Grammar** Adjectives, T41	**Independent Writing** Write a Descriptive Sentence Revise/Final Draft, T50 **Grammar** Adjectives, T51	**Independent Writing** Write a Descriptive Sentence Prepare/Present/Evaluate/Publish, T58 **Grammar** Adjectives, T59

DIFFERENTIATE TO ACCELERATE

 A C T Scaffold to **A**ccess **C**omplex **T**ext

Qualitative · Quantitative
Reader and Task
TEXT COMPLEXITY

IF ▶ the text complexity of a particular section is too difficult for children

THEN ▶ see the references noted in the chart below for scaffolded instruction to help children Access Complex Text.

	Literature Big Book	Reading/Writing Workshop	Leveled Readers

Quantitative

Literature Big Book

Whose Shoes? A Shoe for Every Job
Lexile 70

"Workers and Their Tools"
Lexile 350

Reading/Writing Workshop

"Tom On Top!"
Lexile 70

Leveled Readers

Approaching Level
Lexile BR

Beyond Level
Lexile 120

On Level
Lexile BR

ELL
Lexile BR

Qualitative

What Makes the Text Complex?

• **Connection of Ideas** Answering Questions in a Text, T22

A C T *See Scaffolded Instruction in Teacher's Edition, T22.*

What Makes the Text Complex?
Foundational Skills

• Decoding with short *o*, T28–T29
• Identifying high-frequency words, T29

What Makes the Text Complex?
Foundational Skills

• Decoding with short *o*
• Identifying high-frequency words *you*

See Level Up lessons online for Leveled Readers.

Reader and Task

The Introduce the Concept lesson on pages T10–T11 will help determine the reader's knowledge and engagement in the weekly concept. See pages T12–T13, T23–T27, T44–T45 and T52–T55 for questions and tasks for this text.

The Introduce the Concept lesson on pages T10–T11 will help determine the reader's knowledge and engagement in the weekly concept. See pages T30–T31, T48–T49 and T52–T55 for questions and tasks for this text.

The Introduce the Concept lesson on pages T10–T11 will help determine the reader's knowledge and engagement in the weekly concept. See pages T60–T61, T68–T69, T74–T75, T78–T79 and T52–T55 for questions and tasks for this text.

Monitor and *Differentiate*

IF	you need to differentiate instruction
THEN	use the Quick Checks to assess children's needs and select the appropriate small group instruction focus.

✓ Quick Check

Comprehension Strategy Ask and Answer Questions, T35

Phonemic Awareness/Phonics Short o (initial/medial), T17, T29, T39, T47, T57

High-Frequency Words *you*, T17, T29, T39, T47, T57

If No → | **Approaching** | **Reteach,** pp. T60–T67 |
| **ELL** | **Develop,** pp. T78–T83 |

If Yes → | **On Level** | **Review,** pp. T68–T73 |
| **Beyond Level** | **Extend,** pp. T74–T77 |

Level Up with Leveled Readers

IF	children can read their leveled text fluently and answer comprehension questions
THEN	work with the next level up to accelerate children's reading with more complex text.

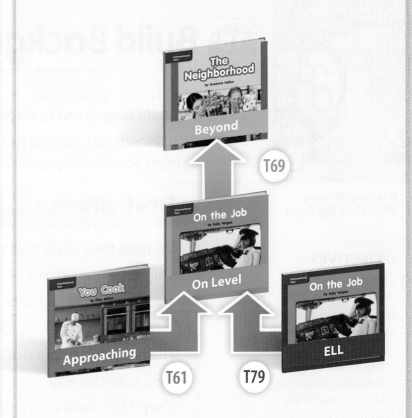

ENGLISH LANGUAGE LEARNERS
SCAFFOLD

| IF | ELL students need additional support | THEN | scaffold instruction using the small group suggestions. |

Reading-Writing Workshop T11 "On the Job!" Integrate Ideas T53	Leveled Reader T78–T79 *On the Job*	Phonological Awareness Onset and Rime Segmentation, T62 Phoneme Isolation, T62 Phoneme Blending, T63 Phoneme Categorization, T63	Phonics, /o/o (initial/ medial), T64–T65	Oral Vocabulary, T80 equipment, uniform, utensils, expect, remained High-Frequency Words, T81 *you*	Writing Shared Writing, T82 Writing Trait: Ideas, T82	Grammar T83 Adjectives

Note: Include ELL Students in all small groups based on their needs.

Materials

Reading/Writing Workshop Big Book
UNIT 4

Literature Big Book
Whose Shoes? A Shoe for Every Job

Visual Vocabulary Cards
equipment
uniform

Response Board

Photo Cards
balloon   olive
barn   otter
blue   ox
green   soup
leaf   spoon
October

Sound-Spelling Cards
octopus

High-Frequency Word Cards
and
can
I
like
see

Think Aloud Cloud

♪ **"If You Take an Octopus to Dinner"**

Reading/Writing Workshop Big Book

OBJECTIVES

CCSS Confirm understanding of a text read aloud or information presented orally or through other media by asking and answering questions about key details and requesting clarification if something is not understood. **SL.K.2**

CCSS Identify real-life connections between words and their use. **L.K.5c**

→ # Introduce the Concept

MINILESSON 10 Mins

Build Background

ESSENTIAL QUESTION
What do people use to do their jobs?

Read aloud the Essential Question. Tell children you are going to read a poem about firefighters and some things they use to do their job.

Firefighters

Up onto their loud, loud truck
The firefighters climb.
They're in an awful hurry,
They move in quick, quick time.
They're going to put out a fire,
Help is on the way.
They'll get there with their water hose
And spray and spray and spray.

What tool did the firefighters use in the poem? (water hose) Explain that this week they will read to find out about different people who work in their community and special things they use to do their jobs.

Oral Vocabulary Words

Use the **Define/Example/Ask** routine to introduce the oral vocabulary words **equipment** and **uniform**.

To introduce the theme "Time for Work," explain that community workers often use special equipment or wear uniforms. Have children name a community worker and tell what kind of uniform that person wears. (Possible response: mail carrier; post office uniform)

Go Digital

"Time for Work"

Video

Photos

Visual Glossary

Visual Vocabulary Cards

Oral Vocabulary Routine

<u>Define:</u> **Equipment** is special tools that someone uses to do a job.

<u>Example:</u> The gardener's equipment includes a shovel and a watering can.

<u>Ask:</u> What kind of equipment does the art teacher use?

<u>Define:</u> A **uniform** is special clothing that workers wear on their jobs.

<u>Example:</u> The baker wears a white uniform with a hat.

<u>Ask:</u> What kind of uniform would you like to wear? Why?

Talk About It: Time for Work

Guide children to discuss how equipment and uniforms help community workers. List children's responses. Display pages 6–7 of the **Reading/Writing Workshop Big Book** and have children do the **Talk About It** activity with a partner.

READING/WRITING WORKSHOP BIG BOOK, pp. 6–7

Collaborative Conversations

Ask and Answer Questions As children engage in partner, small group, and whole group discussions, encourage them to:

→ Ask questions to clarify ideas they do not understand.

→ Ask for help getting information.

→ Wait after asking a question to give others a chance to think.

ENGLISH LANGUAGE LEARNERS SCAFFOLD

Beginning

Recognize Show an image from the Big Book or classroom materials of a person wearing a uniform. Describe the person's clothing. Ask: *Is this (man/woman) wearing a uniform?* Then show an image of someone who is not wearing a uniform and describe his or her clothing. Ask: *Is this (man/woman) wearing a uniform?*

Intermediate

Demonstrate Understanding Display a piece of chalk or marker. Ask: *I use this equipment in the classroom. How can I use the (chalk/marker)?* Elicit more details to support children's answers. Then ask: *What kind of equipment do you use when you play a sport?*

Advanced/Advanced High

Describe Say: *People who help you cross the street near our school are called crossing guards. What kind of uniform do crossing guards wear? What equipment do they use?* Clarify children's responses as needed by providing vocabulary.

→ # Listening Comprehension

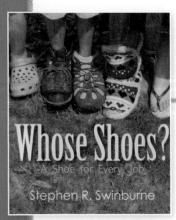

Literature Big Book

ACADEMIC LANGUAGE
cover, letters

 MINILESSON 10 Mins

Read the Literature Big Book

Connect to Concept: Time for Work

Tell children that you will now read about the different kinds of shoes that community workers wear. *What kinds of shoes do you wear when you play outside?*

Concepts of Print

Match Speech to Print; Directionality Display the **Big Book** cover and read aloud the title and subtitle. Tell children you are going to match the words you say to the words on the page. Reread the title and subtitle while pointing to the words. Model directionality as you remind children that we read from left to right and top to bottom.

Genre: Informational Text

Model *Whose Shoes?* is an informational text. Share these characteristics of informational texts with children:

→ Informational text gives facts, or real information, about people, places, or events.

→ Many informational texts include photographs.

Selection Words Preview these words before reading:

flip-flops: summer shoes with V-shaped straps
different: not the same

Set a Purpose for Reading

→ Read aloud the title, subtitle, and author's name.

→ Remind children that the author wrote the words. Point out that for this selection, the author also took the photographs.

→ Ask children to listen as you read the Big Book to find out what kinds of shoes workers wear to do their jobs.

Go Digital

Whose Shoes? A Shoe for Every Job

Model Think Aloud Cloud

Strategy: Ask and Answer Questions

Explain Tell children that they can ask questions before and during reading to help them better understand the text. They can look for answers to their questions in the text and the pictures as they read.

Think Aloud On the cover of the book I see many shoes and I read "A Shoe for Every Job." I wonder what kinds of jobs the author will tell about. I ask myself: *Which jobs will be in the book?* I will read to find out my answer. As I read this book, I will stop after every page or two to ask myself questions about what I am learning. I will look for the answers as I keep reading. This will help me better understand the text.

Model As you read, use the **Think Aloud Cloud** to model the strategy.

Think Aloud On page 6, I see feet without any shoes, but they are not doing a job. I wonder if any of the people in the book will wear no shoes to do their jobs. As I read I will look for the answer to this question.

Respond to Reading

After reading, prompt children to share what they learned about the shoes that workers wear. Discuss which questions they asked themselves while reading and how they answered them. Then have children draw a picture of themselves wearing their favorite pair of shoes from the book.

Make Connections

Use *Whose Shoes?* to discuss the kinds of work people do. Revisit the concept behind the Essential Question *What do people use to do their jobs?* by paging through the Big Book.

Write About It Have children write about their favorite job from the story. Guide them to discuss their choice with a partner.

ENGLISH LANGUAGE LEARNERS SCAFFOLD

Beginning

Respond Orally Display the cover of *Whose Shoes?* Say: *Which shoes would you wear when it's warm?* (flip-flops) Ask: *Which shoes in this photo would you wear when it's cold?* (the different boots) Repeat children's correct answers slowly and clearly to the class, adding details for clarity if possible.

Intermediate

Explain Point to the flip-flops on the cover of *Whose Shoes?* Say: *When would you wear these shoes?* Point to the athletic shoes and ask: *When would you wear these shoes?* Model correct pronunciation as needed.

Advanced/Advanced High

Describe Display the front cover of *Whose Shoes?* and encourage children to describe and ask questions about what they see. Restate children's questions and responses in order to develop their oral language proficiency.

→ # Word Work

Quick Review

Review /n/, /k/: Ask children to tell the initial sound of the *net* and *car* Photo Cards.
Build Fluency: Sound-Spellings: Show the following **Word-Building Cards:** *a, c, i, m, n, p, s, t.* Have children chorally say each sound. Repeat and vary the pace.

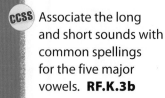

Phonemic Awareness

Phoneme Isolation

Photo Card

① Model Introduce initial sound /o/. Display **Photo Card** for *octopus.* *Listen for the sound at the beginning of this word:* octopus. Octopus *has the /ooo/ sound at the beginning. Say the sound with me: /ooo/.* Say these words and have children repeat: *on, otter, olive.* Emphasize the phoneme /o/.

♪ *Let's play a song. Listen for words with /o/ at the beginning.* Play "If You Take an Octopus to Dinner," and have children listen for /o/. *Let's play the song again and wave our arms like an octopus when we hear words that begin with /o/.* Play or sing the letter song again, encouraging children to join in. Have children wave their arms like an octopus when they hear a word that begins with /o/.

② Guided Practice/Practice Display and name each Photo Card: *October, olive, otter, ox.* Have children repeat. *Tell me the sound at the beginning of the word.* Guide practice with the first word.

Photo Cards

OBJECTIVES

CCSS Isolate and pronounce the initial sounds, medial vowel, and final sounds (phonemes) in three-phoneme words. **RF.K.2d**

CCSS Associate the long and short sounds with common spellings for the five major vowels. **RF.K.3b**

ENGLISH LANGUAGE LEARNERS

Pronunciation
Display and have children name Photo Cards from this lesson to reinforce phonemic awareness and word meanings. Point to a card. Ask: *What do you see?* (an octopus) *What sound is at the beginning of ox?* (/o/) Repeat using Photo Cards with words beginning with /o/.

Go Digital

Phonemic Awareness

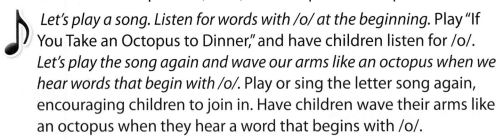

Phonics

ARTICULATION SUPPORT

Demonstrate how to say /o/. Open your mouth and make your lips look like a circle. Put your tongue on the bottom of your mouth. Use your voice to say /o/. Make the sound in the back of your mouth. Place your fingers on your throat. Can you feel the sound? Say *on, off, ox.* Stretch initial /o/. Have children repeat.

Phonics

10 Mins MINILESSON

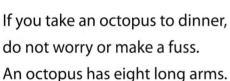

octopus

Sound-Spelling Card

Introduce /o/o

❶ **Model** Display the *Octopus* **Sound-Spelling Card**. Say: *This is the Octopus card. The sound is /o/. The /o/ sound is spelled with the letter o. Say the sound with me: /o/. This is the sound at the beginning of the word* octopus. *Listen: /ooo/,* octopus. *What is the name of this letter?* (*o*) *What sound does this letter stand for?* (/o/)

Display the song "If You Take an Octopus to Dinner" (see **Teacher's Resource Book** online) Read or sing the song with children. Reread the title and point out that the word *octopus* begins with the letter *o*. Model placing a self-stick note below the *O* in *octopus*.

❷ **Guided Practice/Practice** Read each line of the song. Stop after each line and ask children to place self-stick notes below words that begin with *O* or *o* and say the letter name.

If You Take an Octopus to Dinner

If you take an octopus to dinner,
do not worry or make a fuss.
An octopus has eight long arms.
It's one of his many charms.

Wave your arms like an octopus!
O-C-T-O-P-U-S!
Yes! Yes! You'll make a mess
if you take an octopus to dinner.

Corrective Feedback

Sound Error Model the sound /o/ in the initial position, then have children repeat the sound. Say: *My turn. Ox. /ooo/. Now it's your turn.* Have children say the word and isolate initial /o/.

ENGLISH LANGUAGE LEARNERS

Phonemic Awareness: Variations in Languages In some languages, including Spanish, Hmong, and Korean, there is no direct transfer for the /o/ sound. Emphasize the /o/ sound and demonstrate correct mouth position.

YOUR TURN PRACTICE BOOK pp. 101–102

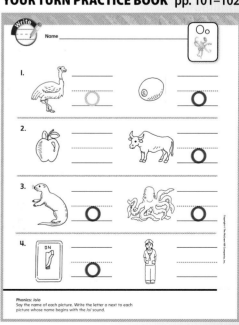

Word Work

 MINILESSON 5 Mins

Handwriting: Write *Oo*

1 Model Say the handwriting cues below as you write and identify the uppercase and lowercase forms of *Oo*. Then trace the letters on the board and in the air as you say /o/.

Circle back, then around all the way.

Circle back, then around all the way.

2 Guided Practice/Practice

→ Say the cues together as children trace both forms of the letter with their index finger. Have them identify the uppercase and lowercase forms of the letter.

→ Have children write *O* and *o* in the air as they say /o/ multiple times.

→ Distribute **Response Boards**. Observe children's pencil grip and paper position, and correct as necessary. Have children say /o/ every time they write the letter *Oo*.

 Daily Handwriting

Throughout the week teach uppercase and lowercase letters *Oo* using the Handwriting models. At the end of the week, have children use the **Your Turn Practice Book** page 108 to practice handwriting.

MINILESSON
5 Mins

High-Frequency Words

you

> ## you
> **High-Frequency Word Card**

❶ **Model** Display page 7 of the **Big Book** *Whose Shoes?* Read aloud the sentence "The first shoes you ever wore were soft and very small." Point to the high-frequency word *you*. Then use the **High-Frequency Word Card** *you* with the **Read/Spell/Write** routine to teach the word.

→ **Read** Point to the word *you* and say the word. *This is the word* you. *Say it with me:* you. You *have red shoes!*

→ **Spell** *The word* you *is spelled y-o-u. Spell it with me.*

→ **Write** *Let's write the word in the air as we say each letter: y-o-u.*

→ Point out to children that the letter *o* in the word *you* has a different sound from the letter *o* in *mop.*

COLLABORATE Have partners create sentences using the word.

❷ **Guided Practice/Practice** Build sentences using High-Frequency Word Cards and teacher-made punctuation cards. Have children point to the high-frequency word *you*. Use these sentences.

`Also online`

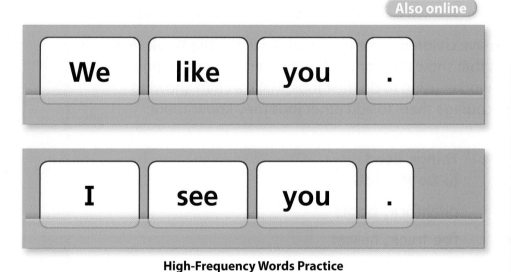

| We | like | you | . |

| I | see | you | . |

High-Frequency Words Practice

Monitor and *Differentiate*

✓ Quick Check

Can children isolate /o/ and match it to the letter *Oo*?

Can children recognize and read the high-frequency word?

⬇

Small Group Instruction

If No →	Approaching	Reteach pp. T62–67
	ELL	Develop pp. T80–83
If Yes →	On Level	Review pp. T70–73
	Beyond Level	Extend pp. T76–77

Language Arts

MINILESSON
10 Mins

Shared Writing

OBJECTIVES

CCSS With guidance and support from adults, recall information from experiences or gather information from provided sources to answer a question. **W.K.8**

CCSS Produce and expand complete sentences in shared language activities. **L.K.1f**

CCSS Sort common objects into categories (e.g., shapes, foods) to gain a sense of the concepts the categories represent. **L.K.5a**

ACADEMIC LANGUAGE

• *descriptive, sentence, adjective*

• Cognates: *adjetivo*

Writing Trait: Ideas

❶ **Model** Tell children that good writers use details to tell about their ideas. The details describe the ideas the writer is writing about.

→ Write and read aloud: *A ballerina wears ballet shoes.*

When I read this sentence, I can picture a ballerina in her pretty ballet shoes. Ballerinas need special shoes when they dance on the tips of their toes.

❷ **Guided Practice/Practice** Ask children what else a ballerina uses. Encourage children to dictate descriptive sentences: *A ballerina uses a tutu. A ballerina uses music.* Read aloud the sentences.

Write a Descriptive Sentence

Focus and Plan Tell children that this week they will learn how to write a descriptive sentence about things people use to do their jobs.

 Brainstorm Have children name jobs they see in the **Big Book**. Point to the pictures that show the worker. Ask children to name things they see each worker using to do their jobs. Make a chart showing their ideas. Encourage them to add other jobs they know about.

Jobs	Things Used to Do the Job
farmer	pitchfork, boots
firefighter	fire truck, helmet
chef	stove, hat

Write Model writing a descriptive sentence using information from the chart. Write and read aloud: *A farmer uses a pitchfork. This sentence tells what a farmer uses to do his or her job.*

Model writing sentences using the other information on the chart. Read aloud the sentences with children.

Grammar

Describing Words (Adjectives)

❶ Model Tell children that an adjective is a describing word that tells more about something.

→ Show **Photo Cards** for balloon and barn. Point to each photo and ask what color each item is. (red)

→ Write red on two self-stick notes. Put each note before the word on the Photo Card. Read aloud as you track the print: *red barn; red balloon. Red is a describing word. It describes the color of these things.*

❷ Guided Practice/Practice Display the Photo Card for *spoon. What color is this spoon?* Write *blue* on a self-stick note. Ask children to put it in the correct place on the Photo Card. Read aloud as you track the print: *blue spoon. Blue is a describing word. It describes the color of the spoon.*

Display the Photo Card for *leaf. What color is this leaf?* Write *green* on a self-stick note. Ask children to put it in the correct place on the Photo Card. As you track the print, have children read aloud with you: *green leaf. Green is a describing word. What does green describe?* (the color of the leaf)

Talk About It

Have partners work together to orally generate sentences with describing words. Encourage them to describe the colors of the things they use to draw or paint.

ENGLISH LANGUAGE LEARNERS SCAFFOLD

Beginning

Explain Display Photo Cards for *blue, green, spoon,* and *leaf.* Have children match the Photo Card with the correct color of each item. Point to the name of the color and encourage children to say the color with you. Allow children ample time to respond.

Intermediate

Practice Display Photo Cards for *spoon* and *leaf. What color is the spoon?* (blue) *What color is the leaf?* (green) Encourage children to say each phrase: *blue spoon, green leaf.* Model correct pronunciation as needed.

Advanced/Advanced High

Practice Display Photo Cards for *spoon* and *leaf.* Have children describe the items in sentences. Ask children to describe the colors of other items in the classroom. Elicit more details to support children's answers.

Daily Wrap Up

• Review the Essential Question and encourage children to discuss it, using the new oral vocabulary words. *What jobs do people do? What tools or equipment do workers use to do their jobs?*

• Prompt children to share the skills they learned. How might they use those skills?

Materials

Reading/Writing Workshop Big Book
UNIT 4

Literature Big Book
Whose Shoes? A Shoe for Every Job

Visual Vocabulary Cards
equipment
uniform

Response Board

a b c

Word-Building Cards

Photo Cards

ant	mop
ball	octopus
bear	nail
fox	sock
giraffe	star
hat	top
jet	

Sound-Spelling Cards
octopus

High-Frequency Word Cards

a	the
and	to
go	we
like	you
see	

Retelling Cards

→ Build the Concept

Oral Language
MINILESSON 10 Mins

Go Digital

Visual Glossary

Category Words

OBJECTIVES

CCSS Use words and phrases acquired through conversations, reading and being read to, and responding to texts. **L.K.6**

CCSS Blend and segment onsets and rimes of single-syllable spoken words. **RF.K.2c**

CCSS Sort common objects into categories (e.g., shapes, foods) to gain a sense of the concepts the categories represent. **L.K.5a**

Develop oral vocabulary

ACADEMIC LANGUAGE

• *category*
• Cognates: *categoría*

ESSENTIAL QUESTION

What do people use to do their jobs?

Remind children that this week they are learning about community workers. They are also learning what kinds of equipment and uniforms the workers use and wear. Ask children to list some jobs that people have in their community.

Read aloud "Firefighters." As you read, have children echo the lines. *In addition to hoses and trucks, what other kinds of equipment do firefighters use?* (ladders, flashlights, helmets)

Phonological Awareness

Onset/Rime Segmentation
Model segmenting onset and rime with the word *truck. I'm going to separate the beginning sounds from the end sounds in truck. Listen: /truk/, /tr/ /uk/.* Have children repeat after you. Model again with *quick. /kwik/, /kw/ /ik/.* Have children repeat the process with other single-syllable words: *fire, /f/ /īər/; way, /w/ /ā/; get, /g/ /et/.*

Review Oral Vocabulary

Use the **Define/Example/Ask** routine to review the oral vocabulary words **equipment** and **uniform**. Prompt children to use the words in sentences.

Vocab
Define
Examp
Ask:

Visual Vocabulary Cards

Category Words: Job Words

❶ Model Use the **Big Book** *Whose Shoes?* to point out job words: *ballerina,* page 14; *farmer,* page 16; *firefighter,* page 18, and *soldier,* page 20. Explain that these are job words. They tell what someone does for work. Point out the photographs that represent each job word. Then ask about each job. *What does a farmer do? What does a firefighter do?*

→ Sing the following song to the tune of "The Farmer in the Dell." Ask children to listen for job words.

> *The chef is in the kitchen,*
> *The chef is in the kitchen,*
> *Hi-ho, so tasty-o,*
> *The chef is in the kitchen.*
>
> *The chef stirs the pot,*
> *The chef stirs the pot,*
> *Hi-ho, so tasty-o,*
> *The chef stirs the pot.*

→ Tell children that *chef* is a job word for someone who cooks. *Chefs work in kitchens. They use pots to cook.* Sing the song again, substituting different job words for *chef, kitchen,* and *pot.* Encourage children to name other job words to add to the song. (Possible answers: clown, circus, ball; teacher, school, book)

❷ Guided Practice/Practice Discuss different jobs, and talk about the clothing, tools, and equipment associated with each job. *What kind of clothing does a chef wear?* (white hat and jacket) *What is a tool that a nurse uses?* (thermometer) *What kind of equipment does a custodian use?* (mop and broom)

→ Encourage children to think of questions they could ask people who have the jobs children have just discussed. Write their suggestions on the board.

ENGLISH LANGUAGE LEARNERS

Understand Help children understand job words for people in the school, such as *teacher, librarian, nurse,* and *custodian.* Describe each job and name a person who holds the job in your school.

LET'S MOVE!

Say different job words from the Big Book *Whose Shoes?* Have children act out what each person might do while performing his or her job.

→ # Listening Comprehension

CLOSE READING

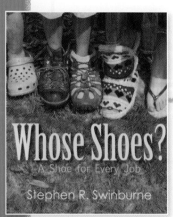

MINILESSON
15
Mins

Reread Literature Big Book

Whose Shoes?
A Shoe for Every Job

Stephen R. Swinburne

Literature Big Book

OBJECTIVES

CCSS With prompting and support, ask and answer questions about key details in a text. **RI.K.1**

CCSS With prompting and support, describe the relationship between illustrations and the text in which they appear (e.g. what person, place, thing, or idea in the text an illustration depicts). **RI.K.7**

• Strategy: Ask and Answer Questions

• Skill: Key Details

Genre: Informational Text

Display *Whose Shoes?* Remind children that informational text contains information about real life. The text tells facts about real people, information, or events. *How do you know that* Whose Shoes? *is informational text?* Have children point to evidence in the text and the pictures to show that this is informational text. (It shows photos of real people; it's about real workers.)

Strategy: Ask and Answer Questions

Remind children that good readers ask and answer questions before and during reading. *As we reread, you can ask yourself questions and look for the answers later in the story.*

Skill: Key Details

Remind children that as they read, they can find important details in the text and in the photos. Point out that photographs sometimes give information that is not in the author's words. *Details in the photographs can help you answer your questions.* As you read, have children listen for evidence in the text to find details.

A C T

Access **C**omplex **T**ext

Connection of Ideas On many pages in this book, the author asks the question "Whose shoes?" and gives the answer on the next page. Children many need help making the connection.

→ To guide children's understanding, read aloud page 13 and point to the picture: *The text asks a question. I will turn the page to find out.* Point out the answer, *ballerina,* on page 14. Flip back and forth to show children that the shoes on page 14 are the same as the shoes on page 13.

Go Digital

Whose Shoes?
A Shoe for
Every Job

Retelling Cards

PAGE 5

CONCEPTS OF PRINT

Track the print as you read aloud the words on this page. Remind children that we read from left to right.

PAGES 6–7

HIGH-FREQUENCY WORDS

Have children identify and read the high-frequency word *you* on page 7.

pp. 6–7

foot/feet, toe/toes: Say each word and then have children echo. Define each word using the photograph on page 6.

PAGES 8–9

KEY DETAILS

Think Aloud I read that when it's cold outside you can wear boots. In the photo I see that there is also snow on the ground. Boots can help you stay warm *and* dry in the snow.

PAGES 10–11

KEY DETAILS

What do the pictures on these pages show? Have children point to the blue shoes on page 10 and the silver shoes on page 11.

pp. 10–11

favorite: Say: *If your favorite shoes are blue, you like those shoes the best. What color are your favorite shoes?*

Listening Comprehension

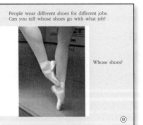

PAGES 12–13

ASK AND ANSWER QUESTIONS

Think Aloud I read that people wear different shoes for different jobs. I see the pretty shoes on page 13. The text asks: "Whose shoes?" I will keep reading to find the answer.

pp. 12–13

whose: Explain that the word *whose* asks who owns something or whom something belongs to. Point to an object on a child's desk. Ask: *Whose (object) is this?*

PAGES 14–15

KEY DETAILS

Remind children to look for details in photographs to learn more information. Point to the cow. Ask: *What is this animal?* (cow) *What do you think cows eat?* (the hay in the photo)

pp. 14–15

ballerina: Tell children that a ballerina is a dancer. Invite a child to show how a ballerina moves.

PAGES 16–17

ASK AND ANSWER QUESTIONS

Think Aloud On page 17, I read "Whose shoes?" I look at the picture. I see part of a truck, big pants, and big boots. I will keep reading to find out whose shoes these are.

PAGES 18–19

ASK AND ANSWER QUESTIONS

Think Aloud When I read the previous page, I asked myself whose shoes those were. I find my answer on page 18. Those shoes belong to a firefighter.

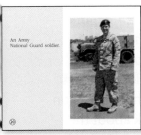

PAGES 20–21

CONCEPTS OF PRINT

Remind children to match the words they say to the words on the page as they read. Track the print on page 20 as you read it aloud, pointing to each word as you say it.

pp. 20–21

Army National Guard soldier: Tell children that soldiers work to keep the United States safe. Say: *This soldier works for the Army National Guard.*

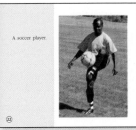

PAGES 22–23

KEY DETAILS

Remind children to look for details in the photographs to help them better understand the text. Ask: *What details do you see on the soccer player's uniform?* (shin guards, shoes, shorts, T-shirt) *What is the soccer player doing?* (kicking a soccer ball)

PAGES 24–25

ASK AND ANSWER QUESTIONS

Think Aloud I wonder what else is part of a construction worker's uniform. I find my answer in the photograph on page 24. A construction worker needs a hard hat to stay safe.

pp. 24–25

construction: Explain that *construction* means "building." Say: *Construction workers build buildings, homes, and offices. Where have you seen a construction worker?*

PAGES 26–27

ASK AND ANSWER QUESTIONS

Point to the shoes on page 27. *How can we find the answer to the question "Whose shoes?"* (Turn the page and keep reading.)

Listening Comprehension

PAGES 28–29

KEY DETAILS

What details help you understand what a chef does? (In the photo I see a kitchen with pots and pans and the man in the picture is holding vegetables. I think a chef cooks food.)

pp. 28–29

Say: *This is a chef. A chef is a person who cooks in a restaurant.* Guide partners in using the photograph on page 28 to talk about the things a chef uses to cook.

PAGES 30–31

AUTHOR'S PURPOSE

Why do you think the author wrote this informational text? (Possible answer: He wanted to show what kinds of shoes different workers wear.)

Text Evidence

Explain Remind children that when they answer a question they need to show where in the story (both words and photographs) they found the answer.

Discuss Say: *The author says you can wear different shoes for different jobs. Whose job do you think needs the toughest shoes? Why?* (Answers may include the National Guard soldier, the shoes protect her feet; the construction worker, the shoes have to help him drive heavy equipment; the firefighter, the shoes have to protect him when he goes into burning buildings.)

Guided Retelling

Tell children that now they will use the **Retelling Cards** to retell the story.

→ Display Retelling Card 1. Based on children's needs, use either the Modeled, Guided or ELL retelling prompts. The ELL prompts contain support for English language learners based on levels of language acquisition. Repeat with the rest of the cards, using the prompts as a guide.

→ Discuss the story. Have children tell about their favorite worker. Ask children why that worker is their favorite.

→ Have children share one new thing they learned about a worker's uniform or equipment from reading *Whose Shoes?*

Model Fluency

Reread page 15 of *Whose Shoes?* emphasizing the intonation. Point to the question mark. Remind children that when they read a sentence that asks a question, they should raise their voice at the end. Then reread the page, and have children repeat after you. Continue reading other pages, modeling the correct intonation for a question.

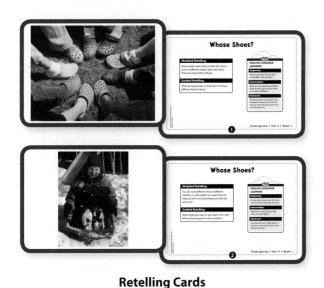

Retelling Cards

YOUR TURN PRACTICE BOOK p. 103

→ # Word Work

Quick Review
Build Fluency: Sound-Spellings: Show the following **Word-Building Cards:** *c, i, m, n, o, p, s, t.* Have children chorally say each sound. Repeat and vary the pace.

MINILESSON 5 Mins

Phonemic Awareness

OBJECTIVES

CCSS Associate the short sounds with common spellings for the five major vowels. **RF.K.3b**

CCSS Read common high-frequency words by sight. **RF.K.3c**

Phoneme Isolation

Photo Card

❶ **Model** Show the *Octopus* **Photo Card** and say the word. *Octopus has the /o/ sound at the beginning: /ooo/, octopus. Say the sound with me: /o/.* Tell children to listen for /o/ in the middle of the word. Display the *Mop* Photo Card. Have children say *mop* with you. *Mop has the /o/ sound in the middle. Listen: /m/ /ooo/ /p/, mop.* Emphasize the medial sound. *Let's say /o/ because we hear /o/ in the middle of mop: /o/.*

❷ **Guided Practice/Practice** Say each of the following words and have children repeat. Have them say /o/ if they hear the sound in the middle of the word. Guide children with the first word.

box   fit   hat   lock   mat   mop   not   sit   top

Then show Photo Cards for *nail, sock, top, hat, fox, mop.* Have children say the name of each picture with you. Ask them to tell whether or not they hear /o/ in the middle of the word.

Go Digital

MINILESSON 5 Mins

Phonics

ELL

ENGLISH LANGUAGE LEARNERS

High-Frequency Words: Reinforce Meaning Display the High-Frequency Word Card *you.* Reinforce the meaning of the word by pointing to the word as you ask the following questions. Have children respond.

- Can *you* jump?
- Can *you* walk?
- Can *you* sing?
- Can *you* dance?

Review Short /o/ *o*

Sound-Spelling Card

❶ **Model** Display the *Octopus* **Sound-Spelling** Card. *This is the letter* o. *The letter* o *stands for /o/ as in* octopus. *What is the letter?* (o) *What sound does the letter* o *stand for?* (/o/)

❷ **Guided Practice/Practice** Have children listen as you say some words. Ask them to write the letter *o* on their **Response Boards** if the word begins with /o/. Guide practice with the first two words.

sock   on   ill   ant   odd   tip   ox   past   olive

Repeat for medial /o/ *o* using the *Mop* Photo Card and the following words: *big, shop, pat, job, hop, ten, pot, sip.*

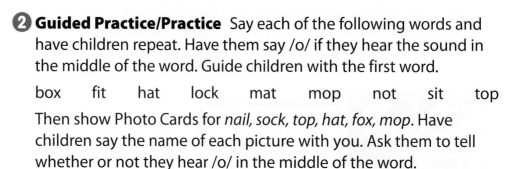

Phonemic Awareness

Phonics

High-Frequency Word Routine

Handwriting

Blend Words with /o/o

❶ Model Place **Word-Building Cards** *o* and *n* in a pocket chart. Point to the letter *o*. Say: *This is the letter* o. *The letter* o *stands for /o/. Say /o/. This is the letter* n. *The letter* n *stands for /n/. Say /n/. Listen as I blend the sounds together: /ooon/. Now blend the sounds with me to read the word.*

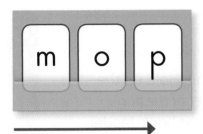

❷ Guided Practice/Practice Use Word-Building Cards or write *mop*. Point to the letter *m* and have children say the sound. Point to the letter *o* and have children say the sound. Point to the letter *p* and have children say the sound. Then move your hand from left to right under the word, and have children blend and read the word *mop*. Repeat with *top* and *pot*.

MINILESSON

5 Mins

High-Frequency Words

you

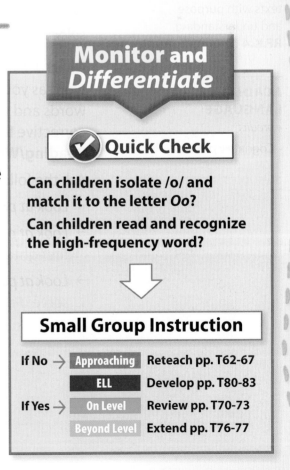

you

High-Frequency Word Card

❶ Guided Practice Display the **High-Frequency Word Card** *you*. Use the **Read/Spell/Write** routine to teach the word. Ask children to close their eyes, picture the word in their minds, and then write it the way they see it. Have children self-correct by checking the High-Frequency Word Card.

❷ Practice Add the high-frequency word *you* to the word bank.

→ Have partners create sentences using the word.

→ Have children count the number of letters in the word and then write the word again.

Cumulative Review Review words: *to, and, go, the, a, see, we, like.*

→ Repeat the **Read/Spell/Write** routine. Mix the words and have children chorally say each one.

Monitor and *Differentiate*

✓ **Quick Check**

Can children isolate /o/ and match it to the letter *Oo*?

Can children read and recognize the high-frequency word?

⬇

Small Group Instruction

If No →	Approaching	Reteach pp. T62-67
	ELL	Develop pp. T80-83
If Yes →	On Level	Review pp. T70-73
	Beyond Level	Extend pp. T76-77

→ # Shared Read

Reading/Writing Workshop Big Book and Reading/Writing Workshop

OBJECTIVES

CCSS Read common high-frequency words by sight. **RF.K.3c**

CCSS Read emergent-reader texts with purpose and understanding. **RF.K.4**

ACADEMIC LANGUAGE

• *predict*

• Cognates: *predecir*

MINILESSON
10 Mins

"Tom on Top!"

Model Skills and Strategies

Model Book Handling Demonstrate book handling. Hold up the book and turn to the front cover. *This is the front cover of the book.* Then display the back cover. *This is the back cover of the book.* Model turning the pages of the book.

Model Concepts About Print Continue reading the story aloud. *As I read each word aloud, I will use my finger to point out the word on the page.* Track the print with your finger so children can begin to develop a speech-to-print match. *Now let's read together. I will point to each word as we read it. I start at the top of the page and move to the bottom of the page.* Continue reading and tracking the print. Encourage children to chime in.

Predict Read the title together and look at the photograph. Ask children to predict what the selection will be about and where the selection will take place.

Read Have children chorally read the story with you. Point to each word as you read it together. Help children sound out the decodable words and say the sight words. If children have difficulty, provide corrective feedback and guide them page by page using the student **Reading/Writing Workshop**.

Ask the following:

→ *Look at page 9. What do you see on the page?* (a firehouse)

→ *Look at page 11. What kind of worker is this? Tell about her job.* (a firefighter; she helps to fight fires)

→ *Look at page 14. Why is the fireman holding a pot?* (He is helping to serve dinner for the firefighters.)

Go Digital

"Tom On Top!"

"Tom On Top!"

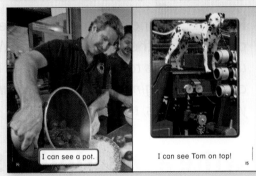
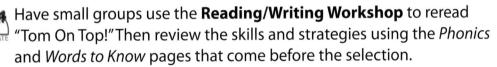

READING/WRITING WORKSHOP, pp. 8–15

Rereading

Have small groups use the **Reading/Writing Workshop** to reread "Tom On Top!" Then review the skills and strategies using the *Phonics* and *Words to Know* pages that come before the selection.

→ Tell children that as they reread, they can ask themselves questions. Explain that they can find the answers in the words. Remind them that they can also look for details in the photographs to help them answer questions.

→ Have children use page 7 to review the high-frequency word *you.*

→ Have children use page 6 to review that the letter *o* can stand for the sound /o/. Have them identify and name each picture. Guide them to blend the sounds to read the words.

ELL

ENGLISH LANGUAGE LEARNERS

Reinforce Vocabulary Display the **High-Frequency Word Cards** *you, I, the, we.* Point to classroom objects and groups of children as you use the high-frequency words in sentences such as the following: *You are sitting on a chair. Where are you sitting?* (I am sitting on a chair.) *I can see Juana hop. Can you see Juana hop?* (Yes, we can see Juana hop.) *I can go to the shelf. Can you go to the shelf?* (Yes, we can go to the shelf.) *We can go many places. Can we go to the lunch room?* (Yes, we can go to the lunch room.)

→ # Language Arts

 MINILESSON
10 Mins

Interactive Writing

Go Digital

Writing

I see a fish.

Grammar

OBJECTIVES

CCSS Use a combination of drawing, dictating, and writing to compose informative/explanatory texts in which they name what they are writing about and supply some information about the topic. **W.K.2**

CCSS Produce and expand complete sentences in shared language activities. **L.K.1f**

CCSS Sort common objects into categories (e.g., shapes, foods) to gain a sense of the concepts the categories represent. **L.K.5a**

ACADEMIC LANGUAGE

- *descriptive, sentence, details, adjective*
- Cognates: *detalles, adjetivo*

Writing Trait: Ideas

Review Remind children that writers use describing words to give details about the things in a story. Write and read aloud: *A carpenter uses noisy tools to build. When I read this sentence, I can imagine a carpenter banging on nails with a hammer or using a very loud drill. Can you picture this, too?*

Write a Descriptive Sentence

Discuss Display the Jobs chart from Day 1. Point to and read aloud the information in the chart. Guide children to choose one job to write about, such as the chef.

Model/Apply Grammar Tell children that you will work together to write a descriptive sentence that tells about a job, using the chart.

What things does a chef need? (a stove, a big hat) *Why does a chef need a stove?* (to cook with) *Why does a chef need a big hat?* (to cover the hair during cooking)

Write these sentences on sentence strips: *A chef uses a stove. A chef uses a hat.*

Read the sentences together, tracking the print. Model how to add a descriptive word to the second sentence. *What can we say about the hat? How can we describe it?* (tall, white) Cut the sentence strip between *a* and *hat*. Write *white* on another piece of sentence strip. Ask children where *white* goes in the sentence. Guide them to put the adjective before the noun. Track the print as you read aloud the sentence: *A chef uses a white hat.*

Write Use the chart to have children help you create another descriptive sentence. Point to and say *firefighter*. Ask which word in the second column names something a firefighter uses. (fire truck) Write and read aloud this sentence frame: *A _____ uses a _____.* Guide children to complete the sentence frame. Write the words. Share the pen with children and have them write the letters they know. Read aloud the completed sentence.

Grammar

MINILESSON 5 Mins

Describing Words (Adjectives)

❶ Review Explain to children that a describing word tells more about something. It is also called an *adjective*. Remind children that the names of colors are describing words. Colors can be used to describe naming words, or nouns.

→ Show **Photo Cards** for *hat* and *star*. Write and read aloud the following sentences:

> *There is a purple hat.*
> *I see a yellow star.*

Ask children to name the words that describe the things in each picture. (purple, yellow)

❷ Guided Practice Tell children that there are other ways to describe something.

Write and read aloud: *I see a round toy. She picks up a big box.*

Ask children which word describes the toy (round) and which word describes the box (big). Explain that shape and size are other ways to describe something. Ask children to help you draw a picture for each sentence. Point out how the adjective helps you see a clearer picture of the object it describes. *In the first sentence, the toy can be any shape, but the word round helps me know what shape it is.*

❸ Practice Have children work with a partner. Provide each pair with drawing paper, crayons, and describing words that tell shape, size, and color. Have pairs think of objects that can be used for each describing word. Ask partners to draw a picture of each object. Have partners label their drawings with the adjective(s) that describes their object. Offer help with writing as needed.

Talk About It

Have partners work together to orally generate sentences with adjectives. Encourage them to describe objects in the classroom.

ENGLISH LANGUAGE LEARNERS

Use Visuals Display Photo Cards for *ant, ball, bear, giraffe, jet,* and *plate.* Help children use describing words or gestures to describe each photo. For *small,* they can put two fingers close together; for *big,* they can spread their arms wide. Help children use words or sentences as well as they can to describe each photo.

Daily Wrap Up

- Discuss the Essential Question and encourage children to use the oral vocabulary words. *Which workers wear uniforms? Why do they need uniforms?*

- Prompt children to review and discuss the skills they used today. How do those skills help them?

Materials

Reading/Writing Workshop Big Book
UNIT 4

Interactive Read-Aloud Cards

Visual Vocabulary Cards
utensils
expect
remained

Photo Cards
box   mop
chin   pig
fish   six
fox   mix
mix   sock
       top

Word-Building Cards

go

High-Frequency Word Cards
go
you

Response Board

♪ "If You Take an Octopus to Dinner"

Puppet

I wonder...

Think Aloud Cloud

→ # Build the Concept

 MINILESSON 10 Mins

Oral Language

OBJECTIVES

CCSS With prompting and support, ask and answer questions about key details in a text. **RL.K.1**

CCSS Identify real-life connections between words and their use. **L.K.5c**

Develop oral vocabulary

ACADEMIC LANGUAGE
tale

ESSENTIAL QUESTION

Remind children that this week they are talking and learning about what people use to do their jobs. Guide children to discuss the Essential Question, using information from the **Big Book** and the weekly rhyme.

Remind children about the job of a firefighter in "Firefighters." Say the rhyme and have children join in.

Oral Vocabulary

Review last week's oral vocabulary words, as well as *equipment* and *uniform* from Day 1. Use the **Define/Example/Ask** routine to introduce *utensils, expect,* and *remained*.

Oral Vocabulary Routine

Define: **Utensils** are tools we use to cook or eat something.

Example: They used forks because these were the best utensils for eating pieces of watermelon.

Ask: What kind of utensil would you use to stir soup?

Define: If you think something will happen, you **expect** it.

Example: I expect that we will read a new book today.

Ask: What do you expect to do the next time you go to the playground?

Define: Something that **remained** in a place stayed there.

Example: The baby kangaroo remained in its mother's pouch for a long time.

Ask: Who remained at home today instead of coming to school?

Visual Vocabulary Cards

Go Digital

Visual Glossary

"Little Juan and the Cooking Pot"

Think Aloud Cloud

→ Listening Comprehension

Read the Interactive Read Aloud

NILESSON 10 Mins

Genre: Tale

Tell children you will be reading a *tale*, which is like a fable. Remind them that a fable is a fiction story that teaches a lesson. Display the Interactive **Read-Aloud Cards**.

Read the title. Tell children that this tale comes from Puerto Rico. Point to the island on a map. Then explain that a cooking pot is a very big pot that can hold a lot of food.

Interactive Read-Aloud Cards

Strategy: Ask and Answer Questions

Remind children that good readers ask themselves questions as they read. This helps them understand what is happening with the characters and plot of the story. Then they can look for answers in the pictures and words of the story. Use the **Think Aloud Cloud** to model asking and answering questions as you read.

Think Aloud I read about a character named Abuela Carmen, but I'm not sure who this is. I wonder who could Abuela Carmen be? I will read on to find out. Oh, I see. Abuela Carmen is Little Juan's grandmother. I answered my question and I understand now.

Read "Little Juan and the Cooking Pot." Pause to model the strategy of asking and answering questions. After each card, have children turn to a partner and share a question they have about a detail in the story.

Make Connections

COLLABORATE
Guide partners to connect "Little Juan and the Cooking Pot" with *Whose Shoes?* Discuss how both texts show the things people use to do their jobs.

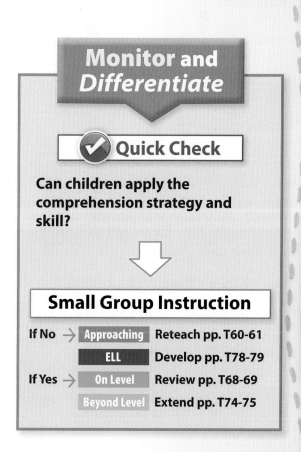

ELL

ENGLISH LANGUAGE LEARNERS

Reinforce Meaning As you read "Little Juan and the Cooking Pot," make meaning clear by pointing to specific characters, places, or objects in the illustrations, demonstrating word meanings, paraphrasing text, and asking children questions. For example, on Card 2, point to the pot. Say: *This is a pot.* Repeat with *apron* and *hat.*

Monitor and *Differentiate*

✓ **Quick Check**

Can children apply the comprehension strategy and skill?

⬇

Small Group Instruction

If No →	Approaching	Reteach pp. T60–61
	ELL	Develop pp. T78–79
If Yes →	On Level	Review pp. T68–69
	Beyond Level	Extend pp. T74–75

→ # Word Work

Quick Review
Build Fluency: Sound-Spellings: Show the following **Word-Building Cards:** *a, c, i, m, n, o, p, s, t*. Have children chorally say each sound. Repeat and vary the pace.

MINILESSON
5 Mins

Phonemic Awareness

Puppet

Phoneme Blending

❶ Model Use the puppet to demonstrate how to blend phonemes to make words. *The puppet is going to say sounds in a word: /o/ /ks/. It can blend the sounds to make a word: /oooks/ ox. When the puppet blends the sounds together, it makes the word* ox. Repeat with *odd, pop.*

❷ Guided Practice/Practice Have children blend sounds to form words. *The puppet is going to say the sounds in a word. Listen to the puppet as it says each sound. Repeat the sounds, then blend them to say the word.* Guide practice with the first word.

/r/ /o/ /k/   /o/ /d/   /ch/ /o/ /p/   /j/ /o/ /g/   /t/ /i/ /p/

/n/ /o/ /t/   /o/ /n/   /sh/ /o/ /p/   /m/ /a/ /d/   /f/ /i/ /sh/

/j/ /o/ /b/   /k/ /ī/ /t/   /f/ /ē/ /t/   /h/ /a/ /t/   /g/ /ā/ /t/

♪ Review initial /o/. Play and sing "If You Take an Octopus to Dinner." Have children clap when they hear initial /o/. Demonstrate as you sing with them.

OBJECTIVES

CCSS Isolate and pronounce the initial, medial vowel, and final sounds in three-phoneme words. **RF.K.2d**

CCSS Demonstrate basic knowledge of one-to-one letter-sound correspondences by producing the primary or many of the most frequent sounds for each consonant. **RF.K.3a**

Blend phonemes to make words

Go Digital

Phonemic Awareness

c a t
Phonics

A A
a a
Handwriting

Phonics

Word-Building Card

Review Short /o/o

❶ **Model** Display **Word-Building Card** o. *This is the letter* o. *The letter* o *stands for /ooo/, the sound you hear in the middle of* mop. *Say the sound with me: /ooo/. I will write the letter* o *because* mop *has the /ooo/ sound in the middle.*

❷ **Guided Practice/Practice** Tell children that you will say some words that have /o/ in the middle and some words that do not. Have children say /o/ and write the letter o on their **Response Boards** when they hear /o/ in the middle of the word. Guide practice with the first word.

hit   top   fox   kit   not   pan   lock

Blend Words with Short o and n, p, t, c, m

❶ **Model** Display Word-Building Cards n, o, t. *This is the letter* n. *It stands for /n/. This is the letter* o. *It stands for /o/. This is the letter* t. *It stands for /t/. Let's blend the three sounds together: /nnnooot/. The word is* not. Continue with *pot, cot, mop.*

❷ **Guided Practice/Practice** Write the following words and sentences. Have children read each word, blending the sounds. Guide practice with the first word.

pop   top   tot   not   pot

Write these sentences and prompt children to read the connected text, sounding out the decodable words: *We can see the top. The pot is not on top. The tot is on the cot.*

Remind children that the letter *o* is called a *vowel*. The vowels they are learning about this year are *a, e, i, o,* and *u.* Every word, syllable, or word part in a longer word, must have a vowel. The rest of the letters in the alphabet, such as *m, s, p, t, n,* and *c* are called *consonants.* Words are made up of vowels and consonants. The word *mop* is made up of the vowel *o* and the consonants *m* and *p.*

Corrective Feedback

Sound Error Model the sound that children missed, then have them repeat. For example, for the word *top,* say: *I hear three sounds in* top. *What are the three sounds?* Return to the beginning of the word. *Let's start over.* Blend the word with children again.

YOUR TURN PRACTICE BOOK p. 104

→ # Word Work

Go Digital

Photo Cards

MINILESSON 5 Mins Phonics

Picture Sort

① Model Remind children that the letter *o* can stand for /o/. Place the **Word-Building Card** *o* in one column in a pocket chart and point to it. *What is this letter?* (o) *What sound does it stand for?* (/o/)

Hold up the **Photo Card** for *top*. *Here is the picture for* top. Top *has the /o/ sound in the middle. Listen, /t/ /ooo/ /p/. I will place* top *under the letter* o *because the letter* o *stands for /o/.*

Repeat with medial /i/ *i* and the Photo Card for *mix*.

② Guided Practice/Practice Display and name the following Photo Cards: *box, chin, fish, fox, mop, pig, six, sock*. Have children say the picture name and the sound in the middle of the word. Have them tell under which letter the Photo Card should be placed. Guide children with the first word.

Photo Cards

Phonics

High-Frequency Word Routine

OBJECTIVES

CCSS Read common high-frequency words by sight. **RF.K.3c**

Sort picture names by medial phonemes

ACADEMIC LANGUAGE

sort

High-Frequency Words

you

❶ Guided Practice Display the **High-Frequency Word Card** *you*. Review the word using the **Read/Spell/Write** routine.

❷ Practice Point to the High-Frequency Word Card *you* and have children read it. Repeat with last week's word *go*.

Build Fluency

Word Automaticity Write the following sentences and have children chorally read aloud as you track the print. Repeat several times.

> Can *you* go?
> *You* and I can go.
> *You* and I can see Tom.
> Can *you* nap on the mat?

Read for Fluency Chorally read the **Take-Home Book** in the **Your Turn Practice Book,** pages 105–106, with children. Then have children reread the book to review high-frequency words and build fluency.

YOUR TURN PRACTICE BOOK pp. 105–106

Monitor and Differentiate

✓ **Quick Check**

Can children blend phonemes to make words and sort words by medial /o/o and medial /i/ i?

Can children read and recognize the high-frequency word?

⬇

Small Group Instruction

If No →	Approaching	Reteach pp. T62-67
	ELL	Develop pp. T80-83
If Yes →	On Level	Review pp. T70-73
	Beyond Level	Extend pp. T76-77

→ Language Arts

Reading/Writing Workshop Big Book

OBJECTIVES

CCSS Use a combination of drawing, dictating, and writing to compose informative/ explanatory texts in which they name what they are writing about and supply some information about the topic. **W.K.2**

CCSS Produce and expand complete sentences in shared language activities. **L.K.1f**

CCSS Sort common objects into categories (e.g., shapes, foods) to gain a sense of the concepts the categories represent. **L.K.5a**

ACADEMIC LANGUAGE

• *sentence, adjective*
• Cognates: *adjetivo*

MINILESSON
10 Mins

Independent Writing

Writing Trait: Ideas

1 Practice Tell children that they will write a descriptive sentence about a worker and draw a picture for the sentence.

2 Guided Practice Share the Readers to Writers page in the **Reading/Writing Workshop**. Read the model sentences aloud.

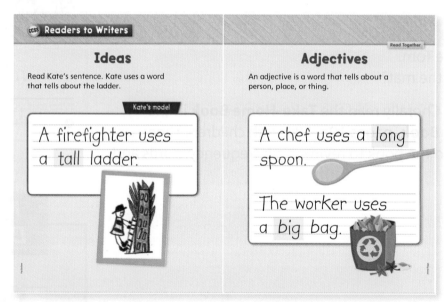

CCSS Readers to Writers

Ideas

Read Kate's sentence. Kate uses a word that tells about the ladder.

Kate's model

A firefighter uses a tall ladder.

Adjectives   *Read Together*

An adjective is a word that tells about a person, place, or thing.

A chef uses a long spoon.

The worker uses a big bag.

READING/WRITING WORKSHOP BIG BOOK, pp. 18–19

Write a Descriptive Sentence

Model Write: *A chef uses a _____ _____.* Point to the blanks and say: *I will write about something that a chef uses. I will write a describing word to tell what it looks like.* Write *long spoon* in the blanks. *This sentence tells about something that the chef uses at work. The word* long *tells what the spoon looks like.*

Prewrite

Brainstorm Have children work with a partner to choose a worker to write about. Ask them to think of the tools that worker uses.

Go Digital

Present the Lesson

We share toys.

Writing

I see a fish.

Grammar

Draft

Ask children to write about a job and describe something that's needed to do the job. Guide them in using this sentence frame: *A _____ uses a _____ _____.* Help them write the name of the worker and an adjective to describe what she/he uses on the job. Then have children draw a picture for their sentence.

Apply Writing Trait As children work, ask them to describe more details about what the worker uses on the job.

Apply Grammar After children write their sentences, ask them to point to the describing words (adjectives).

Grammar

Describing Words (Adjectives)

❶ Review Remind children that an adjective is a describing word that tells more about something, such as its color, shape, or size.

Write and read aloud the following sentences:

> *I like my blue shoes.*
> *I eat a square cracker.*
> *I sit under a tall tree.*

Ask children to name the adjective in each sentence (blue, square, tall) and tell if it describes color, shape, or size.

❷ Guided Practice/Practice Write the following words on separate sticky notes: *big, small, round, gray, red, blue, white, shirt, ball, elephant,* and *rabbit.* Read the words aloud. Ask children to raise their hands when they hear you say a describing word. Put adjectives in one column. Show *ball.* Ask which adjectives can describe it. Write and read aloud each combination that children make, such as *small ball, round ball, red ball, white ball.* Point out that more than one adjective might describe some items.

Have children work in groups. Ask children to put together more combinations of adjectives and nouns. Have children write each combination and draw a picture of it.

Talk About It

Have partners work together to orally generate sentences with adjectives. Encourage children to create sentences with more than one adjective.

Daily Wrap Up

- Review the Essential Question and encourage children to discuss it, using the oral vocabulary words *equipment* and *uniform. What do workers use to do their jobs? Where might you find each worker?*

- Prompt children to review and discuss the skills they used today. Guide them to give examples of how they used each skill.

Materials

Reading/Writing Workshop Big Book
UNIT 4

Reading/Writing Workshop
UNIT 4

Literature Big Book
Whose Shoes? A Shoe for Every Job

Interactive Read-Aloud Cards

Word-Building Cards

Visual Vocabulary Cards
you

High-Frequency Word Cards
you

Photo Cards
astronaut
cat
doctor
dog
horse
nurse
tiger
umpire

Puppet

→ # Extend the Concept

Oral Language

MINILESSON **10** Mins

OBJECTIVES

CCSS Blend and segment onsets and rimes of single-syllable spoken words. **RF.K.2c**

CCSS Use words and phrases acquired through conversations, reading and being read to, and responding to texts. **L.K.6**

Develop oral vocabulary

ESSENTIAL QUESTION

Remind children that this week they have been talking and reading about the things people use to do their jobs. Have them recite the rhyme "Firefighters" and tell about what firefighters use to do their jobs. *What kind of shoes do clowns wear to do their job in* Whose Shoes?

Phonological Awareness
Onset/Rime Segmentation

We can break words into beginning and end parts. Listen: time: /t/ /īm/. Have children repeat. Repeat the routine with *dime:* /d/ /īm/. Guide children to segment the beginning and end sounds in the following words: *bed* (/b/ /ed/); *red* (/r/ /ed/); *ride* (/r/ /īd/); *side* (/s/ /īd/).

Review Oral Vocabulary

Reread the Interactive Read Aloud Use the **Define/Example/Ask** routine to review the oral vocabulary words *equipment, uniform, utensils, expect,* and *remained.* Then have children listen as you reread "Little Juan and the Cooking Pot."

→ *What is Little Juan supposed to borrow from his grandmother?* (her big pot and cooking utensils)

→ *What does Little Juan expect the pot to do?* (walk)

Go Digital

Visual Glossary

"Little Juan and the Cooking Pot"

Category Words

Category Words: Job Words

❶ Explain/Model Chant the following jingle:

> *A ballerina dances.*
> *A soccer player kicks.*
> *A firefighter rescues.*
> *A clown does silly tricks.*

→ Repeat the first line of the jingle and ask children which word is a job word, or a word that describes what someone does for work. (ballerina) Repeat with the remaining lines. Guide children to name more job words, and then add them to the jingle. (Possible answers: A construction worker builds; A clerk pays the bills.)

❷ Guided Practice Display the **Photo Cards** for *astronaut, cowboy, doctor, nurse,* and *umpire*. Review the job words that go with each card. What does an astronaut do for work? What do you think an astronaut's job is like? What tools does an astronaut use? What does an astronaut wear?

→ Have children think about workers in the community that they know or see every day. Ask them to identify job words for these people. (Possible answers: store clerk, school crossing guard, bus driver, coach)

LET'S MOVE!

Form pairs and have children pretend they are one of the workers on the Photo Cards. Have partners take turns acting out the worker doing his or her job. Children should try to guess which job their partner is doing.

YOUR TURN PRACTICE BOOK p. 107

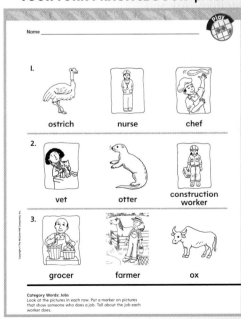

→ **Listening Comprehension**

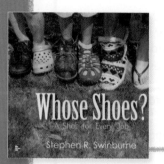

Literature Big Book

OBJECTIVES

CCSS With prompting and support, describe the relationship between illustrations and the text in which they appear (e.g., what person, place, thing, or idea in the text an illustration depicts). **RI.K.7**

- Understand the characteristics of informational text
- Use the text feature labels to gather information
- Apply the comprehension strategy: Ask and Answer Questions
- Make connections across texts

ACADEMIC LANGUAGE

- *photograph, labels*
- Cognates: *fotografía*

MINILESSON
10 Mins

Read "Workers and Their Tools"

"Whose Shoes? A Shoe for Every Job"

Genre: Informational Text

Display "Workers and Their Tools" on pages 32–36 of the **Big Book** and read aloud the title. Explain to children that this informational text gives information about real workers and the tools they use.

Set a Purpose for Reading

Read aloud the first sentence on page 32. Tell children to listen as you continue reading the selection about different workers and the tools they use to do their jobs.

Strategy: Ask and Answer Questions

Remind children that good readers ask and answer questions as they read. Have children look at page 32. *The text asks: What other tools does a chef use? We can find the answer by looking at the photographs: a knife and a frying pan.*

Text Feature: Labels

Explain Point to the labels on page 32. *Labels give more information about photographs. These labels name the tools in the photographs.* Read the labels aloud and have children echo read.

Apply Turn to page 33 and read it aloud. *What does the label in each photograph tell you?* (the name of the object: boots, ax, helmet)

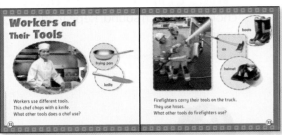

LITERATURE BIG BOOK PAGES 32–33

KEY DETAILS

Point to the large photograph on page 32. *What tools do you see in the photograph of the chef in the kitchen?* (stove, fryer, knife, pan, hat, white coat)

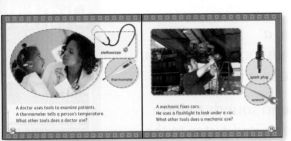

LITERATURE BIG BOOK PAGES 34–35

ASK AND ANSWER QUESTIONS

Point to and read aloud the labels on page 34. *What does a doctor use a stethoscope for?* (to examine a patient; to listen to someone's heart and lungs)

LITERATURE BIG BOOK PAGE 36

KEY DETAILS

Look at the bottom photograph of the girls doing an activity. What tools are the girls using for their activity? (Possible answers: buckets, spoons, containers, measuring cups)

ENGLISH LANGUAGE LEARNERS

Reinforce Meaning As you read aloud the text, make the meaning clear by pointing to details in the photographs. Ask children questions and elicit language.

Retell and Respond

Have children discuss the selection by asking the following questions:

→ *How do hoses help firefighters?* (They spray water to put out fires.)

→ *Why do mechanics need tools?* (to help them fix cars)

Make Connections

Have children recall the selections they have read this week.

→ *The selections this week have told about tools. Which kind of shoes does a ballerina use as a tool to help her dance?* (ballet slippers)

Write About It Write about one of the tools Little Juan's mother uses to cook.

CONNECT TO CONTENT

Tools on the Job Review with children the different tools people use to do their jobs. Have partners choose a worker and think about other tools they may use. Have partners share their ideas with the class.

Word Work

Quick Review

Build Fluency: Sound-Spellings:
Show the following **Word-Building Cards:** *a, c, i, m, n, o, p, s, t.* Have children chorally say each sound. Repeat and vary the pace.

Phonemic Awareness

Puppet

OBJECTIVES

CCSS Distinguish between similarly spelled words by identifying the sounds of letters that differ. **RF.K.3d**

CCSS Read common high-frequency words by sight. **RF.K.3c**

• Blend phonemes to make words

• Blend letter sounds to make words

Phoneme Blending

❶ Model *The puppet is going to say the sounds in a word. Listen: /b/ /o/ /ks/. It can blend these sounds together: /boooks/,* box. *Now say the word with the puppet:* box. Repeat with *lock.*

❷ Guided Practice/Practice Have children blend sounds to form words. *The puppet is going to say the sounds in a word. Listen to the puppet as it says each sound. Repeat the sounds, then blend them to say the word.* Guide practice with the first word.

/p/ /o/ /t/   /m/ /o /m/   /t/ /o/ /t/   /k/ /o/ /t/   /r/ /o/ /k/

Phonics

Blend Words with *Short o, a* and *m, p, t*

❶ Guided Practice Display **Word-Building Cards** *t, o, p.* Point to the letter *t.* *This is the letter* t. *It stands for /t/. Say: /t/. This is the letter* o. *It stands for /o/. Listen as I blend the two sounds together /tooo/. Say: /tooo/. This is the letter* p. *It stands for /p/. Listen as I blend the three sounds: /tooop/,* top. *Now you say it. Let's change* o *to* a. *Use the same routine to blend* tap.

❷ Practice Display Word-Building Cards *n, o, t.* Have children blend the word. Change the letters to make the following words and have children blend: *tot, cot, pot, pop, top, mop.*

Write *not, tot, cot* in a list and ask children which letters are the same in all three words. (*ot*) Point out how all of the words end with the same sound, /ot/. Ask children which letters are different. (*n, t, c*) Discuss the sound each letter stands for and how it changes the word. Repeat with *pop, top, mop.*

Go Digital

Phonemic Awareness

Phonics

Handwriting

Visual Glossary

High-Frequency Word Routine

Dictation

Review Dictate the following sounds for children to spell. Have them repeat the sound and then write the letter that stands for the sound.

/o/   /k/   /n/   /i/   /t/   /p/   /a/

Dictate the following words for children to spell: *can, pit, mop, tan.* Model for children how to segment each word to scaffold the spelling.

When I say the word can, *I hear three sounds: /k/ /a/ /n/. I know the letter* c *stands for /k/, the letter* a *stands for /a/, and the letter* n *stands for /n/. I will write* c, a, n *to spell the word* can.

When children finish, write the letters and words for them to self-correct.

MINILESSON
5 Mins

High-Frequency Words

Visual Vocabulary Card

you

Practice Say the word *you* and have children write it. Then display the **Visual Vocabulary Card** *you* and follow the Teacher Talk on the back.

Build Fluency Build sentences in a pocket chart using **High-Frequency Word Cards** and **Photo Cards**. Use an index card to create a punctuation card for a period. Have children chorally read the sentences as you track the print. Then have them identify the word *you.*

> The doctor can see *you.*
>
> *You* can go to the farm.
>
> *You* and I like toys.

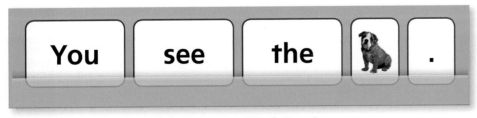

High-Frequency Words Practice

Have partners create sentences using the word *you.*

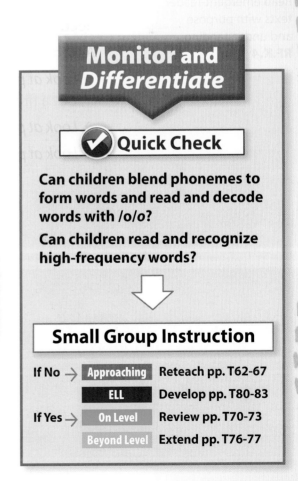

Monitor and Differentiate

✔ **Quick Check**

Can children blend phonemes to form words and read and decode words with /o/o?

Can children read and recognize high-frequency words?

Small Group Instruction

If No →	Approaching	Reteach pp. T62-67
	ELL	Develop pp. T80-83
If Yes →	On Level	Review pp. T70-73
	Beyond Level	Extend pp. T76-77

→ # Shared Read

Reading/Writing Workshop Big Book and Reading/Writing Workshop

---

OBJECTIVES

CCSS Read common high-frequency words by sight. **RF.K.3c**

CCSS Read emergent-reader texts with purpose and understanding. **RF.K.4**

MINILESSON
10 Mins

Read "Tom On Top!"

Model Skills and Strategies

Model Book Handling Demonstrate book handling. Point to the front cover of the book. *This is the front cover of the book.* Then display the back cover of the book. *This is the back cover of the book.* Model turning the pages of the book.

Model Concepts About Print Remind children how to develop speech to print matching. *When I say each word in the sentence, I will point to it. As I read, I will move from left to right, like this.* Move your finger from left to right along a sentence. *I will read the words at the top of the page first and move to the bottom of the page.*

Reread Review each rebus and remind children what it stands for. Then have children chorally read the story. Children should sound out the decodable words and say the sight words. Offer support as needed using the student **Reading/Writing Workshop**.

Ask the following:

→ *Look at page 12. What is this firefighter doing?* (using a hose to put out a fire)

→ *Look at page 13. Who wears this hat?* (the firefighter)

→ *Look at page 15. What is Tom doing?* (standing on the truck)

Go Digital

"Tom On Top!"

"Tom On Top!"

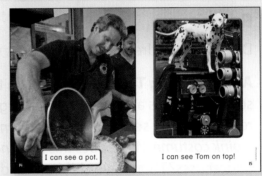

READING/WRITING WORKSHOP, pp. 8–15

Fluency: Intonation

❶ Explain Tell children that as you read the story, you will change your voice in different ways. Explain that your tone will change in different ways when you read sentences that end with a period, a question mark, or an exclamation point. Point out the different kinds of punctuation in the story.

❷ Model Model reading page 9 of "Tom On Top!" and point to the question mark at the end of the sentence. *When I read a sentence that ends with a question mark, I change my tone so that my voice goes higher, like this.* Read the question with proper intonation. Then point out the difference in intonation by reading sentences that end with a period or an exclamation point.

❸ Guided Practice Read the title and have children echo you. Then read each sentence in the story and have children repeat it using proper intonation.

→ # Language Arts

MINILESSON
10 Mins

Independent Writing

Write a Descriptive Sentence

Revise

Distribute children's draft sentences with drawings from Day 3.

Apply Writing Trait Ideas Explain that as writers revise, they make sure their ideas are clear by checking the words they used. Write and read aloud the sentence: *A ballet dancer wears red ballet shoes and a pink costume. What does this sentence tell you about what a ballet dancer uses?* Then have children read the sentences they wrote and check for the following:

→ Who is the worker?

→ Did I write about what the worker uses to do the job?

→ Does my sentence have a descriptive word?

Apply Grammar Explain that writers can use adjectives to give more details. Write and read aloud: *A farmer wears boots.* Show the **Big Book** picture of the farmer. Ask children what adjectives they can use to describe the boots. (tall, black) Write: *A farmer wears tall boots.*

Peer Edit Have children work with a partner to do a peer edit. Ask partners to check that the sentences have describing words. Partners should read the sentences aloud to see if there are any missing words. Provide time for children to make revisions to their sentences.

Final Draft

After children have edited their own papers and finished their peer edits, have them write their final drafts. Explain that they should leave the same amount of space between each word and keep their letters the same size. As children work, conference with them to provide guidance.

OBJECTIVES

CCSS With guidance and support from adults, respond to questions and suggestions from peers and add details to strengthen writing as needed. **W.K.5**

CCSS Produce and expand complete sentences in shared language activities. **L.K.1f**

Revise sentences

ACADEMIC LANGUAGE

• *revise, draft, detail, adjective*
• Cognates: *revisar, detalles, adjetivo*

Go Digital

Writing

I see a fish.

Grammar

Grammar

Describing Words (Adjectives)

1 Review Remind children that an adjective is a describing word that tells more about something, such as its color, shape, or size.

Write this sentence on a sentence strip: *He cuts the _____ paper.*

Have children give adjectives that can be used to describe paper. (any color, shape, or size) Write their suggestions on sentence strips and cut them to separate the words.

2 Guided Practice Ask children to choose an adjective that describes size and put the word in the sentence strip. For example: *He cuts the tiny paper.* Read the completed sentence aloud. Have children read along with you.

Repeat this procedure, asking children to choose an adjective that describes shape and then color. In each case, remind children that these words are adjectives because they describe something.

3 Practice Have children work in small groups. Provide each group with their own copies of the sentence frame: *We play with _____ toys.* Ask children to choose a word that describes a size, shape, or color and write it in the sentence frame. Have children read aloud the sentences they made. Provide support as needed.

Talk About It

Have partners work together to orally generate sentences with adjectives. Encourage them to use adjectives to describe the kinds of food they like to eat.

ENGLISH LANGUAGE LEARNERS

Picture Cards and Sentences Provide descriptive sentences that go with the images on the **Photo Cards** for *cat, dog, horse,* and *tiger.* Hold up a Photo Card for the animal as you say the sentence aloud, such as *The tiger has black stripes.*

Daily Wrap Up

- Review the Essential Question and encourage children to discuss it, using the oral vocabulary words.

- Prompt children to discuss the skills they practiced and learned today. Guide them to share examples of each skill.

Go Digital

www.connected.mcgraw-hill.com
RESOURCES
Research and Inquiry

→ **Wrap Up the Week**
Integrate Ideas

RESEARCH AND INQUIRY

Time for Work

OBJECTIVES

CCSS Participate in shared research and writing projects (e.g., explore a number of books by a favorite author and express opinions about them). **W.K.7**

CCSS With guidance and support from adults, recall information from experiences or gather information from provided sources to answer a question. **W.K.8**

ACADEMIC LANGUAGE
research

Make a Jobs Board

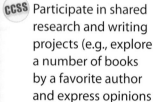 Tell children that today, as part of a small group, they will do a research project to make a poster about a job and the tools needed for that job. Groups will work together to create a job board of the different posters. Review the steps in the research process below.

STEP 1 **Choose a Topic**

Have groups brainstorm the different jobs that people do. Tell children to think about the jobs people do in schools, stores, at hospitals, and so on. If possible, invite some parents to talk about their jobs.

STEP 2 **Find Resources**

Talk about locating and using resources. Guide children to use this week's selections as resources. Also consider web sites and library books about jobs or workers as resources. Have children use the Research Process Checklist online.

STEP 3 **Keep Track of Ideas**

Have children list their ideas by drawing pictures or writing words. If children have outside resources, provide self-stick notes so they can bookmark the pages.

Collaborative Conversations

Provide Details As children engage in discussions with a partner, in a small group, and as a whole class, encourage them to:

→ give details to express their thoughts, feelings, and ideas clearly.

→ use details to describe people, places, things, and events.

→ give details when asking about something they do not understand.

STEP 4 **Create the Project: Jobs Board**

Explain the characteristics of a poster:

→ **Information** These posters will give information about a worker and the tools he or she uses on the job.

→ **Text** Explain that each poster will have a sentence that identifies the worker and names at least one of the tools shown. Provide these sentence frames:

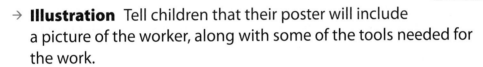
I am a _____. I use a _____.

→ **Illustration** Tell children that their poster will include a picture of the worker, along with some of the tools needed for the work.

Have groups work together to create their informational poster for the Jobs Board.

→ Prompt children to complete their sentence frames. Encourage children who can generate more writing to do so.

→ Remind children to include details in their illustrations so viewers understand what the workers do and what they use to do their jobs.

Groups can combine their posters to create the Jobs Board.

I am a doctor. I use a stethoscope.

ENGLISH LANGUAGE LEARNERS
SCAFFOLD

Beginning	**Intermediate**	**Advanced/Advanced High**
Elaborate Allow children to point to and identify details on posters with single-word names. Restate the information using a complete sentence. Then elicit more information and, again, refashion the child's answer into a complete sentence.	**Identify** As groups work on their posters, prompt them to talk about and identify all of the details they are adding to their illustration. Tell children to imagine that other students are viewing their poster and asking questions about those details.	**Describe** Direct children to include describing words as they tell about the details in their poster. For example: I am a Firefighter. I use <u>black</u> boots.

Materials

Reading/Writing Workshop Big Book
UNIT 4

Literature Big Book
Whose Shoes? A Shoe for Every Job

Interactive Read-Aloud Cards

Word-Building Cards

Visual Vocabulary Cards

High-Frequency Word Cards

a
and
go
like
see
the
to
we
you

Photo Cards

ax
camel
car
lemon
light
moon
moth
nail

nut
ostrich
otter
ox
paint
peach
pig
pizza
sock
tiger
toys

Response Board

"If You Take an Octopus to Dinner"

→ Integrate Ideas

TEXT CONNECTIONS

OBJECTIVES

CCSS With prompting and support, identify basic similarities in and differences between two texts on the same topic (e.g., in illustrations, descriptions, or procedures). **RI.K.9**

CCSS Participate in collaborative conversations with diverse partners about *kindergarten topics and texts* with peers and adults in small and larger groups. **SL.K.1**

- Make connections among texts
- Make connections to the world

Text to Text

Remind children that, all week, they have been reading selections about the things people use to do their jobs. Tell them that now they will think about how the selections are alike and different. Model comparing *Whose Shoes? A Shoe for Every Job* with another selection from the week.

Think Aloud In *Whose Shoes? A Shoe for Every Job*, I saw lots of different kinds of shoes. Different kinds of workers use those shoes to do their jobs. In "Workers and Their Tools" I learned about the different tools that workers use on the job. Both selections showed the tools and equipment needed to do different kinds of work.

Guide children to compare the types of workers and equipment they have read about and seen in the selections from the week, including the Leveled Readers.

Text to Self

Have children tell what job they might like to have when they are older. Ask: *What equipment would you use to do your job?*

Text to World

Talk about the different kinds of workers that children have seen around town. Ask: *What workers do you see at school, in your neighborhood, and in between? What kinds of equipment do they use?*

TALK ABOUT READING

OBJECTIVES

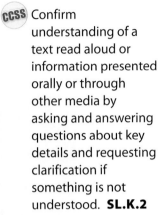

CCSS Confirm understanding of a text read aloud or information presented orally or through other media by asking and answering questions about key details and requesting clarification if something is not understood. **SL.K.2**

Becoming Readers

Talk with children about the genres, strategy, and skill they have learned about this week. Prompt them to discuss how this knowledge helps them to read and understand selections.

→ Remind children that one genre they learned about is informational text. Recall with them some of the characteristics of informational text.

→ Talk with children about the strategy of asking and answering questions. *How did pausing to ask and answer questions about illustrations or text help you understand what you were reading?*

→ Point out that children learned to look for key details in the words and photos to help them understand the text. *Why is it important to look closely at photographs when you are reading informational text?*

RESEARCH AND INQUIRY

OBJECTIVES

CCSS Participate in shared research and writing projects (e.g., explore a number of books by a favorite author and express opinions about them). **W.K.7**

Wrap Up the Project

Guide partners to share information from their poster and to point out details in their illustrations. Encourage children to use words and phrases they learned this week. Have children use the Presenting and Listening checklists online.

→ # Word Work

Quick Review

Build Fluency: Sound-Spellings: Show the following **Word-Building Cards:** *a, c, i, m, n, o, p, s, t.* Have children chorally say each sound. Repeat and vary the pace.

MINILESSON 5 Mins

Phonemic Awareness

OBJECTIVES

CCSS Spell simple words phonetically, drawing on knowledge of sound-letter relationships. **L.K.2d**

CCSS Read common high-frequency words by sight. **RF.K.3c**

Categorize words with the same initial phoneme

Phoneme Categorization

❶ **Model** Display **Photo Cards** for *otter, ox, nail. Listen for which picture names begin with the same sound.* Say the picture names. Otter *and* ox *both begin with /o/.* Nail *does not begin with /o/.* Nail *does not belong.*

❷ **Guided Practice/Practice** Show children sets of Photo Cards. Name the pictures. Have children repeat and then identify the picture in each set that does not begin with the same sound. Guide practice with the first set of words.

pizza, paint, nut	car, pig, camel	ostrich, otter, ax
tiger, sock, toys	pizza, peach, moon	moth, lemon, light

MINILESSON 5 Mins

Phonics

Read Words with Short *o, a* and *c, m, p, t*

❶ **Guided Practice** Remind children that the letter *o* can stand for the sound /o/. Repeat for *a.* Display **Word-Building Cards** *p, o, t.* Point to the letter *p. The letter* p *stands for the sound /p/. Say /p/. Point to the letter* o. *The letter* o *stands for the sound /o/. Say /ooo/. The letter* t *stands for /t/. Say /t/. Let's blend the sounds to make the word: /pooot/* pot. *Let's change the* p *to* c. *Blend and read* cot.

❷ **Practice** Write the words and sentences for children to read:

mop   top   tap   cap

Pam sat on the mat.	I am not on the mat.
I am on the cot.	Sam can see the mop.

Remove words from view before dictation.

♪ Review initial /o/ *o.* Have children write the letter *o* on their **Response Boards.** Play and sing "If You Take an Octopus to Dinner." Have children hold up and show the letter *o* on their boards when they hear initial /o/. Demonstrate as you sing with children.

Go Digital

Phonemic Awareness

m	a
n	t	p

Phonics

Handwriting

Visual Glossary

Dictation

❶ **Review** Dictate the following sounds for children to spell. As you say each sound, have children repeat it and then write the letter on their **Response Boards** that stands for the sound.

/k/   /n/   /i/   /o/   /p/   /s/   /m/   /a/

Dictate the following words for children to spell. Model for children how to use sound boxes to segment each word to scaffold the spelling. *I will say a word. You will repeat the word, then think about how many sounds are in the word. Use your Sound Boxes to count the sounds. Then write one letter for each sound you hear.*

mop   can   on   sip   map   pin

Then write the letters and words for children to self-correct.

MINILESSON
5 Mins

High-Frequency Words

you

Visual Vocabulary Card

❶ **Review** Display **Visual Vocabulary Card** *you*. Have children **Read/Spell/Write** the word. Use the Partner Talk on the back of the card.

Distribute one of the following **High-Frequency Word Cards** to children: *you, go, and, to, the, a, see, we, like*. Tell children that you will say some sentences. *When you hear a word that is on your card, stand and hold up your word card.*

Tom *and I like the* park.
Would *you like to* work with us?
Jenna can *go* with us.
Did *you* want *to* ride along?
Did she *see* them?
We want *a* treat.

❷ **Build Fluency: Word Automaticity** Display High-Frequency Word Cards *you, go, and, to, the, a, see, we,* and *like.* Point to each card, at random, and have children read the word as quickly as they can.

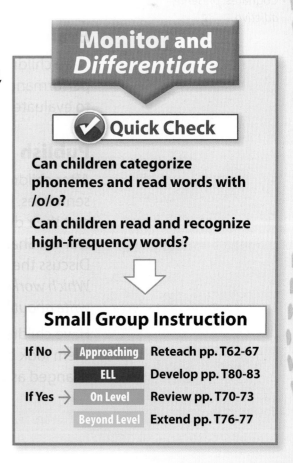

Monitor and *Differentiate*

✔ **Quick Check**

Can children categorize phonemes and read words with /o/o?

Can children read and recognize high-frequency words?

⬇

Small Group Instruction

If No →	**Approaching**	Reteach pp. T62-67
	ELL	Develop pp. T80-83
If Yes →	**On Level**	Review pp. T70-73
	Beyond Level	Extend pp. T76-77

→ # Language Arts

MINILESSON
10 Mins

Independent Writing

Write a Descriptive Sentence

Prepare

Tell children that they will present their finished sentences with drawings from Day 4 to the class. Hold up an example from Day 4 and read it aloud, tracking the print. Then say: *I held my picture up high so everyone could see it. I read my sentence slowly enough so everyone could understand me.*

Present

Have children take turns standing up and reading their sentences aloud. Remind children to show everyone their pictures and to read their sentences slowly so everyone can understand them. Encourage the rest of the class to listen quietly and to wait until the presenter has finished before asking any questions.

Evaluate

Have children discuss their own presentations and evaluate their performances, using the presentation rubric. Use the teacher's rubric to evaluate children's writing.

Publish

After children have finished presenting, collect their drawings and sentences. Create wall collages of workers. Have children help you sort their drawings into groups so each collage shows the same worker. Share some sentences and drawings from each collage. Discuss the tool or equipment children chose to write for each worker. *Which worker did most of you write about? Which tool did most of you write about?*

Have children add their writing to their Writer's Portfolio. Then have them look back at their previous writing and discuss how they have changed as writers throughout the year.

**Go
Digital**

Writing

I see a fish.

Grammar

Grammar

Describing Words (Adjectives)

1 Review Remind children that an adjective is a describing word that tells more about something, such as its color, shape, or size.

List adjectives that tell color, shape, or size (red, blue, yellow, green; round, square, triangle, rectangle; big, little, tall, short). Ask children to name something that each adjective can describe.

2 Review Practice Write and read aloud this sentence:

I found a _____ *box.* Ask children to name adjectives that can be used in the sentence frame.

Have children work with a partner to think of describing words that can be used for a box. Ask the pairs if more than one adjective can be used to describe a box.

Circulate to help children express their thoughts and to offer corrective feedback as needed.

Wrap Up the Week

- Review blending words with initial and medial /o/o.
- Remind children that describing words tell more about something.
- Use the High-Frequency Word Cards to review the Words to Know.
- Remind children that they can write descriptive sentences to give more details about their ideas.

Approaching Level

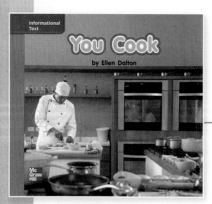

Leveled Reader

OBJECTIVES

CCSS With prompting and support, ask and answer questions about key details in a text. **RI.K.1**

CCSS With prompting and support, identify the main topic and retell key details of a text. **RL.K.2**

CCSS With prompting and support, ask and answer questions about unknown words in a text. **RI.K.4**

Leveled Reader:
You Cook

Leveled Reader

Before Reading

Preview and Predict

Have children point to the title and author's name on their copies of the book. Read the title and the name of the author as children follow along. Discuss the cover photo. *How is this kitchen like or unlike the kitchen at your house? What tools do you use in a kitchen?* Preview the photo on each page with children, and identify the rebus pictures. Ask: *What do you think this book will be about?*

Review Genre: Informational Text

Explain to children that informational text is about real people, places, or events and usually has photographs instead of illustrations.

Model Concepts of Print

Have children turn to page 2. Ask them to put their finger on the first word in the sentence. Have them point to each word as you model pointing and slowly reading each word on the page.

Review High-Frequency Words

Point to the high-frequency word *You* on page 2 of the story and read it aloud. Ask children to say the word aloud, and then find and point to the word on each of the pages in the book.

Essential Question

Set a purpose for reading. Say: *Let's read the book to find out what tools the people in these kitchens use to do their jobs.*

During Reading

Guided Comprehension

As children whisper-read *You Cook*, monitor and provide guidance by correcting blending and modeling the strategy and skill.

Strategy: Ask and Answer Questions

Remind children that as they read they can ask questions about things they don't understand and look for answers in the text and pictures.

Skill: Key Details

Tell children that the key details in the text and photographs will help them understand what the book is mostly about. Explain that they can find key details by looking at the photographs and reading the sentences.

Think Aloud The words on page 2 don't tell me why a bowl is needed. When I look at the photo on page 2, I see a bowl with food in it. The photo shows me what the bowl is needed for. The cook needs the bowl to put food in. This is a key detail in the book.

Guide children to talk about each kitchen item and why cooks use it. Ask them to point to the parts of the photos that give them details about using tools in the kitchen.

After Reading

Respond to Reading

→ *What are some things that you need in a kitchen?* (Possible answers: bowl, knife, pot, spoon, cup, mop, cook)

→ *Look at the pictures. What is a mop used for in the kitchen?* (cleaning the floor)

→ *What does a cook do in a kitchen?* (A cook uses tools to cook food.)

Retell

Have children take turns retelling the story. Help them make a personal connection by asking: *Have you ever made anything in the kitchen? What tools did you use to make your food?*

Model Fluency

Read the story aloud, pointing to the rebus on each page as you say that word with extra emphasis.

Apply Have children practice reading aloud as they point to each word and rebus.

LITERACY ACTIVITIES

Have children complete the activities on the inside back cover of the reader.

Level Up

IF Children read *You Cook* Approaching Level with fluency and correctly answer the Respond to Reading questions,

THEN Tell children that they will read another story about what tools people use to do their jobs.

- Have children page through *On the Job* On Level as you preview with them the different places people work.

- Have children read the story, monitoring their comprehension and providing assistance as necessary.

→ Approaching Level
Phonological Awareness

TIER 2

ONSET AND RIME SEGMENTATION

OBJECTIVES

(CCSS) Blend and segment onsets and rimes of single-syllable spoken words. **RF.K.2c**

 I Do Reread the poem "The Firefighters." Model segmenting onset and rime with the word *truck*. *I'm going to separate the beginning sounds from the end sound in* truck. *Listen:* /truck/, /tr/ /uk/. Have children repeat after you.

 We Do Model segmenting onset and rime again with *quick*. Have children help you separate the beginning sound from the end sound: quick, /kw/ /ik/.

 You Do Have children segment other single-syllable words from the poem and from theme-related words: *fire, way, get, job, tool.*

TIER 2

PHONEME ISOLATION

OBJECTIVES

(CCSS) Isolate and pronounce the initial, medial vowel, and final sounds (phonemes) in three-phoneme words. **RF.K.2d**

 I Do Display the *Octopus* **Photo Card**. *This is an octopus. The first sound I hear in* octopus *is* /ooo/. Have children repeat the word with you, emphasizing the initial sound. Repeat for medial /o/ using the *Top* Photo Card.

 We Do Display the *Olive* Photo Card. Name the photo and have children repeat the name. *What is the first sound in* olive? (/o/) Say the sound together. Repeat for medial /o/ using the *Fox* Photo Card.

 You Do Display the *Otter* Photo Card. Have children name it and say the initial sound. Repeat for medial /o/ using the *Sock* Photo Card.

You may wish to review Phonological Awareness and Phonemic Awareness with **ELL** using this section.

PHONEME BLENDING

OBJECTIVES

CCSS Isolate and pronounce the initial, medial vowel, and final sounds (phonemes) in three-phoneme words. **RF.K.2d**

 I Do

Listen as the puppet says the sounds in a word: /k/ /o/ /t/. Now the puppet will blend the sounds to make a word: /kooot/, cot. The puppet blended the sounds to make the word cot. *Repeat with* ox, nod.

We Do

The puppet is going to say the sounds in a word. Listen to the puppet, then blend the sounds to say the word. Have the puppet say /o/ /n/. Have children repeat. *Now let's blend the sounds and say the word with the puppet: /o/ /n/, /ooonnn/, on.* Repeat with *mom.*

You Do

Have the puppet say the following sounds. Ask children to blend the sounds and say the words:

/r/ /o/ /b/ rob   /o/ /ks/ ox   /d/ /o/ /t/ dot   /p/ /o/ /d/ pod   /o/ /d/ odd

PHONEME CATEGORIZATION

OBJECTIVES

CCSS Isolate and pronounce the initial, medial vowel, and final sounds (phonemes) in three-phoneme words. **RF.K.2d**

 I Do

Display the *Otter, October,* and *Insect* **Photo Cards**. Say each picture name, emphasizing the initial sound. Otter *and* October *begin with /o/.* Insect *does not begin with /o/.* Insect *does not belong.*

 We Do

Display the *Alligator, Olive,* and *Ax* Photo Cards. Have children name each picture with you, emphasizing the initial sound. *Which word does not have the same beginning sound?* (Olive) Repeat the routine with the *Pen, Seal,* and *Pear* Photo Cards.

 You Do

Display and name the *Ant, Apple,* and *Table* Photo Cards. Have children name each picture and tell which one does not have the same initial sound. (Table) Repeat the routine with these sets of Photo Cards: *Inch, Penny, Invitation; Mouse, Tiger, Turtle; Six, Ox, Sock.*

ELL ENGLISH LANGUAGE LEARNERS

For the **ELLs** who need **phonics**, **decoding**, and **fluency** practice, use scaffolding methods as necessary to ensure students understand the meaning of the words. Refer to the Language Transfer Handbook for phonics elements that may not transfer in students' native languages.

Approaching Level

Phonics

SOUND-SPELLING REVIEW

OBJECTIVES

 Associate the long and short sounds with common spellings (graphemes) for the five major vowels. **RF.K.3b**

 I Do Display **Word-Building Card** *c*. Say the letter name and the sound it stands for: *c, /k/*. Repeat for *m, a, s, p, t, i, n*.

 We Do Display Word-Building Cards one at a time and together say the letter name and the sound that each letter stands for.

 You Do Display Word-Building Cards one at a time and have children say the letter name and the sound that each letter stands for.

CONNECT *o* TO /o/

OBJECTIVES

 Associate the long and short sounds with common spellings (graphemes) for the five major vowels. **RF.K.3b**

 I Do Display the *Ostrich* **Sound-Spelling Card**. *The letter* o *can stand for /o/, the sound at the beginning of* ostrich. *What is this letter? What sound does it stand for? I will write* o *when I hear /o/ in these words:* answer, operate, itch, on, opera. Repeat for medial /o/ using *Box* **Photo Card** *and* pond, bike, doll, sock.

 We Do *Ox begins with /o/. Let's write* o. *With children, write* o *when they hear /o/. Say:* object, invite, occupy, oblong. Repeat for medial /o/ using *hop, said, top, rock*.

 You Do Have children write the letter *o* if a word begins with /o/: *odd, if, am, ox, it*. Repeat for medial /o/ using *bond, pal, lock, black*.

RETEACH

OBJECTIVES

 Associate the long and short sounds with common spellings (graphemes) for the five major vowels. **RF.K.3b**

 I Do Display **Reading/Writing Workshop**, p. 6. Point to the *Octopus* **Sound-Spelling Card**. *The letter* o *stands for the /o/ sound you hear at the beginning of* octopus. Say *octopus*, emphasizing /o/.

 We Do Have children name each picture in row 1. Repeat the name, emphasizing initial /o/. Repeat for row 2, emphasizing the medial sound.

 You Do Guide children in reading the words in row 3. Then have them read the words in row 4, offering assistance as needed.

BLEND WORDS WITH /o/ o

OBJECTIVES

Associate the long and short sounds with common spellings (graphemes) for the five major vowels. **RF.K.3b**

 I Do Display **Word-Building Cards** *p, o, t. This is the letter* p. *It stands for /p/. This is the letter* o. *It stands for /o/. This is the letter* t. *It stands for /t/. Listen as I blend all three sounds: /pooot/,* pot. *The word is* pot. *Repeat for* on.

 We Do *Let's blend more sounds to make words. Make the word* not. *Let's blend /nnnooot/,* not. Have children blend to read the word. Repeat with the word *mom. Let's blend /mmmooommm/,* mom.

 You Do Distribute sets of Word-Building Cards with *c, n, o, t, p,* and *m.* Write: *cot, mop,* and *not.* Have children form the words and then blend and read the words.

REREAD FOR FLUENCY

OBJECTIVES

Read emergent-reader texts with purpose and understanding. **RF.K.4**

 I Do Turn to p. 8, and read aloud the title. *Let's read the title together.* Page through the book. Ask children what they see in each picture. Ask children to find the high-frequency word *you* on p. 9.

 We Do Then have children chorally read the story. Have them point to each word as they read. Provide corrective feedback as needed. After reading, ask children to recall what Tom sees.

 You Do Have children reread "Tom on Top!" with a partner for fluency.

BUILD FLUENCY WITH PHONICS

Sound/Spelling Fluency

Display the following **Word-Building Cards**: *m, a, s, p, t, i, n, c,* and *o.* Have children chorally say each sound. Repeat and vary the pace.

Fluency in Connected Text

Write the following sentences. *Tom and Tim sit on a cot. Mom and the cat like to nap.* Have children read the sentences and identify the words with /o/.

→ Approaching Level

High-Frequency Words

TIER 2

RETEACH WORDS

OBJECTIVES
 Read common high-frequency words by sight. **RF.K.3c**

 I Do Display the **High-Frequency Word Card** *you* and use the **Read/Spell/Write** routine to reteach the word.

 We Do Have children turn to p. 7 of **Reading/Writing Workshop** and discuss the first photo. Then read aloud the first sentence. Reread the sentence with children. Then distribute index cards with the word *you* written on them. Have children match their word card with the word *you* in the sentence. Use the same routine for the other sentence on the page.

 You Do Write the sentence frame *You and I can go to the ___.* Have children copy the sentence frame on their **Response Boards**. Then have partners work together to read and orally complete the frame by talking about a place they might go together.

CUMULATIVE REVIEW

OBJECTIVES
Read common high-frequency words by sight. **RF.K.3c**

 I Do Display the **High-Frequency Word Cards** *I, can, the, we, see, a, like, to, and, go.* Use the **Read/Spell/Write** routine to review words. Write sentences such as *We like to go to the top! Can you see Tom and the cat?*

 We Do Chorally read the sentences. Then guide children to create a sentence as a class using the High-Frequency Words.

 You Do Have partners create sentences using the High-Frequency Words. Remind them to refer to the High-Frequency Word Cards as needed. Then have them write the words on their **Response Boards**.

Oral Vocabulary

REVIEW WORDS

OBJECTIVES

Identify real-life connections between words and their use. **L.K.5c**

Develop oral vocabulary: *equipment, uniform, utensils, expect, remained*

Use the **Define/Example/Ask** routine to review words. Use the following definitions and provide examples:

equipment	**Equipment** means tools that someone uses to do a job.
uniform	A **uniform** is special clothing that workers wear on their jobs.
utensils	**Utensils** are tools we use to make or cook something.
expect	If you think something will happen, you **expect** it.
remained	Something that **remained** in a place stayed there.

We Do

Ask questions to build understanding. *What equipment do you need to make a pie? What does a police officer's uniform look like? Which utensils do you use to make soup? What time do you expect to be home today? Why might you remain inside if it is very cold outside?*

You Do

Have children complete these sentence frames: *People who build houses use equipment like ____. A firefighter's uniform includes ____. An example of a utensil is ____. I expect my team will ____. I remained home because ____.*

Comprehension

SELF-SELECTED READING

OBJECTIVES

With prompting and support, ask and answer questions about key details in a text. **RI.K.1**

Apply the strategy and skill to reread the text

Read Independently

Help children select a nonfiction text with photographs to read for sustained silent reading. Remind children to use photographs to help understand information in the text. Guide them to ask and answer questions as they read to help them understand information.

Read Purposefully

Before reading, have children point to a photograph they would like to learn more about. Tell them to select a photograph they think will help them answer questions about the text. After reading, discuss the photograph they identified. *Point to important details in the photograph. How did the photograph help you understand something you read? What questions did you ask and answer to help understand the information?*

→ On Level

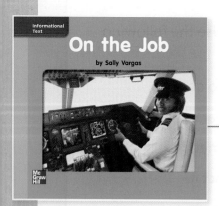

Leveled Reader

OBJECTIVES

CCSS With prompting and support, ask and answer questions about key details in a text. **RI.K.1**

CCSS With prompting and support, identify the main topic and retell key details of a text. **RI.K.2**

CCSS With prompting and support, ask and answer questions about unknown words in a text. **RI.K.4**

Leveled Reader:
On the Job

Go Digital

Leveled Reader

Before Reading

Preview and Predict

Read the title and the name of the author. Have children talk about what they see on the cover. Ask: *What do you think this book is about?* Preview the photos in the book and allow children to confirm or change their predictions.

Review Genre: Informational Text

Explain that informational text is about real people, places, or events. Ask: *What does this book give information about?* (jobs) *How can you tell?*

Model Concepts of Print

Open the book to the first page and say: *Can someone tell me where I should start to read? Where should I read after I finish this page?* Have children track their fingers over the text in their books on page 2 in the direction they will read it.

Review High-Frequency Words

Point out the word *You* on page 2. Have children go through the rest of the book and point to the word *You* on each page.

Essential Question

Set a purpose for reading. Say: *Let's read the book to find out where people do their jobs and what tools they use to do their jobs.*

During Reading

Guided Comprehension

As children whisper-read *On the Job*, remind them to ask questions about words they don't know. Provide guidance for children by correcting blending and modeling the strategy and skill.

Strategy: Ask and Answer Questions

Remind children that as they read they can ask questions about things they don't understand and look for answers in the text and pictures.

Skill: Key Details

Remind children that they can learn more about the topic of an informational text by reading the text and looking carefully at the photographs. This will help them find the key details.

Think Aloud On page 2, I read the sentence and look at the photograph. The key details in the photograph are the bus driver and the student getting on the bus. The sentence and the photograph tell me that being a bus driver is one kind of job.

Guide children to find the key details in the photographs and the sentences to help them talk about what people do in their jobs.

After Reading

Respond to Reading

→ *Who works on a train?* (a conductor)

→ *What tools does a person need to do his or her job on a boat?* (Possible answers: a net, a fishing line, hooks, waterproof clothing)

→ *Why might someone need a ladder to do a job?* (to reach up high while painting)

→ *Why do people do different jobs?* (There are different things that need to be done.)

Retell

Have children take turns retelling the story. Help them make personal connections by asking: *What are some jobs you have seen people do? What tools do they need to do their jobs?*

Model Fluency

Read the sentences one at a time and have children chorally repeat.

Apply Have children practice reading with partners. Encourage them to emphasize the last word in each sentence.

LITERACY ACTIVITIES

Have children complete the activities on the inside back cover of the reader.

Level Up

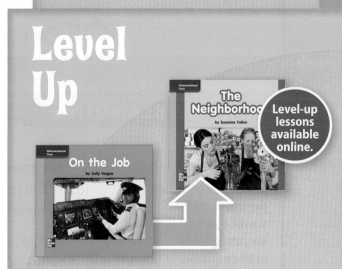

IF Children read *On the Job* On Level with fluency and correctly answer the Respond to Reading questions,

THEN Tell children that they will read another story about what tools people use to do their jobs.

• Have children page through *The Neighborhood* Beyond Level as you talk about what jobs people do in a city and the tools they use.

• Have children read the story, monitoring their comprehension and providing assistance as necessary.

On Level

Phonemic Awareness

PHONEME ISOLATION

OBJECTIVES

CCSS Isolate and pronounce the initial, medial vowel, and final sounds (phonemes) in three-phoneme words. **RF.K.2d**

 I Do Display the *Octopus* **Photo Card**. *This is an* octopus. *The first sound is /ooo/. Say it with me.* Repeat for medial /o/ using the *Lock* Photo Card.

 We Do Say *ox* and have children repeat. *What is the first sound in* ox? Say the sound together. Continue with *olive, ant,* and *inch.* Repeat for medial /o/ using the words *sat, tin,* and *hot.*

 You Do Say these words and have children tell the initial sound in each: *am, if, odd, ant, on.* Repeat for medial /o/ using the words *pit, hop, man,* and *dot.*

PHONEME BLENDING

OBJECTIVES

CCSS Isolate and pronounce the initial, medial vowel, and final sounds (phonemes) in three-phoneme words. **RF.K.2d**

 I Do *Listen as the puppet says the sounds in* mop: /m/ /o/ /p/. *The puppet will blend the sounds together to make a word:* /mmmooop/, mop. *When the puppet blends the sounds together, it makes the word* mop. Repeat with *ox, pot.*

 We Do *The puppet is going to say the sounds in a word. Listen to the puppet, then blend the sounds to say the word.* Have the puppet say /t/ /o/ /p/. Have children repeat. *Now let's blend the sounds and say the word with the puppet:* /t/ /o/ /p/, /tooop/, top. Repeat with *sock.*

 You Do Have the puppet say the following sounds. Ask children to blend the sounds and say the words: /r/ /o/ /k/; /h/ /o/ /p/; /m/ /o/ /m/; /o/ /d/.

PHONEME CATEGORIZATION

OBJECTIVES

CCSS Isolate and pronounce the initial, medial vowel, and final sounds (phonemes) in three-phoneme words. **RF.K.2d**

 I Do Display and name the *Ostrich, October,* and *Anchor* **Photo Cards**. Ostrich *and* October *begin with* /o/. Anchor *does not.* Anchor *does not belong.*

 We Do Display the *Inch, Invitation,* and *Olive* Photo Cards. Together, name each picture. *Which word does not have the same beginning sound?*

 You Do Display and name the *Otter, Pig,* and *Ox* Photo Cards. Have children tell which picture does not have the same initial sound. Repeat with: *Inch, Sock, Invitation; Man, Dog, Doll; Penguin, Pumpkin, Octopus.*

Phonics

REVIEW PHONICS

OBJECTIVES

(CCSS) Associate the long and short sounds with common spellings (graphemes) for the five major vowels. **RF.K.3b**

Display **Reading/Writing Workshop**, p. 6. Point to the *Octopus* **Sound-Spelling Card**. *Which letter stands for the /o/ sound you hear at the beginning of* octopus? *The letter is* o.

Have children say the name of each picture in rows 1 and 2. Then ask them to identify the words with /o/ at the beginning and in the middle.

Have children read each word in rows 3 and 4. Repeat, asking them to raise their hands if they hear /o/ in the middle of the word, keeping their hands lowered if they hear /o/ in the beginning of the word.

PICTURE SORT

OBJECTIVES

(CCSS) Associate the long and short sounds with common spellings (graphemes) for the five major vowels. **RF.K.3b**

Display **Word-Building Cards** *i* and *o* in a pocket chart. Then show the *Sock* Photo Card. Say /s/ /o/ /k/, *sock*. Tell children that the sound in the middle is /o/. *The letter* o *stands for* /o/. *I will put the* Sock **Photo Card** *under the letter* o. Show the *Fish* Photo Card. Say /f/ /i/ /sh/, fish. Tell children that the sound in the middle is /i/. The letter *i* stands for /i/. *I will put the* Fish *Photo Card under the* i.

Show the *Box* Photo Card and say *box*, /b/ /o/ /ks/. Have children repeat. Then have them tell the sound they hear in the middle of *box*. Ask them if they should place the photo under the *i* or the *o*. (o)

Continue the activity using the *Fox, Pig, Mix, Mop, Chin,* and *Lock* Photo Cards. Have children say the picture name and the sounds in the name. Then have them place the card under the *i* or *o*.

→ On Level

Phonics

BLEND WORDS WITH SHORT *o*

OBJECTIVES

 Associate the long and short sounds with common spellings (graphemes) for the five major vowels. **RF.K.3b**

 I Do Write *n, o, t.* This is the letter n. *It stands for /n/. Say it with me: /nnn/. This is the letter* o. *It stands for /o/. Say it with me: /ooo/. This is the letter* t. *It stands for /t/. Say it with me: /t/. I'll blend the sounds together to read the word:* /nnnooot/, not.

 We Do Write *on* and *Tom.* Guide children to blend sound by sound to read each word.

 You Do Write the following words and have children blend sound by sound to read each word.

mom   pop   mop   pot   ox

REREAD FOR FLUENCY

OBJECTIVES

 Read emergent-reader texts with purpose and understanding. **RF.K.4**

 I Do Point to the title "Tom on Top!" on p. 8 of **Reading/Writing Workshop** and indicate the exclamation point. *When we read something that ends with an exclamation point, we read with excitement.* Read the title with excitement and have children repeat using their voices in the same way. Work with children to read for accuracy and expression.

 We Do Read p. 9. Then have children chorally read the page with you. Continue choral reading the remainder of the story.

You Do Have partners reread "Tom on Top!" Provide time to listen as children read the pages. Comment on their accuracy and expression and provide corrective feedback by modeling proper fluency.

High-Frequency Words

REVIEW WORDS

OBJECTIVES

 Read common high-frequency words by sight. **RF.K.3c**

 I Do Use the **High-Frequency Word Card** *you* with the **Read/Spell/Write** routine to review the word.

We Do Have children turn to p. 7 of **Reading/Writing Workshop**. Discuss the photographs and read aloud the sentences. Point to the word *you* and have children read it. Then chorally read the sentences. Have children frame the word *you* in the sentences and read the word.

You Do Say the word *you*. Ask children to close their eyes, picture the word, and write it as they see it. Have children self-correct.

Reteach previously introduced high-frequency words using the **Read/ Spell/Write** routine.

Fluency Point to the High-Frequency Word Cards *I, can, see, you, we, a, the, and like, to, go* in random order. Have children chorally read. Repeat at a faster pace.

Comprehension

SELF-SELECTED READING

OBJECTIVES

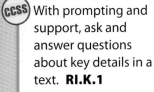 With prompting and support, ask and answer questions about key details in a text. **RI.K.1**

Apply the strategy and skill to reread the text.

Read Independently

Have children select a nonfiction text with photographs to read for sustained silent reading. Remind children that photographs contain important details about the information in the text. Explain that the photographs can help them ask and answer questions before, during, and after reading.

Read Purposefully

Before reading, ask children to point out a photograph they would like to learn more about as they read. Tell them to ask and answer questions about the text and the photograph as they read. After reading, invite children to explain how the photograph included a detail that helped them answer a question they had about the information in the selection.

→ Beyond Level

Leveled Reader

OBJECTIVES

 With prompting and support, ask and answer questions about key details in a text. **RI.K.1**

With prompting and support, identify the main topic and retell key details of a text. **RI.K.2**

Demonstrate understanding of the organization and basic features of print. **RF.K.1**

Leveled Reader:
The Neighborhood

Leveled Reader

Before Reading

Preview and Predict

Ask children to point to the title on the cover of their books. Read it aloud as children point to each word. Ask children to point to the name of the author. Read it aloud and ask: *What does the author do?* Ask children what they think the book will be about. Then preview each page in the book with children. Did they confirm their predictions?

Review Genre: Informational Text

Remind children that informational text gives the reader facts and details about a topic. Point out that informational text may use photos to help explain the topic and give more facts to the reader.

Essential Question

Set a purpose for reading by saying: *Let's read to find out the kinds of jobs people do in a city and the tools they use.*

During Reading

Guided Comprehension

As children whisper-read *The Neighborhood,* monitor and provide guidance by correcting blending and modeling the strategy and skill. Stop periodically to ask open-ended questions, such as *What does a mail carrier do? What does a vet do?*

Strategy: Ask and Answer Questions

Remind children that as they read they can ask questions about things they don't understand and look for answers in the text and pictures. This will help them to better understand the topic.

Skill: Key Details

Remind children that the key details in the text and photographs help them understand the main topic of the book. Explain that they can find key details by looking at the photographs and reading the sentences.

Think Aloud When I read page 5, I am not sure how a vet takes care of pets. I look at the picture. The picture shows the vet examining a dog like a doctor would. She even has a stethoscope to listen to the dog's heartbeat. These key details help me understand that a vet is like a doctor for animals.

Guide children to use the text and photographs to find key details about what kind of tools are used for each job. Have children point to evidence in the text and photographs to support their statements.

After Reading

Respond to Reading

→ *The book says the firefighter keeps us safe. How does the firefighter do this?* (by putting out fires) *What tools does the firefighter need to put out fires?* (Possible answers: hose, water, ladder, special clothing)

→ *What tools does a person need to work in a flower shop?* (Possible answers: flowers, vases, scissors, water, ribbons)

→ *Look at page 8. What tools will the people need to eat their lunch?* (Possible answers: knife, fork, plate, napkins)

Retell

Have children take turns retelling the text. Help them make a personal connection by asking: *What do you need to do your job as a student?*

Gifted and Talented

EVALUATING Have children choose a job or career that they know about. Challenge children to verbalize the tools a person doing that job would need to get the job done.

HAVE children make a poster that shows themselves doing the job and using the tool. Have them label the picture with the job and the tool being used.

LITERACY ACTIVITIES

Have children complete the activities on the inside back cover of the reader.

Beyond Level

Phonics

REVIEW

 OBJECTIVES

Associate the long and short sounds with common spellings (graphemes) for the five major vowels. **RF.K.3b**

 I Do Display **Reading/Writing Workshop**, p. 6. Point to the *Octopus* **Sound-Spelling Card**. *What is the sound at the beginning of* octopus? *What letter can stand for* /o/? *The letter is* o.

 We Do Have children say the name of each picture. Then ask children to share other words they know that begin with /o/.

 You Do Have partners read each word. Ask them to write the words on their **Response Boards**, underlining the letter in each word that stands for /o/.

Fluency Have children turn to p. 8 in **Reading/Writing Workshop** and reread "Tom on Top!" for fluency.

Innovate Have children create a new page for "Tom on Top!" using the sentence frame *Tom can see* ___. to name something else Tom can see in the firehouse.

High-Frequency Words

REVIEW

 OBJECTIVES

Read common high-frequency words by sight. **RF.K.3c**

 I Do Create the **High-Frequency Word Cards** for *put* and *work*. Introduce the words using the **Read/Spell/Write** routine.

 We Do Display the High-Frequency Word Cards for *and, can, you,* and *the*. Have children help you complete the following sentence frames using the High-Frequency Word Cards: *Can you put the pot on the* ___? *Pop and Mom work at the* ___.

 You Do Have partners write sentences using the High-Frequency Words *put* and *work* on their Response Boards. Have them read their sentences.

Vocabulary

ORAL VOCABULARY: SYNONYMS

OBJECTIVES

With guidance and support from adults, explore word relationships and nuances in word meaning. **L.K.5**

Develop oral vocabulary: Synonyms

 I Do Review the meanings of the oral vocabulary words *equipment* and *uniform. A synonym is a word that means almost the same thing as another word. A synonym* for equipment *is* tools. *Tools are items that help people do work.* "People use tools like hammers to build furniture." *A synonym for* uniform *is* outfit. *An* outfit *is a set of clothes worn for a specific purpose.* "Each child must wear a jacket as part of the school outfit."

 You Do Work with children to think of sentences using the new words *tools* and *outfit.*

 We Do Have partners draw a picture that shows a person wearing an outfit and using tools. For example, they could draw a firefighter wearing boots and a hat while using a hose. Ask children to write a caption about their picture.

 Extend Have partners tell a story about two people working together. Have children talk about their uniforms or outfits and explain why they are wearing them. Encourage them to use *tools* and *outfits* in their skit.

Comprehension

SELF-SELECTED READING

OBJECTIVES

With prompting and support, ask and answer questions about key details in a text. **RI.K.1**

Apply the strategy and skill to reread the text.

Read Independently

Have children select a nonfiction text with photographs for sustained silent reading. Remind them that asking and answering questions about text and photographs as they read can help them understand important information.

Read Purposefully

Before reading, ask children to choose a photograph they think will help answer questions about key details in the selection. After reading, invite children to explain how details in the photograph helped them answer a question they had about the text.

 Independent Study Challenge children to create a book poster that illustrates the new facts they learned or found interesting. Invite them to share their posters with the class.

English Language Learners

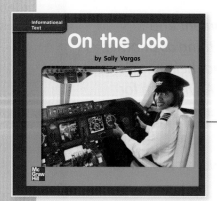

Leveled Reader

OBJECTIVES

 With prompting and support, ask and answer questions about key details in a text. **RI.K.1**

 With prompting and support, identify the main topic and retell key details of a text. **RI.K.2**

 Read emergent-reader texts with purpose and understanding. **RF.K.4**

Shared Read:
On the Job

Go Digital

Leveled Reader

Before Reading

Preview and Predict

Read the title *On the Job*. Ask: *What's the title? Say it again.* Repeat with the author's name. Point to the cover and say: *Where is the title? Where is the author's name?* Discuss each page with children, and identify the rebus pictures *bus, horse, boat, plane, bike, ladder,* and *train.* Then point to the labels. Use simple language to describe each picture. Follow up with questions, such as: *Who is using these tools?*

Essential Question

Set a purpose for reading: *Let's read the book to find out what tools people use to do their jobs.* Encourage children to ask questions about ideas, photos, or words they are unsure about. Model asking for clarification: *I see the word* plane *on page 5. The man works on the plane.* Point to the photo of the flight attendant and say that he helps people on the plane. Return to the Essential Question by discussing the things he needs to do his job.

During Reading

Interactive Question Response

Pages 2–3 Point to the photo on page 2. *I see a bus. Can you point to the bus?* Point to the driver. *This person works on the bus. What does she do?* (She drives the bus.) Point to the sentence and ask children to read it aloud with you. Point to the horse in the photo on page 3. Ask: *Who uses the horse to do a job?* (the farmer/rancher) Talk about how the rancher uses a horse.

Pages 4–5 Point to the photo and label on page 4. *This is a boat. Who can tell me what the man is doing on the boat?* (fishing) *What tool does he need to get the fish?* (net) *Let's read this page together.* Point to the text on page 5 and ask children to read it with you. Ask: *What does the person working on the plane do?* (helps passengers)

Pages 6–7 Point to the label on page 6. *What is the label pointing to?* (bike) *The police officer is on a bike. What does the bike help the police do?* (get around, move from place to place) Read the sentence aloud with children. Point to the label on page 7. Ask: *What does this label point to?* (ladder) *How do people use ladders?* (to climb up to reach things)

Page 8 Point to the train. Say: *This is a train. Who is working on the train?* (Children should point to the train conductor.) *What work does this person do?* (helps people on the train) Ask children to read aloud the sentence as you monitor their reading.

After Reading

Respond to Reading

→ *What are the people in the book doing?* (jobs)

→ *Name some of the things that people need to do their jobs.* (Possible answers: bus, horse, boat, plane, bike, ladder, train)

→ *Which job would you like to do?* (Answers will vary.)

Retell

Let's retell the book together. What does a bus driver need to do a job? (bus) Continue to name each of the other jobs shown in the book. As you name each job, have children name each thing the person uses to do his or her job.

Model Fluency

As you read each sentence, track the print and have children chorally repeat it. Point to each rebus as you emphasize the word that corresponds to it.

Apply Ask children to read with a partner. Encourage children to take turns reading a page aloud, concentrating on the last word in each sentence.

Level Up

IF Children read *On the Job* **ELL Level** with fluency and correctly answer the Respond to Reading questions,

THEN Tell children that they will read a more detailed version of the story.

• Have children page through *On the Job* **On Level** and conduct a picture walk to describe each picture in simple language.

• Have children read the story, monitoring their comprehension and providing assistance as necessary.

LITERACY ACTIVITIES

Have children complete the activities on the inside back cover of the reader.

→ English Language Learners
Vocabulary

PRETEACH ORAL VOCABULARY

CCSS

OBJECTIVES
Speak audibly and express thoughts, feelings, and ideas clearly. **SL.K.6**

LANGUAGE OBJECTIVE
Preview vocabulary

 I Do Display the images from the **Visual Vocabulary Cards** and follow the routine to preteach the oral vocabulary words.

 We Do Display each image again and explain how it illustrates or demonstrates the word. Model using sentences to describe the image.

 You Do Display the word *uniform* again and have children talk to a partner about people who wear uniforms. They may name sports teams, police, or people in other specialty jobs.

Beginning	Intermediate	Advanced/High
Have children draw a picture of someone in a uniform. Prompt children to talk about their drawings.	Ask partners to talk about people in *uniform*.	Ask children to use one of the words in an oral sentence of their own.

PRETEACH ELL VOCABULARY

CCSS

OBJECTIVES
Speak audibly and express thoughts, feelings, and ideas clearly. **SL.K.6**

LANGUAGE OBJECTIVE
Preview ELL vocabulary

 I Do Display the images from the **Visual Vocabulary Cards** one at a time to preteach the ELL vocabulary words *work* and *machine*. Follow the routine. Say each word and have children repeat it. Define each word in English.

We Do Display each image again and incorporate the words in a short discussion about the images. Model using sentences to describe the image.

 You Do Display the word *machine* again and have children say it. Provide children with opportunities to use the word in a sentence by providing this sentence frame: *A machine can* _____.

Beginning	Intermediate	Advanced/High
Have children draw a picture of a machine. Ask questions about the drawing to elicit language.	Ask pairs of children to work together to talk about why machines are useful.	Ask children to give additional examples of ways to complete the sentence frame *Machines can* _____.

High-Frequency Words

REVIEW WORDS

OBJECTIVES

Read common high-frequency words by sight (e.g., *the, of, to, you, she, my, is, are, do, does*). **RF.K.3c**

LANGUAGE OBJECTIVE

Review high-frequency words

 I Do Display the **High-Frequency Word Card** for *you*. Read the word. Use the **Read/Spell/Write** routine to teach the word. Have children write the word on their **Response Boards**.

 We Do Write a sentence that uses the week's high-frequency word: *You can see me.* Track print as children read the sentence. Point to the word *you*.

 You Do Display a sentence frame: *You can _____.* Ask children to point to the word *you* and say it aloud. Then work with children to read and complete the sentence frame.

Beginning	Intermediate	Advanced/High
Ask children to name something they can do by themselves.	Have children complete the sentence frame and read it to a partner.	Ask children to write the word *you* and use it in a sentence.

REVIEW CATEGORY WORDS

OBJECTIVES

Identify real-life connections between words and their use (e.g., note places at school that are colorful). **L.K.5c**

LANGUAGE OBJECTIVE

Use category words

 I Do Display the **Visual Vocabulary Card** for Job Words and say the words aloud. Define the words in English, and then in Spanish, if appropriate, identifying any cognates.

 We Do Ask children to read the words on the card with you. Use the sentence frame to have children talk about the words with you: *We see a _____.* Ask children to tell what each person does in his or her job.

 You Do Have children work in pairs. Ask one child to hold up a card and have the other child complete the sentence frame *I see a _____* by naming the job on the card.

Beginning	Intermediate	Advanced/High
Have children talk about what they see in each photo.	Have partners talk about the different jobs pictured on the card.	Have partners list other words that fit the category.

→ English Language Learners
Writing

SHARED WRITING

OBJECTIVES

CCSS Use a combination of drawing, dictating, and writing to narrate a single event or several loosely linked events, tell about the events in the order in which they occurred, and provide a reaction to what happened. **W.K.3**

LANGUAGE OBJECTIVE

Contribute to a shared writing project

 I Do Review the words *pitchfork, boots, fire truck, helmet, stove,* and *hat* from the Whole Group Shared Writing project as ideas for tools used by farmers, firefighters, and chefs. Model writing a sentence: *A chef can use a pan.*

 We Do With children, choose one of the people and one of the tools. Review with children what the tool does and why people need it for their job. Ask children to help you write a sentence: *A farmer can use a shovel.*

 You Do Have children write a sentence about a worker and a tool they use on the job. Provide them with a sentence frame: *A _____ can use a _____.*

Beginning	Intermediate	Advanced/High
Prompt children to complete the sentence frame by filling in the first blank for them: *A farmer can use a ___.*	Ask pairs to work on the sentence frame together and read them aloud.	Ask children to complete the sentence frame on their own; then complete it again with another tool and job.

WRITING TRAIT: IDEAS

OBJECTIVES

CCSS Use a combination of drawing, dictating, and writing to narrate a single event or several loosely linked events, tell about the events in the order in which they occurred, and provide a reaction to what happened. **W.K.3**

LANGUAGE OBJECTIVE

Use ideas in writing

 I Do Tell children that good writers get ideas for their writing from what they read. Say: *I can write about what I read. Reading gives me good ideas.*

 We Do Show the **Big Book** *Whose Shoes?* Ask: *Why do people in different jobs wear different shoes?* Point out ideas in the text and photographs that show when and why people wear different shoes.

 You Do Have children look the Big Book for ideas for a sentence about shoes people wear on the job. Provide the sentence frame *A _____ wears _____.*

Beginning	Intermediate	Advanced/High
Point to the pictures in the selection and ask: *What kind of shoes does a ballerina wear?*	Ask children to work with a partner to complete the sentence frame.	Ask children to complete the sentence frame and write more than one sentence.

Grammar

DESCRIBING WORDS (ADJECTIVES)

OBJECTIVES

 Identify real-life connections between words and their use (e.g., note places at school that are colorful). **L.K.5.c**

LANGUAGE OBJECTIVE

Identify and use adjectives correctly

Language Transfers Handbook

Spanish, Haitian Creole, Hmong, Korean, and Vietnamese speakers place nouns preceding adjectives when speaking and writing. For example, they may say *I saw a car red* instead of *I saw a red car*. Guide children to use the proper word order when using nouns and adjectives.

I Do — Review with children that adjectives are describing words. Say the following sentence: *The tall chef cooks.* Say it again and have children repeat it. Say: *The adjective in this sentence is* tall. Tall *is a word that describes or tells about the chef.*

We Do — Say the following sentences. Guide children to tell the describing word (adjective) in each.

I have a nice *teacher.*
The brown *dog ran to fetch the ball.*
The nurse is funny.
I see a strong *firefighter.*

You Do — Say the following sentence frame:

The shoes are _____.

Pair children and have them orally complete the sentence frame by providing details from this week's readings. Circulate, listen in, and take note of each child's language use and proficiency.

Beginning	Intermediate	Advanced/High
Use the pictures in *Whose Shoes?* to prompt children to complete the sentence frame.	Ask children to use *Whose Shoes?* or shoes of their classmates to think of describing words.	Ask children to complete the sentence frame without help, and have them read it aloud.

PROGRESS MONITORING

Weekly Assessment

Use your Quick Check observations and the assessment opportunities identified below to evaluate children's progress in key skill areas.

✔ TESTED SKILLS CCSS		Quick Check Observations	Pencil and Paper Assessment
PHONEMIC AWARENESS/ PHONICS /o/ (initial/medial) **RF.K.3b**	o	Can children isolate /o/ and match it to the letter *Oo*?	Practice Book, pp. 101–102, 104
HIGH-FREQUENCY WORDS *you* **RF.K.3c**	you	Can children recognize and read the high-frequency word?	Practice Book, pp. 105–106
COMPREHENSION Key Details **RI.K.1, RI.K.7**		As you read *Whose Shoes? A Shoe for Every Job* with children, can they identify and discuss key details using the photos and the text?	Practice Book, p. 103

Quick Check Rubric

Skills	1	2	3
PHONEMIC AWARENESS/ PHONICS	Does not connect the sound /o/ with the letters *Oo*.	Usually connects the sound /o/ with the letters *Oo*.	Consistently connects the sound /o/ with the letters *Oo*.
HIGH-FREQUENCY WORDS	Does not identify the high-frequency word.	Usually recognizes the high-frequency word with accuracy, but not speed.	Consistently recognizes the high-frequency word with speed and accuracy.
COMPREHENSION	Does not identify key details using the photos and text.	Usually identifies key details using the photos and text.	Consistently identifies key details using the photos and text.

Go Digital! www.connected.mcgraw-hill.com

Using Assessment Results

✓ TESTED SKILLS	If ...	Then ...
PHONEMIC AWARENESS/ PHONICS	**Quick Check Rubric:** Children consistently score 1 or **Pencil and Paper Assessment:** Children get 0–2 items correct	... reteach tested Phonemic Awareness and Phonics skills using Lessons 16–17 in the *Tier 2 Phonemic Awareness Intervention Online PDFs* and Lesson 18 in the *Tier 2 Phonics/ Word Study Intervention Online PDFs.*
HIGH-FREQUENCY WORDS	**Quick Check Rubric:** Children consistently score 1	... reteach tested skills by using the High-Frequency Word Cards and asking children to read and spell the word. Point out any irregularities in sound-spellings.
COMPREHENSION	**Quick Check Rubric:** Children consistently score 1 or **Pencil and Paper Assessment:** Children get 0–1 items correct	... reteach tested skill using Lessons 13–15 in the *Tier 2 Comprehension Intervention Online PDFs.*

Response to Intervention

Use the children's assessment results to assist you in identifying children who will benefit from focused intervention.

Use the appropriate sections of the *Placement and Diagnostic Assessment* to designate children requiring:

TIER 2 **Tier 2 Intervention Online PDFs**

TIER 3 **WonderWorks Intervention Program**

→ Phonemic Awareness

→ Phonics

→ Vocabulary

→ Comprehension

→ Fluency

WEEKLY OVERVIEW

Literature Big Book

Listening Comprehension

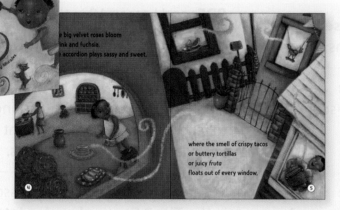

What Can You Do with a Paleta?, 4–32
Genre Fiction

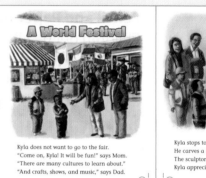

"A World Festival," 33–36
Genre Fiction

Interactive Read-Aloud Cards

"Cultural Festivals"
Genre Informational Text

Oral Vocabulary

cultures   tradition

appreciate   prefer

proud

Minilessons   ✔ TESTED SKILLS CCSS

✔ **Comprehension Strategy** .... Ask and Answer
Questions, T95

✔ **Comprehension Skill** .... Character, Setting,
Events, T104

👉 **Go Digital**

www.connected.mcgraw-hill.com

Big Book and Little Book
Reading/Writing Workshop

Shared Reading

"Sid," 22–29

Genre Fiction

High-Frequency Word do, T99

Minilessons ✓ TESTED SKILLS CCSS

✓ **Phonics** .... d (initial/final), T97

Writing Trait .... Word Choice, T100

Grammar .... Adjectives, T101

Differentiated Text

Approaching   **On Level**   **Beyond**   **ELL**

TEACH AND MANAGE

What You Do

INTRODUCE

Weekly Concept

Meet Your Neighbors

Reading/Writing Workshop
Big Book 20–21

TEACH AND APPLY

Listening Comprehension

Big Book
What Can You Do with a Paleta?
Genre Fiction
Paired Read "A World Festival"
Genre Fiction

Minilessons
Strategy: Ask and Answer Questions
Skill: Character, Setting, Events

Shared Reading

Reading/Writing Workshop
"Sid"

Minilessons
/d/*d*, High-Frequency Word: *do*
Writing, Grammar

 Go Digital

 Interactive Whiteboard

 Interactive Whiteboard

 Mobile

What Your Students Do

WEEKLY CONTRACT

PDF Online

 **Go Digital** Online To-Do List

PRACTICE AND ONLINE ACTIVITIES

Your Turn Practice Book, pp. 109–116

Leveled Readers

Online Activities

 Mobile

WEEK 2 →

DIFFERENTIATE

Small Group Instruction
Leveled Readers

Mobile

INTEGRATE

Research and Inquiry
Our Neighbors Display,
pp. T134–T135

Text Connections
Compare Characters'
Experiences, p. T136

Talk About Reading
Becoming Readers, p. T137

Online
Research

WORKSTATION CARDS

⑪ Globes and Maps
SOCIAL ST

1. Point to the land. 2. Point to the water.

3. Dis

⑪ Word Puzzles for Dd
PHONICS/WORD STUDY

Use puzzle pieces to make words.

d

im

1. Write d.   2. Write a word ending.

d im

3. Make words.

Go Digital! www.connected.mcgraw-hill.com • Interactive Games and Activities • Grade K   11

② Favorite Foods
WRITING

Think of things you like to eat and drink.

1. Talk ab... those foods.   2. Draw a favorite food.

3. W

More Activities on back of cards

⑲ Read with Expression
READING

Good readers read with feeling.

1. Read aloud a book.   2. Don't read too fast.

3. Switch roles. Read and reread the book.

Go Digital! www.connected.mcgraw-hill.com • Interactive Games and Activities • Grade K   19

DEVELOPING READERS AND WRITERS

Write About Reading • Analytical Writing

Write to Sources and Research

Respond to Reading, T95, T143, T151, T157, T161

Connect to Essential Question, T95, T127

Character, Setting, Events, 104

Research and Inquiry, T134

Teacher's Edition

Literature Big Book
What Can You Do with a Paleta?
Paired Read: *"A World Festival"*

Interactive Whiteboard

Leveled Readers
Responding to Texts

Writing Process • Independent Writing

Informational Text
Menu Writing, T122–T123, T132, T140

Conferencing Routines
Peer Conferences, T132

Interactive Whiteboard

Teacher's Edition

Leveled Workstation Card
Favorite Foods, Card 2

Writing Traits • Shared and Interactive Writing

Writing Trait:
Word Choice
Menu Writing, T100, T114

Teacher's Edition

Reading/Writing Workshop

Word Choice,
p. 32

Adjectives,
p. 33

Interactive Whiteboard

Leveled Workstation Card
Favorite Foods, Card 2

Grammar and Spelling/Dictation

Grammar
Describing Words
(Adjectives), T101

Spelling/Dictation
Words with *d* and *a, i, m, n, p, s, t,* T129, T139

Interactive Whiteboard

Teacher's Edition

Online Grammar Games

Handwriting

SUGGESTED LESSON PLAN

		DAY 1	**DAY 2**
✔ **TESTED SKILLS** CCSS			

READING

Whole Group

Teach and Model

Literature
Big Book

Reading/
Writing
Workshop

DAY 1

Build Background Meet Your Neighbors, T92
Oral Vocabulary Words appreciate, cultures, T92
✔ **Listening Comprehension**
• Genre: Fiction
• Strategy: Ask and Answer Questions, T95
Big Book *What Can You Do with a Paleta?*
✔ **Word Work**
Phonemic Awareness:
• Phoneme Isolation, T96
Phonics:
• Introduce /d/d, T97
Handwriting Dd, T98
High-Frequency Word do, T99

Practice *Your Turn* 109–110

DAY 2

Oral Language Meet Your Neighbors, T102
✔ **Category Words** Food Words, T103
✔ **Listening Comprehension**
• Genre: Fiction
• Strategy: Ask and Answer Questions, T104
• Skill: Character, Setting, Events
• Guided Retelling
• Model Fluency, T109
Big Book *What Can You Do with a Paleta?*
✔ **Word Work**
Phonemic Awareness:
• Phoneme Blending, T110
Phonics:
• Blend Words with /d/d, T111
High-Frequency Word do, T111
Shared Reading "Sid," T112–T113

Practice *Your Turn* 111

DIFFERENTIATED INSTRUCTION Choose across the week to meet your student's needs.

Small Group

Approaching Level

Leveled Reader *My Neighbors*, T142–T143
Phonological Awareness
Sentence Segmentation, T144 **TIER 2**
Phonics Sound-Spelling Review, T146 **TIER 2**
High-Frequency Words Reteach Words, T148 **TIER 2**

Leveled Reader *My Neighbors,* T142–T143
Phonemic Awareness
Phoneme Isolation, T144 **TIER 2**
Phonics Connect *d* to /d/, T146 **TIER 2**
High-Frequency Words Cumulative Review, T148 **TIER 2**

On Level

Leveled Reader *Neighborhood Party*, T150–T151
Phonemic Awareness Phoneme Isolation, T152

Leveled Reader *Neighborhood Party*, T150–T151
Phonemic Awareness Phoneme Blending, T152
Phonics Review Phonics, T153
High-Frequency Words Review Words, T155

Beyond Level

Leveled Reader *Parade Day*, T156–T157
Phonics Review, T158

Leveled Reader *Parade Day*, T156–T157
High-Frequency Words Review, T158

English Language Learners

Leveled Reader *Neighborhood Party*, T160–T161
Phonological Awareness
Sentence Segmentation, T144 **TIER 2**
Phonics Sound-Spelling Review, T146 **TIER 2**
Vocabulary Preteach Oral Vocabulary, T162
Writing Shared Writing, T164

Leveled Reader *Neighborhood Party*, T160–T161
Phonemic Awareness
Phoneme Isolation, T144 **TIER 2**
Phonics Connect *d* to /d/, T146 **TIER 2**
Vocabulary Preteach ELL Vocabulary, T162

LANGUAGE ARTS

Whole Group

Writing and Grammar

Shared Writing
Writing Trait: Word Choice, T100
Write a Menu, T100
Grammar Adjectives, T101

Interactive Writing
Writing Trait: Word Choice, T114
Write a Menu, T114
Grammar Adjectives, T115

DAY 3

DAY 4

DAY 5 Review and Assess

Oral Language Meet Your Neighbors, T116
Oral Vocabulary prefer, proud, tradition, T116
✓**Listening Comprehension**
• Genre: Informational Text
• Strategy: Ask and Answer Questions, T117
• Make Connections, T117
Interactive Read Aloud "Cultural Festivals," T117
✓**Word Work**
Phonemic Awareness
• Phoneme Blending, T118
• Picture Sort, T120
Phonics
• Blend Words with *d* and *a, i, m, n*, T119
High-Frequency Word do, T121

Practice *Your Turn* 112–114

Oral Language Meet Your Neighbors, T124
✓**Category Words** Food Words, T125
✓**Listening Comprehension**
• Genre: Fiction
• Strategy: Ask and Answer Questions, T126
• Text Features: Environmental Print
• Make Connections, T127
Big Book Paired Read: "A World Festival," T126
✓**Word Work**
Phonemic Awareness:
• Phoneme Segmentation, T128
Phonics
• Blend Words with *d* and *a, i, m, p, s, t*, T128
High-Frequency Word do, T129
Shared Reading "Sid," T130–T131
Integrate Ideas Research and Inquiry, T134–T135

Practice *Your Turn* 115

Integrate Ideas
• Text Connections, T136
• Talk About Reading, T137
• Research and Inquiry, T137
✓**Word Work**
Phonemic Awareness:
• Phoneme Segmentation, T138
Phonics
• Read Words with *d* and *a, i, m, n, p, s*, T138
High-Frequency Word do, T139

Practice *Your Turn* 116

Leveled Reader *My Neighbors*, T142–T143
Phonemic Awareness
Phoneme Blending, T145
Phonics Reteach, T146
High-Frequency Words Reteach Words, T148

Leveled Reader *My Neighbors*, T142–T143
Phonemic Awareness
Phoneme Segmentation, T145
Phonics Blend Words with /d/d, T147
Oral Vocabulary Review Words, T149

Leveled Reader Literacy Activities, T143
Phonemic Awareness
Phoneme Segmentation, T145
Phonics Reread for Fluency, T147
Build Fluency with Phonics, T147
Comprehension: Self-Selected Reading, T149

Leveled Reader *Neighborhood Party*, T150–T151
Phonemic Awareness
Phoneme Segmentation, T152
Phonics Picture Sort, T153

Leveled Reader *Neighborhood Party*, T150–T151
Phonics Blend Words with /d/d, T154
Reread for Fluency, T154

Leveled Reader Literacy Activities, T151
Comprehension Self-Selected Reading, T155

Leveled Reader *Parade Day*, T156–T157
Vocabulary Oral Vocabulary: Synonyms, T159

Gifted and Talented

Leveled Reader *Parade Day*, T156–T157
Phonics Innovate, T158

Leveled Reader Literacy Activities, T157
Comprehension Self-Selected Reading, T159

Gifted and Talented

Leveled Reader *Neighborhood Party*, T160–T161
Phonemic Awareness
Phoneme Blending, T145
Phonics Reteach, T146
High-Frequency Words Review Words, T163
Writing Writing Trait: Word Choice, T164

Leveled Reader *Neighborhood Party*, T160–T161
Phonemic Awareness
Phoneme Segmentation, T145
Phonics Blend Words with /d/d, T147
High-Frequency Words Review Category Words, T163
Grammar Adjectives, T165

Leveled Reader Literacy Activities, T161
Phonemic Awareness
Phoneme Segmentation, T145
Phonics Reread for Fluency, T147
Build Fluency with Phonics, T147

Independent Writing
Writing Trait: Word Choice, T122
Write a Menu
Prewrite/Draft, T122–T123
Grammar Adjectives, T123

Independent Writing
Write a Menu
Revise/Final Draft, T132
Grammar Adjectives, T133

Independent Writing
Write a Menu
Prepare/Present/Evaluate/Publish, T140
Grammar Adjectives, T141

DIFFERENTIATE TO ACCELERATE

Qualitative — Quantitative

Reader and Task

TEXT COMPLEXITY

IF ➤ the text complexity of a particular section is too difficult for children

THEN ➤ see the references noted in the chart below for scaffolded instruction to help children Access Complex Text.

Literature Big Book	Reading/Writing Workshop	Leveled Readers

	Literature Big Book	Reading/Writing Workshop	Leveled Readers	
Quantitative	*What Can You Do with a Paleta?* **Lexile** 890 Paired Selection: "A World Festival" **Lexile** 390	"Sid" **Lexile** 340	**Approaching Level** **Lexile** BR **Beyond Level** **Lexile** 100	**On Level** **Lexile** 100 **ELL** **Lexile** BR
Qualitative	**What Makes the Text Complex?** • **Sentence Structure** Sentences Across Pages, T104 **A C T** *See Scaffolded Instruction in Teacher's Edition, T104.*	**What Makes the Text Complex?** **Foundational Skills** • Decoding with *d*, T110–T111 • Identifying high-frequency words, T111	**What Makes the Text Complex?** **Foundational Skills** • Decoding with *d* • Identifying high-frequency words *do* *See Level Up lessons online for Leveled Readers.*	
Reader and Task	The Introduce the Concept lesson on pages T92–T93 will help determine the reader's knowledge and engagement in the weekly concept. See pages T94–T95, T105–T109, T126–T127 and T134–T137 for questions and tasks for this text.	The Introduce the Concept lesson on pages T92–T93 will help determine the reader's knowledge and engagement in the weekly concept. See pages T112–T113, T130–T131 and T134–T137 for questions and tasks for this text.	The Introduce the Concept lesson on pages T92–T93 will help determine the reader's knowledge and engagement in the weekly concept. See pages T142–T143, T150–T151, T156–T157, T160–T161 and T134–T137 for questions and tasks for this text.	

Nathan Love

Monitor and *Differentiate*

IF ▶ you need to differentiate instruction

THEN ▶ use the Quick Checks to assess children's needs and select the appropriate small group instruction focus.

✓ **Quick Check**

Comprehension Strategy Ask and Answer Questions, T117

Phonemic Awareness/Phonics /d/*d* (initial/final), T99, T111, T121, T129, T139

High-Frequency Words *do,* T99, T111, T121, T129, T139

If No →	**Approaching**	**Reteach,**	pp. T142–T149
	ELL	**Develop,**	pp. T160–T165
If Yes →	**On Level**	**Review,**	pp. T150–T155
	Beyond Level	**Extend,**	pp. T156–T159

Level Up with Leveled Readers

IF ▶ children can read their leveled text fluently and answer comprehension questions

THEN ▶ work with the next level up to accelerate children's reading with more complex text.

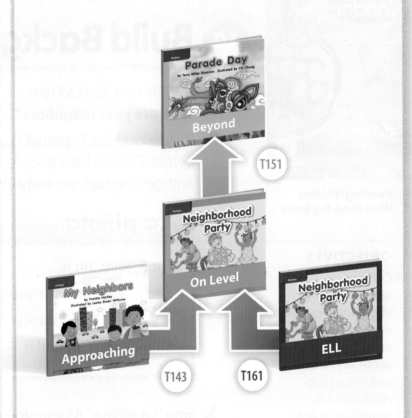

ENGLISH LANGUAGE LEARNERS
ELL SCAFFOLD

IF ELL students need additional support **THEN** ▶ scaffold instruction using the small group suggestions.

Reading-Writing Workshop T93 "Hello, Neighbor!"	Leveled Reader T160–T161 *Neighborhood Party*	Phonological Awareness	Phonics, /d/d, (initial/final), T146–T147	Oral Vocabulary, T162 cultures, appreciate, prefer, tradition, proud	Writing Shared Writing, T164	Grammar T165 Adjectives
Integrate Ideas T135		Sentence Segmentation, T144 Phoneme Isolation, T144 Phoneme Blending, T145 Phoneme Segmentation, T145		**High-Frequency Words,** T163 *do*	Writing Trait: Word Choice, T164	

Note: Include ELL Students in all small groups based on their needs.

Materials

Reading/Writing Workshop Big Book
UNIT 4

Literature Big Book
What Can You Do with a Paleta?

Visual Vocabulary Cards
cultures
appreciate

Response Board

Photo Cards
carrots
deer
dime
dish
dog
doll
grapes
pizza

Sound-Spelling Cards
dolphin

do
High-Frequency Word Cards
a
do
like
see
you

I wonder...
Think Aloud Clouds

♪ "La piñata"
"Did You See a Dolphin?"

Reading/Writing Workshop Big Book

OBJECTIVES

CCSS Confirm understanding of information presented orally by asking and answering questions about key details and requesting clarification if something is not understood. **SL.K.2**

CCSS Describe familiar people, places, things, and events, and with prompting and support, provide additional detail. **SL.K.4**

→ # Introduce the Concept

MINILESSON 10 Mins

Build Background

ESSENTIAL QUESTION
Who are your neighbors?

Read aloud the Essential Question. *We are going to sing a song about a piñata.* Explain how people hit piñatas at parties to break them open and get the toys or candy inside.

La piñata

Hit it, hit it, hit it,

See that you don't miss it!

Try to find the distance

so that you can find it.

♪ Sing "La piñata." As you sing each line, have children echo and pretend to hit a piñata. Tell children that piñatas were invented in Mexico, but now people around the world enjoy them. *Where might you find a piñata in your neighborhood?* Tell children that this week they will learn about people in their neighborhoods.

Oral Vocabulary Words

Use the **Define/Example/Ask** routine to introduce the oral vocabulary words **cultures** and **appreciate**.

To introduce the theme "Meet Your Neighbors," explain that neighbors may come from different cultures. *It is fun to have different cultures in my neighborhood. I learn many things from neighbors about the world.*

Go Digital

Meet Your Neighbors

Video

Visual Glossary

Visual Vocabulary Cards

Oral Vocabulary Routine

<u>Define:</u> **Cultures** include the language, holidays, and special foods shared by groups of people.

<u>Example:</u> My family celebrates holidays from the Chinese and German cultures.

<u>Ask:</u> What special food or holiday from a culture can you name?

<u>Define:</u> When you **appreciate** something, you respect or value it.

<u>Example:</u> I appreciate that you eat lunch with me.

<u>Ask:</u> Who do you appreciate in your neighborhood? Why?

Talk About It

Guide children to discuss the cultures in their neighborhood, such as the music, foods, holidays, or traditions. List their responses. Display pages 20–21 of the **Reading/Writing Workshop Big Book** and have the children do the **Talk About It** activity with a partner.

READING/WRITING WORKSHOP BIG BOOK, pp. 20–21

Collaborative Conversations

Be Open to All Ideas As children engage in partner, small group, and whole group discussions, tell them:

→ That all ideas, questions, or comments are important.

→ To ask a question if something is unclear.

→ To respect the opinions of others.

ENGLISH LANGUAGE LEARNERS SCAFFOLD

Beginning

Use Visuals Explain that the picture shows two families from a neighborhood saying hello to each other. *Do the people in the families look happy?* (yes) Point to the pie that the mother in the blue shirt is holding. *Is this a pie?* (yes) *Maybe the two families will eat pie together!*

Intermediate

Describe Have children describe what is going on in the picture. *How many people are in the picture? Who is holding a pie?* Correct grammar and pronunciation as needed.

Advanced/Advanced High

Discuss Have children elaborate on what they think the two families might do together. Which children might play together? Elicit more details to support children's answers.

→ Listening Comprehension

Literature Big Book

OBJECTIVES

CCSS Actively engage in group reading activities with purpose and understanding. **RL.K.10**

CCSS Follow words from left to right, top to bottom, and page by page. **RF.K.1a**

- Strategy: Ask and Answer Questions
- Connect Big Book to Weekly Concept

ACADEMIC LANGUAGE

- *illustrations*
- Cognates: *ilustraciónes*

MINILESSON
10 Mins

Read the Literature Big Book

Connect to Concept: Meet Your Neighbors

Tell children that you will now read about a neighborhood where people can buy *paletas*, or flavored ice treats. *What fun treats can you get in your neighborhood?*

Concepts of Print

Directionality Display the **Big Book** cover and read aloud the title. Remind children that we read from left to right and make a return sweep to the left. Model these motions with your finger as you reread the title.

Genre: Fiction

Model *What Can You Do with a Paleta?* is a fiction story. Share these characteristics of fiction with children:

→ The events and characters are made up by the author.

→ Stories often have illustrations, or drawings, to show what happens.

> **Story Words** Preview these words before reading:
>
> **wagon:** a cart with wheels
> *sarape:* Spanish word for a brightly colored shawl
> *barrio:* Spanish word meaning "neighborhood"

Set a Purpose for Reading

→ Identify and read aloud the title and the names of the author and the illustrator.

→ Remind children that the author wrote the words in the story and the illustrator drew the pictures.

→ Ask children to listen as you read aloud the Big Book to learn about the characters' neighborhood.

Go Digital

What Can You Do with a Paleta?

Think Aloud Cloud

Strategy: Ask and Answer Questions

Explain Tell children that they can ask and answer questions before and while they read to help them better understand the text.

Think Aloud As I read this book, I will stop after every page or two to ask myself questions about what I am learning. I will look for the answers as I keep reading. This will help me to better understand the story.

Model As you read, use the **Think Aloud Cloud** to model the strategy.

Think Aloud Before I begin reading, I wonder about the characters on the cover. I ask myself a question: *What is their neighborhood like?* I will begin reading to find my answer. The book tells me the neighborhood is called a *barrio*. It has roses, music, and yummy *paletas*.

Respond to Reading

After reading, prompt children to share what they learned about *paletas*. Discuss which questions they asked themselves while reading and how they answered them. Then have children draw a picture of themselves with a paleta, doing one of the things from the story.

Make Connections

Use *What Can You Do with a Paleta?* to discuss the culture and types of people in this neighborhood. Revisit the concept behind the Essential Question *Who are your neighbors?* by paging through the **Big Book**.

Write About It
Have children write about a neighbor or place in their neighborhood.

→ # Word Work

Quick Review

Review /k/ /o/: Ask children to tell the initial sound of the *camel* and *octopus* Photo Cards.

Build Fluency: Sound-Spellings: Show the following **Word-Building Cards:** *a, c, i, m, n, o, p, s, t.* Have children chorally say each sound. Repeat and vary the pace.

MINILESSON
5 Mins

Phonemic Awareness

Phoneme Isolation

1 **Model** Introduce initial sound /d/. Display the **Photo Card** for *dolphin. Listen for the sound at the beginning of* dolphin. *Dolphin has the /d/ sound at the beginning. Say the sound with me: /d/.* Say these words and have children repeat: *doll, dish, deer.* Emphasize the phoneme /d/.

Photo Card

♪ *Let's play a song. Listen for words with /d/ at the beginning.* Play "Did You See a Dolphin?" Have children listen for initial /d/. *Let's listen to the song again and raise a hand when we hear words that begin with /d/.* Play or sing the letter song again, encouraging children to join in. Have children raise their hands when they hear a word that begins with /d/.

2 **Guided Practice/Practice** Display and name each Photo Card: *deer, dime, dog, doll. Say each picture name with me. Tell me the sound at the beginning of the word.* Guide practice with the first word.

Photo Cards

ARTICULATION SUPPORT

Demonstrate how to say /d/. Open your mouth a little. Put the front of your tongue just behind your top front teeth. Use your voice and flick your tongue down to say /d/. Say *dog, day, dive.* Emphasize initial /d/. Have children repeat.

Go Digital

Phonemic Awareness

Dd
dolphin
Sound-Spelling Cards

MINILESSON
10 Mins

Phonics

dolphin

Sound-Spelling Card

Introduce /d/ d

❶ Model Display the dolphin **Sound-Spelling Card**. Say: *This is the Dolphin card. The sound is /d/. The /d/ sound is spelled with the letter* d. *Say the sound with me: /d/. This is the sound at the beginning of the word* dolphin. *Listen: /d/, /d/, /d/, dolphin. What is the name of this letter?* (d) *What sound does this letter stand for?* (/d/)

Display "Did You See a Dolphin?" (see Teacher's Resource Book online) Read or sing the song with children. Reread the title and point out that the word *did* begins and ends with the letter *d*. Model placing a self-stick note below the *d* in *Did* and *Dolphin*.

❷ Guided Practice/Practice Read each line of the song. Stop after each line and ask children to place self-stick notes below words that begin with *D* or *d* and say the letter name.

Did You See a Dolphin?

Did you see a dolphin diving in the deep?

Dipping and diving, swiftly she swims.

Do dolphins ever sleep?

Do dolphins ever sleep?

Corrective Feedback

Sound Error Model the sound /d/ in the initial position, then have children repeat the sound. *Say: My turn.* Doll. */d/. Now it's your turn.* Have children say the words *dig* and *dish* and isolate the initial sound.

ELL
ENGLISH LANGUAGE LEARNERS

Phonemic Awareness: Minimal Contrasts Focus on articulation. Make the /d/ sound and point out your mouth position. Have children repeat. Use the articulation photos. Children may have difficulty distinguishing between /d/ and /p/ in words such as *dip* and *did*.

Phonemic Awareness: Variations in Language In some languages, including Cantonese and Korean, there is no direct transfer for the /d/ sound. Emphasize the /d/ sound and demonstrate correct mouth position.

YOUR TURN PRACTICE BOOK pp. 109–110

→ # Word Work

5 Mins MINILESSON

Handwriting: Write *Dd*

❶ Model Say the handwriting cues below as you write and identify the uppercase (capital) and lowercase forms of *Dd*. Identify the forms of the letter for children. Then trace the letters on the board and in the air as you say /d/.

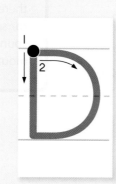

Straight down. Go back to the top. Around and in at the bottom.

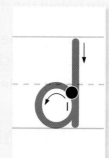

Circle back and around. Go to the top line. Straight down.

❷ Guided Practice/Practice

→ Say the cues together as children trace both forms of the letter with their index fingers. Have them identify the uppercase (capital) and lowercase forms of the letter.

→ Have children write *D* and *d* in the air as they say /d/ multiple times.

→ Distribute **Response Boards**. Observe children's pencil grip and paper position, and correct as necessary. Have children say /d/ every time they write the letter *Dd*.

 Daily Handwriting

Throughout the week teach uppercase and lowercase letters *Dd* using the Handwriting models. At the end of the week, have children use **Your Turn Practice Book** page 116 to practice handwriting.

Go Digital

Handwriting

| the | is |
| you | do |

High-Frequency Word Routine

High-Frequency Words

do

do

High-Frequency Word Card

① Model Display the book *What Can You Do with a Paleta?* Read the title. Point to the high-frequency word *do.* Then use the **High-Frequency Word Card** *do* with the **Read/Spell/Write** routine to teach the word.

→ **Read** Point to the word *do* and say the word. *This is the word* do. *Say it with me:* do. Do *you like school?*

→ **Spell** *The word* do *is spelled d-o. Spell it with me.* Point out that the letter *d* stands for /d/ as in *do.*

→ **Write** *Let's write the word in the air as we say each letter: d-o.*

→ Let children know that the letter *o* in the word *do* has a different sound from the /o/ sound in *dot.*

→ Have partners create sentences using the word.

② Guided Practice/Practice Build sentences using High-Frequency Word Cards, **Photo Cards**, and teacher-made punctuation cards. Have children point to the high-frequency word *do.* Use these sentences.

Also online

| Do | you | like | | ? |

| Do | you | like | | ? |

High-Frequency Words Practice

Monitor and Differentiate

✓ **Quick Check**

Can children isolate /d/ and match it to the letter *Dd*?

Can children recognize and read the high-frequency word?

↓

Small Group Instruction

If No →	Approaching	Reteach pp. T144-149
	ELL	Develop pp. T162-165
If Yes →	On Level	Review pp. T155-155
	Beyond Level	Extend pp. T158-159

→ # Language Arts

MINILESSON
10 Mins

Shared Writing

Writing Trait: Word Choice

1 Model Tell children that our senses help us describe our world with words. Write and read aloud examples from the **Big Book**. For example: *Where the big velvet roses bloom red and pink and fuchsia. Where the accordion plays sassy and sweet.* Point out the words that tell what the roses look like, how the roses feel, and how the accordion music sounds.

2 Guided Practice/Practice Write and read aloud more Big Book examples: *where the smell of crispy tacos or buttery tortillas or juicy fruta floats out of every window.* Ask: Which words make you think of one of your senses. (smell) Have children name the describing words that tell about smell, taste, and feel. (buttery, juicy, crispy)

Write a Menu

Focus and Plan Tell children that this week they will make a menu. Explain that a menu shows a list of food and drinks.

Brainstorm Make a two-column chart. Ask children to name their favorite food or drink. List their responses in column one. Then have children describe the food and list their descriptions in the second column. Encourage children to use all their senses to describe the foods.

Food and Drink	Description
chicken	delicious
rice	brown
oranges	juicy
lemonade	cold

Write Model writing a phrase about a food in the list. *I can take a food and a describing word and write them together:* delicious chicken. *This would be a good item on a menu.* Use the list to write other phrases for menu items. Read aloud the phrases with children.

MINILESSON
5 Mins

Grammar

Describing Words (Adjectives)

1 **Model** Explain to children that describing words can also come after the naming word. Write and read aloud: *The tomatoes are red. The peaches are soft. Which words describe the fruit in each sentence?* (red, soft) Underline the adjectives and read the sentences aloud with children.

2 **Guided Practice/Practice** Ask children to think of describing words for ice cream. Write sentences using some of the children's responses, such as *Ice cream is soft. The ice cream is vanilla.* Read aloud the sentences with children.

Write and read aloud these sentences:

> *The tortillas are round.*
>
> *The tortillas are soft.*
>
> *The bread is fresh.*
>
> *The bread is tasty.*

Ask children to name the describing word in each sentence. Have children create their own sentences using more describing words about food.

Talk About It

COLLABORATE

Have partners work together to orally describe fruits, using adjectives. Encourage them to tell how the fruit feels, tastes, and smells.

ENGLISH LANGUAGE LEARNERS SCAFFOLD

Beginning

Explain Help children understand the meaning of some adjectives by showing a real object, such as an apple. *What color is the apple?* Guide children in describing the apple by saying: *The apple is red.* Model correct pronunciation as needed.

Intermediate

Practice Write and read: *The banana is _____.* Ask children to name a describing word to complete the sentence. Write other fruits for children to describe. Allow children ample time to respond.

Advanced/Advanced High

Practice Have children focus on one sense at a time as they describe a fruit, such as *I see an orange. It feels bumpy. It tastes sweet. It is round. It smells fresh.* Elicit more details to support children's answers.

Daily Wrap Up

- Review the Essential Question and encourage children to discuss it, using the new oral vocabulary words. *What different kinds of food do you see in your neighborhood?*

- Prompt children to share the skills they learned. How might they use those skills?

Materials

Reading/Writing Workshop Big Book
UNIT 4

Literature Big Book
What Can You Do with a Paleta?

Visual Vocabulary Cards
cultures
appreciate

Word-Building Cards

Response Board

Photo Cards
apple
astronaut
boots
butter
carrots
cheese
corn
cowboy

doctor
egg
fish
jacket
juice
nurse
pie
pizza
sandwich
shirt
umbrella
umpire
vegetables
vest

Retelling Cards

Sound-Spelling Cards
dolphin

Puppet

♪ **"La piñata"**

High-Frequency Word Cards
a	see
and	the
do	to
go	we
like	you

→ Build the Concept

⏱ MINILESSON 10 Mins

Oral Language

OBJECTIVES

CCSS Use words and phrases acquired through conversations, reading and being read to, and responding to texts. **L.K.6**

CCSS Sort common objects into categories (e.g., shapes, foods) to gain a sense of the concepts the categories represent. **L.K.5a**

• Segment sentences into words

• Develop oral vocabulary

ESSENTIAL QUESTION

Who are your neighbors?

Remind children that this week they are learning about neighbors and neighborhoods. They are also learning about cultures and how to appreciate many different kinds of people.

Sing the song, "La piñata." As you sing, have children echo the lines. Say: *Think about what we read in the book. What kinds of food might someone serve at a party in the barrio?* (*paletas, tacos, tortillas*)

Phonological Awareness

Sentence Segmentation

Let's say the first line of the song and clap for each word. Clap the first sentence with children. *Let's say the line again and I am going to hold up a finger for each time we say a word.* "Hit it, hit it, hit it." *How many words did I count?* (6) *Let's say the second line. You will clap and I will count.* "See that you don't miss it!" *How many words did I count?* (6) Continue clapping the song with children and counting the words.

Review Oral Vocabulary

Use the **Define/Example/Ask** routine to review the oral vocabulary words **cultures** and **appreciate**. Prompt children to use the words in sentences.

Visual Vocabulary Cards

Go Digital

Visual Glossary

Category Words

Category Words: Food Words

❶ Model Use the **Big Book** *What Can You Do with a Paleta?* to point out food words: *tacos, tortillas,* page 5; *paleta,* page 6. Explain that food words name things we eat. Tell children that the words in the story are Spanish food words. Point out the illustrations of paletas on pages 8 and 10. *I can look at the pictures for clues to figure out what paleta is. What is another food word for* paleta? (popsicle, ice pop) Explain that a *paleta* is a frozen treat made from fresh fruit. Have children share what they know about the other foods in the story.

→ Ask children to use food words in sentences. *Describe a time you tried a new food. What did you eat? What did it taste like?* For example: *I ate cheesy tacos. They were spicy and yummy.*

❷ Guided Practice/Practice Tell children you will say some words. If the word is a food word, they will say "yum."

fish	cheese	shoe	cut	rice
desk	doll	egg	lettuce	strawberry

→ Ask groups of children to sort food from other objects. Gather small food items, such as a piece of fruit, health bars, and nuts, as well as small classroom items such as crayons, paint brushes, books, etc.

→ Give each group of children some food items and some classroom items.

→ Have children sort the food from the classroom objects.

→ Discuss with children how they decided to group the objects.

LET'S MOVE!

Have children act out scenes from the Big Book *What Can You Do with a Paleta?* Have children act out licking a paleta, cooling off with a paleta, and giving a paleta to a friend.

ENGLISH LANGUAGE LEARNERS

Understand Help children understand the food words *tortillas, tacos,* and *paleta* from the Big Book. Discuss with children what the different foods are. Have them draw a picture of each food. Then help them add labels to their drawings.

→ # Listening Comprehension

Literature Big Book

 MINILESSON **15** Mins

Reread Literature Big Book

Genre: Fiction

Display *What Can You Do with a Paleta?* Review that fiction stories contain events that could happen in real life, but the stories are made up. *How do you know that this book is fiction?* Have children point to evidence in the text and pictures to show that it is fiction. (Pictures are drawings, not photographs; characters don't look real.)

Strategy: Ask and Answer Questions

Remind children that good readers ask and answer questions before they read and while they read. *As we reread, you can ask questions and look for the answers later in the story.*

Skill: Character, Setting, Events

Tell children that when they read a story it is important to pay attention to characters, setting, and events. Characters are the people or animals in a story. *Look for the characters in the illustrations as we read.* The setting is where and when the story happens, and the events are what happens in the story. *Pay attention to what the characters do and what happens to them.* As you read, have children listen for evidence in the text that tells about the characters, settings, and events.

Go Digital

What Can You Do with a Paleta?

Retelling Cards

OBJECTIVES

 With prompting and support, ask and answer questions about key details in a text. **RL.K.1**

 With prompting and support, identify characters, settings, and major events in a story. **RL.K.3**

- Strategy: Ask and Answer Questions
- Skill: Character, Setting, Events

ACADEMIC LANGUAGE

- *fiction*
- Cognates: *ficción*

Access Complex Text

Sentence Structure Some sentences in *What Can You Do with a Paleta?* continue over a range of pages. Children may become confused about what is part of a sentence or where a sentence begins and ends.

→ Point out that the text on pages 4–6 is all one sentence. Guide children to look for capital letters that begin sentences, along with periods, exclamation points, or question marks that end sentences. Model how to flip the pages back and forth to find the beginning and ending of a complete thought.

PAGES 4–5

CONCEPTS OF PRINT

Remind children to read from left to right and top to bottom, and to use a return sweep. Point out that this sentence continues on page 6.

Point out that this sentence continues on page 6.

pp. 4–5

accordion: Tell children that an accordion is a musical instrument. Pantomime playing an accordion and point to the one in the picture. Ask children if they have ever heard an accordion. If so, where?

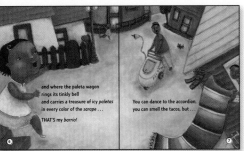

PAGES 6–7

CHARACTER, SETTING, EVENTS

Point to the character on page 6. Say: *This character is telling us the story. The setting is her barrio, which means "neighborhood" in Spanish.* Have children identify the neighborhood sound the character hears. (tinkly bell)

pp. 6–7

treasure: Explain that if something is a *treasure*, it is very special. The girl thinks that paletas are a kind of treasure.

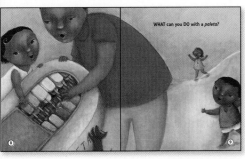

PAGES 8–9

HIGH-FREQUENCY WORDS

Have children identify and read the high-frequency word **do** on page 9.

PAGES 10–11

CHARACTER, SETTING, EVENTS

Remind children that events are what happens in the story. Point to the brother on page 11. Ask: *What does the girl do to her brother?* (scares him with her purple and green tongue)

pp. 10–11

paint your tongue: Point to the girl's tongue on page 10. Pantomime painting your tongue with a *paleta.* Say: *The girl says you can "paint your tongue" because the* paleta *makes her tongue green when she eats it.*

Listening Comprehension

PAGES 12–13

ASK AND ANSWER QUESTIONS

Think Aloud I read that the girl has to decide which kind of *paleta* she wants. I wonder: What else can you do with a *paleta*? I will keep reading to find out the answer.

pp. 12–13

decisions: When I make decisions, I choose to do one thing or another thing. Today I made a decision to wear (blue). What decision would you make about the paletas? Which flavor would you choose?

PAGES 14–15

ASK AND ANSWER QUESTIONS

Think Aloud When I was reading earlier, I asked myself: What else can you do with a *paleta*? I find my answer on page 15. I learn you can make new friends. I will continue to ask and answer questions as I read.

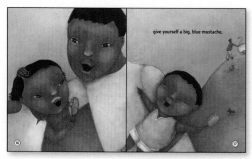

PAGES 16–17

CHARACTER, SETTING, EVENTS

Remind children that they can learn about the characters by looking at the illustrations. Display page 16. Ask: *Which color* paleta *did the girl choose?* (blue) *What does this tell you about the character?* (She likes blue *paletas*.)

pp. 16–17

mustache: Point to the blue mustache on the girl. Explain that this is a pretend mustache made by the *paleta*. A real mustache is hair that grows between the mouth and the nose. Have children use their fingers to pantomime having mustaches.

PAGES 18–19

ASK AND ANSWER QUESTIONS

Think Aloud The girl says you can create a masterpiece with *paletas*. I know that a masterpiece is a kind of art. I ask myself: What kind of art does the girl make? I look at the illustrations to find my answer. She makes colorful swirls.

PAGES 20–21

PHONICS

Remind children that they have learned about words with the initial /d/ sounds. Ask them to find the word with initial /d/ on page 21. (does)

pp. 20–21

cool off: When I need to "cool off," I am too hot. I drink cold water to cool off. What else can I do if I am too hot? (use a fan; sit in the shade)

PAGES 22–23

CHARACTER, SETTING, EVENTS

What is happening on these pages? What are the characters doing? (The girl's Tío, or uncle, is telling a story about baseball to her and her brother. They are listening carefully.)

pp. 22–23

Have volunteers act out pitching, catching, and hitting to help explain the game of baseball.

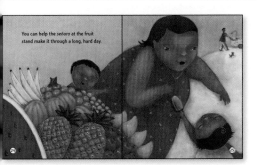

PAGES 24–25

CHARACTER, SETTING, EVENTS

We read earlier that the setting for this story is the girl's barrio, or neighborhood. Read aloud page 24 and point to the woman on page 25. *Who is this character in the barrio?* (a woman who sells fruit)

pp. 24–25

make it through: Tell children that when people need to "make it through" a workday, they are tired and need help. Ask children what helps them make it through a hard day at school.

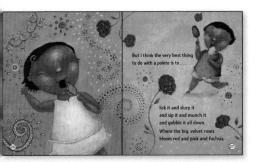

PAGES 26–27

HIGH-FREQUENCY WORD

Have children identify and read the high-frequency word **do** on page 27.

pp. 26–27

slurp, sip, munch, gobble: Tell children that these words are all noises we can make when we eat. Make slurping and munching sounds. Have children mimic you.

Listening Comprehension

CLOSE READING

ELL

PAGES 28–29

CONCEPTS OF PRINT

Remind children that we read from left to right and top to bottom, with a return sweep. Model tracking the print as you read page 28 aloud.

pp. 28–29

house, window, door, neighbors: Say each word and have children echo you. Define each word using the illustrations.

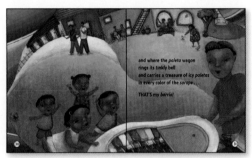

PAGES 30–31

AUTHOR'S PURPOSE

Why do you think the author wrote this fiction story? (Possible answer: She wanted to tell a fun story about a tasty treat; she wanted to show what a barrio is like.)

PAGE 32

ASK AND ANSWER QUESTIONS

At the end of page 32 is a question: Which is YOUR favorite? *My favorite flavor is* (strawberry). *What is yours?*

Text Evidence

Explain Remind children that when they answer a question, they need to show where in the story (both words and illustrations) they found the answer.

Discuss *How do you know there are many smells in the barrio?* (On page 5, the author says you can smell tacos, tortillas, and *fruta*. The illustrations show smells coming out of the windows.)

Guided Retelling

Tell children that now they will use the **Retelling Cards** to retell the story.

→ Display Retelling Card 1. Based on children's needs, use either the Guided or ELL retelling prompts. The ELL prompts contain support for English language learners based on levels of language acquisition. Repeat with the rest of the cards, using the prompts as a guide.

→ Discuss the story. After retelling, have children tell what they think is the best thing to do with a *paleta*.

→ Have children act out an event from the story with a partner.

Model Fluency

Reread pages 10–11 of *What Can You Do with a Paleta?* emphasizing the expression used when reading a sentence that ends with an exclamation point. Explain that exclamation points show strong feeling, such as excitement. Then reread the sentence on pages 10–11, and have children repeat it and mimic your tone. Repeat with the sentence on page 21.

Retelling Cards

YOUR TURN PRACTICE BOOK p. 111

→ # Word Work

Quick Review

Build Fluency: Sound-Spellings: Show the following **Word-Building Cards:** *a, c, d, i, m, n, o, p, s, t.* Have children chorally say each sound. Repeat and vary the pace.

MINILESSON **5 Mins**

Phonemic Awareness

Puppet

Phoneme Blending

1 Model Use the puppet to demonstrate how to blend phonemes to make words. *The puppet is going to say sounds in a word, /d/ /i/ /g/. It can blend those sounds to make a word: /diiig/* dig. *When the puppet blends the sounds together, it makes the word* dig. *Listen as the puppet blends more sounds to make a word.* Model phoneme blending with the following:

/d/ /i/ /sh/   /d/ /e/ /s/ /k/

2 Guided Practice/Practice *The puppet is going to say the sounds in a different word: /d/ /i/ /p/. Say the sounds. Let's blend the sounds and say the word with the puppet: /diiip/,* dip. Tell children to listen as the puppet says the sounds in words. Have them repeat the sounds, and then blend them to say the word.

/d/ /o/ /k/ dock   /d/ /a/ /sh/ dash   /d/ /i/ /m/ dim   /d/ /o/ /t/ dot

OBJECTIVES

CCSS Demonstrate basic knowledge of one-to-one letter-sound correspondences by producing the primary or many of the most frequent sounds for each consonant. **RF.K.3a**

CCSS Read common high-frequency words by sight. **RF.K.3c**

MINILESSON **5 Mins**

Phonics

Dd

dolphin

Sound-Spelling Card

Review /d/ *d*

1 Model Display the *Dolphin* **Sound-Spelling Card**. Say: *This is the letter* d. *The letter* d *stands for the sound /d/ as in the word* dolphin. *What is the letter?* (d) *What sound does the letter* d *stand for?* (/d/)

2 Guided Practice/Practice Have children listen as you say some words. Ask them to write the letter *d* on their **Response Boards** if the word begins with /d/. Do the first two words with children.

dance	cap	desk	deer
nest	door	tape	dust

Go Digital

Phonemic Awareness

c a t

Phonics

the | is
you | do

High-Frequency Word Routine

A A
a o

Handwriting

Blend Words with /d/ *d*

❶ Model Place **Word-Building Cards** *d, i, p* in a pocket chart. Point to the letter d. *This is the letter* d. *The letter* d *stands for /d/. Say: /d/. This is the letter* i. *The letter* i *stands for /i/. Say: /i/. This is the letter* p. *The letter* p *stands for /p/. Say: /p/. Listen as I blend the sounds together: /diiip/. Now blend the sounds with me to read the word.*

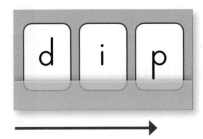

❷ Guided Practice/Practice Use Word-Building Cards or write *dot*. Point to the letter *d* and have children say the sound. Point to the letter *o* and have children say the sound. Point to the letter *t* and have children say the sound. Move your hand from left to right under the word, and have children blend and read *dot*.

MINILESSON
5 Mins

High-Frequency Words

do

do

High-Frequency Word Card

❶ Guided Practice Display the **High-Frequency Word Card** *do*. Use the **Read/Spell/Write** routine to teach the word. Ask children to close their eyes, picture the word in their minds, and then write it the way they see it. Have children self-correct by checking the High-Frequency Word Card.

❷ Practice Add the high-frequency word *do* to the word bank.

→ Have partners create sentences using the word.

→ Have children count the number of letters in the word and then write the word again.

Cumulative Review Review words: *a, and, go, like, see, the, to, we, you.*

→ Repeat the **Read/Spell/Write** routine. Mix the words and have children chorally say each one.

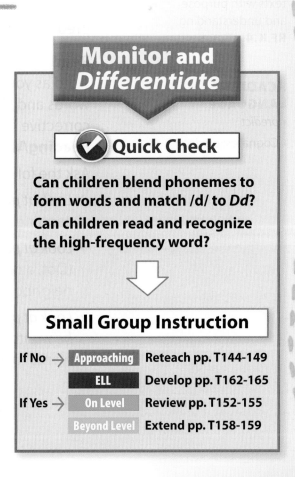

Monitor and *Differentiate*

✓ **Quick Check**

Can children blend phonemes to form words and match /d/ to *Dd*?

Can children read and recognize the high-frequency word?

⬇

Small Group Instruction

If No →	Approaching	Reteach pp. T144-149
	ELL	Develop pp. T162-165
If Yes →	On Level	Review pp. T152-155
	Beyond Level	Extend pp. T158-159

→ # Shared Read

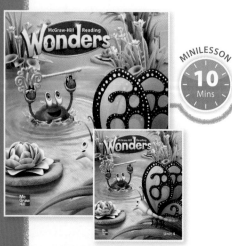

Reading/Writing Workshop Big Book and Reading/Writing Workshop

OBJECTIVES

CCSS Read common high-frequency words by sight. **RF.K.3c**

CCSS Read emergent-reader texts with purpose and understanding. **RF.K.4**

ACADEMIC LANGUAGE
• *predict*
• Cognates: *predecir*

MINILESSON 10 Mins

Read "Sid"

Model Skills and Strategies

Model Book Handling Demonstrate book handling. Hold up and point to the front cover of the book. *This is the front cover of the book.* Point to the back cover of the book. *This is the back cover of the book.* Model turning the pages of the book.

Model Concepts About Print Model reading a page from the story as you track the print with your finger or a pointer, moving from left to right. Point out that we read from the top of the page to the bottom of the page. Next, invite children to echo the sentence that you read as you track the print. Then invite a volunteer to come up to the **Big Book** and read the sentence. Continue having volunteers come up to the Big Book and echo read.

Predict Read the title together. Encourage children to describe the illustration. Invite them to tell what is happening in the picture and predict what the story will be about.

Read Have children chorally read the story with you. Point to each word as you read it together. Help children sound out the decodable words and say the sight words. If children have difficulty, provide corrective feedback and guide them page by page using the student **Reading/Writing Workshop**.

Ask the following:

→ *Look at page 23. What is this family doing?* (moving to a new home; carrying some of their belongings into the home)

→ *Look at page 27. Who is knocking on the family's front door?* (Dot, a neighbor. She wants to welcome the new family to the neighborhood. She's bringing them muffins to eat.)

→ *Look at page 28. Who is knocking on the door now? What do you think he wants to play?* (Possible answer: Tod, a neighbor; he probably wants to play ball with Sid.)

Go Digital

"Sid"

"Sid"

READING/WRITING WORKSHOP, pp. 22–29

Rereading

Have small groups use the **Reading/Writing Workshop** to reread "Sid". Then review the skills and strategies using the *Phonics* and *Words to Know* pages that come before the selection.

→ As they reread, have children ask themselves questions. Encourage them to reread the text and look closely at the illustrations to find the answers. Have them describe the characters, the setting, and the events that take place in the story.

→ Have children use page 21 to review the high-frequency word *do*.

→ Have children use page 20 to review that the letter *d* can stand for the sound /d/. Encourage them to identify and name each picture that begins or ends with the sound /d/. Guide them to blend the sounds to read the words.

ENGLISH LANGUAGE LEARNERS

Reinforce Vocabulary Display the **High-Frequency Word Cards** *do, we, you, can, see, the*. Point to classroom objects and groups of children as you use the high-frequency words in sentences such as the following: *I can hear a dog barking outside. Do you hear a dog barking outside?* (Yes, we can hear a dog barking outside.) *I can see the classroom door opening. Do you see the classroom door opening?* (Yes, we can see the classroom door opening.) *I can do the puzzle. Can you do the puzzle?* (Yes, we can do the puzzle.)

→ # Language Arts

 MINILESSON 10 Mins

Interactive Writing

Go Digital

Writing

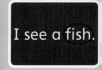

I see a fish.

Grammar

OBJECTIVES

CCSS Use a combination of drawing, dictating, and writing to compose informative/ explanatory texts in which they name what they are writing about and supply some information about the topic. **W.K.2**

CCSS Produce and expand complete sentences in shared language activities. **L.K.1f**

• Recognize describing words (adjectives)

• Dictate words for a menu

ACADEMIC LANGUAGE

• *description, chart, adjective*

• Cognates: *adjetivo*

Writing Trait: Word Choice

Review Tell children that good writers choose the right words to describe things. Write and read aloud: *I like cold, vanilla ice cream.* Tell children that *cold* and *vanilla* are describing words that tell about the ice cream.

Write a Menu

Discuss Display the chart from Day 1 and read it aloud. Invite children to add more favorite foods and drinks to the chart. Guide children to choose foods for a menu.

Model/Apply Grammar Tell children that you will work together to write a menu for a restaurant. Point to and read aloud the name of a food or drink in the first column. Write the name of the food. For example, *I like rice, so I will write rice on our menu.*

Write the following frame: _____ *rice*

Model how to choose a word to describe the food you chose. Point out a word that describes rice in the second column of the chart. Remind children that these describing words are called adjectives. Write *brown rice* and read it aloud, tracking the print.

Write Have children help you select items for a menu. Start with the food you modeled (brown rice) and have children choose other foods and drinks from the chart. Help children choose a describing word for each food and drink. *How else can we describe lemonade?* (sweet, sour) Write the words as children dictate. Share the pen with children and have them write the letters they know.

MINILESSON
5 Mins

Grammar

Describing Words (Adjectives)

1 Review Remind children that we can use our senses to help us choose good describing words.

→ Write and read aloud these sentences:

I have a black cat.
My cat feels soft.
My little cat purrs.

Have children identify the describing word in each sentence. (black, soft, little)

2 Guided Practice Tell children that describing words are helpful. *If we lose something, we can describe it to other people who can help us find it.* Show the **Photo Card** for *vest*. Write and read aloud this sentence frame: *I lost my _____ vest.* Ask children to help you describe the vest. Guide them to describe the color. (yellow) Point to the blank, fill it in, and read aloud: *I lost my yellow vest.*

Provide other sentence frames, such as *I lost my _____ jacket.* Show the Photo Card for *jacket*. Read aloud the completed sentence. Ask children to point to the describing word in the sentence.

3 Practice Have children work in pairs. Provide each group with the sentence frame *I lost my _____ _____.* Show the Photo Cards for *boots* and *shirt*. Guide children in creating sentences that describe the item on each Photo Card. Have pairs read their sentences aloud.

Talk About It

Have partners work together to orally generate sentences with adjectives. Encourage them to create sentences describing the clothes they are wearing.

ENGLISH LANGUAGE LEARNERS

Use Visuals Ask children to draw or describe foods they love. Have them describe the ingredients. List the foods on the board and read the list together. To reinforce the meaning of English words for foods, use the Photo Cards for *apple, butter, carrots, cheese, corn, egg, fish, juice, pie, pizza, sandwich, vegetables.* Model correct pronunciation as needed.

Daily Wrap Up

- Discuss the Essential Question and encourage children to use the oral vocabulary words. *What foods from other cultures have you tried?*

- Prompt children to share the skills they learned. How might they use those skills?

Materials

Reading/Writing
Workshop Big Book
UNIT 4

Interactive Read-Aloud
Cards

**Visual
Vocabulary
Cards**
proud
tradition
prefer

Photo Cards
deer
dime
dinosaur
door
octopus
olive
otter
ox

Word-Building Cards

**High-Frequency
Word Cards**
a   see
and   the
do   to
go   we
like   you

Response Board

**"Did You See
a Dolphin?"**

Puppet

→ # Build the Concept

MINILESSON
10 Mins
Oral Language

OBJECTIVES

CCSS Actively engage in group reading activities with purpose and understanding. **RL.K.10**

CCSS Identify real-life connections between words and their use. **L.K.5c**

Develop oral vocabulary

ACADEMIC LANGUAGE

• *informational text*
• Cognates: *texto informativo*

ESSENTIAL QUESTION

Remind children that this week they are talking and learning about who their neighbors are. Guide children to discuss the Essential Question using information from the **Big Book** and the weekly song.

Remind children that their neighbors might celebrate many different holidays. Sing the song "La Piñata" and have children join in.

Oral Vocabulary

Review last week's oral vocabulary words, as well as *cultures* and *appreciate* from Day 1. Then use the **Define/Example/Ask** routine to introduce *proud, tradition,* and *prefer*.

Oral Vocabulary Routine

Define: When you are **proud**, you feel good about yourself or something you have done.

Example: Josh is proud that he read the book all by himself.

Ask: What makes you feel proud?

Define: A **tradition** is a belief or habit that is repeated in a family.

Example: It is a tradition to go sledding on New Year's Day.

Ask: What is a holiday tradition you enjoy?

Define: When you **prefer** something, you like it more than something else.

Example: Some children prefer math to science.

Ask: Do you prefer singing or dancing? Why?

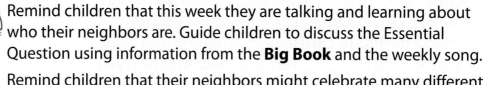

Visual Vocabulary Cards

Go Digital

Visual Glossary

"Cultural Festivals"

Think Aloud Cloud

Listening Comprehension

Read the Interactive Read Aloud

NILESSON
10 Mins

Genre: Informational Text

Tell children you will be reading an informational text. Remind them that *informational text* gives true information, or facts, about a topic. Display the **Interactive Read-Aloud Cards**.

Read the title. Point out that cultural festivals are held to celebrate important events and holidays.

Interactive Read-Aloud Cards

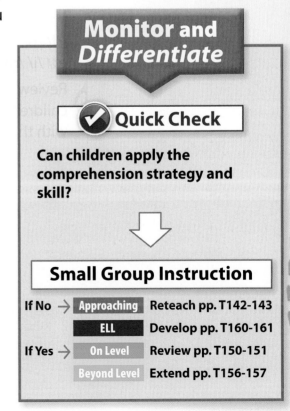

Strategy: Ask and Answer Questions

Remind children that good readers ask themselves questions as they read. This helps them understand the information in the text. Use the **Think Aloud Cloud** to model asking and answering questions as you read the selection.

Think Aloud I read that some holidays and festivals go on for a whole week! That sounds like fun. I wonder what festivals go on for that long. Who celebrates those holidays? I will keep reading to find out the answer.

Read "Cultural Festivals." Pause to model using the strategy of asking and answering questions.

Make Connections

COLLABORATE
Guide partners to connect "Cultural Festivals" with *What Can You Do with a Paleta?* Discuss how both texts tell us more about the cultures in our neighborhoods. Remind children that one selection is fiction and the other is informational text.

ELL

ENGLISH LANGUAGE LEARNERS

Reinforce Meaning As you read "Cultural Festivals," make meaning clear by pointing to specific people, places, or objects in the photographs, demonstrating word meanings, paraphrasing text, and asking children questions. For example, on Card 1, point to a fan. Say: *This is a fan.* Repeat with *dress* and *costume*.

Monitor and *Differentiate*

✓ **Quick Check**

Can children apply the comprehension strategy and skill?

⬇

Small Group Instruction

If No →	**Approaching**	Reteach pp. T142-143
	ELL	Develop pp. T160-161
If Yes →	**On Level**	Review pp. T150-151
	Beyond Level	Extend pp. T156-157

→ # Word Work

Quick Review

Build Fluency: Sound-Spellings: Show the following **Word-Building Cards:** *c, d, i, m, n, o, t.* Have children chorally say each sound. Repeat and vary the pace.

MINILESSON 5 Mins ## Phonemic Awareness

Puppet

OBJECTIVE

CCSS Isolate and pronounce the initial, medial vowel, and final sounds in three-phoneme words. **RF.K.2d**

CCSS Demonstrate basic knowledge of one-to-one letter-sound correspondences by producing the primary or many of the most frequent sounds for each consonant. **RF.K.3a**

Blend phonemes to make words

Phoneme Blending

① **Model** Use the puppet to demonstrate how to blend phonemes to make words. *The puppet is going to say sounds in a word: /d/ /o/ /t/. It can blend those sounds to make a word: /dooot/ dot. Now the puppet is going to say the sounds in a new word: /m/ /a/ /d/. When the puppet blends the sounds together, it makes the word* mad. Explain that the word *mad* has the /d/ sound at the end. *Listen as the puppet blends more sounds to make words.* Model blending with initial and final /d/ with the following:

/d/ /i/ /sh/   /s/ /a/ /d/   /m/ /u/ /d/   /d/ /i/ /p/

② **Guided Practice/Practice** *The puppet is going to say the sounds in a different word. Listen as it says each sound: /d/ /i/ /m/. Let's say the sounds and then blend them together: /d/ /i/ /m/, /diiim/. Let's all say the word:* dim. Repeat with the word *nod.* Tell children that the puppet is going to say the sounds in words. Have children repeat the sounds, then blend them to say the words. Guide practice with the first word.

/d/ /o/ /t/   /p/ /o/ /d/   /d/ /u/ /k/   /r/ /e/ /d/
/d/ /i/ /m/   /d/ /a/ /d/   /h/ /i/ /d/   /d/ /ē/ /p/

♪ Review initial /d/. Play and sing "Did You See a Dolphin?" Have children clap when they hear initial /d/. Demonstrate as you sing with them.

Go Digital

Phonemic Awareness

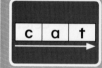

Phonics

Handwriting

Phonics

LESSON 10 Mins

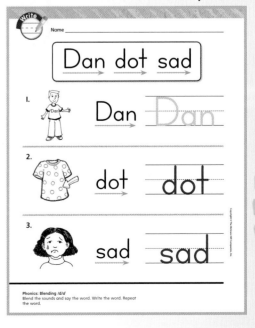

d

Word-Building Card

Review /d/ *d*

1 Model Display **Word-Building Card** *d*. *This is the letter* d. *The letter* d *stands for /d/, the sound you hear at the end of* sad. *Say the sound with me: /d/. I will write the letter* d *because* sad *has the /d/ sound at the end.*

2 Guided Practice/Practice Tell children that you will say some words that have /d/ at the end and some words that do not. Have children say /d/ and write the letter *d* on their **Response Boards** when they hear /d/ at the end of the word. Guide practice with the first word.

had   sit   lid   cap   mad   man   sad

Blend Words with *d* and *a, i, m, n*

1 Model Display Word-Building Cards *d, a, d*. *This is the letter* d. *It stands for /d/. This is the letter* a. *It stands for /a/. This is the letter* d. *It stands for /d/. Let's blend the three sounds together: /daaad/. The word is* dad. Continue with *mad, pad, sad.*

2 Guided Practice/Practice Write the following words. Have children read each word blending the sounds. Guide practice with the first word.

mad   Dan   did   dim   dip

Write these sentences and prompt children to read the connected text, sounding out the decodable words: *I am not mad. Dad can see the top. Did you sit on the mat?*

Corrective Feedback

Sound Error Model the sound that children missed, then have them repeat. For example, for the word *mad*, tap under the letter *d* and ask: *What's the sound?* Return to the beginning of the word. *Let's start over.* Blend the word with children again.

YOUR TURN PRACTICE BOOK p. 112

→ # Word Work

MINILESSON
5 Mins

Phonics

Photo Cards

Picture Sort

❶ Model Remind children that the letter *d* stands for /d/. Place the **Word-Building Card** *d* on the left side of a pocket chart. *What is the letter?* (*d*) *What sound does it stand for?* (/d/)

Hold up the *Deer* **Photo Card**. *Here is the picture for* deer. Deer *has the /d/ sound at the beginning. I will place* deer *under the letter* d *because the letter* d *stands for /d/.*

Use the same routine for /o/ *o* and the Photo Card for *octopus*.

❷ Guided Practice/Practice Display and name the following Photo Cards: *dime, dinosaur, door, olive, otter, ox*. Have children say the picture name and the sound at the beginning of the word. Have them tell which letter the Photo Card should be placed under. Guide children with the first word.

Photo Cards

MINILESSON 5 Mins

High-Frequency Words

do

1 Guided Practice Display the **High-Frequency Word Card** *do*. Review the word using the **Read/Spell/Write** routine.

2 Practice Point to the High-Frequency Word Card *do* and have children read it. Repeat with previous weeks' words *a, and, go, like, see, the, to, we, you.*

Build Fluency

Word Automaticity Write the following sentences and have children chorally read aloud as you track the print. Repeat several times.

> Do you see the cat?
> I can see Tim and Matt.
> Do you like Pam and Dan?
> Do you nap on the mat?

Read for Fluency Distribute pages 113–114 of the **Your Turn Practice Book** and help children assemble their Take-Home Books. Chorally read the Take-Home Book with children. Then have children reread the book to review high-frequency words and build fluency.

YOUR TURN PRACTICE BOOK pp. 113–114

Monitor and Differentiate

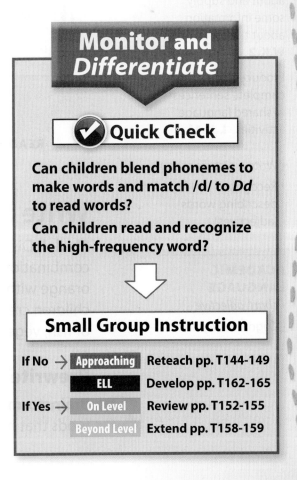

✓ **Quick Check**

Can children blend phonemes to make words and match /d/ to *Dd* to read words?

Can children read and recognize the high-frequency word?

⬇

Small Group Instruction

If No →	**Approaching**	Reteach pp. T144-149
	ELL	Develop pp. T162-165
If Yes →	**On Level**	Review pp. T152-155
	Beyond Level	Extend pp. T158-159

→ # Language Arts

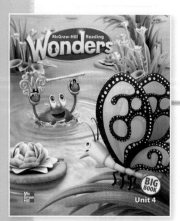
MINILESSON 10 Mins

Independent Writing

Writing Trait: Word Choice

① Practice Tell children that they will make picture menus of their favorite meals. They will draw and label their favorite foods.

② Guided Practice Share the Readers to Writers page in the **Reading/Writing Workshop**. Read the model sentences aloud.

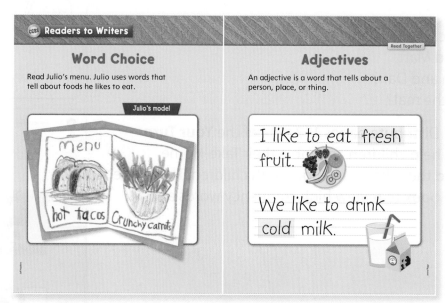

READING/WRITING WORKSHOP BIG BOOK, pp. 32–33

Write a Menu

Model Display the chart from Day 1. Point to and read aloud different combinations of foods and their descriptions. Then, draw a wedge of an orange with a drop of juice dripping from it. Label it *juicy orange*. Have children create a picture menu for a balanced meal that includes meat or fish, vegetables, fruit, pasta or rice, and a drink.

Prewrite

Brainstorm Have children work with a partner to choose four different foods that make up a good meal.

OBJECTIVES

CCSS Use a combination of drawing, dictating, and writing to compose informative/explanatory texts in which they name what they are writing about and supply some information about the topic. **W.K.2**

CCSS Produce and expand complete sentences in shared language activities. **L.K.1f**

• Write a picture menu
• Recognize describing words (adjectives)

ACADEMIC LANGUAGE
• *chart, adjective*
• Cognates: *adjetivo*

Go Digital

Present the Lesson

Writing

I see a fish.

Grammar

Draft

Ask children to draw a picture menu of their favorite meal. Guide children in drawing pictures and making labels for each food or drink on their menu. Help children write labels to describe the food. Encourage children who can generate more writing to do so.

Apply Writing Trait As children label their menus, have them tell you more about each of their favorite foods and drinks.

Apply Grammar Tell children to point to and tell you the describing word they wrote for each food or drink.

Grammar

Describing Words (Adjectives)

1 Review Remind children that an adjective is a describing word that tells more about something. Remind them that we use our senses to help us to choose good describing words.

Write and read aloud the following sentences:

> I like fluffy bread.
> My friend likes crunchy carrots.

Ask children to name the describing word in each sentence.

2 Guided Practice/Practice Write and read aloud this sentence from the **Big Book**: *The paleta wagon rings its tinkly bell.*

Ask children to name the describing word in the sentence. (tinkly) Have children dictate other describing words for a bell. (little, loud, shiny) Write the words on self-stick notes and substitute them for *tinkly*. Read aloud the new sentences.

Write and read aloud this sentence from the Big Book: *It has icy paletas.*

Have partners name the describing word in the sentence. (icy) Have partners think of other describing words that might fit. (colorful, cold, delicious, juicy, bright) Help children write the words on self-stick notes and substitute their own words for *icy*. Ask children to share their new sentences with the class.

Talk About It

Have partners work together to orally generate sentences with adjectives. Encourage children to describe the things they ate for breakfast.

Daily Wrap Up

- Review the Essential Question and encourage children to discuss, using the oral vocabulary words *cultures* and *appreciate*. *What do you know about other cultures? What do you appreciate about other cultures?*

- Prompt children to review and discuss the skills they used today. Guide them to give examples of how they used each skill.

Materials

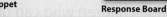

Reading/Writing Workshop Big Book
UNIT 4

Reading/Writing Workshop
UNIT 4

Literature Big Book
What Can You Do with a Paleta?

Interactive Read-Aloud Cards

Word-Building Cards

Visual Vocabulary Cards

High-Frequency Word Cards
do

Puppet

Response Board

Photo Cards
berries   vegetable
cheese   watermel
egg
grapes
lemon
peach
pear
sandwich
soup

→ # Extend the Concept

MINILESSON
10 Mins

Oral Language

OBJECTIVES

CCSS Demonstrate understanding of spoken words, syllables, and sounds (phonemes). **RF.K.2**

CCSS Use words and phrases acquired through conversations, reading and being read to, and responding to texts. **L.K.6**

Develop oral vocabulary

ESSENTIAL QUESTION

Remind children that this week they have been talking and reading about who their neighbors are. Have them sing "La Piñata" and think about the celebration in this song. Then ask them to tell about the neighborhood in *What Can You Do with a Paleta?*

Phonological Awareness

Sentence Segmentation

Repeat from the song: "See that you don't miss it!" Say: *We can break this sentence into its words. Listen as I say the sentence and clap for each part.* Clap once for each word as you say the sentence. Have children echo and mimic. Then say: *I'm going to say another line from the song:* "Hit it; hit it; hit it." Have a child repeat the line and clap for each part of the sentence. Then have the entire class echo and mimic.

Review Oral Vocabulary

Reread the Interactive Read Aloud Use the **Define/Example/Ask** routine to review the oral vocabulary words *cultures, appreciate, proud, tradition,* and *prefer.* Then have children listen as you reread "Cultural Festivals."

→ *What are special ways of celebrating Cinco de Mayo?* (People have parades and listen to mariachi music. They eat tacos and spicy soup at street fairs.)

→ *What is a tradition during Diwali?* (giving gifts to friends and family)

Go Digital

Visual Glossary

"Cultural Festivals"

Category Words

Category Words: Food Words

1 **Explain/Model** Read aloud the following poem about food:

> *One bite, two bites, I am eating a paleta.*
> *Three bites, four bites, the flavor is so yummy.*
>
> *Five bites, six bites, I love to eat paleta.*
> *Seven bites, eight bites, the paleta is in my tummy.*

→ Reread the first line of the poem and ask children which word is a food word, or a word that names something we eat. (paleta) Then challenge children to name other food words. Repeat the poem using the new food words in place of *paleta*. Invite children to read the poem aloud with you.

2 **Guided Practice** Display the **Photo Cards** for *cheese, egg, sandwich, soup,* and *yogurt. What do these pictures have in common?* (They are all food words.) Talk about each food word. Then work with children to create sentences using the food words from the Photo Cards. (Possible answers: I like Swiss cheese; I ate a peanut butter and jelly sandwich.)

→ Ask children to identify food words that are part of a sandwich. Point to the bread, jelly, and peanut butter on the Photo Card for *sandwich*. Work with children to name other sandwich ingredients. (Possible answers: bun, cheese, mustard, lettuce, tomato, ham, turkey)

LET'S MOVE!

Give directions for children to act out. For example: *Crack an egg. Bite into an apple. Scoop up the cereal. Knead the dough. Stir the soup.* Then call out the direction words in random order, more quickly this time, and have children act them out. For example: *Bite. Scoop. Stir. Crack. Knead.*

YOUR TURN PRACTICE BOOK p. 115

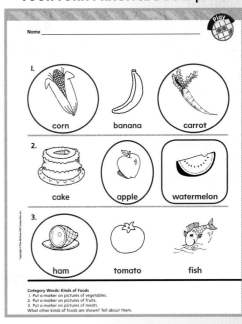

→ # Listening Comprehension

CLOSE READING

Literature Big Book

MINILESSON
10 Mins

Read "A World Festival"

Genre: Fiction

Display "A World Festival" on pages 33–36 of the **Big Book** and read aloud the title. Remind children that fiction stories can tell about places that seem real, but the story and the characters are not real.

Set a Purpose for Reading

Read aloud page 33. Tell children to listen as you continue reading the story so they can learn what happens when Kyla and her family go to a World Festival.

Strategy: Ask and Answer Questions

Remind children that good readers ask and answer questions as they read. Have children look at page 33. *We can ask: What will be at the festival? The text and illustrations tell us the answer: crafts, shows, and music from different countries around the world.*

Text Feature: Environmental Print

Explain Tell children that environmental print is the writing we see on signs, buildings, and products. *We can learn more about a story from the environmental print shown in the illustrations.*

Apply Have children look closely at the illustration on page 33. *What signs do you see at the festival?* (World Festival banner; food and drink sign)

Go Digital

What Can You Do with a Paleta?

LITERATURE BIG BOOK PAGE 33

CHARACTER, SETTING, EVENTS

Where does the story take place? (at a World Festival in Kyla's neighborhood) *Who doesn't want to go to the fair?* (Kyla)

OBJECTIVES

CCSS With prompting and support, identify characters, settings, and major events in a story. **RL.K.3**

CCSS Ask and answer questions about unknown words in a text. **RL.K.4**

- Understand the characteristics of fiction
- Use the text feature environmental print to gather information
- Apply the comprehension strategy: Ask and Answer Questions
- Make connections across texts

ACADEMIC LANGUAGE
environmental print

Kyla stops to watch a sculptor from Africa.
He carves a mask out of wood.
The sculptor is careful as he works.
Kyla appreciates his masks.

Kyla discovers a puppet show.
Puppets move with rods and strings.
The puppets dance across water.
The puppets act out a story from Vietnam.

LITERATURE BIG BOOK PAGES 34–35

ASK AND ANSWER QUESTIONS

Which country is the puppet show from? (Vietnam) Point to Vietnam on a map or globe. Then point to the United States to show the waters and land between the two countries.

Model how to use clues to figure out the meaning of *carves*. Then have partners ask and answer questions to figure out the meaning of *sculptor*.

Kyla hears trumpets.
A band plays a Mexican song.
They dance and clap to the music.
Kyla and her brother do not want to leave.
"Can we come again next year?" she asks.

LITERATURE BIG BOOK PAGE 36

CHARACTER, SETTING, EVENTS

What do Kyla and her family do last at the festival? (They dance and clap to a Mexican band playing music.) Point to Mexico on a map. Then point to your state. Have children trace a path from Mexico to your state.

Retell and Respond

Have children discuss the story by asking the following questions:

→ *What does the festival have?* (It has crafts, shows, and music from different countries around the world.)

→ *What does the man from Africa make?* (wooden masks)

Make Connections

OLLABORATE

Have children recall the selections they have read this week.

→ The selections this week told about neighborhoods. *What is another name for neighborhood?* (barrio) *What did the girl buy?* (paletas)

Write About It Write about one of the celebrations you read about in "Cultural Festivals."

SOCIAL STUDIES CONNECT TO CONTENT

Different Cultures Around the World Review with children cultures that were described in the story. Encourage children to tell about other cultures they know about. Display a map or globe and point out the different countries being discussed. Explain to children that a globe is a model of Earth.

 → **Word Work**

MINILESSON 5 Mins

Phonemic Awareness

OBJECTIVES

CCSS Isolate and pronounce the initial, medial vowel, and final sounds in three-phoneme words. **RF.K.2d**

CCSS Spell simple words, phonetically, drawing on knowledge of sound-letter relationships. **L.K.2d**

CCSS Read common high-frequency words by sight. **RF.K.3c**

- Segment words into phonemes
- Blend letter sounds to make words

Phoneme Segmentation

❶ **Model** Use **Sound Boxes** and markers. *Listen for how many sounds are in this word:* sad. *Say the word with me:* sad. *There are three sounds in* sad. *Say the sounds in* sad *with me: /s/ /a/ /d/. Let's place a marker for each sound in a sound box.* Demonstrate for children how to use the Sound Boxes. Repeat for *dad.*

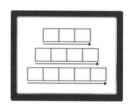
Sound Box

❷ **Guided Practice/Practice** Distribute Sound Boxes and markers. Say each word. Have children repeat the word and say each sound as they place a marker in a box. Then have them tell the number of sounds in the word. Guide practice with the first word.

mad, /m/ /a/ /d/	dot, /d/ /o/ /t/	duck, /d/ /u/ /k/
dig, /d/ /i/ /g/	pad, /p/ /a/ /d/	sit, /s/ /i/ /t/

MINILESSON 5 Mins

Phonics

Blend Words with *d* and *a, i, m, p, s, t*

❶ **Guided Practice** Display **Word-Building Cards** *p, a, d.* Point to the letter *p. This is the letter* p. *The letter* p *stands for /p/. Say /p/. This is the letter* a. *The letter* a *stands for /a/. Listen as I blend the two sounds together /paaa/. Say /paaa/. This is the letter* d. *The letter* d *stands for /d/. Listen as I blend the three sounds /paaad/,* pad. *Now you say it. Let's change* p *to* s. Use the same routine to blend *sad.*

❷ **Practice** Write *did* and *dad.* Have children blend the words. Ask children to tell which letter is the same. (*d*) Ask children to tell which letters are different. (*i* and *a*) Discuss the sounds each letter stands for and how it changes the word. Repeat with *mad, mat.*

Go Digital

Phonemic Awareness

Phonics

Handwriting

Visual Glossary

High-Frequency Word Routine

Dictation

Review Dictate the following sounds for children to spell. Have them repeat the sound and then write the letter that stands for the sound.

/d/   /k/   /n/   /i/   /o/   /t/

Dictate the following words for children to spell: *dip, did, mad, dot*. Model for children how to segment each word to scaffold the spelling.

When I say the word dip, *I hear three sounds: /d/ /i/ /p/. I know the letter* d *stands for /d/, the letter* i *stands for /i/, and the letter* p *stands for /p/. I will write* d, i, p.

When children finish, write the letters and words for them to self-correct.

High-Frequency Words

do

Visual Vocabulary Card

Practice Say the word *do* and have children write it. Then display the **Visual Vocabulary Card** *do* and follow the Teacher Talk routine on the back.

Build Fluency Build sentences in a pocket chart using **High-Frequency Word Cards**, **Photo Cards** and teacher made punctuation cards. Have children chorally read the sentences as you track the print. Then have them identify the word *do*.

> *Do* you see the sky?
>
> *Do* you like berries?
>
> *Do* you like vegetables?
>
> *Do* you like to juggle?

Have partners create sentences using the word *do*.

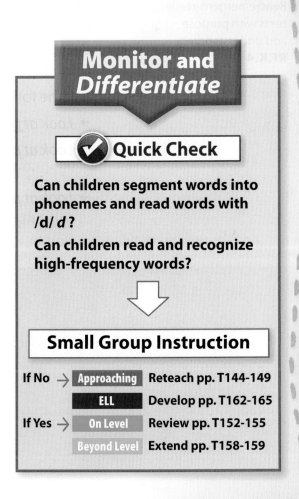

Monitor and Differentiate

✓ **Quick Check**

Can children segment words into phonemes and read words with /d/ *d*?

Can children read and recognize high-frequency words?

⬇

Small Group Instruction

If No →	Approaching	Reteach pp. T144-149
	ELL	Develop pp. T162-165
If Yes →	On Level	Review pp. T152-155
	Beyond Level	Extend pp. T158-159

→ # Shared Read

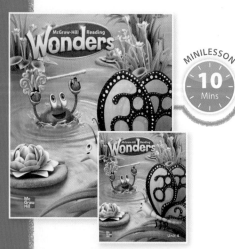

Reading/Writing Workshop Big Book and Reading/Writing Workbook

OBJECTIVES

CCSS Read common high-frequency words by sight. **RF.K.3c**

CCSS Read emergent-reader texts with purpose and understanding. **RF.K.4**

MINILESSON
10 Mins

Read "Sid"

Model Skills and Strategies

Model Book Handling Demonstrate book handling. Hold up the book and point to the front cover. *This is the front cover of the book.* Point to the back cover. *This is the back cover.* Model turning the pages of the book.

Model Concepts About Print Point to the cover. Read the title while reminding children how you read from left to right. Then model reading each sentence of the story, tracking the print as you read. *Remember that when I read each sentence, I begin on the left and move to the right.* Finally, invite a volunteer to come up to the **Big Book** and model reading from left to right, tracking the print with his or her finger.

Reread Review each rebus and discuss what it stands for. Then have children chorally read the story. Children should sound out the decodable words and say the sight words. Offer support as needed using the student **Reading/Writing Workshop**.

Ask the following:

→ *Look at page 24. What does Sid see?* (his new house)

→ *Look at page 25. Who is knocking or tapping on the front door?* (a neighbor named Dan)

→ *Look at page 29. What are new friends Sid and Tod doing?* (playing ball)

Go Digital

"Sid"

"Sid"

READING/WRITING WORKSHOP, pp. 22–29

Fluency: Intonation

1 Explain Explain that you change the tone of your voice when you read sentences that end with a period, question mark, or exclamation point. Point out different kinds of punctuation in the story, including the title.

2 Model Model reading pages 22 and 23 of "Sid." Point to the question mark on page 23. *When I read page 23, I notice how the sentence ends with a question mark. When I read the question, I change my tone so that my voice goes higher, like this.* Read the question with appropriate intonation. Then point out differences in intonation by reading other sentences in the story that end with other types of punctuation.

3 Guided Practice Read the title and encourage children to echo you. Then read each sentence in the story and have children repeat it using proper intonation. Finally, invite the class to choral read the story as you listen for proper intonation.

→ # Language Arts

MINILESSON 10 Mins Independent Writing

Write a Menu

Revise

Distribute the children's picture menus from Day 3.

Apply Writing Trait Word Choice Explain that as writers revise, they can choose different words that better describe what they are writing about. Write and read aloud the label *cold lemonade*. Suggest to children other words that can describe the lemonade you like. (tangy, sweet, icy, pink) Tell children you think *tangy* best describes your favorite lemonade, so you will change *cold* to *tangy*. Write and read aloud: *tangy lemonade*.

Help children decide whether they can think of better describing words for their menus. Then have children read the labels they wrote and check for the following:

→ Does this word describe what I like about this food?

→ What might be a better word to use?

→ Do my pictures describe the food?

→ Do I have enough on my menu for a meal?

Apply Grammar Review that a describing word is called an *adjective*. Have children share some of the describing words on their menus.

Peer Edit Have children work in pairs to do a peer edit. Ask partners to check that the menus give an adjective that makes the food sound delicious. Partners should read the labels aloud to see if there is another adjective they can suggest. Provide time for children to make revisions to their menus.

Final Draft

After children have edited their own papers and finished their peer edits, have them write their final draft. Explain that the drawing and the label that goes with it should be next to each other. Tell children to write neatly so that people can read their menu. As children work, conference with them to provide guidance.

OBJECTIVES

 CCSS With guidance and support from adults, respond to questions and suggestions from peers and add details to strengthen writing as needed. **W.K.5**

CCSS Produce and expand complete sentences in shared language activities. **L.K.1f**

- Revise labels for a menu
- Recognize describing words (adjectives)

ACADEMIC LANGUAGE

- *revise, draft, adjective*
- Cognates: *revisar, adjetivo*

Grammar

ONE LESSON
5 Mins

Describing Words (Adjectives)

1 Review Remind children that we use our senses to help us choose good describing words, or adjectives. Show the **Photo Card** for *watermelon*. Ask children to name some adjectives that describe a watermelon. (red, green, juicy, sweet)

2 Guided Practice Display the Photo Card for *berries*, which shows strawberries, blueberries, raspberries, blackberries, and cranberries. Tell children to think of one of the fruits pictured. Try to guess which fruit they are thinking of by asking questions: *Is it round? Is it smooth? Is it bumpy? Is it red? Is it dark?*

Write the answer to each question in the following sentence frame:

> *The fruit is _____.*

3 Practice Have children work in pairs to repeat the above exercise with the Photo Card for *vegetables*. First, ask children to name adjectives that describe the vegetables they see. (orange, red, green, long, smooth, shiny, flowery, leafy, skinny) Record responses on chart paper. Then have children use these adjectives in a sentence frame: *Is it _____?*

Tell them to guess which vegetable their partner is thinking of. Write answers in this sentence frame: *The vegetable is _____.* Ask children to read aloud each sentence they make and have them guess the vegetable. Provide support as needed.

Talk About It

Have partners work together to orally generate sentences with adjectives. Encourage them to create sentences about why a particular food is their favorite. Read aloud this sentence frame: *I like _____ because it is _____.*

ENGLISH LANGUAGE LEARNERS

Picture Cards and Describing Words Display Photo Cards for *grapes, lemon, peach,* and *pear*. Work with children to name describing words (adjectives) that tell about the fruit. Have children use a phrase or sentence with the adjective and fruit as well as they can. For example: *purple grapes* or *The grapes are purple.*

Daily Wrap Up

- Review the Essential Question and encourage children to discuss it, using the oral vocabulary words.

- Prompt children to discuss the skills they practiced and learned today. Guide them to share examples of each skill.

☞ **Go** Digital

www.connected.mcgraw-hill.com
RESOURCES
Research and Inquiry

→ **Wrap Up the Week**

Integrate Ideas

RESEARCH AND INQUIRY

Meet Your Neighbors

OBJECTIVES

 Participate in shared research and writing projects (e.g., explore a number of books by a favorite author and express opinions about them). **W.K.7**

 With guidance and support from adults, explore a variety of digital tools to produce and publish writing, including in collaboration with peers. **W.K.6**

ACADEMIC LANGUAGE
• *research, Internet*
• Cognates: *internet*

Make a Display

Tell children that today they will do a research project with a partner to make a display about people or places in their neighborhood. Review the steps in the research process below.

STEP 1 Choose a Topic

Guide partners to talk about people who live in their neighborhood. Have them think about neighbors who come from different places. Prompt partners to discuss neighborhood places, such as stores and restaurants, that come from different cultures.

STEP 2 Find Resources

Talk about locating and using resources to collect information. Encourage children to gather details by asking questions. Guide children to use maps and the Internet as resources, too. Have children use the Research Process Checklist online.

STEP 3 Keep Track of Ideas

Have children list their ideas by drawing pictures or writing words. Help children write words that may be unfamiliar because they are names of countries or states.

Collaborative Conversations

Listen Carefully As children engage in discussions with a partner, in a small group, or as a whole class, encourage them to:

→ look at the person who is speaking.

→ listen to the words the speaker is saying.

→ respect others by not interrupting them.

→ repeat classmates' ideas to check understanding.

We know the Vermas. They are nice.

STEP 4 **Create the Project:
Our Neighbors Display**

Explain the characteristics of the project:

→ **Information** This display will give information about people or places in the neighborhood.

→ **Text** Tell pairs that their portion of the display will have a sentence that describe their illustration. Provide this sentence frame:

These/This are/is the _____ .

→ **Illustration** Direct children to draw a picture of the person or place.

Direct children to work with a partner to choose someone or something in their neighborhood that they will represent in the display.

→ Guide children to use the research from the Internet sources and digital tools to produce and publish their writing.

→ Guide children to name the person or thing in the first sentence.

→ Encourage children who can write more about their topic to do so.

→ Encourage children to include details in their illustration.

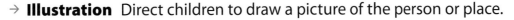

ELL ENGLISH LANGUAGE LEARNERS SCAFFOLD

Beginning	Intermediate	Advanced/Advanced High
Use Sentence Frames Pair children with more fluent speakers. Provide sentence frames to help children describe their illustration. For example: Our picture shows _____. It is from _____.	**Discuss** Guide children to focus on what is interesting about having people or things in the neighborhood (such as restaurants) from different cultures. You might also ask how children know that people are from cultures that are different from their own.	**Describe** Prompt children to use adjectives to describe details in their pictures. Use the details and adjectives as springboards for additional questions that help fully describe the cultural aspects of children's pictures.

Materials

Reading/Writing Workshop Big Book
UNIT 4

Literature Big Book
What Can You Do with a Paleta?

Interactive Read-Aloud Cards

Word-Building Cards

Visual Vocabulary Cards
do

High-Frequency Word Cards
a	see
and	the
do	to
go	we
like	you

Photo Cards
banana
celery
cherry
olive
pea
soup
yogurt

Response Board

"Did You See a Dolphin?"

→ Integrate Ideas

TEXT CONNECTIONS

Connect to Essential Question

OBJECTIVES

 With prompting and support, compare and contrast the adventures and experiences of characters in familiar stories. **RL.K.9**

 Participate in collaborative conversations with diverse partners about *kindergarten topics and texts* with peers and adults in small and larger groups. **SL.K.1**

- Make connections among texts
- Make connections to the world

Text to Text

Remind children that, all week, they have been reading selections about neighbors. Tell them that now they will connect the texts, or think about how the selections are alike and different. Model comparing *What Can You Do with a Paleta?* with "A World Fair."

 Think Aloud In *What Can You Do with a Paleta?* the girl seems so happy to tell about her neighborhood. The pictures show me that the neighborhood is very colorful and friendly. The character in "A World Fair" isn't happy at first, but by the end of the story, she *is* happy. The fair seemed colorful and friendly too.

Guide children to compare the characters' experiences in "A World Fair" with the events and fairs featured in "Cultural Festivals," as well as in the Leveled Readers from the week.

Text to Self

Have children discuss any festivals or holidays they have been a part of. *What traditions does your family have?*

Text to World

Talk about the extra interest that different cultures add to a neighborhood. Ask: *Why is it fun and interesting to have people from many different cultures in a neighborhood?*

TALK ABOUT READING

OBJECTIVES

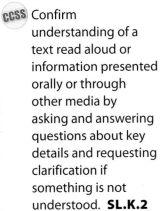

CCSS Confirm understanding of a text read aloud or information presented orally or through other media by asking and answering questions about key details and requesting clarification if something is not understood. **SL.K.2**

Becoming Readers

Talk with children about the genres, strategy, and skill they have learned about this week. Prompt them to discuss how this knowledge helps them to read and understand selections.

→ Note that one genre that children learned about this week is fiction. Recall with children some of the characteristics of fiction.

→ Talk with children about the strategy of asking and answering questions. *How did pausing to ask and answer questions about neighbors help you to understand the selections?*

→ Remind children that they learned about character, setting, and events. *What did you learn about the characters by looking at the illustrations in* What Can You Do with a Paleta? *What did you learn about the setting? What did you learn about the events?*

RESEARCH AND INQUIRY

OBJECTIVES

CCSS Participate in shared research and writing projects (e.g., explore a number of books by a favorite author and express opinions about them). **W.K.7**

Wrap Up the Project

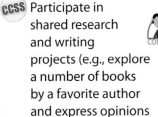

Guide partners to share their pictures on the bulletin board and to tell about what they've shown by pointing out details and describing them. Encourage children to use words and phrases they learned this week. Have children use the Presenting and Listening checklists online.

 # Word Work

 MINILESSON 5 Mins

Phonemic Awareness

OBJECTIVES

CCSS Spell simple words phonetically, drawing on knowledge of sound-letter relationships. **L.K.2d**

CCSS Read common high-frequency words by sight. **RF.K.3c**

• Segment words into phonemes
• Blend sounds to read words with /d/ *d*

Phoneme Segmentation

❶ **Model** Use **Sound Boxes** and markers. *Listen to this word:* dip. *Say it with me:* dip. *Say the sounds in* dip *with me:* /d/ /i/ /p/. *Let's place a marker for each sound in a box:* /d/ /i/ /p/. Repeat for *Don*.

❷ **Guided Practice/Practice** Distribute Sound Boxes and markers. Say each word. Have children repeat the word and say each sound as they place a marker in a box. Then have them tell the number of sounds in the word. Guide practice with the first word.

mud, /m/ /u/ /d/	dock, /d/ /o/ /k/	Dan, /d/ /a/ /n/
dim, /d/ /i/ /m/	nod, /n/ /o/ /d/	sad, /s/ /a/ /d/

 MINILESSON 5 Mins

Phonics

Read Words with *d* and *a, i, m, n, p, s*

❶ **Guided Practice** Remind children that the letter *d* can stand for the sound /d/. Display **Word-Building Cards** *m, a, d.* Point to the letter *m. The letter* m *stands for the sound* /m/. *Say* /mmm/. *The letter* a *stands for the sound* /a/. *Say* /aaa/. *The letter* d *stands for* /d/. *Say* /d/. *Let's blend the sounds to make the word:* /mmmaaad/ mad. *Let's change* m *to* s. Blend and read *sad* with children.

❷ **Practice** Write these words and sentences for children to read:

Dan   pad   dim   did

I am sad.	Don can see the mat.
Did you like the cat?	Dad can see Pam and Dot.

Remove words from view before dictation.

♪ Review initial /d/ *d*. Have children write the letter *d* on their **Response Boards**. Play and sing "Did You See a Dolphin?" Have children hold up and show the letter *d* on their boards when they hear initial /d/. Demonstrate as you sing with children.

Go Digital

Phonemic Awareness

Phonics

Handwriting

Visual Glossary

Dictation

1 **Review** Dictate the following sounds for children to spell. As you say each sound, have children repeat it and then write the letter that stands for the sound.

/d/   /k/   /n/   /i/   /o/   /t/

2 **Dictate** the following words for children to spell. Model for children how to use sound boxes to segment each word to scaffold the spelling. *I will say a word. You will repeat the word, then think about how many sounds are in the word. Use your Sound Boxes to count the sounds. Then write one letter for each sound you hear.*

sad   cat   dot   sip   pad   dim

Then write the letters and words for children to self-correct.

MINILESSON

5 Mins

High-Frequency Words

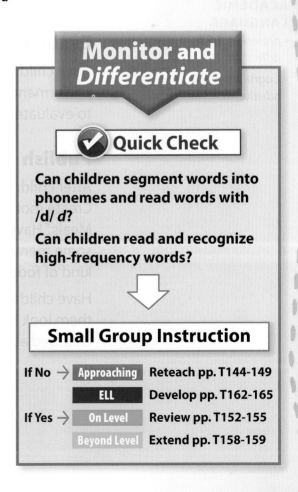

do

Visual Vocabulary Card

1 **Review** Display **Visual Vocabulary Card** *do*. Then choose a Partner Talk activity on the back.

Distribute one of the following **High-Frequency Word Cards** to children: *and, do, go, to, you*. Tell children that you will say some sentences. *When you hear the word that is on your card, stand and hold up your word card.*

Do birds fly in the sky?
You can see the sun.
Do you want *to go* with us.
Tim *and* Don will come.
I want *to* give this *to* her.

2 **Build Fluency: Word Automaticity** Display High-Frequency Word Cards *do, you, go, and, to, the, a, see, we,* and *like*. Point to each card, at random, and have children read the word as quickly as they can.

Monitor and Differentiate

✓ Quick Check

Can children segment words into phonemes and read words with /d/ d?

Can children read and recognize high-frequency words?

⬇

Small Group Instruction

If No →	Approaching	Reteach pp. T144-149
	ELL	Develop pp. T162-165
If Yes →	On Level	Review pp. T152-155
	Beyond Level	Extend pp. T158-159

Language Arts

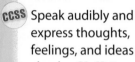 **Independent Writing**

Write a Menu

Prepare

Tell children that they will present their finished picture menus from Day 4 to the class. Hold up an example from Day 4 and read it aloud, tracking the print. *I pointed to the picture when I read the label. I read my label with feeling so everyone knows how much I like this food.*

Present

Have children take turns standing up and reading their picture menus aloud. Remind children to point to the pictures and to read their labels with feeling so everyone can understand how they feel about the food. Encourage the rest of the class to listen quietly and to wait until the presenter has finished before asking any questions.

Evaluate

Have children discuss their own presentations and evaluate their performances, using the presentation rubric. Use the teacher's rubric to evaluate children's writing.

Publish

After children have finished presenting, collect their picture menus. Create mobiles for the menus and label the mobiles "Our Favorite Meals." Have children help you attach the menus onto string. Share some menus from each mobile. Discuss how many children liked each kind of food and the different words each person used to describe it.

Have children add their writing to their Writer's Portfolio. Then have them look back at their previous writing and discuss how they have changed as writers throughout the year.

OBJECTIVES

CCSS Speak audibly and express thoughts, feelings, and ideas clearly. **SL.K.6**

CCSS Produce and expand complete sentences in shared language activities. **L.K.1f**

• Make a presentation
• Recognize describing words (adjectives)

ACADEMIC LANGUAGE

• *present, publish, adjective*
• Cognates: *presente, adjetivo*

Go Digital

Writing

I see a fish.

Grammar

Grammar

Describing Words (Adjectives)

1 **Review** Remind children that an adjective is a describing word that tells more about something. Explain to children that sometimes the adjective will come before the naming word. Other times the adjective may come after the naming word. Show the **Photo Card** for *soup.* Write and read aloud the following sentence: *The soup is red.* Have children tell what the describing word is. (red) *What does it describe?* (the soup)

2 **Review/Practice** Write and read aloud this sentence frame:

The _____ is _____.

Point to the first blank and tell children that the name of a food goes there. Point to the second blank and tell children a describing word goes there. Write *soup* and *red* on self-stick notes to fill in the blanks and read *The soup is red.*

Have children work in groups. Show groups the Photo Cards for *banana, celery, cherry, olive, pea,* and *yogurt.* Have children choose a food to describe. Provide the sentence frame above and self-stick notes. Circulate to help children write their adjectives and to offer corrective feedback as needed. Guide children to think of multiple describing words for each food.

Wrap Up the Week

- Review blending words with initial and final /d/ *d.* Remind children that describing words give details about something.

- Use the **High-Frequency Word Cards** to review the **Words to Know**.

- Remind children that they can choose many different words to describe one thing.

→ Approaching Level

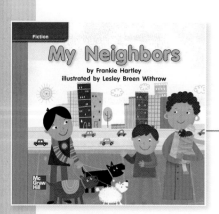

Leveled Reader

OBJECTIVES

CCSS With prompting and support, ask and answer questions about key details in a text. **RL.K.1**

CCSS With prompting and support, retell familiar stories, including key details. **RL.K.2**

CCSS With prompting and support, identify characters, settings, and major events in a story. **RL.K.3**

CCSS Read emergent-reader texts with purpose and understanding. **RF.K.4**

Leveled Reader:
My Neighbors

Leveled Reader

Before Reading

Preview and Predict

Show children the cover of the book. Read the title and the names of the author and illustrator. Discuss the cover illustration. Say: *Think about the title. Where might this story take place?* Preview each illustration and identify the rebus pictures. Ask children what they think the story will be about.

Review Genre: Fiction

Remind children that fiction is a made-up story. Say: *A fiction story has characters and events.* Ask children to name some of their favorite fiction stories and tell what happens to the characters.

Model Concepts of Print

Model for children how to read the text on page 2, while you track your finger under each word.

Review High-Frequency Words

Point to the high-frequency word *do* on page 2 of the story. Then ask children to look through the rest of the book to find the word *do*.

Essential Question

Set a purpose for reading. Say: *Let's read the book to find out who the boy's neighbors are.* Remind children to use the rebuses and illustrations as they read.

During Reading

Guided Comprehension

As children read *My Neighbors,* monitor and provide guidance by correcting blending and modeling the strategy and skill.

Strategy: Ask and Answer Questions

Remind children that as they read they can ask questions about things they don't understand and look for answers in the text and pictures.

Skill: Character, Setting, and Events

Explain to children that they can learn a lot about a story by thinking about the characters, setting, and events. Explain that characters are the people in a story. The setting is where and when the story takes place. The events are the things that happen in the story.

Think Aloud On page 2, I see from the picture that the boy and his mom are the main characters. The baker is another character. The setting is their neighborhood. The event is that the boy and his mother are buying bread.

Guide children to talk about the events happening on each page. Ask children to read the sentence and look at the illustration. Then have them describe the event they see the characters taking part in.

After Reading

Respond to Reading

→ *What are the boy and his mother doing on page 3?* (shopping for fruit)

→ *Who do the boy and his mother meet in their neighborhood on page 4?* (a boy walking dogs)

→ *Why is it fun to meet different people in your neighborhood?* (You can talk to the different people and see what they are doing each day.)

Retell

Have children take turns retelling the story. Help them make a personal connection by asking: *Who do you see in your neighborhood?*

Model Fluency

Reread the story aloud, pausing after each page and have children choral-read with you.

Apply Have children practice reading aloud and emphasizing different words as they point to each word and rebus.

LITERACY ACTIVITIES

Have children complete the activities on the inside back cover of the reader.

Level Up

Level-up lessons available online.

IF Children read *My Neighbors* **Approaching Level** with fluency and correctly answer the Respond to Reading questions,

THEN Tell children that they will read another story about who their neighbors are.

- Have children page through *Neighborhood Party* **On Level** as you preview what children know about the people in their neighborhood.

- Have children read the story, monitoring their comprehension and providing assistance as necessary.

→ Approaching Level

Phonological Awareness

SENTENCE SEGMENTATION

OBJECTIVES

 Demonstrate understanding of spoken words, syllables, and sounds (phonemes). **RF.K.2**

 I Do Remind children that all sentences are made of words. Say the line from the song "La Piñata," *See that you don't miss it!* Say the sentence again. Have children clap the words while you holding up a finger and count each word. *There are six words in this sentence.*

 We Do Repeat the line and have children hold up fingers and count the words in the sentence as you say them.

 You Do Say the first part of the last line of the song: *Try to find the distance...* Have children clap for each word. Repeat the line and have children hold up a finger for each word. Ask how many words. (5)

PHONEME ISOLATION

OBJECTIVES

 Isolate and pronounce the initial, medial vowel, and final sounds (phonemes) in three-phoneme words. **RF.K.2d**

 I Do Display the *Dolphin* **Photo Card**. *This is a dolphin. The first sound I hear in* dolphin *is /d/.* Have children repeat the word with you, emphasizing the initial sound. Then have them say the first sound with you: /d/. Repeat for final /d/ using the *Bird* Photo Card.

 We Do Display the *Dinosaur* Photo Card. Name the photo and have children repeat it. *What is the first sound in* dinosaur? (/d/) Say the sound together. Repeat for final /d/ using the *Cloud* Photo Card.

 You Do Display the *Door* Photo Card. Have children say the name, then say the initial sound: *door*, /d/. Repeat for final /d/ using the *Hand* Photo Card.

You may wish to review Phonological Awareness and Phonemic Awareness with **ELL** using this section.

PHONEME BLENDING

OBJECTIVES

 Isolate and pronounce the initial, medial vowel, and final sounds (phonemes) in three-phoneme words. **RF.K.2d**

 Listen as the puppet says the sounds in a word: /d/ /o/ /t/. Now the puppet will blend the sounds together to make a word: /dooot/, dot. The puppet blended the sounds /dooot/ to make the word dot. Repeat with *bad, dock.*

 The puppet will say the sounds in a word. Listen to the puppet, then blend the sounds to say the word. Have the puppet say /d/ /i/ /m/. Have children repeat. *Now let's blend the sounds and say the word with the puppet:* /d/ /i/ /m/, /diiimmm/, dim. Repeat with *pad.*

 Have the puppet say the following sounds. Ask children to blend the sounds and say the words:

/d/ /u/ /k/ duck   /d/ /a/ /b/ dab   /s /a/ /d/ sad   /d/ /i/ /d/ did

PHONEME SEGMENTATION

OBJECTIVES

 Isolate and pronounce the initial, medial vowel, and final sounds (phonemes) in three-phoneme words. **RF.K.2d**

 Use the **Sound Boxes** and markers. *Listen as I say a word:* mad. *Say the word with me:* mad. *There are three sounds in* mad: /m/ /a/ /d/. *I'll place a marker for each sound:* /m/ /a/ /d/. Point to the sounds in turn and have children say them with you. Repeat for *dip.*

 Distribute Sound Boxes and markers. *Listen as I say a word:* dim. *Say the word with me:* dim. *Say the sounds with me:* /d/ /i/ /m/. *How many sounds do you hear?* (3) *Now place a marker for each sound.* Repeat for the word *dad.*

 Say the word *sad.* Have children repeat the word, then say its sounds. Have them tell the number of sounds, then place a marker for each sound. Continue with the words *dot, day, had, red,* and *deck.*

ELL ENGLISH LANGUAGE LEARNERS

For the **ELLs** who need **phonics**, **decoding**, and **fluency** practice, use scaffolding methods as necessary to ensure students understand the meaning of the words. Refer to the Language Transfer Handbook for phonics elements that may not transfer in students' native languages.

→ Approaching Level

Phonics

SOUND-SPELLING REVIEW

OBJECTIVES

CCSS Demonstrate basic knowledge of one-to-one letter-sound correspondences by producing the primary or many of the most frequent sounds for each consonant. **RF.K.3a**

 I Do Display **Word-Building Card** o. Say the letter name and the sound it stands for: /o/ o. Repeat for *m, a, s, p, t, i, n, c.*

 We Do Display Word-Building Cards one at a time and together say the letter name and the sound that each letter stands for.

 You Do Display Word-Building Cards one at a time and have children say the letter name and the sound that each letter stands for.

CONNECT *d* TO /d/

OBJECTIVES

CCSS Demonstrate basic knowledge of one-to-one letter-sound correspondences by producing the primary or many of the most frequent sounds for each consonant. **RF.K.3a**

 I Do Display the *Dolphin* **Sound-Spelling Card**. *The letter* d *stands for /d/ at the beginning of* dolphin. *Say the name of the letter and the sound it stands for.* (d, /d/) *I'll write* d *when I hear /d/:* dance, deep, mile, desk, tool. Repeat for final /d/ using the *Cloud* **Photo Card** and the words *head, glad, gate, muffin, kid.*

 We Do *Day begins with /d/. Let's write* d. With children, write *d* when they hear /d/. Say: *sail, dish, dash, poem.* Repeat for final /d/ using *hop, said, camp, head, feed.*

 You Do Have children write the letter *d* if a word begins with /d/: *date, pear, sick, disk, down, talk.* Repeat for final /d/ using *small, wet, read, weed, green, sad.*

RETEACH

OBJECTIVES

CCSS Isolate and pronounce the initial, medial vowel, and final sounds (phonemes) in three-phoneme words. **RF.K.2d**

 I Do Display **Reading/Writing Workshop**, p. 20. The letter *d* stands for the /d/ sound you hear at the beginning of *dolphin.* Say *dolphin,* emphasizing /d/.

 We Do Have children name each picture in row 1. Repeat the name, emphasizing /d/. Repeat for row 2, emphasizing the final sound.

 You Do Guide children in reading the words in row 3. Then have them read the words in row 4, offering assistance as needed.

BLEND WORDS WITH /d/ d

OBJECTIVES

 Isolate and pronounce the initial, medial vowel, and final sounds (phonemes) in three-phoneme words. **RF.K.2d**

 I Do Display **Word-Building Cards** d, o, t. *This is the letter* d. *It stands for* /d/. *This is the letter* o. *It stands for* /o/. *This is the letter* t. *It stands for* /t/. *Listen as I blend all three sounds:* /dooot/, dot. *The word is* dot. *Repeat for* pod.

 We Do *Now let's blend more sounds to make words.* Make the word *dim. Let's blend* /diiimmm/, dim. Have children blend to read the word. Repeat with the word *sad. Let's blend* /saaad/, sad.

You Do Distribute sets of Word-Building Cards with *d, i, a, m,* and *p.* Write: *pad, dim, dip, mad,* and *mid.* Have children form the words and then blend and read the words.

REREAD FOR FLUENCY

OBJECTIVES

 Read emergent-reader texts with purpose and understanding. **RF.K.4**

I Do Turn to p. 22 of the **Reading/Writing Workshop** and read aloud the title. *Let's read the title together.* Page through the book. Ask children what they see in each picture. Ask children to find the high-frequency word *do* on pp. 23 and 24.

 We Do Then have children open their books and chorally read the story. Have children point to each word as they read. Provide corrective feedback as needed. After reading, ask children to recall the people who welcomed Sid's family to their new home.

 You Do Have children reread "Sid" with a partner for fluency.

BUILD FLUENCY WITH PHONICS

Sound/Spelling Fluency

Display the following **Word-Building Cards**: *m, a, s, p, t, l, n, c, o,* and *d.* Have children chorally say each sound. Repeat and vary the pace.

Fluency in Connected Text

Write the following sentences. *The cat did not like Dad! Don and Sid sit on top. Did you see the dot on the map?* Have children read the sentences and identify the words with /d/d.

→ Approaching Level

High-Frequency Words

TIER 2

RETEACH WORDS

OBJECTIVES

CCSS Read common high-frequency words by sight. **RF.K.3c**

I Do Display **High-Frequency Word Card** *do* and use the **Read/Spell/Write** routine to reteach the word.

We Do Have children turn to p. 21 of **Reading/Writing Workshop** and discuss the first photo. Then read aloud the first sentence. Reread the sentence with children. Have children point to the word *do* in the sentence. Use the same routine for the other sentence on the page.

You Do Write the sentence frame *Do you like to ___?* Have children copy the sentence frame on their **Response Boards**. Then have partners work together to read and orally complete the frame by asking each other to name things they like to do.

CUMULATIVE REVIEW

OBJECTIVES

CCSS Read common high-frequency words by sight. **RF.K.3c**

I Do Display the **High-Frequency Word Cards** *I, can, the, we, see, a, like, to, and, go, you, do*. Use the **Read/Spell/Write** routine to review words. Write sentences such as: *Dan and Sid do not like to mop. Can you see the pin on the cap?*

We Do Chorally read the sentences. Then guide children to create a sentence as a class using the High-Frequency Words.

You Do Have partners create sentences using the High-Frequency Words. Remind them to refer to the High-Frequency Word Cards as needed. Then have them write the words on their **Response Boards**.

Oral Vocabulary

REVIEW WORDS

CCSS **OBJECTIVES**

Identify real-life connections between words and their use. **L.K.5c**

Develop oral vocabulary: *cultures, appreciate, proud, tradition, prefer*

 I Do

Use the **Define/Example/Ask** routine to review words. Use the following:

cultures   **Cultures** are the languages, holidays, and special foods shared by groups of people.

appreciate   When you **appreciate** something, you respect it or value it.

proud   When you are **proud**, you feel good about yourself or something you have done.

tradition   A **tradition** is a belief or habit that is repeated in a family.

prefer   When you **prefer** something, you like it more than something else.

 We Do

Ask questions to build understanding. *What have you learned about cultures in books you have read? Why do you appreciate your school? What is something you have done at school that you are proud of? What is a new tradition in your family? Which do you prefer to eat—fruit or vegetables? Why?*

 You Do

Have children complete these sentence frames: *We can learn about new cultures by ___. I appreciate a new box of crayons because ___. My family was proud because ___. A summer tradition is ___. I prefer hot days to cool days when I want to ___.*

Comprehension

SELF-SELECTED READING

CCSS **OBJECTIVES**

With prompting and support, ask and answer questions about key details in a text. **RL.K.1**

Apply the strategy and skill to reread the text.

Read Independently

Help children select a story with illustrations for sustained silent reading. Remind children that they can use illustrations to help them understand what is happening with the characters, setting, and events in a story. Tell children to ask and answer questions before, during, and after reading.

Read Purposefully

Before reading, help children identify an illustration of a character they want to find out more about. After reading, guide children to discuss the illustration. Have them explain how the illustration helped them understand the story. *Why did you want to learn more about the character? How did the picture help you answer questions as you read?*

→ On Level

Leveled Reader

OBJECTIVES

CCSS With prompting and support, ask and answer questions about key details in a text. **RL.K.1**

CCSS With prompting and support, retell familiar stories, including key details. **RL.K.2**

CCSS With prompting and support, identify characters, settings, and major events in a story. **RL.K.3**

CCSS Read emergent-reader texts with purpose and understanding. **RF.K.4**

Leveled Reader:
Neighborhood Party

Go Digital

Leveled Reader

Before Reading

Preview and Predict

Show children the cover of the book. Read the title and the names of the author and illustrator. Ask children what the author and illustrator do. Have children talk about what they see on the cover. Preview the illustrations inside the book and allow children to predict what they will learn. Say: *This book is about a neighborhood party. What do you see in the illustrations that make it look like a party?*

Review Genre: Fiction

Review with children that fiction is a made-up story that has characters, events, and settings.

Model Concepts of Print

Model how to point to each word as you read a page of text. Tell children to point to the words as you read each page in the book.

Review High-Frequency Words

Point out the word *do* on page 2. Ask children to use the word in a sentence of their own.

Essential Question

Set a purpose for reading: *Who do you think lives in this neighborhood? Let's read the book to find out who the neighbors in this city apartment building are.*

During Reading

Guided Comprehension

As children whisper-read, monitor and provide guidance by correcting blending and modeling the strategy and skill.

Strategy: Ask and Answer Questions

Remind children that as they read they can ask questions about things they don't understand and look for answers in the text and pictures.

Skill: Characters, Setting, and Events

Remind children that characters are the people in a story, the setting is the place, and the events are what happens in the story. Explain that the illustrations will help children identify the characters, setting, and events in a story.

Think Aloud Looking at the illustration on page 2, I see some of the characters. They are on the roof of an apartment building. This is the setting of the story. A man is bringing food for the party. The text tells me some of this, and I understand more when I look at the illustration.

Guide children to discuss the text and illustration on each page and talk about what the characters are doing.

After Reading

Respond to Reading

→ *What kinds of foods are at the party at the apartment building?* (tacos, soup, chips, dip, hot dogs, dumplings)

→ *Who are the people at the party?* (the neighbors in the building)

→ *What makes all the foods at the party different from each other?* (They are from different cultures, or different countries.)

Retell

Have children take turns retelling the story. Help them make personal connections by asking: *What are some foods that you would like to share with your neighbors?*

Model Fluency

As you read the first few pages, have children chorally repeat each sentence.

Apply Have children practice reading with partners. Encourage them to use expression in their voices as they read.

LITERACY ACTIVITIES

Have children complete the activities on the inside back cover of the reader.

Level Up

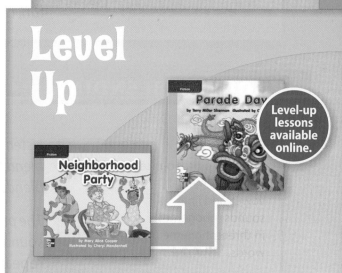

Level-up lessons available online.

IF Children read *Neighborhood Party* On Level with fluency and correctly answer the Respond to Reading questions,

THEN Tell children that they will read another story about who their neighbors are.

• Have children page through *Parade Day* Beyond Level as you talk about what the children see at a community parade.

• Have children read the story, monitoring their comprehension and providing assistance as necessary.

→ **On Level**

Phonemic Awareness

PHONEME ISOLATION

OBJECTIVES

CCSS Isolate and pronounce the initial, medial vowel, and final sounds (phonemes) in three-phoneme words. **RF.K.2d**

 I Do Display the *Dolphin* **Photo Card**. *This is a dolphin. The first sound is /d/. Say it with me.* Repeat for final /d/ using the *Hand* Photo Card.

 We Do Say *dug* and have children repeat. *What is the first sound in* dug? (/d/) Repeat with *cap, deer,* and *pin.* Repeat for final sounds with *tip, hid, mom.*

 You Do Say these words and have children tell the initial sound: *ox, man, dog, dim, tan, can.* Repeat for final sounds using the words *pad, pat, cap, ram.*

PHONEME BLENDING

OBJECTIVES

CCSS Isolate and pronounce the initial, medial vowel, and final sounds (phonemes) in three-phoneme words. **RF.K.2d**

 I Do *Listen as the puppet says the sounds in a word: /d/ /a/ /sh/. The puppet will blend the sounds together to make a word: /daaash/,* dash. *When the puppet blends the sounds together, it makes the word* dash. Repeat with *dish, had.*

 We Do *The puppet will say sounds in a word. Repeat the sounds, then blend the sounds to say the word.* Have the puppet say /d/ /i/ /m/. Guide children to repeat the sounds and blend them to make *dim.*

 You Do Have the puppet say the following sounds. Ask children to repeat the sounds and then blend them to say the word: /d/ /u/ /k/ duck; /s/ /a/ /d/ sad; /n/ /o/ /d/ nod; d/ /u/ /g/ dug.

PHONEME SEGMENTATION

OBJECTIVES

CCSS Isolate and pronounce the initial, medial vowel, and final sounds (phonemes) in three-phoneme words. **RF.K.2d**

 I Do Use the **Sound Boxes** and markers. *Listen as I say a word:* mad. *Say it with me. There are three sounds in* mad: /m/ /a/ /d/. *I'll place a marker in a box for each sound.* Repeat for *did.*

 We Do *Listen as I say a word:* dad. *Say the word with me:* dad. *Say the sounds with me:* /d/ /a/ /d/. *Now place a marker for each sound.* Repeat for the word *dot.*

 You Do Say *dot.* Have children repeat the word, then say its sounds. Have them place a marker in a box for each sound and tell how many sounds in the word. Continue with *duck, bad, dig,* and *bed.*

Phonics

REVIEW PHONICS

OBJECTIVES

CCSS Demonstrate basic knowledge of one-to-one letter-sound correspondences by producing the primary or many of the most frequent sounds for each consonant. **RF.K.3a**

Display **Reading/Writing Workshop**, p. 20. Point to the *Dolphin* **Sound-Spelling Card**. *What letter stands for the* /d/ *sound you hear at the beginning of* dolphin? *The letter is* d.

Have children say the name of each picture in rows 1 and 2. Then ask them to identify the words with /d/ in the beginning and the words with /d/ at the end.

Have children read each word in rows 3 and 4. Repeat, asking them to raise their hands if they hear /d/ at the beginning of the word, keeping their hands lowered if they hear /d/ at the end of the word.

PICTURE SORT

OBJECTIVES

CCSS Isolate and pronounce the initial, medial vowel, and final sounds (phonemes) in three-phoneme words. **RF.K.2d**

Display **Word-Building Cards** *d* and *t* in a pocket chart. Then show the *Door* Photo Card. Say *door.* Tell children that the sound at the beginning is /d/. *The letter* d *stands for* /d/. *I will put the* Door *Photo Card under the letter* d. Show the *Top* Photo Card and say the name. Tell children that the sound at the beginning of *top* is /t/. *The letter* t *stands for* /t/. *I will put the* Top *Photo Card under the* t.

Show the *Deer* Photo Card and say the picture name. Have children repeat. Then have them tell the sound they hear at the beginning of *deer.* Ask them if they should place the photo card under the *d* or the *t.*

Continue using Photo Cards for *Toe, Dime,* and *Teeth.* Have children say the picture name and the initial sound. Then have them place the card under the *d* or *t.*

→ ## On Level

Phonics

BLEND WORDS WITH /d/d

OBJECTIVES

 Isolate and pronounce the initial, medial vowel, and final sounds (phonemes) in three-phoneme words. **RF.K.2d**

 I Do Write *d, i, p. This is the letter* d. *It stands for /d/. Say it with me: /d/. This is the letter* i. *It stands for /i/. Say it with me: /iii/. This is the letter* p. *It stands for /p/. Say it with me: /p/. I'll blend the sounds together to read the word:* /diiip/, dip.

 We Do Write *pad* and *did*. Guide children to blend the words sound by sound to read each word.

 You Do Write the following words and have children blend the words sound by sound to read each word.

mad   Dan   dot   Sid   dim

REREAD FOR FLUENCY

OBJECTIVES

 Read emergent-reader texts with purpose and understanding. **RF.K.4**

 I Do Point to the title "Sid" on p. 22 of **Reading/Writing Workshop**. Read the title and have children repeat. Work with them to read for accuracy and expression. Model reading page 26: *When I read,* "Dot and Dan can sip," *I read all the way to the end of the sentence before pausing. This makes my reading sound natural, as if I were talking.*

 We Do Read p. 23. Point to the question mark and explain that your voice goes up when asking a question. Then have children chorally read the page with you. Continue chorally reading the remainder of the pages.

 You Do Have partners reread "Sid." Provide time to listen as children read the pages. Comment on their accuracy and expression and provide corrective feedback by modeling proper fluency.

High-Frequency Words

REVIEW WORDS

OBJECTIVES

 Read common high-frequency words by sight. **RF.K.3c**

 Use the **High-Frequency Word Card** *do* with the **Read/Spell/Write** routine to review the word.

 Have children turn to p. 21 of **Reading/Writing Workshop**. Discuss the photographs and read aloud the sentences. Point to the word *do* and have children read it. Then chorally read the sentences. Have children frame the word *do* in the sentences and read the word.

 Say the word *do*. Ask children to close their eyes, picture the word, and write it as they see it. Have children self-correct.

Reteach previously introduced high-frequency words using the **Read/Spell/Write** routine.

Fluency Point to the **High-Frequency Word Cards** *I, can, the, we, see, a, like, to, and, go, you,* and *do* in random order. Have children chorally read. Repeat at a faster pace.

Comprehension

SELF-SELECTED READING

OBJECTIVES

 With prompting and support, ask and answer questions about key details in a text. **RL.K.1**

Apply the strategy and skill to reread the text

Read Independently

Have children select a story with illustrations to read for sustained silent reading. Remind them that the illustrations can help them understand key details about characters, setting, and plot. Explain that the illustrations can also help them ask and answer questions before, during, and after reading.

Read Purposefully

Before reading, ask children to point out an illustration of a character or a setting they would like to learn more about. Tell them that during reading, they should ask and answer questions about the story and the illustrations. Have them focus on ways the illustration can help them answer their questions. After reading, guide children in a discussion about how the illustration helped them answer a question about the character or setting.

→ # Beyond Level

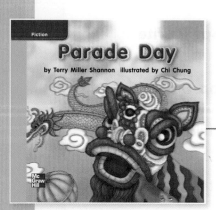

Leveled Reader

OBJECTIVES

(CCSS) With prompting and support, ask and answer questions about key details in a text. **RL.K.1**

(CCSS) With prompting and support, retell familiar stories, including key details. **RL.K.2**

(CCSS) With prompting and support, name the author and illustrator of a story and define the role of each in telling the story. **RL.K.6**

Leveled Reader:
Parade Day

Go Digital

Leveled Reader

Before Reading

Preview and Predict

Ask children to point to the title on the cover of their books. Read it aloud as children point to each word. Ask children to point to the name of the author and the illustrator. Read each one aloud and ask: *What does the author do? What does the illustrator do?* Have children look at the picture on the cover and ask them what they think the book will be about. Have them preview each page. Did they confirm their predictions?

Review Genre: Fiction

Have children recall that fiction stories are make-believe. Explain that the characters and events in the stories are made up by the author. Ask children whether they think the events in this story *could* take place in real life.

Essential Question

Remind children of the Essential Question: *Who are your neighbors?* Have children set a purpose for reading by saying: *Let's read to find out who the neighbors are in this story.*

During Reading

Guided Comprehension

As children whisper-read *Parade Day,* monitor and provide guidance by correcting blending and modeling the strategy and skill.

Strategy: Ask and Answer Questions

Remind children that as they read they can ask questions about things they don't understand and look for answers in the text and pictures.

Skill: Character, Setting, and Events

Review with children that the people in a story are the characters, the place where the characters are is the setting, and the things that happen in the story are the events. Model how to use illustrations to learn more about the characters, setting, and events in the story.

Think Aloud When I read page 3, I know that Dean sees Mr. Grant and that Jada wants to make music. I can see from the illustration that Jada and Dean are watching the men playing music march by. One of the men must be Mr. Grant. Jada and Dean are the main characters and the event is that they are watching Mr. Grant play music in the parade.

Guide children to read the text and look at the illustrations in the book. Ask them to describe the event that is happening in each picture. Ask them to say where they think the parade is taking place.

After Reading

Respond to Reading

→ *Who are the characters in the story?* (The main characters are Dean and Jada. The other characters are the people in the parade.)

→ *What is the setting of the story?* (a neighborhood parade)

→ *Why do you think Jada wants to do everything she sees in the parade?* (Possible answer: She is very excited about the parade and everything looks fun to her.)

Retell

Have children take turns retelling the story. Help them make a personal connection by asking: *Have you ever been to a parade in your community? What did you see there? Did you see any of your neighbors?*

Gifted and Talented

EVALUATING Ask children to plan a community parade of their own. Have them think about what the parade would commemorate and where it would be held. Encourage them to think about what they would like to include in their parade, such as music or performances.

HAVE children draw a picture of their parade showing the way they planned it and the events they chose to feature. Ask children to share their pictures with the class.

LITERACY ACTIVITIES

Have children complete the activities on the inside back cover of the reader.

Beyond Level

Phonics

REVIEW

OBJECTIVES

 Demonstrate basic knowledge of one-to-one letter-sound correspondences by producing the primary or many of the most frequent sounds for each consonant. **RF.K.3a**

I Do Display **Reading/Writing Workshop**, p. 20. Point to the *Dolphin* **Sound-Spelling Card**. *What is the sound at the beginning of* dolphin? *What letter can stand for /d/? The letter is* d.

We Do Have children say the name of each picture. Then ask them to share other words they know that begin with /d/.

You Do Have partners read each word. Ask them to write the words on their **Response Boards**, underlining the letter in each word that stands for /d/.

Fluency Have children reread the story "Sid" for fluency.

Innovate Have children create a new page for "Sid" by completing the frame ___ *can tap, tap, tap on a* ___ . with the name of a new person who comes to visit and what that person taps.

High-Frequency Words

REVIEW

OBJECTIVES

 Read common high-frequency words by sight. **RF.K.3c**

I Do Create index cards for *buy* and *grow*. Introduce the words using the **Read/Spell/Write** routine.

We Do Display the High-Frequency Word Cards for *do, the, you, and, to, like,* and *can*. Have partners create sentence frames using the High-Frequency Word Cards: *Do you like to buy* ___? *Don and Tim can grow the* ___ . Then have them complete the sentence frames.

You Do Have partners write sentences using the High-Frequency Words *buy* and *grow* on their **Response Boards**. Have them read their sentences.

Vocabulary

OBJECTIVES

 With guidance and support from adults, explore word relationships and nuances in word meanings. **L.K.5**

Develop oral vocabulary: Synonyms

 I Do Review the meanings of the oral vocabulary words *prefer* and *appreciate*. *A synonym is a word that means almost the same thing as another word. A synonym for* prefer *is* favor. *When you favor something, you like it better.* I favor sneakers over boots. *A synonym for* appreciate *is* value. *To value something is to be grateful for it.* Teachers value their students.

 We Do Work with children to create sentences using the new words *favor* and *value*.

 You Do Have children work with a partner to think of three or four people or things they value. Then have partners think of another synonym for *appreciate* and describe why they value the person or thing they chose.

Gifted and Talented **Extend** Have partners create a short poem describing something they favor. They should use *favor* and *value* in their poems. Explain that the poems do not have to rhyme. Ask children to share their poems.

Comprehension

OBJECTIVES

 With prompting and support, ask and answer questions about key details in a text. **RL.K.1**

Apply the strategy and skill to reread the text.

Read Independently

Have children select a story with illustrations for sustained silent reading. Remind them that asking and answering questions about the story and illustrations can help them understand the characters, setting, and events.

Read Purposefully

Before reading, ask children to choose an illustration of a character or setting they would like to learn more about. Remind them to use the illustration to ask and answer questions. After reading, have children explain how details in the illustration helped them answer questions.

Gifted and Talented **Independent Study** Have children choose one illustration from the books they read this week. Challenge them to use the details in the picture to predict what they think might happen next. Encourage them to ask and answer questions, then write a few sentences describing what they think will happen.

English Language Learners

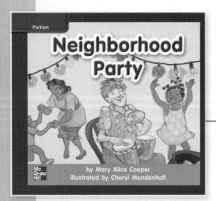

Leveled Reader

OBJECTIVES

 With prompting and support, ask and answer questions about key details in a text. **RL.K.1**

With prompting and support, retell familiar stories, including key details. **RL.K.2**

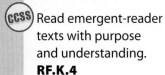 Read emergent-reader texts with purpose and understanding. **RF.K.4**

Shared Read:
Neighborhood Party

Go Digital

Leveled Reader

Before Reading

Preview and Predict

Show children the cover of the book. Read aloud the title as you point to it. Ask children to tell about a party they have been to. Point out and name things in the cover illustration. Have children repeat, using the language pattern, "*This is a _____.*" Walk children through the book and identify the rebus pictures: *tacos, soup, chips, dip, hot dogs, dumplings,* and *drums.* Say each word and ask children to point to the item in the illustration and to the label.

Essential Question

Set a purpose for reading: *Let's find out who the neighbors are. Let's find out what food the neighbors bring to the party.* Encourage children to ask questions or ask for help to clarify what they do not understand as they read.

During Reading

Interactive Question Response

Pages 2–3 Point to the illustration on page 2. Ask: *What do these people bring to the party?* (tacos) As children respond, reinforce the language pattern in the story. Say: *We do need tacos.* Read the sentence with children, having them point to each word as they read it. Point to the illustration on page 3. *Look at the picture. What does the woman bring to the party to share?* (soup) Reinforce the language pattern. Say: *We do need soup.* Have children read the sentence.

Pages 4–5 Point to the illustration and label on page 4. (Note: If the English words *chips* and *dip* are not familiar to children, bring in examples to show them.) Say: *The labels on this picture say* chips. *Who brings the chips?* (Encourage children to answer in full sentences: "The man brings the chips.") *What does the boy on page 5 bring?* (The boy brings dip.) Read the sentences on pages 4 and 5 with children.

Pages 6–7 Point to the illustration and label on page 6. Ask: *What are the labels pointing to?* (hot dogs and plate) *Who will eat these hot dogs?* (all the people at the party) Read aloud the sentence with children. Point to the illustration on page 7 and the labels pointing to the dumplings and the plate. *What are the labels pointing to?* (dumplings and plate) Point to the woman holding the plate. Ask: *What do the characters say they do need?* Read the sentence with children.

Page 8 Point to the illustration. Say: *This man brings drums. What can the man do with the drums at the party?* (Encourage children to respond in a full sentence: "The man can make music.") *What do you think the party will be like with drums?* (Possible answers: The party will be loud/fun.) Monitor children as they whisper-read the sentence.

After Reading

Respond to Reading

To reinforce children's use of English, encourage them to answer in full sentences. Prompt if necessary.

→ *What are the people doing on the roof?* (The people are having a party.)

→ *What kinds of foods do people bring to the party?* (Possible answers: The people bring tacos/soup/chips/dip/hot dogs/dumplings.)

→ *Why is it fun to have a party with your neighbors?* (Possible answer: You can talk to them/get to know them/share food.)

Retell

Let's retell the book together. What are the people in the book doing? (They are having a party.) *What are the people sharing with each other?* (They are sharing different kinds of foods.)

Model Fluency

As you read each sentence, track the print and have children chorally repeat it. Stop occasionally to point to a rebus or to discuss a picture.

Apply Ask partners to practice reading the book together. Encourage children to repeat a line when they have difficulty with a word.

LITERACY ACTIVITIES

Have children complete the activities on the inside back cover of the reader.

Level Up

IF Children read *Neighborhood Party* **ELL Level** with fluency and correctly answer the Respond to Reading questions,

THEN Tell children that they will read a more detailed version of the story.

• Have children page through *Neighborhood Party* **On Level** and discuss who the neighbors are and what they are sharing.

• Have children read the story, monitoring their comprehension and providing assistance as necessary.

→ English Language Learners
Vocabulary

PRETEACH ORAL VOCABULARY

OBJECTIVES

CCSS Speak audibly and express thoughts, feelings, and ideas clearly. **SL.K.6**

LANGUAGE OBJECTIVE

Preview vocabulary

 I Do Display the images from the **Visual Vocabulary Cards** and follow the routine to preteach the oral vocabulary words.

 We Do Display each image again and explain how it illustrates or demonstrates the word. Model using sentences to describe the image.

You Do Display the word *appreciate* again and have children talk to a partner to name different things they appreciate.

Beginning	Intermediate	Advanced/High
Have children draw a picture of something they appreciate. Ask questions to elicit language.	Provide the following sentence frame: *I appreciate _____.*	Ask children a question using one of the words and have them answer in a complete sentence.

PRETEACH ELL VOCABULARY

OBJECTIVES

CCSS Speak audibly and express thoughts, feelings, and ideas clearly. **SL.K.6**

LANGUAGE OBJECTIVE

Preview ELL vocabulary

I Do Display the images from the **Visual Vocabulary Cards** one at a time to preteach the ELL vocabulary words *potluck* and *celebrate*, then follow the routine. Say each word and have children repeat it. Define each word in English.

 We Do Display each image again and incorporate the word in a short discussion about the image. Model using sentences to describe the image.

 You Do Have children talk to a partner to name different things they would like to bring to a potluck. Provide the sentence frame: *I could bring _____.*

Beginning	Intermediate	Advanced/High
Model completing the sentence frame. Guide children to tell what they could bring to a potluck.	Have pairs work together to come up with a list of food.	Ask children to make a sentence of their own that incorporates both words.

High-Frequency Words

REVIEW WORDS

CCSS

OBJECTIVES

Read common high-frequency words by sight (e.g., *the, of, to, you, she, my, is, are, do, does*). **RF.K.3c**

LANGUAGE OBJECTIVE

Review high-frequency words

 I Do Display the **High-Frequency Word Card** for *do*. Read the word. Use the **Read/Spell/Write** routine to teach the word. Have children write the word on their **Response Boards**.

 We Do Say sentences that show the word used in a question and a statement: *Do you like snakes? I do not like snakes.* Read each sentence with children. Explain to them that the word *do* can be used to ask a question.

 You Do Ask children to work with partners to come up with oral sentences using the word *do*. Write the sentences on the board and ask volunteers to circle the word *do* in each.

Beginning	Intermediate	Advanced/High
Help children say and write the word *do* on paper.	Have partners ask each other questions that start with "Do you ____?"	Ask children to name more things to complete the sentence frame: *Do you ____?*

REVIEW CATEGORY WORDS

CCSS

OBJECTIVES

Identify real-life connections between words and their use (e.g., note places at school that are colorful). **L.K.5c**

LANGUAGE OBJECTIVE

Use category words

 I Do Display the following **Photo Cards** and say each word aloud: *apple, carrots, egg, pizza, sandwich.* Define the words in English, and then in Spanish, if appropriate, identifying any cognates.

 We Do Provide sentence frames to help children talk about the foods: *I like _____ because _____; I do not like _____ because _____.*

 You Do Have children work with a partner to use the sentence frames with other kinds of foods.

Beginning	Intermediate	Advanced/High
Have children draw a picture of a food they like. Ask questions about the picture.	Have partners talk about their favorite foods.	Have children create their own oral sentences about food.

→ English Language Learners
Writing

SHARED WRITING

OBJECTIVES

CCSS Use a combination of drawing, dictating, and writing to narrate a single event or several loosely linked events, tell about the events in the order in which they occurred, and provide a reaction to what happened. **W.K.3**

LANGUAGE OBJECTIVE

Contribute to a shared writing project

 Review the words *chicken, rice, oranges,* and *lemonade* from the chart in the Whole Group Shared Writing project. Model writing a sentence: *I like to eat chicken.*

 Have children select one of the foods and help you write a sentence about it. Provide the following sentence frame: *You like to eat _____ .*

 Provide partners with a sentence frame: *We like to eat _____ .* Ask them to discuss foods they like, and agree on one to add to the sentence frame.

Beginning	Intermediate	Advanced/High
Provide children with pictures to help them identify foods in English.	Have partners list foods they like to help them express their ideas.	Ask children to add adjectives to their sentence to describe their favorite food.

WRITING TRAIT: WORD CHOICE

OBJECTIVES

CCSS With guidance and support from adults, respond to questions and suggestions from peers and add details to strengthen writing as needed. **W.K.5**

LANGUAGE OBJECTIVE

Choose the best words when writing

 Explain that good writers choose the best words to talk about their topic. They choose words that help readers picture what is happening in the story.

 Point to the **Big Book** selection *What Can You Do with a Paleta?* Help children find descriptive words from the story. Ask: *What are the tortillas like?* (buttery) *What are the tacos like?* (crispy)

 Have children think of a favorite food. Then have them work with a partner to write a list of words that describe their favorite foods.

Beginning	Intermediate	Advanced/High
Show children pictures of different types of foods and help them think of describing words for them.	Ask children to find examples of describing words in familiar texts.	Ask children to use adjectives to write a sentence about their favorite food.

Grammar

DESCRIBING WORDS (ADJECTIVES)

OBJECTIVES

Identify real-life connections between words and their use (e.g., note places at school that are colorful). **L.K.5c**

LANGUAGE OBJECTIVE

Recognize and use adjectives correctly

Language Transfers Handbook

Cantonese and Korean speakers place adjectives following nouns in their native language. Children may need help with the correct order of words, such as in the sentence *This is a lesson new.*

 I Do

Review that an adjective is a describing word that tells about something, such as its color, shape, or size. Say the following sentence: *I think pizza is tasty.* Say the sentence again and have children repeat it. Say: *Tasty is an adjective. It describes or tells about the word* pizza.

We Do

Say the following sentences. Guide children to tell the describing word (adjective) in each.

I ate hot *soup.*

You drank fresh *water.*

The cookie tastes sweet.

 You Do

Use the following sentence frame:

My lunch was _____ .

Pair children and have them orally complete the sentence frame by providing details from this week's readings. Circulate, listen in, and take note of each child's language use and proficiency.

Beginning	Intermediate	Advanced/High
Ask children what they had for lunch. Prompt them to describe how it tasted.	Have children list describing words from this week's selections before completing the sentence frame.	Ask children to complete the sentence frame with little or no help and read their sentence aloud.

PROGRESS MONITORING

Weekly Assessment

Use your Quick Check observations and the assessment opportunities identified below to evaluate children's progress in key skill areas.

✔ TESTED SKILLS CCSS	Quick Check Observations	Pencil and Paper Assessment
PHONEMIC AWARENESS/ PHONICS **d** /d/ (initial/final) **RF.K.3a**	Can children isolate /d/ and match it to the letter *Dd*?	Practice Book, pp. 109–110, 112
HIGH-FREQUENCY WORDS *do* **do** **RF.K.3c**	Can children recognize and read the high-frequency word?	Practice Book, pp. 113–114
COMPREHENSION Character, Setting, Events **RL.K.3**	As you read *What Can You Do with a Paleta?* with children, can they use the text and illustrations to identify and discuss characters, setting, and events?	Practice Book, p. 111

Quick Check Rubric

Skills	1	2	3
PHONEMIC AWARENESS/ PHONICS	Does not connect the sound /d/ with the letters *Dd*.	Usually connects the sound /d/ with the letters *Dd*.	Consistently connects the sound /d/ with the letters *Dd*.
HIGH-FREQUENCY WORDS	Does not identify the high-frequency word.	Usually recognizes the high-frequency word with accuracy, but not speed.	Consistently recognizes the high-frequency word with speed and accuracy.
COMPREHENSION	Does not use the text and illustrations to identify and discuss characters, setting, and events.	Usually uses the text and illustrations to identify and discuss characters, setting, and events.	Consistently uses the text and illustrations to identify and discuss characters, setting, and events.

Go Digital! www.connected.mcgraw-hill.com

Using Assessment Results

TESTED SKILLS	If ...	Then ...
PHONEMIC AWARENESS/ PHONICS	**Quick Check Rubric:** Children consistently score 1 or **Pencil and Paper Assessment:** Children get 0–2 items correct	... reteach tested Phonemic Awareness and Phonics skills using Lessons 16–17 and 27–29 in the ***Tier 2 Phonemic Awareness Intervention Online PDFs*** and Lesson 20 in the ***Tier 2 Phonics/Word Study Intervention Online PDFs.***
HIGH- FREQUENCY WORDS	**Quick Check Rubric:** Children consistently score 1	... reteach tested skills by using the High-Frequency Word Cards and asking children to read and spell the word. Point out any irregularities in sound-spellings.
COMPREHENSION	**Quick Check Rubric:** Children consistently score 1 or **Pencil and Paper Assessment:** Children get 0–1 items correct	... reteach tested skill using Lessons 22–30 in the ***Tier 2 Comprehension Intervention Online PDFs.***

Response to Intervention

Use the children's assessment results to assist you in identifying children who will benefit from focused intervention.

Use the appropriate sections of the ***Placement and Diagnostic Assessment*** to designate children requiring:

 Tier 2 Intervention Online PDFs

 WonderWorks Intervention Program

→ Phonemic Awareness

→ Phonics

→ Vocabulary

→ Comprehension

→ Fluency

WEEKLY OVERVIEW

Literature Big Book

Listening Comprehension

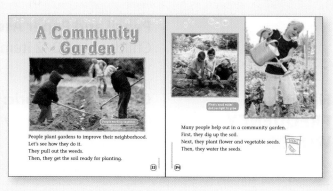

Roadwork, 4–32
Genre Informational Text

"A Community Garden," 33–36
Genre Informational Text

Interactive Read-Aloud Cards

"The Bundle of Sticks"
Genre Fable

Oral Vocabulary

community	harvest
improve	quarrel
confused	

Minilessons ✔ **TESTED SKILLS** CCSS

✔ **Comprehension Strategy**......... Ask and Answer
Questions, T177

✔ **Comprehension Skill**.............. Key Details, T186

☞ **Go**
Digital

www.connected.mcgraw-hill.com

WEEK 3

PITCH IN

Essential Question
How can people help to make your community better?

Big Book and Little Book
Reading/Writing Workshop

Shared Reading

Mom and I go to a ___. beach 37

"I Can, You Can!" 36–43

Genre Fiction

High-Frequency Words to, and, go, you, do, T181

Minilessons ✓ TESTED SKILLS CCSS

✓ **Phonics** .... Review
i, n, c, T179; o, d, T192

Writing Traits .... Word Choice, T182

Grammar .... Adjectives, T183

Differentiated Text

Approaching   **On Level**   **Beyond**   **ELL**

TEACH AND MANAGE

What You Do

INTRODUCE

Weekly Concept

Pitch In

**Reading/Writing Workshop
Big Book, 34–35**

TEACH AND APPLY

Listening Comprehension

Big Book
Roadwork
Genre Informational Text
Paired Read "A Community Garden"
Genre Informational Text

Minilessons
Strategy: Ask and Answer Questions
Skill: Key Details

Shared Reading

Reading/Writing Workshop
"I Can, You Can!"

Minilessons
Review *i, n, c, o, d* High-Frequency
Words: *to, and, go, you, do*
Writing, Grammar

Go Digital

 Interactive Whiteboard

 Interactive Whiteboard

Mobile

What Your Students Do

WEEKLY CONTRACT

PDF Online

PRACTICE AND ONLINE ACTIVITIES

Your Turn Practice Book, pp. 117–126

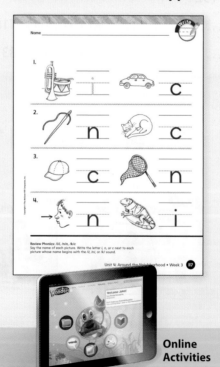

Leveled Readers

Go Digital

Online To-Do List

Online Activities

Mobile

WEEK 3 →

DIFFERENTIATE

Small Group Instruction
Leveled Readers

 **Mobile**

INTEGRATE

Research and Inquiry
Community Plan, pp. T216–T217

Text Connections
Compare Processes, p. T218

Talk About Reading
Becoming Readers, p. T219

 Online Research

WORKSTATION CARDS

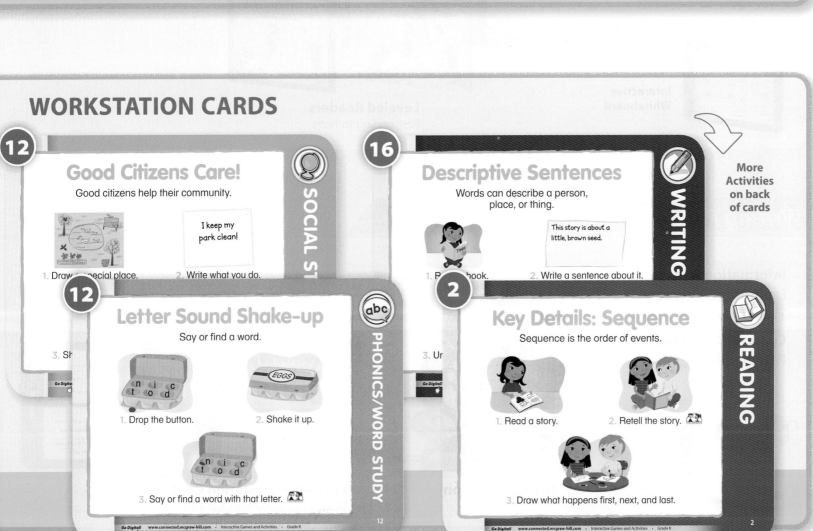

12 Good Citizens Care!
Good citizens help their community.

I keep my park clean!

1. Draw a special place.   2. Write what you do.

SOCIAL ST

12 Letter Sound Shake-up
Say or find a word.

3. Sh

EGGS

1. Drop the button.   2. Shake it up.

3. Say or find a word with that letter.

PHONICS/WORD STUDY   12

More Activities on back of cards

16 Descriptive Sentences
Words can describe a person, place, or thing.

This story is about a little, brown seed.

1. P   book.   2. Write a sentence about it.

WRITING

2 Key Details: Sequence
Sequence is the order of events.

3. Ur

1. Read a story.   2. Retell the story.

3. Draw what happens first, next, and last.

READING   2

Go Digital! www.connected.mcgraw-hill.com • Interactive Games and Activities • Grade K

DEVELOPING READERS AND WRITERS

Write About Reading • Analytical Writing

Write to Sources and Research

Respond to Reading, T177, T225, T233, T239, T243

Connect to Essential Question, T177, T209

Key Details, 186

Research and Inquiry, T216

Teacher's Edition

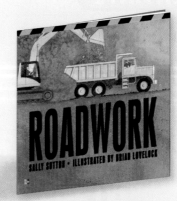

Literature Big Book
Roadwork
Paired Read: *"A Community Garden"*

Interactive Whiteboard

Leveled Readers
Responding to Texts

Writing Process • Independent Writing

Informational Text
Expository Sentences,
T204–T205, T214, T222

Conferencing Routines
Peer Conferences, T214

Interactive Whiteboard

Teacher's Edition

Leveled Workstation Card
Descriptive Sentences, Card 16

Writing Traits • Shared and Interactive Writing

Writing Trait:
Word Choice
Expository Sentences, T182, T196

Teacher's Edition

Word Choice, p. 46

Adjectives, p. 47

Reading/Writing Workshop

Interactive Whiteboard

Leveled Workstation Card
Descriptive Sentences, Card 16

Grammar and Spelling/Dictation

Grammar
Describing Words
(Adjectives), T183

Spelling/Dictation
Words with *a, i, o, n, c, d, p, t,*
T211, T221

Interactive Whiteboard

Teacher's Edition

Online Grammar Games

Handwriting

SUGGESTED LESSON PLAN

	DAY 1	**DAY 2**

READING

Whole Group

Teach and Model

Literature
Big Book

Reading/
Writing
Workshop

DAY 1

Build Background Pitch In, T174
Oral Vocabulary community, improve, T174
✔ **Listening Comprehension**
• Genre: Informational Text
• Strategy: Ask and Answer Questions, T177
Big Book *Roadwork*
✔ **Word Work**
Phonemic Awareness
• Phoneme Identity, T178
Phonics
• Review /i/i, /n/n, /k/c, T179
Handwriting Write Sentences with *c, d, i, n, o,* T180
High-Frequency Words and, do, go, to, you, T181

Practice *Your Turn* 117

DAY 2

Oral Language Pitch In, T184
✔ **Category Words** Position Words, T185
✔ **Listening Comprehension**
• Genre: Informational Text
• Strategy: Ask and Answer Questions, T186
• Skill: Key Details
• Guided Retelling
• Model Fluency, T191
Big Book *Roadwork*
✔ **Word Work**
Phonemic Awareness
• Phoneme Blending, T192
Phonics
• Blend Words with /i/i, /o/o, /n/n, /d/d, T193
High-Frequency Words and, do, go, to, you, T193
Shared Reading "I Can, You Can!" T194–T195

Practice *Your Turn* 118

DIFFERENTIATED INSTRUCTION Choose across the week to meet your student's needs.

Small Group

Approaching Level

Leveled Reader *We Clean!* T224–T225
Phonemic Awareness
Recognize Rhyme, T226 ②
Phonics Sound-Spelling Review, T228 ②
High-Frequency Words Reteach Words, T230 ②

Leveled Reader *We Clean!* T224–T225
Phonemic Awarenesss
Phoneme Identity, T226 ②
Phonics Connect Sounds to Spellings, T228 ②
High-Frequency Words
Cumulative Review, T230 ②

On Level

Leveled Reader *Can You Fix It?* T232–T233
Phonemic Awareness
Phoneme Identity, T234

Leveled Reader *Can You Fix It?* T232–T233
Phonemic Awareness Phoneme Blending, T234
Phonics Review Phonics, T235
High-Frequency Words Review Words, T237

Beyond Level

Leveled Reader *Helping Mom,* T238–T239
Phonics Review, T240

Leveled Reader *Helping Mom,* T238–T239
High-Frequency Words Review, T240

English Language Learners

Leveled Reader *Can You Fix It?,* T242–T243
Phonemic Awareness
Recognize Rhyme, T226 ②
Phonics Sound-Spelling Review, T228 ②
Vocabulary Preteach Oral Vocabulary, T244
Writing Shared Writing, T246

Leveled Reader *Can You Fix It?,* T242–T243
Phonemic Awareness
Phoneme Identity, T226 ②
Phonics Connect Sounds to Spellings, T228 ②
Vocabulary Preteach ELL Vocabulary, T244

LANGUAGE ARTS

Whole Group

Writing and Grammar

Shared Writing
Writing Trait: Word Choice, T182
Write an Expository Sentence, T182
Grammar Adjectives, T183

Interactive Writing
Writing Trait: Word Choice, T196
Write an Expository Sentence, T196
Grammar Adjectives, T197

WEEK 3 →

DAY 3	DAY 4	DAY 5 Review and Assess

READING

Oral Language Pitch In, T198
Oral Vocabulary confused, harvest, quarrel, T198
✓**Listening Comprehension**
• Genre: Fable
• Strategy: Ask and Answer Questions, T199
• Make Connections, T199
Interactive Read Aloud
"The Bundle of Sticks," T199
✓**Word Work**
Phonemic Awareness
• Phoneme Blending, T200
Phonics
• Review /i/i, /o/o, /n/n, /k/c, /d/d, T201
• Picture Sort, T202
High-Frequency Words and, do, go, to, you, T203

Practice *Your Turn* 119–122

Oral Language Pitch In, T206
✓**Category Words** Position Words, T207
✓**Listening Comprehension**
• Genre: Informational Text
• Strategy: Ask and Answer Questions, T208
• Text Feature: Captions
• Make Connections, T209
Big Book Paired Read: "A Community Garden," T208
✓**Word Work**
Phonemic Awareness
• Phoneme Segmentation, T210
Phonics
• Blend Words with *a, i, o, n, c, d, p, t,* T210
High-Frequency Words and, do, go, to, you, T211
Shared Reading "I Can, You Can!" T212–T213
Integrate Ideas Research and Inquiry, T216–T217

Practice *Your Turn* 123–125

Integrate Ideas
• Text Connections, T218
• Talk About Reading, T219
• Research and Inquiry, T219
✓**Word Work**
Phonemic Awareness
• Phoneme Segmentation, T220
Phonics
• Read Words with Short
i, o, n, c, d, p t, T220
High-Frequency Words and, do, go, to, you, T221

Practice *Your Turn* 126

DIFFERENTIATED INSTRUCTION

Leveled Reader *We Clean!* T224–T225
Phonemic Awareness
Phoneme Blending, T227
Phonics Reteach, T228
High-Frequency Words Cumulative Review, T230

Leveled Reader *We Clean!* T224–T225
Phonemic Awareness
Phoneme Segmentation, T227
Phonics Blend Words with /i/i, /n/n, /k/c, /o/o, /d/d, T229
Oral Vocabulary Review Words, T231

Leveled Reader Literacy Activities, T225
Phonemic Awareness
Phoneme Segmentation, T227
Phonics
Reread for Fluency, T229
Build Fluency with Phonics, T229
Comprehension Self-Selected Reading, T231

Leveled Reader *Can You Fix It?* T232–T233
Phonemic Awareness
Phoneme Segmentation, T234
Phonics Picture Sort, T235

Leveled Reader *Can You Fix It?* T232–T233
Phonics Blend Words with /i/i, /n/n, /k/c, /o/o, /d/d, T236
Reread for Fluency, T236

Leveled Reader Literacy Activities, T233
Comprehension Self-Selected Reading, T237

Leveled Reader *Helping Mom,* T238–T239
Vocabulary Oral Vocabulary: Synonyms, T241

Gifted and Talented

Leveled Reader *Helping Mom,* T238–T239
Phonics Innovate, T240

Leveled Reader Literacy Activities, T239
Comprehension Self-Selected Reading, T241

Gifted and Talented

Leveled Reader *Can You Fix It?* T242–T243
Phonemic Awareness Phoneme Blending, T227
Phonics Reteach, T228
High-Frequency Words Review Words, T245
Writing Writing Trait: Word Choice, T246

Leveled Reader *Can You Fix It?* T242–T243
Phonemic Awareness
Phoneme Segmentation, T227
Phonics Blend Words with /i/i, /n/n, /k/c, /o/o, /d/d, T229
High-Frequency Words Review Category Words, T245
Grammar Adjectives, T247

Leveled Reader Literacy Activities, T243
Phonemic Awareness
Phoneme Segmentation, T227
Phonics
Reread for Fluency, T229
Build Fluency with Phonics, T229

LANGUAGE ARTS

Independent Writing
Writing Trait: Word Choice, T204
Write an Expository Sentence
Prewrite/Draft, T204–T205
Grammar Adjectives, T205

Independent Writing
Writing an Expository Sentence
Revise/Final Draft, T214
Grammar Adjectives, T215

Independent Writing
Writing an Expository Sentence
Prepare/Present/Evaluate/Publish, T222
Grammar Adjectives, T223

DIFFERENTIATE TO ACCELERATE

 A C T Scaffold to **A**ccess **C**omplex **T**ext

IF the text complexity of a particular section is too difficult for children

THEN see the references noted in the chart below for scaffolded instruction to help children Access Complex Text.

Qualitative Quantitative
Reader and Task
TEXT COMPLEXITY

Literature Big Book	Reading/Writing Workshop	Leveled Readers

	Literature Big Book	Reading/Writing Workshop	Leveled Readers
Quantitative	*Roadwork* **Lexile** 40 Paired Selection: "A Community Garden" **Lexile** 330	"I Can, You Can!" **Lexile** 180	**Approaching Level** **Lexile** BR **Beyond Level** **Lexile** 290	**On Level** **Lexile** 60 **ELL** **Lexile** BR

Qualitative	**What Makes the Text Complex?** • **Specific Vocabulary** Sounds Words, T186 **A C T** *See Scaffolded Instruction in Teacher's Edition, T186.*	**What Makes the Text Complex?** **Foundational Skills** • Decoding with *i, o, d, n*, T192–T193 • Identifying high-frequency words, T193	**What Makes the Text Complex?** **Foundational Skills** • Decoding with *i, o, d, n* • Identifying high-frequency words *and, do, go, to, you* *See Level Up lessons online for Leveled Readers.*

Reader and Task	The Introduce the Concept lesson on pages T174–T175 will help determine the reader's knowledge and engagement in the weekly concept. See pages T176–T177, T187–T191, T208–T209 and T216–T219 for questions and tasks for this text.	The Introduce the Concept lesson on pages T174–T175 will help determine the reader's knowledge and engagement in the weekly concept. See pages T194–T195, T212–T213 and T216–T219 for questions and tasks for this text.	The Introduce the Concept lesson on pages T174–T175 will help determine the reader's knowledge and engagement in the weekly concept. See pages T224–T225, T232–T233, T238–T239, T242–T243 and T216–T219 for questions and tasks for this text.

Monitor and *Differentiate*

IF you need to differentiate instruction

THEN use the Quick Checks to assess children's needs and select the appropriate small group instruction focus.

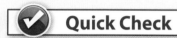 **Quick Check**

Comprehension Strategy Ask and Answer Questions, T199

Phonemic Awareness/Phonics Review /i/i, /n/n, /k/c, /o/o, /d/d, T181, T193, T203, T211, T221

High-Frequency Words *to, and, go, you, do,* T181, T193, T203, T211, T221

If No →	**Approaching**	**Reteach,** pp. T224–T231
	ELL	**Develop,** pp. T242–T247
If Yes →	**On Level**	**Review,** pp. T232–T237
	Beyond Level	**Extend,** pp. T238–T241

Level Up with Leveled Readers

IF children can read their leveled text fluently and answer comprehension questions

THEN work with the next level up to accelerate children's reading with more complex text.

ENGLISH LANGUAGE LEARNERS
SCAFFOLD

IF ELL students need additional support **THEN** scaffold instruction using the small group suggestions.

Reading-Writing Workshop T175 "Let's Help Out!"	Leveled Reader T242–T243 *Can You Fix It?*	Phonological Awareness	Phonics,	Oral Vocabulary, T244	Writing	Grammar
Integrate Ideas T217		Recognize Rhyme, T226 Phoneme Identity, T226 Phoneme Blending, T227 Phoneme Segmentation, T227	Review /i/i, /n/n, /k/c, /o/o, /d/d, T228–T229	community, improve, confused, harvest, quarrel **High-Frequency Words,** T245 *to, and, go, you, do*	Shared Writing, T246 Writing Trait: Word Choice, T246	T247 Adjectives

Note: Include ELL Students in all small groups based on their needs.

Materials

Reading/Writing Workshop Big Book
UNIT 4

Literature Big Book
Roadwork

Visual Vocabulary Cards
community
improve

Response Board

Photo Cards

camel	inchworm
car	ink
carrots	insect
comb	nail
dime	nest
doll	net
door	newspaper
inch	night
	nose
	olive
	otter
	ox

 Ii
insect

Sound-Spelling Cards
insect
camel
nest

 and

High-Frequency Word Cards
and
can
do
go
like
the
to
we
you

 I wonder…

Think Aloud Cloud

"Kim Hears an Insect"
"I've Been Working on the Railroad"

Reading/Writing Workshop Big Book

OBJECTIVES

CCSS Confirm understanding of information presented orally by asking and answering questions about key details and requesting clarification if something is not understood. **SL.K.2**

CCSS Describe familiar people, places, things, and events, and with prompting and support, provide additional detail. **SL.K.4**

→ # Introduce the Concept

MINILESSON 10 Mins

Build Background

ESSENTIAL QUESTION

How can people help to make your community better?

Read aloud the Essential Question. Tell children that you are going to sing a song about one way people helped to improve their community, by working on a railroad.

> ## I've Been Working on the Railroad
>
> I've been working on the railroad,
> all the live-long day.
> I've been working on the railroad,
> just to pass the time away.
> Can't you hear the whistle blowin'?
> Rise up so early in the morn.
> Can't you hear the captain shoutin'?
> "Dinah, blow your horn!"

Sing the song with children. *How do trains and railroads help communities?* Tell children that this week, they will learn how people help their own communities.

Oral Vocabulary Words

Use the **Define/Example/Ask** routine to introduce the oral vocabulary words **community** and **improve**.

To introduce the theme "Pitch In," explain that it's important to care about your community and help when you can. Explain that *pitch in* means "to do your part." *How do you pitch in and help at home?*

Go Digital

Pitch In

Video

Visual Glossary

Oral Vocabulary Routine

<u>Define:</u> A **community** is a group of people who work, play, or live together.

<u>Example:</u> Playing sports is a great way for people in a community to have fun together.

<u>Ask:</u> What do you enjoy about our community?

<u>Define:</u> To **improve** is to make something better.

<u>Example:</u> You can improve at sports by practicing every day.

<u>Ask:</u> How could our class improve?

Visual Vocabulary Cards

Talk About It: Pitch In

Have children discuss ways to help out in a community. List children's responses. Have partners discuss ways that volunteers can improve a community. Display pages 34–35 of the **Reading/Writing Workshop Big Book** and have children do the **Talk About It** activity with a partner.

READING/WRITING WORKSHOP BIG BOOK, pp. 34–35

Collaborative Conversations

Provide Details As children engage in partner, small group, and whole group discussions, encourage them to:

→ Give details to express their thoughts, feelings, and ideas clearly.

→ Use details to describe people, places, things, and events.

→ Give details when asking about things they do not understand.

ELL

ENGLISH LANGUAGE LEARNERS SCAFFOLD

Beginning

Use Visuals Explain that the children in the photograph are working to make their community a better place by helping to paint a mural, or a big picture. Point out that the children are painting a picture of the earth. *Are these children helping? Are they making the community a nicer place?*

Intermediate

Describe Ask children to describe what is happening in the picture. Ask them to tell about what the children are doing and what tools they are using. Correct grammar and pronunciation as needed.

Advanced/Advanced High

Discuss Have children elaborate on how the children in the photograph are helping. Ask: *How does their work help the community?* Elicit details to support children's answers.

→ # Listening Comprehension

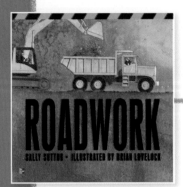

Literature Big Book

OBJECTIVES

 Actively engage in group reading activities with purpose and understanding. **RI.K.10**

Follow words from left to right, top to bottom, and page by page. **RF.K.1a**

• Strategy: Ask and Answer Questions

• Connect Big Book to Weekly Concept

ACADEMIC LANGUAGE

• *illustrations*

• Cognates: *ilustraciónes*

MINILESSON 10 Mins

Read the Literature Big Book

Connect to Concept: Pitch In

Tell children that you will now read about road workers and how roads are made. *What workers help your community?*

Concepts of Print

Directionality; Match Print to Speech Display the **Big Book** cover. Remind children that we read from left to right and use a return sweep back to the left. Model reading from left to right with your finger as you read aloud the title. Point out that the words you say match the words on the page.

Genre: Informational Text

Model *Roadwork* is an informational text. Remind children of the characteristics of informational text:

→ Informational text tells facts, or true information, about real life places and events.

> **Selection Words** Preview these words before reading:
>
> **roadwork:** work done to fix or build a road
> **roadbed:** area where a road is built
> **machine:** a tool that makes work easier

Set a Purpose for Reading

→ Read aloud the title and the names of the author and illustrator.

→ Remind children that the author wrote the words and the illustrator drew the pictures.

→ Tell children to listen as you read aloud the Big Book to learn about making roads.

Go Digital

Roadwork

I wonder...

Model Think Aloud Cloud

Strategy: Ask and Answer Questions

Explain Remind children that they can ask and answer questions before they read and while they are reading to help them better understand the text.

Think Aloud As I read this book, I will pause after every few pages to ask myself questions about what I am learning. I will look for the answers as I keep reading. This will help me to better understand the text.

Model As you read, use the **Think Aloud Cloud** to model the strategy.

Think Aloud Before I begin reading, I wonder what is in the truck on the cover of the book. I ask myself the questions: *What is in the truck? What is it for?* I will begin reading to find my answer. The truck is filled with dirt that the workers will use to build the road.

Respond to Reading

After reading, prompt children to share what they learned about roadwork. Discuss which questions they asked while reading and how they answered them. Then have children draw one of the steps in making a road. Encourage them to tell the class about what is happening in their picture.

Make Connections

Use *Roadwork* to discuss the ways that people improve their communities. Revisit the concept behind the Essential Question *How can people help to make your community better?* by paging through the **Big Book**.

Write About It Have children write about one of the steps the workers took to make the new road. Discuss how this work will help their community.

→ # Word Work

Quick Review

Review /i/, /k/, /n/: Ask children to tell the initial sound of the *insect*, *car*, and *net* Photo Cards.
Build Fluency: Sound-Spellings: Show the following **Word-Building Cards:** *a, c, d, i, m, n, o, p, s, t.* Have children chorally say each sound. Repeat and vary the pace.

 Phonemic Awareness

MINILESSON — 5 Mins

Phoneme Identity

Photo Card

OBJECTIVES

CCSS Isolate and pronounce the initial sounds, in words. **RF.K.2d**

CCSS Demonstrate basic knowledge of one-to-one letter-sound correspondences by producing the primary or many of the most frequent sounds for each consonant. **RF.K.3a**

① Model Display the **Photo Cards** *car, camel, carrots. I will say three picture names:* car, camel, carrots. *Say the names with me:* car, camel, carrots. *Which sound is the same in* car, camel, carrots? *Yes, the first sound, /k/, is the same.* Repeat with the Photo Cards *inch, ink, insect* and *nest, newspaper, night.*

② Guided Practice/Practice Show children sets of the Photo Cards. Name the pictures with children and have them identify the sound that is the same in each set.

comb, camel, car	nose, nail, net	insect, inchworm, inch
ox, otter, olive	door, dime, doll	

Go Digital

Phonemic Awareness

Phonics

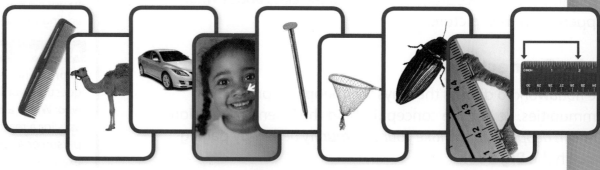

Photo Cards

 **ELL**

ENGLISH LANGUAGE LEARNERS

Phonemic Awareness: Minimal Contrasts Because there is no direct sound-symbol match for short vowels in Spanish and other languages, provide additional practice in pronouncing and blending /a/, /i/, and /o/. List the words *pat, pit, pot; tap, tip, top; an, in, on.* Say the words slowly for children to repeat. Use the articulation photos.

ARTICULATION SUPPORT

If children need additional support, refer to Articulation Support in Volume 3: page T14 for /i/; page T96 for /n/; page T178 for /k/. Refer to Volume 4: page T14 for /o/; page T96 for /d/.

Phonics

10 Mins

Ii

insect

Sound-Spelling Card

Review /i/ *i*, /n/ *n*, /k/ *c*

1 Model Display the *Insect* **Sound-Spelling Card**. Say: *This is the letter* i. *The letter* i *can stand for the sound /i/ as in the word* insect. *What is the letter?* (*i*) *What sound does the letter* i *stand for?* (/i/) Repeat for /n/ *n* and /k/ *c* with the *Nest* and *Camel* Sound-Spelling Cards.

2 Guided Practice/Practice Have children listen as you say some words. Ask them to write the letter *i* on their **Response Boards** if the word begins with /i/. Do the first two words with children.

in   dig   it   road   is   inch   tip   iguana

Repeat for /n/ *n* and /k/ *c*.

not   pack   nest   seal   nose   nail   paint   nice
cut   cast   make   road   cap   mix   comb   cow

♪ Review /i/*i*. Have children write the letter *i* on their Response Boards. Play "Kim Hears an Insect." Have children show their Response Boards with the letter *i* when they hear /i/.

Corrective Feedback

Sound Error Model the sound /i/ in the initial position, then have children repeat the sound. Say: *My turn.* Inch. /i/ /i/ /i/. *Now it's your turn.* Have children say the word *inch* and isolate the initial sound and write the letter *i*. Repeat for /n/*n* and /k/*c* if necessary.

ENGLISH LANGUAGE LEARNERS

Phoneme Variations in Language: In some languages, including Vietnamese and Hmong, there is no direct transfer for the /i/ sound. Emphasize the /i/ sound and demonstrate correct mouth position.

YOUR TURN PRACTICE BOOK p. 117

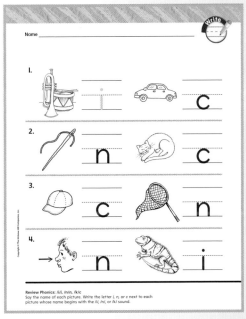

→ # Word Work

MINILESSON
5
Mins

Handwriting: Write Sentences with *c, d, i, n, o*

OBJECTIVES

CCSS Write a letter or letters for most consonant and short-vowel sounds. **L.K.2c**

CCSS Demonstrate basic knowledge of one-to-one letter-sound correspondences by producing the primary or many of the most frequent sounds for each consonant. **RF.K.3a**

CCSS Read common high-frequency words by sight. **RF.K.3c**

❶ **Model** Review handwriting and letter sound correspondence with the letters *i, n, c, o,* and *d.*

→ Write the following sentence. *Can dad sit on the mat?* Read the sentence with children and track the print.

→ *I hear the /k/ sound in the word* can. *I know that the letter* c *stands for /k/. I will underline the letter* c *because it stands for /k/. Which word has the sound /d/?* (dad) *Which letter stands for /d/?* Underline the letter *d* at the beginning and end of *dad.* Continue asking children which word has the sound /i/ and which letter stands for the sound (sit, *i*); /o/ (on, *o*) and /n/ (on, *n*). Underline the letters that stand for the sounds and read the words with children.

❷ **Guided Practice/Practice**

→ Write the following sentence for children to copy: *Tom did not see the cap.* Give them ample time to write the sentence. Chorally read the sentence.

→ Ask children to identify which words have the sound /o/. (Tom, not) Have them underline the letter that stands for the sound (*o*) and read the words. Ask children to identify words with the following sounds and to underline the letter that stands for the sound: /d/ (did, *d*); /i/ (did, *i*); /n/ (not, *n*) and /k/ (cap, *c*).

→ Have children check that the words in their sentences are separated by spaces. Remind them that all sentences begin with a capital letter and have end punctuation. Have them correct as needed.

 **Daily Handwriting**

Throughout the week review writing words and sentences with *Cc, Ii, Nn, Oo, Dd.* At the end of the week, have children use the **Your Turn Practice Book** page 126 to practice writing words.

Go Digital

Handwriting

| the | is |
| you | do |

High-Frequency Word Routine

High-Frequency Words

and, do, go, to, you

1 Model Display and read page 18 of the **Big Book** *Roadwork*. Ask children to point to the high-frequency words *to* and *and*. Then use sentences on the **Visual Vocabulary Cards** to review *you*, *do*, and *go*. Ask children to point to the High-Frequency Words in the sentence. Use the **High-Frequency Word Cards** and the **Read/Spell/Write** routine to review all of the words.

→ **Read** Point to the word *to* and say the word. *This is the word* to. *Say it with me:* to. *We ride* to *work.*

→ **Spell** *The word* to *is spelled t-o. Spell it with me.*

→ **Write** *Let's write the word in the air as we say each letter: t-o.*

2 Guided Practice/Practice Build sentences using High-Frequency Word Cards, **Photo Cards**, and teacher-made punctuation cards. Have children point to the high-frequency words *and, do, go, to* and *you*. Use these sentences: *Do you like celery? We go to a farm. We like grapes.*

→ Have partners create sentences using the word.

→ # Language Arts

MINILESSON
10 Mins

Shared Writing

OBJECTIVES

CCSS With guidance and support from adults, recall information from experiences or gather information from provided sources to answer a question. **W.K.8**

CCSS Produce and expand complete sentences in shared language activities. **L.K.1f**

• Make a chart
• Recognize describing words (adjectives)

ACADEMIC LANGUAGE
• *chart, adjective*
• Cognates: *adjetivo*

Writing Trait: Word Choice

❶ Model Tell children that writers choose their words carefully to describe the people and things they are writing about. Point to the construction workers in the first pages of the **Big Book**. Write and read aloud: *These workers use heavy tools. The word* heavy *is a good word choice because it describes the tools.*

❷ Guided Practice/Practice Write and read aloud this sentence: *The workers fix old roads. Which word describes the roads?* (old)

Write an Expository Sentence

Focus and Plan Tell children that this week they will learn how to write a sentence about a worker in their community.

COLLABORATE

Brainstorm Make a two-column chart to list community workers and how they help to make their community better. Have children describe how these workers help their community.

Workers	How They Help
vet	helps sick animals
librarian	helps find interesting books
crossing guard	helps cross a busy street
gardener	helps plant crops and flowers

Write Model writing a sentence, using ideas from the chart. Write this sentence frame: *The vet helps _____ animals.* Point to the word *sick* and write the word on a self-stick note. Fill in the sentence frame and read the sentence aloud. Point out that *sick* is a describing word.

Model writing sentences using the other workers on the chart. Read aloud the sentences with children.

Go Digital

Writing

I see a fish.

Grammar

Grammar

Describing Words (Adjectives)

❶ **Model** Remind children that an adjective can come before or after a naming word.

Write and read aloud these sentences:

The cat is sad.

It is a black cat.

What is the naming word in the first sentence? (cat) *What is the describing word?* (sad) *What is the naming word in the second sentence?* (cat) *What is the describing word?* (black)

❷ **Guided Practice/Practice** Tell children that adjectives are useful for sorting things. Use manipulatives of different colors and shapes. Ask children to sort the manipulatives into different groups by color. Point out that you need to use adjectives to tell how you are sorting the objects. Emphasize the color name as you say: *The blue ones go here. The red ones go there.*

Have children work in pairs. Ask children to sort the manipulatives by shape. Write and read: *This group is _____.* Ask pairs to read aloud the sentence with the correct shape for each group.

Talk About It

Have partners work together to orally generate sentences with adjectives. Encourage one partner to describe something in the classroom, using adjectives for the object's shape and size.

ENGLISH LANGUAGE LEARNERS SCAFFOLD

Beginning

Explain Gather manipulatives that have different colors. Hold up each one and ask children what color it is. Write and read: *This is a ___ one.* Guide children in saying the sentence with the correct color adjective. Allow children ample time to respond.

Intermediate

Practice Point to a manipulative and ask children to answer questions about it. For example: *What shape is it? Is this one big or small?* Allow children ample time to respond.

Advanced/Advanced High

Practice Have children use sentences, as they are able, to tell where each type of manipulative should go: *The blue ones go here. The yellow ones go here.* Elicit more details to support children's answers.

Daily Wrap Up

- Review the Essential Question and encourage children to discuss it, using the new oral vocabulary words. *What workers do you know in your community? How do they help to make your community better?*

- Prompt children to share the skills they learned. How might they use those skills?

Materials

Reading/Writing Workshop Big Book
UNIT 4

Literature Big Book
Roadwork

Visual Vocabulary Cards
community
improve

Response Board

Word-Building Cards

dolphin

Sound-Spelling Cards
dolphin
octopus

"Nellie's Nest" and "I've Been Working on the Railroad"

Retelling Cards

Puppet

→ Build the Concept

MINILESSON 10 Mins

Oral Language

OBJECTIVES

CCSS Recognize rhyming words. **RF.K.2a**

CCSS Identify real-life connections between words and their use (e.g., note places at school that are colorful). **L.K.5c**

Develop oral vocabulary

ACADEMIC LANGUAGE
• *sequence*
• Cognates: *secuencia*

ESSENTIAL QUESTION

How can people help to make your community better?

Remind children that this week they are learning about ways people can improve their communities. Point out that people can help their communities in big or small ways.

Sing with children "I've Been Working on the Railroad." Ask: *How could we change the song to be about building a road for cars?*

Phonological Awareness
Recognize Rhyme

Tell children that the words *day* and *away* rhyme in "I've Been Working on the Railroad." Words that rhyme have the same ending sounds. Repeat *day* and *away* and have children tell you a new word that rhymes with them. (Possible responses: play, stay, clay) Say: *Listen carefully to these three words and tell me which one does not rhyme:* blow, wind, snow (wind) Which words do rhyme? (blow, snow) Repeat this routine with *page, book, look*.

Review Oral Vocabulary

Use the **Define/Example/Ask** routine to review the oral vocabulary words **community** and **improve**. Prompt children to use the words in sentences.

Vocab
Define
Examp
Ask:

Visual Vocabulary Cards

Go Digital

Visual Glossary

Category Words

Category Words: Position Words

❶ Model Use the **Big Book** *Roadwork* to discuss position words. Point to the word *down* on page 9. Explain that this is a position word. It describes where someone or something is. Guide children in using position words to answer questions about the illustrations: page 8, *Where is the dump truck?* (in front of the loader; under the loader); page 10, *In what direction is the bulldozer going?* (up); page 11, *Where is the dump truck dumping rocks?* (down the hill; in back of the truck); and page 18, *Where is the woman in the red jacket sitting?* (next to the woman in the yellow jacket)

Sing the following song to the tune of "The Bear Went Over the Mountain." Ask children to listen for position words.

> *The trucks went over the bridge,*
> *To get to the next town.*
>
> *The red truck got there first,*
> *And beat the rest to town.*
>
> *The blue truck got there last,*
> *Because it ran out of gas.*

→ Sing the first two lines of the song again and ask children how the trucks got to town. (They went over the bridge.) Repeat with the remaining lines. Tell children that *over, next, first,* and *last* are position words. They tell where the trucks are.

❷ Guided Practice/Practice Have children sit in a circle. Give each child a crayon. Put a chair in the middle of the circle. Give each child a direction that includes a position word. For example: *Madi, put your crayon under the chair. Sam, put your crayon in front of Madi's crayon.*

→ Ask children why *up, down, on, under, next, first,* and *last* are position words. (Possible answer: They tell where someone or something is.)

ENGLISH LANGUAGE LEARNERS

Understand Help children understand the meaning of position words by instructing each child to go to a different place in the classroom. Use a position word as you say where each child is. Have children repeat what you say. For example: *Bridget is at the front of room. Max is next to the door.*

LET'S MOVE!

Play a game of "Simon Says." Give children directions with position words, including *over, under, front,* and *back.* For example: *Simon says, put your hands over your head. Simon says, move to the back of your desk. Simon says, place a hand on your chair. Simon says, put one foot in front of the other.*

→ # Listening Comprehension

CLOSE READING

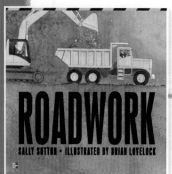

Literature Big Book

OBJECTIVES

 CCSS With prompting and support, ask and answer questions about key details in a text. **RI.K.1**

CCSS With prompting and support, retell key details of a text. **RI.K.2**

• Strategy: Ask and Answer Questions
• Skill: Key Details

ACADEMIC LANGUAGE
• *sequence*
• Cognates: *secuencia*

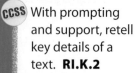

MINILESSON **15** Mins

Reread Literature Big Book

Genre: Informational Text

Display *Roadwork.* Remind children that informational text tells facts, or information, about real things, places, or events. *What makes* Roadwork *informational text?* Have children point to evidence in the text and pictures to show that this is informational text. (The book explains how workers build roads.)

Strategy: Ask and Answer Questions

Remind children that good readers ask and answer questions about things they do not understand before and during reading. *As we reread, you can ask questions about how a road is built and look for the answers later in the selection.*

Skill: Key Details

Remind children that when they read they can find important details in the text and in the illustrations. Point out that informational text often follows a sequence, or order. Details can help us understand the order. We can discuss the order of events by using words such as *first, next,* and *last.* Display page 5 of *Roadwork* and model using sequence words. For example, say: *First, the workers plan the road.* As you read, have children listen for evidence in the text to find details about the sequence.

Go Digital

Roadwork

Retelling Cards

ACT
Access Complex Text

Specific Vocabulary This selection contains many sound words, some of which students may be unfamiliar with. Explain to children that the big, bold words on each page are sound words. Point out that these words sometimes sound like the noise they are naming.

→ Model saying the sound words on page 5 expressively, mimicking the noises as you say *Ping! Bang! Tap!* Have children repeat and echo. Continue as necessary with other examples throughout the selection.

ELL

PAGES 4–5

CONCEPTS OF PRINT

Remind children to read from left to right and top to bottom, with a return sweep. Have a volunteer track the words on the page as you read them.

PAGES 6–7

KEY DETAILS

What are the workers doing on these pages? (digging and moving the earth; clearing a pathway)

pp. 6–7

clear: Tell children that when you *clear* something, you move anything that is in the way. Place a pile of books on your desk. As you pick them up, say: *Watch as I clear my desk.* Say *clear* and have children repeat.

PAGES 8–9

PHONICS

Remind children that they have learned about words with the initial and final /d/ sounds. Ask children to find words on page 9 that have initial and final /d/. (load, dirt, drop, down) *What letter makes the /d/ sound?* (d)

PAGES 10–11

ASK AND ANSWER QUESTIONS

Think Aloud As I read, I wonder how the workers will build the road. I ask myself: *What will the workers do after they lay the groundwork?* I will keep reading to find my answer.

pp. 10–11

groundwork: Explain that *groundwork* is what you do to get ready for something. *What would the groundwork be for drawing a picture?* (gather paper and crayons)

Listening Comprehension

CLOSE READING
ELL

PAGES 12–13

KEY DETAILS

How do the machines pack the ground? (they roll one way and then back) Have children point to the machine that looks like it rolls back and forth.

pp. 12–13

good and hard: Explain to children that *good and hard* is a phrase people use to say something is solid. Knock on the wall of the classroom. Say: *This wall is good and hard.* Have children mimic you.

PAGES 14–15

PHONICS

Remind children that they have learned about words that have the initial and medial /o/ sounds. Ask them to find and read aloud the words with medial /o/ on page 14. (hot, sploshy)

PAGES 16–17

ASK AND ANSWER QUESTIONS

Think Aloud I wonder how the workers make the tar firm and flat. I can find the answer by looking at the illustrations. I see a large machine with rollers. It's pushing down on the tar and making it flat and firm.

pp. 16–17

firm: Explain that if something is *firm,* it is not easy to move. Push against the wall and say: *The wall is firm.* Stomp your foot on the ground: *Is it firm?*

PAGES 18–19

HIGH-FREQUENCY WORDS

Have children identify and read the high-frequency words *to* and *and.*

SHADES OF MEANING

To understand the difference between *gulp* and *slurp,* act out the words. Have children mimic you. Then say the words and have children act them out.

pp. 18–19

milk, sandwich, banana, apple: Use the illustrations to help review and define each word.

ELL

PAGES 20–21

ASK AND ANSWER QUESTIONS

What questions do you have about what we have read so far? Can you find the answers on this page? Or do we need to keep reading?

PAGES 22–23

CONCEPTS OF PRINT

Remind children that the first word in a sentence begins with a capital letter. Read aloud the first three lines on page 22. Ask children to identify the capital letters at the beginning of each sentence. (R, R, D, F)

pp. 22–23

raise, hoist: Explain to children that *raise* and *hoist* have similar meanings: "to lift."

PAGES 24–25

KEY DETAILS

What time of day is it on these pages? How do you know? (It is nighttime. The sky in the picture is dark and the workers are testing the lights.)

pp. 24–25

No one wants a crash: Tell children this sentence means that no one wants someone to have a car accident. Explain that a crash is when two cars bump into each other.

PAGES 26–27

KEY DETAILS

On this page workers are planting trees and other plants. What do they do after they plant them in the ground? How do you know? (Possible answer: They water the plants. The words said that they water them and in the picture I see a worker with a hose.)

Listening Comprehension

CLOSE READING

ELL

PAGES 28–29

ASK AND ANSWER QUESTIONS

Think Aloud As I read these pages, I realize that the workers are cleaning up. The road seems to be finished. I ask myself: What happens next, after the road is done? I will keep reading to find out my answer.

pp. 28–29

Tidy up: Remind children that *tidy up* is another way to say "clean." Model tidying up your desk. Ask: *When do you tidy up your bedroom?*

PAGES 30–31

KEY DETAILS

The workers have finished building the road. What happens next? (People drive on the new road) Encourage children to review the sequence of building a road.

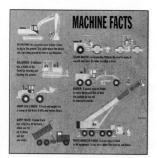

PAGE 32

AUTHOR'S PURPOSE

Why do you think the author included a page with all of the different machines that the workers used? (Possible answer: To help us learn more about how roads are made)

Text Evidence

Explain Remind children that when they answer a question, they need to show where in the story (both words and illustrations) they found the answer.

Discuss *How do you know that the workers test the lights?* (On page 24, the author says they test the lights and watch them shine. I can see the lights in the illustrations.)

Guided Retelling

Tell children that now they will use the **Retelling Cards** to retell the story.

→ Display Retelling Card 1. Based on children's needs, use either the Modeled, Guided or ELL retelling prompts. The ELL prompts contain support for English language learners based on levels of language acquisition. Repeat with the rest of the cards, using the prompts as a guide.

→ Discuss the story. Have children tell which part of road building they think is most interesting.

→ Have children act out a step from building a road with a partner.

Model Fluency

Reread pages 20–21 of *Roadwork* and emphasize the expression used when reading the words printed in large letters, ending with exclamation points. Explain that exclamation points show strong feeling, such as excitement. Then reread the sentences on pages 20–21 and have children repeat them. Encourage them to mimic the sounds the larger words represent.

Retelling Cards

YOUR TURN PRACTICE BOOK p. 118

→ # Word Work

Quick Review

Build Fluency: Sound-Spellings: Show the following **Word-Building Cards:** *a, c, d, i, m, n, o, p, s, t.* Have children chorally say each sound. Repeat and vary the pace.

MINILESSON 5 Mins

Phonemic Awareness

Puppet

Phoneme Blending

❶ Model Use the puppet to demonstrate how to blend phonemes to make words. *The puppet is going to say sounds in a word, /n/ /o/ /d/. It can blend those sounds to make a word: /noood/ nod. When the puppet blends the sounds together, it makes the word* nod. *Listen as the puppet blends more sounds to make a word.* Continue modeling phoneme blending with the following:

/n/ /o/ /t/   /k/ /a/ /n/   /t/ /o/ /p/   /n/ /a/ /p/   /d/ /i/ /p/

❷ Guided Practice/Practice Tell children to listen as the puppet says sounds in words. *Have children repeat the sounds, and then blend them to say the words.* Guide practice with the first word.

/d/ /o/ /t/ dot   /k/ /a/ /p/ cap   /s/ /i/ /p/ sip   /m/ /a/ /n/ man

MINILESSON 5 Mins

Phonics

Review /o/ o and /d/ d

❶ Model Display the *Octopus* **Sound-Spelling Card.** Say: *This is the letter* o. *The letter* o *can stand for the sound /o/ as in the word* octopus. *What is the letter?* (o) *What sound does the letter* o *stand for?* (/o/) Repeat for /d/ d, using the *Dolphin* Sound-Spelling Card.

❷ Guided Practice/Practice Have children listen as you say some words. Ask them to write the letter o on their **Response Boards** if the word begins with /o/. Do the first two words with children.

otter   pit   olive   ox   did   ostrich   nap   octopus

Repeat for /d/ d.

dime   dog   tip   pot   dip   duck   sun   dish

♪ Review /n/ n. Have children write the letter n on their **Response Boards.** Play "Nellie's Nest." Have children show their Response Boards with the letter n when they hear /n/.

OBJECTIVES

CCSS Demonstrate basic knowledge of one-to-one letter-sound correspondences by producing the primary or many of the most frequent sounds for each consonant. **RF.K.3a**

CCSS Read common high-frequency words by sight. **RF.K.3c**

ACADEMIC LANGUAGE
blend

ELL

ENGLISH LANGUAGE LEARNERS

High-Frequency Words: Reinforce Meaning Display the High-Frequency Word Cards *and, do, go, to, you.* Use the words in simple sentences, such as *I give the book to you.* As you say each sentence, point to the words and use gestures to convey meaning. Have children repeat the sentences.

Go Digital

Phonemic Awareness

Phonics

Handwriting

High-Frequency Word Routine

Blend Words with /i/i, /o/o, /n/n, /d/d

❶ Model Place **Word-Building Cards** n, o, and d in a pocket chart. Point to the letter n. *This is the letter n. The letter n stands for /n/. Say /n/. This is the letter o. The letter o stands for /o/. Say /o/. This is the letter d. The letter d stands for /d/. Say /d/. Listen as I blend the sounds together: /noood/. Now blend the sounds with me to read the word.*

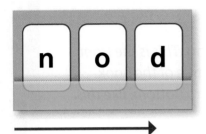

❷ Guided Practice/Practice Use Word-Building Cards or write *did*. Point to the letter *d* and have children say the sound. Point to the letter *i* and have children say the sound. Point to the letter *d* and have children say the sound. Then move your hand from left to right under the word, and have children blend and read the word *did*.

High-Frequency Words

and, do, go, to, you

❶ Guided Practice Display the **High-Frequency Word Card** *and*. Use the **Read/Spell/Write** routine to review the words. Ask children to close their eyes, picture the word in their minds, and then write it the way they see it. Have children self-correct by checking the High-Frequency Word Card. Repeat for *do, go, to, you*.

❷ Practice Review the current words in the word bank.

→ Have partners create sentences using each word.

→ For each word, have children count the number of letters, look at the letters in the word and then write the word again.

Cumulative Review Review words: *the, a, see, we, like*.

→ Repeat the **Read/Spell/Write** routine. Mix the words and have children chorally say each one.

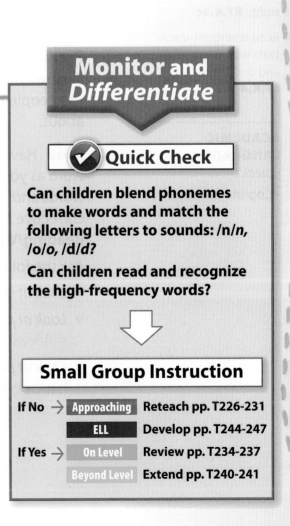

Monitor and *Differentiate*

✓ Quick Check

Can children blend phonemes to make words and match the following letters to sounds: /n/n, /o/o, /d/d?

Can children read and recognize the high-frequency words?

⬇

Small Group Instruction

If No →	Approaching	Reteach pp. T226–231
	ELL	Develop pp. T244–247
If Yes →	On Level	Review pp. T234–237
	Beyond Level	Extend pp. T240–241

→ # Shared Read

Reading/Writing Workshop Big Book and Reading/Writing Workshop

---

OBJECTIVES

CCSS Read common high-frequency words by sight. **RF.K.3c**

CCSS Read emergent-reader texts with purpose and understanding. **RF.K.4**

ACADEMIC LANGUAGE

• *predict*

• Cognates: *predecir*

MINILESSON 10 Mins

Read "I Can, You Can!"

Model Skills and Strategies

Model Book Handling Demonstrate book handling. *This is the front cover of the book. The front cover always includes the title of the book. When I read this page, I read from left to right and top to bottom, like this.* Read the title on the front cover.

Model Concepts About Print Turn to page 37 and point to the first word in the sentence. *The word Mom begins with a capital, or uppercase, letter because it is the first word in the sentence.* Invite volunteers to come up to the **Big Book** and point to the first word in sentences and identify them as capital letters. *As I read each word, I'm going to point to it, like this.* Demonstrate speech to print matching by reading the sentence slowly, tracking the print with your finger. Then invite children to echo read the sentence as you track the print.

Predict Read the title together. Invite children to look closely at the illustration on pages 36 and 37. Encourage them to describe what the people are doing. Then have them predict what the story will be about.

Read Have children chorally read the story with you. Point to each word as you read it together. Help children sound out decodable words and say the sight words. If children have difficulty, provide corrective feedback and guide them page by page using the student **Reading/Writing Workshop**.

Ask the following:

→ *Look at page 37. Where does this story take place?* (on a beach)

→ *Look at page 38. What is the child doing?* (Possible answers: making a sandcastle; patting the sand in the pail)

→ *Look at page 43. Why is everyone happy?* (Possible answer: They are happy because they have built sandcastles.)

Go Digital

"I Can, You Can!"

"I Can, You Can!"

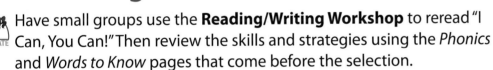

READING/WRITING WORKSHOP, pp. 36–43

Rereading

Have small groups use the **Reading/Writing Workshop** to reread "I Can, You Can!" Then review the skills and strategies using the *Phonics* and *Words to Know* pages that come before the selection.

→ Have children ask themselves questions as they read. Remind them that they can find the answers in the words and the illustrations. If necessary, model how to ask and answer a question. Encourage them to look for details in the illustrations that help to answer their questions.

→ Have children use page 35 to review the high-frequency words *to, and, go, you,* and *do.*

→ Have children use page 34 to review the letters *i, n, c, o,* and *d,* and their corresponding sounds. Guide them to blend the sounds to read the words.

ELL

ENGLISH LANGUAGE LEARNERS

Reinforce Vocabulary Display the **High-Frequency Word Cards** *to, and, go, you, do.* Point to pictures in the classroom and groups of children as you use the high-frequency word in sentences such as the following: *Do you go to the beach?* (Yes, we go to the beach.) *Do you like to run and play?* (Yes, we like to run and play.) *What does the eraser do?* (The eraser wipes chalk off the board.) *When do you come to school?* (We come to school at 8 o'clock.)

→ # Language Arts

MINILESSON 10 Mins

Interactive Writing

Writing Trait: Word Choice

Review Remind children that we can choose describing words to write about workers in our community. Write and read aloud: *The crossing guard helps me cross a busy street.* Ask children what kind of street is being described. (busy)

Write an Expository Sentence

Discuss Display the chart from Day 1. Read aloud the types of workers and how they help. Guide children to choose a worker to write about.

Model/Apply Grammar Tell children that you will work together to write a sentence using the information in the chart.

Write the sentence frame: *The _____ helps _____.*

Model how to choose a worker and how that worker helps to complete the sentence. Point to a worker in the first column and how that worker helps in the second column. Fill in the sentence frame. For example, write: *The librarian helps to find interesting books.* Read the sentence aloud. *What kind of worker is the sentence about?* Point to the word *librarian. What kind of books does the librarian help to find?* (interesting) *The word* interesting *is an adjective, because it describes the kind of books.*

Write Have children help you use the chart to choose another worker to write about, using the above sentence frame.

Guide children to complete the sentence frame. Write the words. Share the pen with children and have them write the letters they know.

OBJECTIVES

CCSS Use a combination of drawing, dictating, and writing to compose informative/ explanatory texts in which they name what they are writing about and supply some information about the topic. **W.K.2**

CCSS Produce and expand complete sentences in shared language activities. **L.K.1f**

- Write an expository sentence
- Recognize describing words (adjectives)

ACADEMIC LANGUAGE

- *description, chart, adjective*
- Cognates: *adjetivo*

Grammar

5 Mins

Describing Words (Adjectives)

❶ Review Remind children that many times an adjective appears right before the naming word, or noun. Explain that sometimes the adjective can appear after the naming word. Show children the construction vehicles in the **Big Book**.

→ Write and read aloud: *The truck is heavy.*

→ *Which word tells about the truck?* (heavy) Point to the word *heavy. Heavy is an adjective because it describes the truck.*

❷ Guided Practice Have children suggest another word to describe the trucks, using pictures from the Big Book.

→ Write the sentence frame: *The truck is _____.*

→ Model adding an adjective to make a new sentence. Write *yellow* on a self-stick note and add it to the sentence. Read aloud the sentence and ask children to name the describing word. (yellow)

❸ Practice Have children work in pairs to make their own sentences by placing self-stick notes with adjectives in the sentence frame. Help children read the sentences they have made. Ask children to name the describing word, or adjective, in each sentence they make.

Talk About It

Have partners work together to orally generate sentences with adjectives. Encourage them to describe things they see on the streets in their neighborhood.

ENGLISH LANGUAGE LEARNERS

Actively Engage Pair English language learners with fluent speakers. Have English language learners choose the adjective to put in the sentence frame about trucks: *The truck is ____.* Have fluent speakers read the sentence aloud. Offer help with reading the sentences as needed. Ask English language learners to repeat the sentences as they are able.

Daily Wrap Up

● Discuss the Essential Question and encourage children to use the oral vocabulary words. *How does a community worker help you? How does a community worker help other people?*

● Prompt children to review and discuss the skills they used today. How do those skills help them?

Materials

Reading/Writing Workshop Big Book
UNIT 4

Interactive Read-Aloud Cards

Visual Vocabulary Cards
harvest
quarrel
confused

Sound-Spelling Cards
camel   nest
dolphin   octopus
insect

Photo Cards
camel
car
comb
corn
cow
deer
dime
dinosaur

dog
dolphin
inch
inchworm
insect
invitation
nail
nest
net
nose
nut
October
octopus
olive
otter

 a b c
Word-Building Cards

 and
High-Frequency Word Cards
and   to
do   you
go

Response Board

Puppet

♪ **"Can Your Camel Do the Can-Can?"**

→ Build the Concept

MINILESSON
10 Mins
Oral Language

OBJECTIVES

CCSS Actively engage in group reading activities with purpose and understanding. **RL.K.10**

CCSS Identify real-life connections between words and their use. **L.K.5c**

Develop oral vocabulary

ACADEMIC LANGUAGE
• fable, characters, plot
• Cognates: *fábula*

ESSENTIAL QUESTION

 Remind children that this week they are talking and learning about how people can make a community better. Guide children to discuss the Essential Question using information from the **Big Book** and the weekly song.

Remind children how the railroad workers in "I've Been Working on the Railroad" help make their community better. Sing the song and have children join in.

Oral Vocabulary

Review last week's oral vocabulary words, as well as *community* and *improve* from Day 1. Then use the **Define/Example/Ask** routine to introduce *harvest, quarrel,* and *confused.*

Oral Vocabulary Routine

Define: During a **harvest**, farmers pick the food they have grown.

Example: The farm workers picked many oranges during the harvest.

Ask: Why is harvest time important to a community?

Define: When people **quarrel**, they argue or disagree with each other.

Example: Please don't quarrel about who will get the red crayon first.

Ask: What can you do to stop a quarrel from starting?

Define: To be **confused** is to be mixed up.

Example: The street signs confused the new driver and he took a wrong turn.

Ask: Have you ever been confused following the rules of a game? Explain.

Vocab
Define
Exampl
Ask:

Visual Vocabulary Cards

Go Digital

Visual Glossary

"The Bundle of Sticks"

I wonder...

Think Aloud Cloud

Listening Comprehension

Read the Interactive Read Aloud

NILESSON 10 Mins

Genre: Fable

Tell children you will be reading a fable. Guide them in recalling that a *fable* is a fiction story that teaches a lesson. Display the **Interactive Read-Aloud Cards**.

Read the title. Point out that a *bundle* of sticks is a lot of sticks all together. It might be held together by a piece of string.

Interactive Read-Aloud Cards

Strategy: Ask and Answer Questions

Guide children in recalling that good readers ask themselves questions as they read. *Asking questions can help us understand important details in a story.* Use the **Think Aloud Cloud** to model asking and answering questions as you read the fable.

Think Aloud I read that Mrs. Sato asked Yuki to break a stick. She broke it easily. I'm confused by this. I wonder why she would ask her to break a stick. I'll read ahead to try to answer my question. I read ahead and I was able to answer my question. Mrs. Sato wanted the children to see that they needed to work together, so they could be strong like a bundle of sticks.

Read "The Bundle of Sticks." Pause to model the strategy as you read.

Make Connections

COLLABORATE

Guide partners to connect "The Bundle of Sticks" with *Roadwork*. Discuss the different ways that the two selections show how people can make their communities better.

ENGLISH LANGUAGE LEARNERS

Reinforce Meaning As you read "The Bundle of Sticks," make meaning clear by pointing to specific characters, places, or objects in the illustrations, demonstrating word meanings, paraphrasing text, and asking children questions. For example, on Card 2, point to the illustration of Yuki breaking the stick and ask: *What is Yuki doing to the stick?* (Yuki is breaking the stick.)

Monitor and *Differentiate*

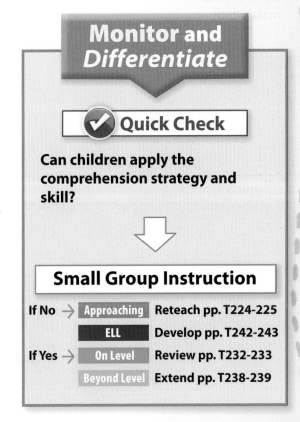

✔ **Quick Check**

Can children apply the comprehension strategy and skill?

⬇

Small Group Instruction

If No →	**Approaching**	Reteach pp. T224-225
	ELL	Develop pp. T242-243
If Yes →	**On Level**	Review pp. T232-233
	Beyond Level	Extend pp. T238-239

→ # Word Work

Phonemic Awareness

Puppet

Phoneme Blending

OBJECTIVES

CCSS Isolate and pronounce the initial, medial vowel, and final sounds in three-phoneme words.
RF.K.2d

CCSS Demonstrate basic knowledge of one-to-one letter-sound correspondences by producing the primary or many of the most frequent sounds for each consonant.
RF.K.3a

• Blend phonemes to make words

• Blend sounds to make words

❶ **Model** *The puppet will say the sounds in a word. Listen: /t/ /o/ /p/. It can blend these sounds to make a word: /tooop/,* top. *Say the word with the puppet:* top. *Repeat with* cat.

❷ **Guided Practice/Practice** Have children blend sounds to form words. *The puppet is going to say the sounds in a word. Listen to the puppet as it says each sound. Repeat the sounds. Then blend the sounds to say the word.* Guide practice with the first word.

/d/ /a/ /d/	/n/ /o/ /t/	/p/ /a/ /d/	/k/ /a/ /n/
/t/ /i/ /p/	/t/ /o/ /m/	/t/ /i/ /n/	/t/ /a/ /n/
/d/ /a/ /n/	/k/ /a/ /p/	/s/ /o/ /k/	/m/ /i/ /s/
/t/ /o/ /s/	/m/ /o/ /p/	/p/ /a/ /k/	/m/ /o/ /s/

Go Digital

Phonemic Awareness

Phonics

Handwriting

Phonics

10 Mins

Review /i/i, /o/o, /n/n, /k/c, /d/d

❶ Model Display the *Nest* **Sound-Spelling Card**. *This is the letter* n. *The letter* n *stands for /n/, the sound you hear at the beginning of* nest. *Say the sound with me /n/. I will write the letter* n *because* nest *has /n/ at the beginning.*

Repeat for /i/i, /o/o, /k/c, /d/d using the *Insect, Octopus, Camel,* and *Dolphin* Sound-Spelling Cards.

❷ Guided Practice/Practice Tell children that you will say words that begin with one of the sounds that were reviewed. Have children say the initial sound and write the letter that stands for that sound on their **Response Boards**. Tell children to hold up and show you their Response Boards after they have written the letter. Guide practice with the first word.

if   desk   olive   cold   night   inch   doll   ox   cat   nose

Blend Words with Short *i, o* and *n, c, d, t*

❶ Model Display **Word-Building Cards** *n, o, d. This is the letter* n. *It stands for /n/. This is the letter* o. *It stands for /o/. This is the letter* d. *It stands for /d/. Let's blend the three sounds together: /n/ /ooo/ /d/, /noood/. The word is* nod. Repeat with *not, cot, tin.*

❷ Guided Practice/Practice Write the following words. Have children read each word, blending the sounds. Guide practice with the first word.

on   tin   Don   did   not

Write these sentences and prompt children to read the connected text, sounding out the decodable words: *Tom can not see Don. Can Dad see the mop?*

Corrective Feedback

Sound Error Model the sound that children missed, then have them repeat. For example, for the word *Don*, tap under the letter *d* and ask: *What's the* sound? Return to the beginning of the word. *Let's start over.* Blend the word with children again.

YOUR TURN PRACTICE BOOK pp. 119–120

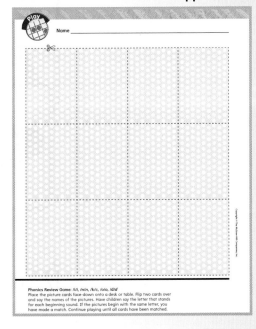

Phonics Review Game: */i/i, /n/n, /k/c, /o/o, /d/d*
Place the picture cards face-down onto a desk or table. Flip two cards over and say the names of the pictures. Have children say the letter that stands for each beginning sound. If the pictures begin with the same letter, you have made a match. Continue playing until all cards have been matched.

→ # Word Work

OBJECTIVES

CCSS Read common high-frequency words by sight. **RF.K.3c**

Sort picture names by initial phoneme

ACADEMIC LANGUAGE
sort

MINILESSON **5** Mins

Phonics

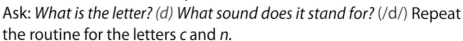

Photo Cards

Picture Sort

❶ **Model** Remind children that the letter *d* stands for /d/. Place the **Word-Building Card** *d* in one column in a pocket chart. Ask: *What is the letter? (d) What sound does it stand for? (/d/)* Repeat the routine for the letters *c* and *n*.

Hold up the *Dolphin* **Photo Card**. *Here is the picture for* dolphin. Dolphin *has the /d/ sound at the beginning. I will place* dolphin *under the letter* d *because the letter* d *stands for /d/.*

Repeat the routine for *the Camel and Nest* Photo Cards.

❷ **Guided Practice/Practice** Name the Photo Cards: *car, comb, corn, cow, deer, dime, dinosaur, dog, nail, net, nose, nut.* Ask children to say the picture name and tell the sound at the beginning of the word. Have them tell which letter the Photo Card should be placed.

Repeat for /i/ *i* and /o/ *o* using the *Insect* and *Octopus* Photo Cards. Have children sort the following Photo Cards: *inch, inchworm, invitation, October, olive, otter.*

Photo Cards

 Review /k/*c*. Have children write the letter *c* on their Response Boards. Play "Can Your Camel Do the Can-Can?" Have children show their Response Boards with the letter *c* when they hear /k/.

Go Digital

Phonics

High-Frequency Word Routine

NILESSON
5 Mins

High-Frequency Words

and, do, go, to, you

1 Guided Practice Display the **High-Frequency Word Cards** and, do, go, to and you. Review the word using the **Read/Spell/Write** routine.

2 Practice Point to the High-Frequency Word Card and. Have children read the word. Repeat with words do, go, to, and you.

Build Fluency

Word Automaticity Write the following sentences and have children chorally read aloud as you track the print. Repeat several times.

> Matt can go in.
> Dan and Tom see the cat.
> Do you see the cat?
> The cat can go to you.

Read for Fluency Distribute pages 121–122 of the **Your Turn Practice Book** and help children assemble their Take-Home Books. Chorally read the Take-Home Book with children. Then have children reread the book to review high-frequency words and build fluency.

YOUR TURN PRACTICE BOOK pp. 121–122

Monitor and Differentiate

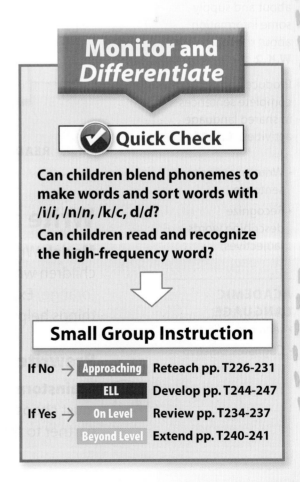

✓ Quick Check

Can children blend phonemes to make words and sort words with /i/i, /n/n, /k/c, d/d?

Can children read and recognize the high-frequency word?

Small Group Instruction

If No →	**Approaching**	Reteach pp. T226-231
	ELL	Develop pp. T244-247
If Yes →	**On Level**	Review pp. T234-237
	Beyond Level	Extend pp. T240-241

→ # Language Arts

Reading/Writing Workshop Big Book

 MINILESSON **10 Mins**

Independent Writing

Writing Trait: Word Choice

❶ **Practice** Tell children that they will write a sentence about a worker they know in their community.

❷ **Guided Practice** Share the Readers to Writers page in the **Reading/Writing Workshop**. Read the model sentences aloud.

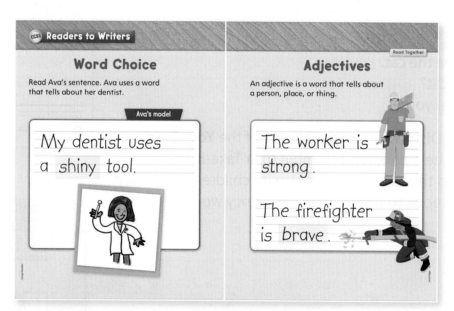

READING/WRITING WORKSHOP BIG BOOK, pp. 46–47

OBJECTIVES

CCSS Use a combination of drawing, dictating, and writing to compose informative/explanatory texts in which they name what they are writing about and supply some information about the topic. **W.K.2**

CCSS Produce and expand complete sentences in shared language activities. **L.K.1f**

- Write an expository sentence
- Recognize describing words (adjectives)

ACADEMIC LANGUAGE

- *sentence, adjective*
- Cognates: *adjetivo*

Write an Expository Sentence

Model Write and read aloud: *The gardener plants orange flowers.* Ask children what word tells us about the kind of flowers that are planted. (orange) Explain to children that using words to describe people and things helps to make sentences more interesting.

Prewrite

 Brainstorm Tell children that before they can begin writing, they must choose a worker to write about. Have children work with a partner to think of a community worker that they are familiar with.

Go Digital

Present The Lesson

Writing

I see a fish.

Grammar

Draft

Guide children in writing a sentence that tells about a community worker they know about. Help children choose words that describe how the worker helps. Have them draw a picture for their sentence. Encourage children who can generate more writing to do so.

Apply Writing Trait As children write and draw, have them tell why they chose that worker. Ask them to share other words they could have used to describe that worker.

Apply Grammar Tell children to point to and tell you the adjective that describes what the worker does.

Grammar

Describing Words (Adjectives)

1 **Review** Remind children that we can use our senses to help us describe things. Write and read: *The music is loud. My pillow is soft.*

Ask children to name the adjective in each sentence. *Which sense would you use to describe music? A soft pillow?* (hearing; touch)

2 **Guided Practice/Practice** Have children look at pictures in the **Big Book**. Ask children what describing words they think of when they look at the pictures. Remind them to think of words using all of their senses. Record children's responses as a list. (dirty, brown, rocky, heavy, loud, bumpy, smooth, black) Write and read aloud a sentence based on the list of adjectives, such as: *The construction site is rocky.*

Have children work in small groups. Ask children to dictate more sentences, using adjectives from the list. Write and read aloud the sentences.

Talk About It

Have partners work together to orally generate sentences with adjectives. Encourage them to describe things they hear in their homes.

Daily Wrap Up

- Review the Essential Question and encourage children to discuss it, using the oral vocabulary words *community* and *improve*. *How does each worker help make the community better? What can you do to improve your community?*

- Prompt children to review and discuss the skills they used today. Guide them to give examples of how they used each skill.

Materials

Reading/Writing Workshop Big Book
UNIT 4

Reading/Writing Workshop
UNIT 4

Literature Big Book
Roadwork

Interactive Read-Aloud Cards

Word-Building Cards

Response Board

and
High-Frequency Word Cards
and   to
do   you
go

Visual Vocabulary Cards
and   to
do   you
go

Photo Cards
ambulance snow
kitten   ant
egg   dog
feather   giraffe
mouse   hippo

♪ **"If You Take an Octopus to Dinner"**

→ Extend the Concept

MINILESSON
10 Mins
Oral Language

OBJECTIVES

CCSS Recognize and produce rhyming words. **RF.K.2a**

CCSS Use words and phrases acquired through conversations, reading and being read to, and responding to texts. **L.K.6**

Develop oral vocabulary

ESSENTIAL QUESTION

Remind children that this week they have been talking and reading about how people can make the community better. Have them sing "I've Been Working on the Railroad." *How are the workers in the song like the workers in the book* Roadwork?

Phonological Awareness
Recognize Rhyme
Sing the first two lines from "I've Been Working on the Railroad." *The words* day *and* away *rhyme. Words that rhyme have the same end sound. Listen:* day, away. *I can say more words with this end sound:* say, may, pay, bay, hay. Tell children you are going to say pairs of words. They should raise their hands if the two words rhyme. Pause between word pairs: *go/get; pad/sad; game/tame, big/buy, tail/nail.*

Review Oral Vocabulary

Reread the Interactive Read Aloud Use the **Define/Example/Ask** routine to review the oral vocabulary words *community, improve, harvest, quarrel,* and *confused.* Then have children listen as you reread "The Bundle of Sticks."

→ *What did the children quarrel about at the beginning of the story?* (They couldn't decide how to participate in the harvest festival.)

→ *What did the class decide to do to improve the community?* (The children made paper lanterns and wrote recipes.)

Go Digital

Visual Glossary

"The Bundle of Sticks"

Category Words

Category Words: Position Words

1 **Explain/Model** Use a book and a desk to demonstrate different position words. For example:

> *The book is* on *the desk.*
> *The book is* off *the desk.*
> *The book is* under *the desk.*
> *The book is* next *to the desk.*
> *The book is* in back *of the desk.*

→ Repeat each sentence and ask children to identify the position word. (on, off, under, next, back) Then have children instruct you to put the book in different positions. Children should use a position word in their sentence. For example: *Put the book in front of the desk.*

2 **Guided Practice** Play a version of "I Spy," using different position words. Give children hints about the location of different objects around the classroom. Have them guess the objects you are thinking of. *I spy something that is in front of my desk. I spy something that is under the flag.*

→ Have children take turns being the person who "spies" different objects around the room. Remind them to use position words in their clues.

LET'S MOVE!

Call out directions that use position words. For example: *Andrew, stand next to the computer. Maria, sit under the window.* Then ask each child to explain where he or she is. Remind children to use a position word in their sentences. For example: *I am next to the computer.*

ENGLISH LANGUAGE LEARNERS

Practice Use a book to further demonstrate position words. Stress the position words as you move the book to a new position. For example: *The book is above my head. Where is the book? The book is next to my feet. Where is the book?* Have children mirror your actions using books of their own.

YOUR TURN PRACTICE BOOK p. 123

Category Words: Position Words
Put a marker on each picture that shows a position word. Name the position shown in each picture.

→ # Listening Comprehension

CLOSE READING

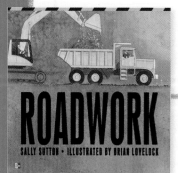

Literature Big Book

OBJECTIVES

CCSS With prompting and support, ask and answer questions about key details in a text. **RI.K.1**

- Understand the characteristics of informational text
- Use the text feature captions to gather information
- Apply the comprehension strategy: Ask and Answer Questions
- Make connections across texts

ACADEMIC LANGUAGE
- *text, captions*
- Cognates: *texto*

MINILESSON
10 Mins

Read "A Community Garden"

Genre: Informational Text

Display "A Community Garden" on pages 33–36 of the **Big Book** and read aloud the title. Remind children that informational text tells about real people, places, and/or things.

Set a Purpose for Reading

Read aloud the first sentence on page 33. Tell children to listen as you continue reading the selection to learn how people volunteer at a community garden to improve their neighborhood.

Strategy: Ask and Answer Questions

Remind children that good readers ask and answer questions as they read. Have children look at page 33. *We can ask: How can people help improve their neighborhood? We can answer: They can plant a garden.* Explain to children that people who help to improve their neighborhoods are good citizens. They work together to make their neighborhoods better.

Text Feature: Captions

Explain Point to the photograph and caption on page 33. *Captions give more information about photographs. This caption tells that the people are working together.* Read aloud the caption and have children echo.

Apply Read aloud the text on page 34. Ask a volunteer to point to the caption on the page. Have children identify the photograph that the caption is describing. (photo of girl watering plants)

Go Digital

Roadwork

LITERATURE BIG BOOK PAGE 33

HIGH-FREQUENCY WORDS

Have children identify and read the high-frequency words *to* and *do* on page 33. Repeat the routine with the word *and* on page 34; the word *go* on page 35; and the word *you* on page 36.

LITERATURE BIG BOOK   PAGES 34–35

KEY DETAILS

What do people do to the seeds after they plant them? (They water the seeds.)

LITERATURE BIG BOOK PAGE 36

ASK AND ANSWER QUESTIONS

Why are the volunteers at the community garden good citizens? (Possible answer: They are helping to improve their neighborhood. They share the vegetables and flowers that grow in the garden.)

Retell and Respond

Have children discuss the text by asking the following questions:

→ *How does a community garden help a neighborhood?* (Possible answer: A garden can make a neighborhood beautiful.)

→ *What happens to the flowers and vegetables?* (People share them.)

Make Connections

Have children recall the selections they have read this week.

→ *How did the workers move the dirt for the new road?* (with a truck)

Write About It Write about how Mrs. Sato's class helped the community.

ENGLISH LANGUAGE LEARNERS

Reinforce Meaning As you read aloud the text, make the meaning clear by pointing to details in the photographs and captions. Ask children questions and elicit language.

 CONNECT TO CONTENT

Community Help Review with children how people can improve their community by making gardens. Have partners discuss the kinds of things they would like to grow in a community garden. Ask: *Why are people who help in a community garden good citizens?*

→ # Word Work

MINILESSON 5 Mins

Phonemic Awareness

OBJECTIVES

CCSS Isolate and pronounce the initial, medial vowel, and final sounds in three-phoneme words. **RF.K.2d**

CCSS Distinguish between similarly spelled words by identifying the sounds of letters that differ. **RF.K.3d**

CCSS Read common high-frequency words by sight. **RF.K.3c**

• Segment words into phonemes
• Blend letter sounds to make words

Phoneme Segmentation

❶ **Model** Use the **Sound Boxes** and markers. *Listen as I say a word:* mad. *Say the word with me:* mad. *Say the sounds in* mad *with me:* /m/ /a/ /d/. *There are three sounds in* mad. *Let's place a marker in a box for each sound:* /m/ /a/ /d/. *Repeat for* pot.

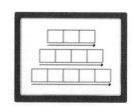

Sound Boxes

❷ **Guided Practice/Practice** Distribute Sound Boxes and markers. Say the word. Have children repeat the word and say each sound as they place a marker in a box. Then have them tell the number of sounds in the word. Guide practice with the first word.

sad, /s/ /a/ /d/   dot, /d/ /o/ /t/   nap, /n/ /a/ /p/
sand, /s/ /a/ /n/ /d/   dip, /d/ /i/ /p/   cap, /k/ /a/ /p/
did, /d/ /i/ /d/   mask, /m/ /a/ /s/ /k/   mop, /m/ /o/ /p/

MINILESSON 5 Mins

Phonics

Blend Words with *a, i, o, n, c, d, p, t*

❶ **Guided Practice** Display **Word-Building Cards** *c, o, t.* Point to the letter *c. This is the letter* c. *It stands for* /k/. *This is the letter* o. *It stands for* /o/. *Listen as I blend the two sounds together* /kooo/. *Say* /kooo/. *This is the letter* t. *The letter* t *stands for* /t/. *Listen as I blend the three sounds:* /kooot/, cot. *Now you say it.* Change *c* to *d.* Repeat with *dot.*

❷ **Practice** Write *pat, pit, pot* . Have children blend the words. Ask children which letters are the same. (p, t) Ask children to tell which letters are different. (*a, i* and *o*) Discuss the sounds each letter stands for and how it changes the word. Repeat for *tap, tip, top.*

♪ Review /o/o. Have children write the letter *o* on their **Response Boards**. Play "If You Take an Octopus to Dinner." Have children show their Response Boards with the letter *o* when they hear /o/.

Go Digital

Phonemic Awareness

Phonics

Handwriting

Visual Glossary

High-Frequency Word Routine

Dictation

1 Review Dictate the following sounds for children to spell. Have them repeat the sound and then write the letter that stands for the sound.

/d/   /k/   /n/   /i/   /o/   /t/   /s/

2 Dictate the following words for children to spell: *pin, cot, nod, dip*. Model for children how to segment each word to scaffold the spelling.

Say: *When I say the word* pin, *I hear three sounds: /p/ /i/ /n/. I know the letter* p *stands for /p/, the letter* i *stands for /i/, and the letter* n *stands for /n/. I will write the letters* p, i, n *to spell the word* pin.

When children finish, write the letters and words for them to self-correct.

MINI LESSON
5 Mins

High-Frequency Words

and, do, go, to, you

Practice Display the **Visual Vocabulary Cards** for *and, do, go, to,* and *you*. Follow the **Read/Spell/Write** routine on the card for each word. Then choose a Teacher Talk activity on the back.

Build Fluency Build sentences in a pocket chart using **High-Frequency Word Cards** and **Photo Cards**. Use an index card to create a punctuation card for a question mark. Have children chorally read the sentences as you track the print. Then have them identify the words *and, do, go, to,* and *you*.

Do you see the bear and the deer?

Can you go to the farm?

Do you see the kitten?

Have partners create sentences using the words *and, do, go, to, you*.

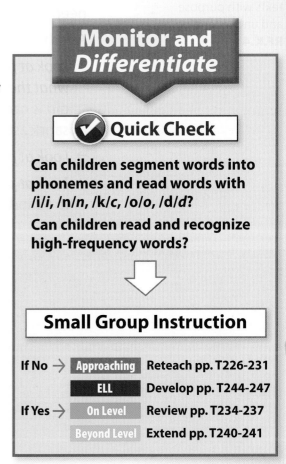

Monitor and Differentiate

✓ Quick Check

Can children segment words into phonemes and read words with /i/i, /n/n, /k/c, /o/o, /d/d?

Can children read and recognize high-frequency words?

⬇

Small Group Instruction

If No →	Approaching	Reteach pp. T226-231
	ELL	Develop pp. T244-247
If Yes →	On Level	Review pp. T234-237
	Beyond Level	Extend pp. T240-241

→ # Shared Read

Reading/Writing Workshop Big Book and Reading/Writing Workshop

OBJECTIVES

CCSS Read common high-frequency words by sight. **RF.K.3c**

CCSS Read emergent-reader texts with purpose and understanding. **RF.K.4**

MINILESSON 10 Mins

Read "I Can, You Can!"

Model Skills and Strategies

Model Book Handling Demonstrate book handling. Display the front cover of the book. *This is the front cover of the book.* Then display the back cover. *This is the back cover of the book.* Model turning the pages of the book.

Model Concepts About Print Point to the word *Can* in the sentence on page 39. *Remember that the word* Can *begins with a capital letter because it is the first word in the sentence.* Invite volunteers to come up to the **Big Book** and point to the capital letter that begins the first word in each sentence.

Reread Review the rebus for *beach* and discuss what it stands for. Then have children chorally reread the story. Help children sound out the decodable words and say the sight words. Offer support as needed using the student **Reading/Writing Workshop**.

Ask the following:

→ *Look at pages 36 and 37. What clues in the illustration help tell you what these people are planning to do?* (They are at a beach. The girl is carrying a pail and shovel. They are probably going to make sandcastles.)

→ *Look at page 40. What is the girl doing?* (She is tipping the pail.)

→ *Look at page 42. How is Don helping?* (He is helping to pat down the sandcastle.)

Go Digital

"I Can, You Can!"

"I Can, You Can!"

READING/WRITING WORKSHOP, pp. 36–43

Fluency: Expression

1 Explain Tell children that as you read the story, you will read with expression, or feeling. They will hear the expression in your voice. Explain that you will emphasize different words and change your voice when you read sentences that end with a period, question mark, or exclamation point.

2 Model Model reading "I Can, You Can!" with expression. *When I read the story, I change my tone when I read sentences with different kinds of punctuation.* Read each sentence with appropriate expression.

3 Guided Practice Invite children to choral read the story with feeling. Have them listen to you first and then echo each sentence. Encourage them to match your intonation and expression.

→ # Language Arts

10 Mins MINILESSON

Independent Writing

Writing an Expository Sentence

Revise

Distribute the children's draft sentences and drawings from Day 3.

Apply Writing Trait Word Choice Explain that as writers revise, they can choose different words that better describe what they are writing about. Write and read aloud: *The gardener plants little trees. I would like to give a better description of the tree. I can describe the kind of tree.* Tell children you think *plant oak trees* is a better description. Write and read aloud: *The gardener plants oak trees.*

Help children decide whether they can think of better words to describe the workers they wrote about. Then have children read the sentences they wrote and check for the following:

→ Did I choose the correct name of the worker?

→ Did I use the best describing words?

→ Did I describe how the worker helps in the community?

→ Does my drawing show what the worker does?

Apply Grammar Explain that the words used to describe people and things are called adjectives. Have children share the adjectives they used in their sentences.

Peer Edit Have children work with a partner to do a peer edit, reading each other's drafts. Partners can read the sentences aloud to see if there is another adjective they can suggest. Ask partners to check that the picture matches any changes made. Provide time for children to make revisions to their sentences.

Final Draft

After children have edited their own papers and finished their peer edits, have them write their final draft. Remind them to write neatly so that readers can read their writing. As children work, conference with them to provide guidance.

OBJECTIVES

CCSS With guidance and support from adults, respond to questions and suggestions from peers and add details to strengthen writing as needed. **W.K.5**

CCSS Produce and expand complete sentences in shared language activities. **L.K.1f**

- Revise an expository sentence
- Recognize describing words (adjectives)

ACADEMIC LANGUAGE
revise, draft, adjective

Go Digital

Writing

I see a fish.

Grammar

Grammar

5 Mins ONLINE LESSON

Describing Words (Adjectives)

1 **Review** Remind children that we use our senses to help us think of describing words. Show the **Photo Card** for *ambulance*. Ask children to use each of their senses to list words that describe an ambulance. (white, red, big, noisy, loud, fast) Point out that all of these describing words are adjectives.

2 **Guided Practice** Show the Photo Card for *kitten*. Ask children to think of each of their senses as they name words that describe a kitten. (small, cute, furry, fluffy, soft, quiet) Record their responses.

Write a sentence about the kitten, using one of the adjectives named: *The kitten is small.*

Write a sentence frame: *The kitten is _____.* Ask children to make another sentence about the kitten. Write and read aloud sentences that children create. Have them point to the adjective in each sentence.

3 **Practice** Have children work in small groups. Distribute the Photo Cards for *egg, feather, mouse, snow;* one to each group. Tell children they will guess which Photo Card the other groups have. Children in each group should give clues about the thing on their Photo Card, using describing words. Children can say: *This thing is _____.* The group that guesses correctly gives clues about their own Photo Card next. Provide support if a group is struggling to guess correctly.

Talk About It

Have partners work together to orally generate sentences with adjectives. Encourage partners to describe places in their community.

Daily Wrap Up

- Review the Essential Question and encourage children to discuss it, using the oral vocabulary words.

- Prompt children to discuss the skills they practiced and learned today. Guide them to share examples of each skill.

☞ **Go** Digital

www.connected.mcgraw-hill.com
RESOURCES
Research and Inquiry

→ ## Wrap Up the Week
Integrate Ideas

RESEARCH AND INQUIRY

Pitch In

OBJECTIVES

CCSS Participate in shared research and writing projects (e.g., explore a number of books by a favorite author and express opinions about them). **W.K.7**

CCSS With guidance and support from adults, recall information from experiences or gather information from provided sources to answer a question. **W.K.8**

ACADEMIC LANGUAGE
research

Make a Community Plan

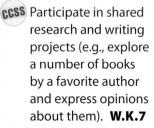

Tell children that today partners will research and make a plan for ways they can make their community better. Review the steps in the research process below.

STEP 1 ### Choose a Topic

Prompt partners to ask each other about things they don't like in their community, such as litter, and how things could be made better.

STEP 2 ### Find Resources

Talk about locating and using resources. Help children find online resources. Direct children to find ideas in the selections from the week. Point out that children can also use their own experience as a resource. Have children use the Research Process Checklist online.

STEP 3 ### Keep Track of Ideas

Have children create a two-column Problem and Solution chart to list their ideas by drawing pictures or writing words. Children may also want to print out pages from the Internet for reference.

Collaborative Conversations

Be Open to All Ideas As children engage in discussions with their partner, in a small group, and as a whole class, tell them to:

→ listen carefully because all ideas, questions, and comments are important.

→ ask a question if something is unclear.

→ respect the opinions of others.

→ give their opinions, even if they are different from those of other people.

We can pick up. Our community will be clean.

STEP 4 **Create the Project:**
Community Plan

Explain the characteristics of the project:

→ **Information** A plan gives information. This plan will show and tell how children plan to improve something in the community.

→ **Text** Note that each community plan should tell what children plan to do. Provide these sentence frames:

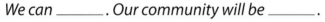
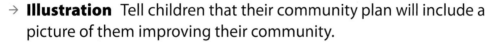
We can _____ . Our community will be _____ .

→ **Illustration** Tell children that their community plan will include a picture of them improving their community.

Have partners work together to create their community plan.

→ Guide children to complete the first sentence by telling what they will do. They should complete the second sentence with a word that describes.

→ Encourage children who can generate more writing to do so.

→ Prompt children to include details in their illustration that show how they will help their community.

ELL **ENGLISH LANGUAGE LEARNERS**
SCAFFOLD

Beginning	**Intermediate**	**Advanced/Advanced High**
Use Sentence Frames Pair children with more fluent speakers. Provide sentence frames to help children talk about their community plan. For example: *In our community, the problem is ____. To fix it, we can ____.*	**Discuss** Encourage children to talk about what happens when people work together. Have them tell about their community plan and how the help of many people will make the job easier.	**Elaborate** Encourage children to elaborate on their community plan by showing and telling about the community before and after the planned improvement. Prompt them to use descriptive words so listeners and readers can "see" the improvement.

Materials

Reading/Writing Workshop Big Book
UNIT 4

Literature Big Book
Roadwork

Interactive Read-Aloud Cards

Word-Building Cards

Visual Vocabulary Cards
and
do
go
to
you

High-Frequency Word Cards
and
do
go
to
you

Photo Cards
bear
gorilla
penguin
rose
tiger
turtle
wolf
zoo

Response Board

"Did You See a Dolphin?"

⊙→ Integrate Ideas

TEXT CONNECTIONS

Connect to Essential Question

OBJECTIVES

 With prompting and support, identify basic similarities in and differences between two texts on the same topic (e.g., in illustrations, descriptions, or procedures). **RI.K.9**

 Participate in collaborative conversations with diverse partners about *kindergarten topics and texts* with peers and adults in small and larger groups. **SL.K.1**

• Make connections among texts

• Make connections to the world

Text to Text

Point out to children that all week they have been reading selections about ways to make communities better. Tell them that now they will connect the texts, or think about how the selections are alike and different. Model comparing *Roadwork* with another selection from the week.

 Think Aloud In *Roadwork*, I saw how the workers worked together to build the road. In "The Bundle of Sticks," I saw how the students worked together, once they learned their lesson from the teacher. In both stories, people got a job done by working together.

Guide children to compare the process of building a road in *Roadwork* with the process of making a garden in "A Community Garden." Then have them compare other selections from the week.

Text to Self

Have children discuss one way that they have made the community a better place. How did it make them feel?

Text to World

Talk about how every single person could do something to make his or her community a better place. *What would happen if no one did anything to make our community better? What would happen if* everyone *did at least one thing to make our community better?*

TALK ABOUT READING

OBJECTIVES

CCSS Confirm understanding of a text read aloud or information presented orally or through other media by asking and answering questions about key details and requesting clarification if something is not understood. **SL.K.2**

Becoming Readers

Talk with children about the genres, strategy, and skill they have learned about this week. Prompt them to discuss how this knowledge helps them to read and understand selections.

→ Remind children that one genre they learned about is informational text. *What features of* Roadwork *help you know that it is informational text?*

→ Talk with children about the strategy of asking and answering questions. *How did pausing to ask and answer questions while we read help you to understand the selections?*

→ Note that children learned to look for key details about the sequence of a selection. *How did noting the order of important events help you better understand what you were reading?*

RESEARCH AND INQUIRY

OBJECTIVES

CCSS Participate in shared research and writing projects (e.g., explore a number of books by a favorite author and express opinions about them). **W.K.7**

Wrap Up the Project

Guide partners to share their community plan and to point out details in their illustrations. Encourage children to use words and phrases they learned this week. Have children use the Presenting and Listening checklists online.

→ # Word Work

Quick Review

Build Fluency: Sound-Spellings: Show the following **Word-Building Cards:** *a, c, d, i, m, n, o, p, s, t.* Have children chorally say each sound. Repeat and vary the pace.

MINILESSON 5 Mins

Phonemic Awareness

Phoneme Segmentation

❶ **Model** Use the **Sound Boxes** and markers. *Listen to this word:* not. *Say the word with me:* not. *Say the sounds in* not *with me: /n/ /o/ /t/. There are three sounds in* not. *Let's place a marker in each box for each sound: /n/ /o/ /t/. Repeat for* cot.

❷ **Guided Practice/Practice** Distribute Sound Boxes and markers. Have children say each sound in the word as they place a marker in each box. Then have them say the word and tell the number of sounds in the word. Guide practice with the first word.

dot, /d/ /o/ /t/	top, /t/ /o/ /p/	on, /o/ /n/	cap, /k/ /a/ /p/
pin, /p/ /i/ /n/	Dan, /d/ /a/ /n/	can, /k/ /a/ /n/	test, /t/ /e/ /s/ /t/

MINILESSON 5 Mins

Phonics

Read Words with Short *i, o, n, c, d, p, t*

❶ **Guided Practice** Display **Word-Building Cards** *n, o, t.* Point to the letter *n. The letter* n *stands for /n/. Say /nnn/. The letter* o *stands for /o/. Say /ooo/. The letter* t *stands for /t/. Say /t/. Let's blend the sounds to make the word: /nnnooot/* not. *Now let's change the* n *to* d. Blend and read the word *dot* with children.

❷ **Practice** Write these words and sentences for children to read:

dip   tin   cot   pit   Don   top

We see Tom.   We like Dan and Tim.
Did you sit on the cot?   Can you nap on a cot?

Remove words from view before dictation.

♪ Review initial /d/d. Have children write the letter *d* on their **Response Boards**. Play and sing "Did You See a Dolphin?" Have children hold up and show the letter *d* on their boards when they hear initial /d/.

Dictation

Review Dictate the following sounds for children to spell. As you say each sound, have children repeat it and then write the letter on their **Response Boards** that stands for the sound.

/i/   /n/   /o/   /k/   /d/   /s/   /t/

Dictate the following words for children to spell. Model for children how to use sound boxes to segment each word to scaffold the spelling. *I will say a word. You will repeat the word, then think about how many sounds are in the word. Use your Sound Boxes to count the sounds. Then write one letter for each sound you hear.*

did   cot   nod   sit   pin   mop

Then write the letters and words for children to self-correct.

High-Frequency Words

and, do, go, to, you

① **Review** Display **Visual Vocabulary Card** *do*. Have children **Read/Spell/Write** the word. Then choose a Partner Talk activity. Repeat with *and, go, to, you*.

Distribute the following **High-Frequency Word Cards** to children: *and, do, go, to, you*. Tell children that you will say some sentences. *When you hear the word that is on your card, stand and hold up your word card.*

Don ***and*** I work on the road.
Do you see the bulldozer?
We will ***go*** across the street.
It's time ***to*** take a break.
Do you want ***to*** help plant flowers?
Let's ***go to*** the library first ***and*** then the playground.

② **Build Fluency: Word Automaticity** Display High-Frequency Word Cards *and, do, go, to* and *you*. Point to each card, at random, and have children read the word as quickly as they can.

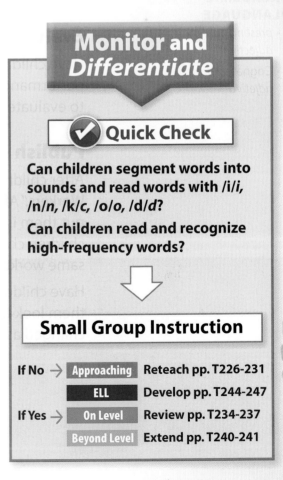

Monitor and *Differentiate*

✔ **Quick Check**

Can children segment words into sounds and read words with /i/*i*, /n/*n*, /k/*c*, /o/*o*, /d/*d*?

Can children read and recognize high-frequency words?

Small Group Instruction

If No →	**Approaching**	Reteach pp. T226-231
	ELL	Develop pp. T244-247
If Yes →	**On Level**	Review pp. T234-237
	Beyond Level	Extend pp. T240-241

Language Arts

MINILESSON
10 Mins
Independent Writing

Writing an Expository Sentence

Prepare

Tell children that they will present their finished sentences and drawings from Day 4 to the class. Hold up an example from Day 4 and read it aloud, tracking the print. *I showed my drawing when I read my sentence. I read my sentence clearly so everyone can understand me.*

Present

Have children take turns standing up and reading their sentences aloud. Remind children to show their drawings and to read their sentences clearly so everyone can understand them. Encourage the rest of the class to listen quietly and to wait until the presenter has finished before asking any questions.

Evaluate

Have children discuss their own presentations and evaluate their performances, using the presentation rubric. Use the teacher's rubric to evaluate children's writing.

Publish

After children have finished presenting, have a parade of "Community Workers." After the parade, collect their sentences with drawings and put them in a "Community Workers" binder. Discuss the workers that children chose and the different ways they chose to describe the same worker.

Have children add their writing to their Writer's Portfolio. Then have them look back at their previous writing and discuss how they have changed as writers throughout the year.

OBJECTIVES

 Speak audibly and express thoughts, feelings, and ideas clearly. **SL.K.6**

 Produce and expand complete sentences in shared language activities. **L.K.1f**

• Present sentences

• Recognize describing words (adjectives)

ACADEMIC LANGUAGE

• *present, publish, adjective*

• Cognates: *presente, adjetivo*

**Go
Digital**

Writing

I see a fish.

Grammar

MINILESSON
5 Mins

Grammar

Describing Words (Adjectives)

1 Review Remind children that an adjective is a describing word. Tell children to use their sense of smell, taste, sight, hearing, and touch to think of describing words.

Show the **Photo Card** for *rose.* Ask children to think of an adjective to describe how it looks (red), how it smells (sweet, flowery, fresh), and how it feels (soft, thorny, pointy).

Write this sentence: *A rose is soft.* Have children point to the describing word in the sentence. Then ask them to dictate other sentences, using describing words.

COLLABORATE

2 Review Practice Show the Photo Card for *zoo.* Have children work in pairs. Provide this sentence frame: *The zoo is _____ .* Have children name adjectives that describe a zoo. (smelly, big, exciting, fun, special) Complete the sentence as they dictate words. Have them point to the describing word in the sentence.

Show Photo Cards for *bear, camel, gorilla, penguin, tiger, turtle,* and *wolf.* Have children say a sentence to describe each of these zoo animals. Guide children to think of each of their senses to help them think of adjectives. Circulate to help children write their sentences, offering corrective feedback as needed.

Wrap Up the Week

- Review blending words with /i/*i*, /n/*n*, /k/*c*, /o/*o*, and /d/*d*.
- Remind children that adjectives are words that describe people and things.
- Use the **High-Frequency Word Cards** to review the Words to Know.
- Remind children that they can choose many different words to describe one thing.

→ Approaching Level

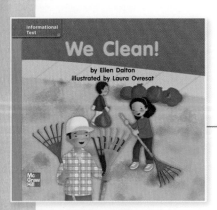

Leveled Reader

OBJECTIVES

(CCSS) With prompting and support, ask and answer questions about key details in a text. **RI.K.1**

(CCSS) With prompting and support, ask questions about unknown words in a text. **RI.K.4**

(CCSS) Read emergent-reader texts with purpose and understanding. **RF.K.4**

Leveled Reader:
We Clean!

Go Digital

Leveled Reader

Before Reading

Preview and Predict

Read the title and the names of the author and illustrator as children follow along by pointing to the words on their copy of the book. Discuss the illustration on the cover. Ask children to predict what the story might be about. Preview each page, identifying the rebus word and reinforcing the vocabulary.

Review Genre: Informational Text

Remind children that informational text gives readers information about a topic. Say: *This book gives information about how some neighbors help to make their community better.*

Model Concepts of Print

Model for children how to read from left to right and from top to bottom, including a return sweep. Use your finger to follow the text on the page as you read aloud.

Review High-Frequency Words

Point to the high-frequency word *you* on each page of the story.

Essential Question

Set a purpose for reading: *Let's find out how people can be good citizens and help to make their community better.*

During Reading

Guided Comprehension

As children whisper-read *We Clean!*, monitor and provide guidance by correcting blending and modeling the strategy and skill.

Strategy: Ask and Answer Questions

Remind children that as they read they can ask questions about things they don't understand, such as an unfamiliar word, and look for answers in the text and pictures.

Skill: Key Details

Explain to children that the selection is about people cleaning an empty lot. Tell children that things happen in order. Remind children to pay attention to key details in the text and illustrations.

Think Aloud I see that the events in this selection happen in order. First people pick up the trash. On page 3, the illustration and text are about people raking the ground. This is a key detail. On page 4, a woman brings bags of dirt. Then on page 5, a boy digs a hole in the ground. I will look for the order of events and key details as I read.

Guide children to talk about why each event must happen in order. Ask children to use the text and the illustrations to help guide their discussion about what the people are doing on each page.

After Reading

Respond to Reading

→ *What do the people need the bags for?* (to pick up litter)

→ *On page 5, the neighbors use shovels. What do they want to do when they dig the hole?* (plant a tree)

→ *How are these people being good citizens ?* (They cleaned up the trash and planted trees.)

Retell

Have children take turns retelling the story. Help them make a personal connection by asking: *How can you make your community better?*

Model Fluency

Read the story aloud, and have children point to each word you read. Then have them echo-read the sentence.

Apply Have children practice tracking each word by pointing to it as they say it aloud.

LITERACY ACTIVITIES

Have children complete the activities on the inside back cover of the reader.

Level Up

IF Children read *We Clean!* **Approaching Level** with fluency and correctly answer the Respond to Reading questions,

THEN Tell children that they will read another story about how people can help to make their community better.

• Have children page through *Can You Fix It?* **On Level** as you build background for what children know about fixing things around the neighborhood.

• Have children read the story, monitoring their comprehension and providing assistance as necessary.

Approaching Level
Phonological Awareness

RECOGNIZE RHYME

TIER 2

OBJECTIVES

CCSS Recognize and produce rhyming words. **RF.K.2a**

 I Do Remind children that rhyming words have the same ending sounds. Tell them that the words *day* and *away* rhyme in "I've Been Working on the Railroad." Repeat *day* and *away. The word may also rhymes with* day *and* away. *Say the words with me:* may, day, away. Have children tell you a new word that also rhymes. (Possible responses: play, stay, clay)

 We Do Say the words *morn* and *horn. Listen to some new words:* train, corn. *Which word does not rhyme with* morn *and* horn? (train)

 You Do *I'll say three words. Tell me which one does not rhyme:* blow, wind, snow. (wind) *Which words do rhyme?* (blow, snow) Repeat this routine with *page, book, look.*

PHONEME IDENTITY

TIER 2

OBJECTIVES

CCSS Isolate and pronounce the initial, medial vowel, and final sounds (phonemes) in three-phoneme words. **RF.K.2d**

 I Do Display the *Nose, Nail,* and *Night* **Photo Cards**. Say the picture names and have children repeat them with you. *What sound is the same in* nose, nail, *and* night? *Yes, the first sound,* /n/, *is the same.* Repeat with the *Deer, Dime,* and *Doctor* Photo Cards.

  We Do Show and name the following sets of Photo Cards. Have children repeat each name in a set with you. Guide them to say the sound that is the same in each set.

Ox Otter Olive	Camera Camel Comb	Nut Nine Night
Inch Insect Invitation	Dog Doll Dolphin	

You Do Show the sets of Photo Cards again. Have children name each picture in a set, then say the sound that is the same.

You may wish to review Phonological Awareness and Phonemic Awareness with **ELL** using this section.

PHONEME BLENDING

OBJECTIVES

 Isolate and pronounce the initial, medial vowel, and final sounds (phonemes) in three-phoneme words. **RF.K.2d**

 I Do *Listen as the puppet says the sounds in a word: /k/ /o/ /d/. Now the puppet will blend the sounds together to make a word: /koood/, cod. The puppet has blended the sounds /koood/ to make the word* cod. *Repeat with* nip, Don.

 You Do *The puppet is going to say the sounds in a word. Listen to the puppet, then blend the sounds to say the word.* Have the puppet say /d/ /o/ /k/. Have children repeat. *Now let's blend the sounds and say the word with the puppet: /d/ /o/ /k/, /doook/, dock. Repeat with* tin.

 We Do Have the puppet say the following sounds. Ask children to blend the sounds and say the words:

/m/ /a/ /d/   /d/ /a/ /n/   /m/ /o/ /p/   /d/ /i/ /p/

PHONEME SEGMENTATION

OBJECTIVES

 Isolate and pronounce the initial, medial vowel, and final sounds (phonemes) in three-phoneme words. **RF.K.2d**

I Do Use the **Sound Boxes** and markers. *Listen as I say a word:* nip. *Say the word with me:* nip. *There are three sounds in* nip: /n/ /i/ /p/. *I'll place a marker for each sound:* /n/ /i/ /p/. Point to the sounds in turn and have children say them with you. Repeat for *dot*.

 You Do Distribute Sound Boxes and markers. *Listen as I say a word:* pin. *Say the word with me:* pin. *Say the sounds with me:* /p/ /i/ /n/. *How many sounds?* (3) *Now place a marker for each sound.* Repeat for the word *pan*.

 We Do Say the word *dad*. Have children repeat the word, then say its sounds. Have them tell the number of sounds they say, then place a marker for each sound. Continue with the words *cot, fad, it, dock, on,* and *bad*.

ELL ENGLISH LANGUAGE LEARNERS

For the **ELLs** who need **phonics**, **decoding**, and **fluency** practice, use scaffolding methods as necessary to ensure students understand the meaning of the words. Refer to the Language Transfers Handbook for phonics elements that may not transfer in students' native languages.

→ # Approaching Level

Phonics

SOUND-SPELLING REVIEW

TIER 2

CCSS

OBJECTIVES

Demonstrate basic knowledge of one-to-one letter-sound correspondences by producing the most frequent sounds for each consonant. **RF.K.3a**

I Do Say the letter name and the sound it stands for. For example: Letter *i* /i/. Repeat for *c, o, n, d, t, p, s, a, m*.

We Do Display **Word-Building Cards** one at a time and together say the letter name and the sound that each letter stands for.

You Do Display Word-Building Cards one at a time and have children say the letter name and the sound that each letter stands for.

CONNECT SOUNDS TO SPELLINGS

TIER 2

CCSS

OBJECTIVES

Demonstrate basic knowledge of one-to-one letter-sound correspondences by producing the primary or many of the most frequent sounds for each consonant. **RF.K.3a**

I Do Display the *Camel* **Sound-Spelling Card.** *The letter* c *can stand for* /k/ *at the beginning of* camel. *What is this letter? What sound does it stand for?* Repeat for /o/o, /n/n, /i/i, and /d/d.

We Do *The word* cub *begins with* /k/. *Let's write* c *on our* **Response Boards.** Continue with the words *date, olive, neck*, and *itch*, guiding children to write the letter that stands for the initial sound in each word.

You Do Say the following words and have children write the letter for the initial sound in the word: *it, odd, desk, name, cape*.

RETEACH

CCSS

OBJECTIVES

Know and apply grade-level phonics and word analysis skills in decoding words. **RF.K.3**

I Do To review letter sounds, display **Reading/Writing Workshop**, p. 34. Point to each picture in rows 1 and 2 and say the picture name.

We Do Have children name each picture in rows 1 and 2. Repeat the name, emphasizing the initial sound. Repeat the names for *can* and *cap*, emphasizing the final sounds. Ask which word ends in /n/. (can)

You Do Guide children in reading rows 3 and 4, offering assistance as needed.

BLEND WORDS WITH /i/*i*, /n/*n*, /k/*c*, /o/*o*, /d/*d*

OBJECTIVES

(CCSS) Isolate and pronounce the initial, medial vowel, and final sounds (phonemes) in three-phoneme words. **RF.K.2d**

 I Do
Display **Word-Building Cards** *n, o,* and *t. This is the letter* n. *It stands for* /n/. *This is the letter* o. *It stands for* /o/. *This is the letter* t. *It stands for* /t/. *Listen as I blend all three sounds:* /nnnooot/, not. *The word is* not. Repeat for *dip.*

 You Do
Now let's blend more sounds to make words. Make the word *din. Let's blend* /d/ /i/ /n/: /diiinnn/, din. Have children blend to read the word. Repeat with the word *cod. Let's blend* /k/ /o/ /d/, /koood/, cod.

 We Do
Distribute sets of Word-Building Cards with *i, n, c, o, d.* Write: *nod, on, in.* Have children form the words and then blend and read the words.

REREAD FOR FLUENCY

OBJECTIVES

(CCSS) Read emergent-reader texts for purpose and understanding **RF.K.4**

 I Do
Turn to p. 36 of the **Reading/Writing Workshop** and read aloud the title. *Let's read the title together.* Page through the book. Ask children what they see in each picture. Ask children to find the high-frequency words *and, go,* and *to* on p. 37.

 You Do
Then have children open their books and chorally read the story. Have children point to each word as they read. Provide corrective feedback as needed. After reading, ask children to recall what the children do on the beach.

 We Do
Have children reread "I Can, You Can!" with a partner for fluency.

BUILD FLUENCY WITH PHONICS

Sound/Spelling Fluency

Display the following Word-Building Cards: *i, n, c, o,* and *d.* Have children chorally say each sound. Repeat and vary the pace.

Fluency in Connected Text

Write the following sentences. *Do you see the pin on the cap? The cat did not sit on the cot. The man can dip the mop in the pan.* Have children read the sentences and identify the words with /i/, /n/, /k/, /o/, and /d/.

→ Approaching Level

High-Frequency Words

RETEACH WORDS

OBJECTIVES

CCSS Read common high-frequency words by sight. **RF.K.3c**

 I Do Display **High-Frequency Word Cards** *to, and, go, you,* and *do* and use the **Read/Spell/Write** routine to reteach the high-frequency words.

 We Do Have children turn to p. 35 of **Reading/Writing Workshop** and read aloud the words in rows 1 and 2 with them. Then read aloud the sentences in rows 3 and 4. Reread the sentences with children. One at a time hold up the High-Frequency Word Cards for *to, and, go, you,* and *do*. Have children say the word on the card. Ask them whether the word is in the sentence. If they say yes, have them touch and say the word in the sentence. Use the same routine for the other sentence on the page.

 You Do Write the sentence frame *Do you like to go to the ____?* Have children copy the sentence frame on their **Response Boards**. Then have partners work together to read and orally complete the frame by asking each other to name places they like to go.

CUMULATIVE REVIEW

OBJECTIVES

CCSS Read common high-frequency words by sight. **RF.K.3c**

 I Do Display the **High-Frequency Word Cards** *I, can, the, we, see, a, like, to, and, go, you, do*. Use the **Read/Spell/Write** routine to review words. Use the High-Frequency Word Cards to create sentences such as *Don and I like to go to the top! Do you see the man tap and dip?*

 We Do Use the **Read/Spell/Write** routine with children to review words. Invite a volunteer to write the word on the board. Offer help as needed. Then guide children to create a sentence as a class using the High-Frequency Word Cards.

 You Do Have children create sentences with a partner. Remind them to refer to the High-Frequency Word Cards as needed. Then have them write the words on their **Response Boards**.

Oral Vocabulary

REVIEW WORDS

OBJECTIVES

CCSS Identify real-life connections between words and their use. **L.K.5c**

Develop oral vocabulary: *community, improve, harvest, quarrel, confused*

 I Do Use the **Define/Example/Ask** routine to review words. Use the following definitions and provide examples:

community A **community** is a group of people who works, plays, or lives together.

improve When you **improve** something, you make it better.

harvest During a **harvest**, farmers pick the food plants they have grown.

quarrel When people **quarrel**, they argue or disagree with each other.

confused To be **confused** is to be mixed up.

 You Do Ask questions to build understanding. *How would you describe your community? What could you do to improve a dry garden? Why is it important for people to work together during a harvest? Why should people not quarrel loudly? Why might you be confused when you learn something new?*

 We Do Have children complete these sentence frames: *One of the good things about our community is ___. I could improve my reading by ___. If I could help with a harvest, I would like to ___. I don't like to hear people quarrel because ___. When I am confused, I usually ___.*

Comprehension

SELF-SELECTED READING

OBJECTIVES

CCSS With prompting and support, ask and answer questions about key details in a text. **RL.K.1**

Apply the strategy and skill to reread the text.

Read Independently

Help children select an informational story with illustrations for sustained silent reading. Provide stories with a clear beginning, middle, and end. Tell children that good readers know the order of events in a story. Remind them to ask and answer questions as they read to figure out what happens first, next, and last.

Read Purposefully

Before reading, help children draw three boxes in a row on a piece of paper. Explain that they should draw a picture in the first box to tell what happens first in the story. Continue with *next* and *last* in the other two boxes. After reading, guide children in a discussion about the order of story events. Ask: *What happened first in the story? What happened next in the story? What happened last in the story?*

→ On Level

Leveled Reader

OBJECTIVES

CCSS With prompting and support, ask and answer questions about key details in a text. **RI.K.1**

CCSS With prompting and support, ask and answer questions about unknown words in a text. **RI.K.4**

CCSS Read emergent-reader texts with purpose and understanding. **RF.K.4**

Leveled Reader:
Can You Fix It?

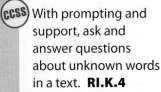
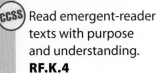
Leveled Reader

Before Reading

Preview and Predict

Read aloud the title and the names of the author and illustrator as children point to the words on their copies of the book. Have children talk about what they see on the cover. Ask them to predict what things the character might fix in the story. Preview each page and help children confirm or change their predictions.

Review Genre: Informational Text

Remind children that informational text gives readers information about a topic. Say: *This book gives information about how someone can fix things.*

Model Concepts of Print

Point out to children that each sentence in the book begins with a capital letter. Ask children to point to the first word in each sentence in the book.

Review High-Frequency Words

Point out the word *you* on page 2. Ask children to identify the word on each page.

Essential Question

Set a purpose for reading: *Let's read the book to find out how somebody can help by fixing things in the community.*

During Reading

Guided Comprehension

As children whisper-read *Can You Fix It?*, provide feedback with any difficult words. Monitor and provide guidance by correcting blending and modeling the strategy and skill.

Strategy: Ask and Answer Questions

Remind children that as they read they can ask questions about unfamiliar words and look for answers in the text and pictures.

Skill: Key Details

Remind children that they should look for key details in the text and pictures to help them understand the story. Explain that key details in a selection often show how the events happened in a certain order.

Think Aloud I use the key details in the selection to help me understand what the woman fixes. First she fixes the car. Then she fixes the sink. Next she fixes the swing in the park.

Guide children to discuss the order of the events. Look at the pictures and text with them and point out key details.

After Reading

Respond to Reading

→ *What kinds of things did the woman fix around her home and neighborhood?* (car, sink, swing, bike, door, roof, pool)

→ *What did the woman fix first?* (a car)

→ *What is the last thing the woman fixes?* (the pool)

→ *How is the woman being a good citizen?* (Possible answer: She is helping to fix things in the community.)

Retell

Have children take turns retelling the story in the correct sequence. Help them make personal connections by asking: *What are some ways you could help your neighbors and make your community better?*

Model Fluency

After you read the first few pages, ask a volunteer to read a page or two with no assistance. Encourage children to follow along in the book as the volunteer reads aloud.

Apply Have children practice reading with partners. Encourage them to read with expression in their voices.

LITERACY ACTIVITIES

Have children complete the activities on the inside back cover of the reader.

Level Up

IF Children read *Can You Fix It?* On Level with fluency and correctly answer the Respond to Reading questions,

THEN Tell children that they will read another story about how people can help to make their community better.

• Have children page through *Helping Mom* Beyond Level as you talk about what a vet does to help animals in a neighborhood.

• Have children read the story, monitoring their comprehension and providing assistance as necessary.

On Level

Phonemic Awareness

PHONEME IDENTITY

OBJECTIVES

 Isolate and pronounce the initial, medial vowel, and final sounds (phonemes) in three-phoneme words. **RF.K.2d**

 Display the *Cube, Cook,* and *Comb* **Photo Cards.** Say the picture names and have children repeat them. Ask children to say the sound that is the same in *cube, cook,* and *comb.* Repeat with the *Nest, Nail, Nine* Photo Cards.

 Show and name the following sets of Photo Cards. Have children repeat each name. Guide them to identify the sound that is the same: *Ox, Otter, Olive; Camera, Car, Comb; Nut, Nurse, Night; Inch, Insect, Ink; Deer, Doll, Dime.*

 Show the sets of Photo Cards again. Have children name each picture in the set then say the sound that is the same.

PHONEME BLENDING

OBJECTIVES

 Isolate and pronounce the initial, medial vowel, and final sounds (phonemes) in three-phoneme words. **RF.K.2d**

 Listen as the puppet says the sounds in a word: /d/ /a/ /d/. The puppet will blend the sounds together to make a word: /daaad/, dad. Say the word: dad.

 Listen to the puppet say sounds in words. Have the puppet say /k/ /a/ /p/. Have children repeat. *Now let's blend the sounds and say the word with the puppet: /k/ /a/ /p/, /kaaap/, cap.* Repeat with *pot, tin.*

 Have the puppet say these sounds. Ask children to blend the sounds and say the words: /d/ /o/ /t/; /t/ /a/ /n/; /k/ /o/ /t/; /n/ /a/ /p/; /d/ /i/ /d/.

PHONEME SEGMENTATION

OBJECTIVES

 Isolate and pronounce the initial, medial vowel, and final sounds (phonemes) in three-phoneme words. **RF.K.2d**

 Use the **Sound Boxes** and markers. *Listen to this word: not. There are three sounds in not: /n/ /o/ /t/. I'll place a marker for each sound: /n/ /o/ /t/.*

 Say the word *dim. Say the sounds with me: /d/ /i/ /m/. How many sounds?* (3) *Place a marker for each sound.* Repeat for *dot* and *cat.*

 Say the word *tin.* Have children repeat the word and say the sounds. Have them place a marker in a box for each sound. Repeat with *on, nip, man.*

Phonics

REVIEW PHONICS

OBJECTIVES

 Demonstrate basic knowledge of one-to-one letter-sound correspondences by producing the primary or many of the most frequent sounds for each consonant. **RF.K.3a**

 I Do To review letter sounds, display **Reading/Writing Workshop**, p. 34. Point to each picture in rows 1 and 2 and say the picture names.

 We Do Have children say the name of each picture. Ask them to identify which picture names begin with /i/, /n/, /k/, /d/, or /o/ and which words end with /n/ and /p/.

You Do Have children read each word in rows 3 and 4. Repeat to practice fluency.

PICTURE SORT /i/*i*, /o/*o*

OBJECTIVES

CCSS Isolate and pronounce the initial, medial vowel, and final sounds (phonemes) in three-phoneme words. **RF.K.2d**

 I Do Display **Word-Building Cards** *i* and *o* in a pocket chart. Then show the *Mop* **Photo Card**. Say /m/ /o/ /p/, mop. *The sound in the middle is /o/. The letter o stands for /o/. I will put the* Mop *Photo Card under the letter* o. Show the *Mix* Photo Card. Say /m/ /i/ /ks/, mix. *The sound in the middle is /i/. The letter i stands for /i/. I will put the* Mix *Photo Card under the* i.

 We Do Show the *Box* Photo Card and say *box,* /b/ /o/ /ks/. Have children repeat, then tell the sound they hear in the middle. Ask them where to place the Photo Card.

 You Do Continue the activity using the *Pig, Top, Fish, Rock,* and *Chin* Photo Cards. Have children say the picture name and the sounds, then place the card under the *i* or *o*.

→ ## On Level

Phonics

BLEND WORDS WITH /i/i, /n/n, /k/c, /o/o, /d/d

OBJECTIVES

 CCSS Isolate and pronounce the initial, medial vowel, and final sounds (phonemes) in three-phoneme words. **RF.K.2d**

 I Do Use **Word-Building Cards** or write *d, o, t*. *This is the letter* d. *It stands for /d/. Say it with me: /d/. This is the letter* o. *It stands for /o/. Say it with me: /ooo/. This is the letter* t. *It stands for /t/. Say it with me: /t/. I'll blend the sounds together to read the word: /dooot/, dot.*

 We Do Write *in* and *mop*. Guide children to blend the words sound by sound to read each word.

 You Do Write the following words and have children blend the words sound by sound to read each word.

cop   did   dip   pop   nip

REREAD FOR FLUENCY

OBJECTIVES

CCSS Read emergent-reader texts with purpose and understanding. **RF.K.4**

 I Do Point to the title "I Can, You Can!" on p. 36 of **Reading/Writing Workshop** and tell children that this is a statement that shows excitement. *When we read a sentence that ends with an exclamation point, our voice shows excitement.* Read the title and have them repeat with the same expression. Work with children to read for accuracy and expression. Model reading a page: *When I read, "I can pat, pat, pat on top," I read all the way to the end of the sentence before pausing. This makes my reading sound smooth and natural, as if I were talking.*

We Do Reread p. 39. Then have children chorally read the page with you. Point to the question mark and explain that when we read a question, our voice goes up at the end. Continue with the remainder of the pages.

 You Do Have children reread "I Can, You Can!" Provide time to listen as children read the pages. Comment on their accuracy and expression and provide corrective feedback by modeling proper fluency.

High-Frequency Words

REVIEW WORDS

OBJECTIVES

Read common high-frequency words by sight. **RF.K.3c**

 I Do Use the **High-Frequency Word Cards** to review the words *to, and, go, you,* and *do* using the **Read/Spell/Write** routine.

 We Do Have children turn to p. 35 of **Reading/Writing Workshop**. Read the sentence in row 3 and have children point to the words *do, you to, go*. Repeat with row 4 with the word *and*.

 You Do Have children read the words in rows 1 and 2. Say the word *you*. Have children close their eyes, picture the word, and write it as they see it. Have children self-correct. Repeat with *to, and, go, do*.

Fluency Point to the **High-Frequency Word Cards** *you, I, can, see, go, and, to, we, like, the, a,* and *do* in random order. Have children chorally read. Repeat at a faster pace.

Comprehension

SELF-SELECTED READING

OBJECTIVES

With prompting and support, ask and answer questions about key details in a text. **RL.K.1**

Apply the strategy and skill to reread the text.

Read Independently

Have children select an informational story with illustrations for sustained silent reading. Provide stories that have a clear beginning, middle, and end. Tell children to identify details that happen first, next, and last in the story to help them better understand it. Remind them to ask and answer questions as they read.

Read Purposefully

Before reading, ask children to draw three boxes in a row. Model how to write *first, next,* and *last* above each box. Then have children write a few words or draw a picture in each box to tell about what happens at the beginning, the middle, and the end of the story. Ask children to share their summaries with the class.

→ # Beyond Level

Leveled Reader

OBJECTIVES

(CCSS) With prompting and support, ask and answer questions about key details in a text. **RL.K.1**

(CCSS) With prompting and support, retell familiar stories, including key details. **RL.K.2**

(CCSS) Ask and answer questions about unknown words in a text. **RL.K.4**

(CCSS) With prompting and support, name the author and illustrator of a story and define the role of each in telling the story. **RL.K.6**

Leveled Reader:
Helping Mom

by Terry Miller Shannon
illustrated by Susan Reagan

Before Reading

Preview and Predict

Read aloud the title. Have children point to the name of the author on the cover of their books. Read it aloud as children point to each word. Ask children to tell what an author does. Repeat the routine with the illustrator's name. Have children preview the illustrations. Then ask: *What do you think the book will be about?*

Review Genre: Fiction

Tell children that like the informational texts they have been reading this week, some fiction stories also give information. Explain that in this story, one of the characters is a vet, a doctor who helps animals.

Essential Question

Remind children of the Essential Question: *How can people help to make your community better?* Have children set a purpose for reading by saying: *Let's read to see how a special place for sick animals can help to make a neighborhood better.*

During Reading

Guided Comprehension

Have children whisper-read *Helping Mom*. Remind them to use picture clues if they are unfamiliar with some of the words they are reading. Monitor and provide guidance by correcting blending and modeling the strategy and skill.

Strategy: Ask and Answer Questions

Remind children that asking questions as they read helps them focus on the story and helps them understand what's happening. They can also ask questions about unfamiliar words and look for answers in the text and pictures.

Go Digital

Leveled Reader

Skill: Key Details

Remind children that they should look for key details in the text and pictures to help them understand the story. Explain that key details in a story often show how the events happened in a certain order.

Think Aloud I use the key details in the story to help me understand what is happening in the story. On page 2, I find out that the girl is going to work with her mother. The illustration shows me that the girl is happy about this. The key details on page 3 tell me that the girl's mother is a vet. On page 4, I learn that the girl helps to take care of the animals by walking the dogs. I will keep reading to see what she does next.

Guide children to discuss the order of the events. Look at the pictures and text with them and point out key details.

After Reading

Respond to Reading

→ *The title of the story is called* Helping Mom. *How does the girl in the book help her mother?* (She helps out at an animal shelter where her mom is a vet.)

→ *What does the girl do after she gives the animals food and water?* (She cleans their cages.)

→ *Why does the girl think the animal shelter is a good place for her?* (Possible answers: she likes helping animals; it makes her feel good to see animals get better)

Retell

Have children take turns retelling the story. Help them make a personal connection by asking: *Have you ever been to an animal shelter or a vet's office? How did the animal shelter help make your community better?*

Gifted and Talented

EVALUATING Ask children to choose one animal that might be at an animal shelter. Have them think about and describe what the animal shelter might do to help the animal.

HAVE children draw a picture of their animal being helped at the animal shelter. Ask them to include a word or phrase that describes what the animal shelter does.

LITERACY ACTIVITIES

Have children complete the activities on the inside back cover of the reader.

→ Beyond Level

Phonics

OBJECTIVES

 Demonstrate basic knowledge of one-to-one letter-sound correspondences by producing the primary or many of the most frequent sounds for each consonant. **RF.K.3a**

 I Do To review letter sounds, display **Reading/Writing Workshop**, p. 34. Point to each picture in rows 1 and 2 and say the picture name.

 We Do Have children say the name of each picture in rows 1 and 2. Then point to and name the *nut* picture. Ask children to say the beginning sound, /n/, then share other words they know that begin with the same sound. Repeat for *can* and *door*.

 You Do Have partners read each word in rows 3 and 4. Ask them to write the words on their **Response Boards**, underlining the letter in each word that stands for /o/.

Fluency Have children reread the story "I Can, You Can!" for fluency.

Innovate Have children create a new page for "I Can, You Can!" using the sentence frame *Can you see the ____?* to name something else that the children might see at the beach.

High-Frequency Words

OBJECTIVES

 Read emergent-reader texts with purpose and understanding. **RF.K.4**

 I Do Create **High-Frequency Word Cards** for *give* and *find*. Introduce the words using the **Read/Spell/Write** routine.

 We Do Display the High-Frequency Word Cards for *to, and, the, I, can, a,* and *do.* Have children help you complete the following sentence frames using the High-Frequency Word Cards: *Do not give the cap to the ____. Dad and I can find the ____.*

 You Do Have partners write sentences using the High-Frequency Words *give* and *find* on their **Response Boards**. Have them read their sentences.

Vocabulary

ORAL VOCABULARY: SYNONYMS

OBJECTIVES

 With guidance and support from adults, explore word relationships and nuances in word meanings. **L.K.5**

Develop oral vocabulary: Synonyms

 I Do Review the meanings of the oral vocabulary words *community* and *quarrel*. Explain that a synonym is a word that means almost the same thing as another word. *A synonym for* community *is* neighborhood. *A neighborhood is a place where people live*. I play with friends from my neighborhood. *A synonym for* quarrel *is* argue. *To argue is to disagree when talking*. I heard the gardeners argue about which flower to plant.

 We Do Work with children to think of sentences using the new words *neighborhood* and *argue*.

 You Do Have partners work together to create sentences. Children should include *argue* and *neighborhood* in their sentences. Ask them to share them.

Gifted and Talented **Extend** *Antonyms are words that have opposite meanings*. Argue *and* agree *are antonyms*. Challenge partners to say more antonyms for *argue*. Ask them to use some of the words in a short skit about neighbors working together.

Comprehension

SELF-SELECTED READING

OBJECTIVES

 With prompting and support, ask and answer questions about key details in a text. **RL.K.1**

Apply the strategy and skill to reread the text.

Read Independently

Have children select an informational story with illustrations for sustained silent reading. Remind them that asking and answering questions before, during, and after reading can help them understand the order of events.

Read Purposefully

Before reading, ask children to draw four boxes in a row. As they read, have them ask and answer questions and write the events in order in the boxes. After reading, ask children to share the text in their boxes with the class.

 Independent Study Have children think about something they read this week about how people make their communities better. Challenge them to write a few sentences stating their opinion about it.

English Language Learners

Leveled Reader

 OBJECTIVES

 With prompting and support, ask and answer questions about key details in a text. **RI.K.1**

With prompting and support, ask and answer questions about unknown words in a text. **RI.K.4**

Read emergent-reader texts with purpose and understanding. **RF.K.4**

Shared Read:
Can You Fix It?

 **Go Digital**

Leveled Reader

Before Reading

Preview and Predict

Make sure children understand the English term "fix it." Tear a piece of paper. Ask: *Can I fix it?* Demonstrate taping the torn piece of paper as you say: *I can fix it.* Show children the cover of the book. Point to the title and then read it aloud as you point to each word. Read it again, asking children to read it with you, while they point to each word. Discuss the cover illustration. Ask: *What can the woman fix?* Encourage children to respond in full sentences, "The woman can fix ___." Walk children through the book, identifying the rebus pictures and having children tell what the woman can fix, using complete sentences. Prompt by asking: *What is the woman fixing on this page?*

Essential Question

Set a purpose for reading: *How can people help their neighbors? How can they help their community? Let's find out how this woman helps to make her community better.* Encourage children to ask questions or ask for help to clarify what they do not understand.

During Reading

Interactive Question Response

Pages 2–3 Point to the illustration on page 2. *The woman is working. What can she fix? Let's read the text to find out.* Read the text aloud with children. Point to the illustration on page 3. *Look at the picture. What is the woman fixing here?* (sink) *Point to the sink. Now point to the label that says* sink.

Pages 4–5 Point to the illustration and label on page 4. *The label on this picture says* swing. *Say the word with me:* swing. *What is the woman doing to the swing?* (fixing it) *Show me how you point to the bike on page 5. Now point to the label that says* bike. *Read this page with me.*

Pages 6–7 Point to the illustration and label on page 6. Ask: *What kind of door is this?* (a door for a dog) *What is the woman doing to the door?* (fixing it) *What do the words on the page say?* (You can fix the door.) Point to the illustration on page 7 and the label pointing to the roof. Ask: *What does this label point to?* (roof) *Where can you find a roof?* (on top of a building) *Let's read this text together.*

Page 8 Point to the illustration. *This is a pool. How does the woman fix the pool?* (She covers the hole.) *Why does she fix the pool?* (so the children can play in it)

After Reading

Respond to Reading

Encourage children to answer in full sentences to practice their English. Ask:

→ *What things does the woman fix around her neighborhood? Point to each thing she fixes as you say it.* (The woman can fix the car/sink/swing/bike/door/roof/pool.)

→ *Who does the woman help when she fixes things?* (She helps friends and people in her neighborhood.)

→ *What is the woman doing on page 8?* (She is fixing the pool.) *What are the other people in the picture doing?* (The kids are waiting to swim; some adults are cooking food)

Retell

Let's retell the book together. What is the woman doing? (The woman is fixing things in her neighborhood.) *Let's retell all the things that the woman fixes in her community.*

Model Fluency

As you read each sentence aloud, track the print and have children repeat each word after you. Stop occasionally to point to a rebus or to discuss a picture.

Apply Ask small groups of children to read together. Encourage children to use the pictures to help them figure out what the text says.

LITERACY ACTIVITIES

Have children complete the activities on the inside back cover of the reader.

Level Up

Level-up lessons available online.

IF Children read *Can You Fix It?* **ELL Level** with fluency and correctly answer the Respond to Reading questions,

THEN Tell children that they will read a more detailed version of the story.

• Have children page through *Can You Fix It?* **On Level** and discuss how people can help make their community better.

• Have children read the story, monitoring their comprehension and providing assistance as necessary.

→ English Language Learners
Vocabulary

OBJECTIVES

 CCSS Speak audibly and express thoughts, feelings, and ideas clearly. **SL.K.6**

LANGUAGE OBJECTIVE

Preview vocabulary

 I Do Display the images from the **Visual Vocabulary Cards** and follow the routine to preteach the oral vocabulary words.

 We Do Display each image again and explain how it illustrates or demonstrates the word. Model using sentences to describe the image.

 You Do Display the word *improve* again. Have children talk to a partner about skills they can improve. Provide a sentence frame for them to use: *We can improve _____.*

Beginning	Intermediate	Advanced/High
Prompt children to talk about things in their community they would like to improve.	Have partners talk about ways they might improve their grades.	Ask children a question that uses one of the words and have them answer the question in a complete sentence.

OBJECTIVES

 CCSS Speak audibly and express thoughts, feelings, and ideas clearly. **SL.K.6**

LANGUAGE OBJECTIVE

Preview ELL vocabulary

 I Do Display images from the **Visual Vocabulary Cards** one at a time to preteach the ELL vocabulary words *repair* and *mechanical* and follow the routine. Say each word and have children repeat it. Define the word in English.

 We Do Display each image again and incorporate the words in a short discussion about the image. Model using sentences to describe the image.

 You Do Display the word *repair* and have children say the word. Provide a sentence frame and ask partners to come up with oral sentences: *I can repair _____.*

Beginning	Intermediate	Advanced/High
Have children draw a picture of something that is broken. Prompt them to discuss how to repair it.	Have partners talk about a time they repaired something.	Ask children to use each of the words in an oral sentence of their own.

High-Frequency Words

REVIEW WORDS

OBJECTIVES

CCSS Read common high-frequency words by sight (e.g., *the, of, to, you, she, my, is, are, do, does*). **RF.K.3c**

LANGUAGE OBJECTIVE

Review high-frequency words

 I Do Display the **High-Frequency Word Cards** for the words for the last five weeks: *to, and, go, you,* and *do.* Read the words. Use the **Read/Spell/Write** routine to teach the words. Have children write the words on their **Response Boards**.

 We Do Ask children to think of a sentence for each of the words. Write these on the board and read them with children. Have them underline the high-frequency words in each sentence.

 You Do Display the High-Frequency Word Cards from the previous five weeks. Display one card at a time as children chorally read them. Mix and repeat. Note words children need to review.

Beginning	Intermediate	Advanced/High
Provide extra practice in reading the words on the cards.	Ask children to locate the words in a reading selection or on another written page.	Ask children to choose three of the five words and use them in oral sentences.

REVIEW CATEGORY WORDS

OBJECTIVES

CCSS Identify real-life connections between words and their use (e.g., note places at school that are colorful). **L.K.5c**

LANGUAGE OBJECTIVE

Use category words

 I Do Write and say words such as *on, off, under, next to,* and *in back of* as children repeat the words. Define each word in English and then in Spanish, if appropriate, identifying any cognates.

 We Do Place a pencil on, under, next to, etc., a book. Work with children to tell where the pencil is.

 You Do Ask partners to choose an object in the room and use position words to tell where it is.

Beginning	Intermediate	Advanced/High
Demonstrate each position word visually as children repeat it chorally after you.	Ask children to use one of the category words or phrases in a complete sentence.	Challenge children to use at least two category words to describe where they are sitting in the room.

→ English Language Learners
Writing

SHARED WRITING

OBJECTIVES

 Use a combination of drawing, dictating, and writing to narrate a single event or several loosely linked events, tell about the events in the order in which they occurred, and provide a reaction to what happened. **W.K.3**

LANGUAGE OBJECTIVE

Contribute to a shared writing project

 I Do Review the words *vet, librarian, crossing guard,* and *gardener* from the Whole Group Shared Writing project as possible ideas. Review the jobs that each person does, such as help sick animals or find books. Model writing a sentence: *A gardener helps plants.*

 We Do Have children help you write a shared sentence about one of the jobs a person does, for example: *A crossing guard helps children.*

 You Do Have pairs of children use the following sentence frame to explain how a worker helps people in the community: *A _____ helps _____.* Then have children write their own sentence.

Beginning	Intermediate	Advanced/High
Reinforce with children what people do in each job. Use picture support whenever possible.	Ask children to work independently to complete the sentence frame.	Challenge children to write more than one sentence about a job.

WRITING TRAIT: WORD CHOICE

OBJECTIVES

 With guidance and support from adults, respond to questions and suggestions from peers and add details to strengthen writing as needed. **W.K.5**

LANGUAGE OBJECTIVE

Choose the best words when writing

I Do Explain to children that writers think about the best words to use when they write. They think about words that describe people, places, and things. They also think about good words to describe actions.

 We Do Point to the **Big Book** *Roadwork*. Remind children that the story tells how workers make roads. Point to pictures in the selection. Ask: *What does this worker do?* Help children choose the best words to describe what they see.

 You Do Have children write a sentence to show what the road workers do in the selection. Provide them with the sentence frame *The road workers _____.*

Beginning	Intermediate	Advanced/High
Help children complete the sentence frame using the illustrations to talk about what road workers do.	Have partners talk about what road workers do.	Have children complete the sentence frame in at least three different ways based on the pictures in the selection.

Grammar

DESCRIBING WORDS (ADJECTIVES)

OBJECTIVES

 Identify real-life connections between words and their use (e.g., note places at school that are colorful). **L.K.5c**

LANGUAGE OBJECTIVE

Recognize and use adjectives correctly

Language Transfers Handbook

Spanish speakers often show comparative and superlative forms by using separate words, such as *more old* instead of *older*. Guide children to use *-er* and *-est* endings when needed.

 I Do Review that an adjective is a describing word that tells about people, places, or things. Adjectives can describe things in many ways, including by their color, shape, size, feel, or taste. Say the following sentence: *The workers are tired.* Say the sentence again and have children repeat it. Say: Tired *is an adjective. It describes the word* workers.

 We Do Say the following sentences. Guide children to tell the describing word (adjective) in each.

This is a great *community.*

We are hard *workers.*

We fixed the bumpy *road.*

You Do Use the following sentence frame:

The workers are _____.

Pair children and have them orally complete the sentence frame by providing descriptive words from this week's readings. Circulate, listen in, and take note of each child's language use and proficiency.

Beginning	Intermediate	Advanced/High
Have children draw a picture of a worker. Prompt them to describe the worker they drew.	Remind children that an adjective describes a person, place, or thing. Ask: *How can you describe these workers?*	Ask children to complete the sentence frame with little or no help and then read the sentence aloud.

PROGRESS MONITORING

Weekly Assessment

Use your Quick Check observations and the assessment opportunities identified below to evaluate children's progress in key skill areas.

✔ TESTED SKILLS CCSS	Quick Check Observations	Pencil and Paper Assessment
PHONICS Review **RF.K.3a, RF.K.3b** **k**	Can children match the letters to sounds: /i/ i, /n/ n, /k/ c, /o/ o, /d/ d?	Practice Book, p. 117
HIGH-FREQUENCY WORDS to, and, go, you, do **RF.K.3c** **go**	Can children recognize and read the high-frequency words?	Practice Book, pp. 121–122
COMPREHENSION Key Details **RI.K.1**	As you read *Roadwork* with children, can they identify key details and discuss the sequence in which they occur?	Practice Book, p. 118

Quick Check Rubric

Skills	1	2	3
PHONICS	Does not connect the sounds /i/, /n/, /k/, /o/, /d/ with the letters *Ii, Nn, Cc, Oo, Dd*.	Usually connects the sounds /i/, /n/, /k/, /o/, /d/ with the letters *Ii, Nn, Cc, Oo, Dd*.	Consistently connects the sounds /i/, /n/, /k/, /o/, /d/ with the letters *Ii, Nn, Cc, Oo, Dd*.
HIGH-FREQUENCY WORDS	Does not identify the high-frequency words.	Usually recognizes the high-frequency words with accuracy, but not speed.	Consistently recognizes the high-frequency words with speed and accuracy.
COMPREHENSION	Does not identify key details and their sequence in the text.	Usually identifies key details and their sequence in the text.	Consistently identifies key details and their sequence in the text.

Go Digital! www.connected.mcgraw-hill.com

Using Assessment Results

TESTED SKILLS	If ...	Then ...
PHONICS	**Quick Check Rubric:** Children consistently score 1 or **Pencil and Paper Assessment:** Children get 0–2 items correct	... reteach tested Phonics skills using Lessons 14, 16–18 and 20 in the ***Tier 2 Phonics/Word Study Intervention Online PDFs.***
HIGH-FREQUENCY WORDS	**Quick Check Rubric:** Children consistently score 1	... reteach tested skills by using the High-Frequency Word Cards and asking children to read and spell the word. Point out any irregularities in sound-spellings.
COMPREHENSION	**Quick Check Rubric:** Children consistently score 1 or **Pencil and Paper Assessment:** Children get 0–1 items correct	... reteach tested skill using Lessons 10–12 in the ***Tier 2 Comprehension Intervention Online PDFs.***

Response to Intervention

Use the children's assessment results to assist you in identifying children who will benefit from focused intervention.

Use the appropriate sections of the ***Placement and Diagnostic Assessment*** to designate children requiring:

 Tier 2 Intervention Online PDFs

 WonderWorks Intervention Program

→ Phonemic Awareness

→ Phonics

→ Vocabulary

→ Comprehension

→ Fluency

SUMMATIVE ASSESSMENT

Unit Assessment

CCSS TESTED SKILLS

✔ COMPREHENSION:	✔ HIGH-FREQUENCY WORDS:	✔ PHONEMIC AWARENESS:	✔ PHONICS:	✔ CATEGORY WORDS:
• Key Details **RI.K.7** • Character, Setting, Events **RL.K.3** • Key Details **RL.K.1**	• *you, do, to, and, go* **RF.K.3c**	• Phoneme Isolation **RF.K.2d** • Phoneme Blending **RF.K.2d** • Phoneme Categorization **RF.K.2d** • Phoneme Segmentation **RF.K.2d**	• o (initial/medial) **RF.K.3b** • d (initial/final) **RF.K.3a**	• Jobs **L.K.5a** • Position **L.K.1e**

Use Multiple Assessments for Instructional Planning

To create instructional profiles for your children, look for patterns in the results from the following assessment.

Running Records

Use the instructional reading level determined by the Running Record calculations for regrouping decisions.

Using Assessment Results

TESTED SKILLS	If ...	Then ...
COMPREHENSION	Children answer 0–3 items correctly ...	... reteach tested skills using the *Tier 2 Comprehension Intervention Online PDFs*
HIGH-FREQUENCY WORDS	Children answer 0–1 items correctly ...	... reteach tested skills using Section 3 of the *Tier 2 Fluency Intervention Online PDFs*
PHONEMIC AWARENESS	Children answer 0–3 items correctly ...	... reteach tested skills using the *Tier 2 Phonemic Awareness Intervention Online PDFs*
PHONICS	Children answer 0–3 items correctly ...	... reteach tested skills using the *Tier 2 Phonics/Word Study Intervention Online PDFs* and Section 2 and 4 of the *Tier 2 Fluency Intervention Online PDFs*
CATEGORY WORDS	Children answer 0–1 items correctly ...	... reteach tested skills using the *Tier 2 Vocabulary Intervention Online PDFs*

Response to Intervention

Use the appropriate sections of the *Placement and Diagnostic Assessment* and children's assessment results to designate children requiring:

 Tier 2 Intervention Online PDFs

 WonderWorks Intervention Program

→ Phonological and Phonemic Awareness

→ Phonics

→ Vocabulary

→ Comprehension

→ Fluency

Using Assessment Results

TESTED SKILLS	If ...	Then ...
COMPREHENSION	Children answer 0–3 items correctly ...	...reteach tested skills using the Tier 2 Comprehension Intervention Online PDFs
HIGH-FREQUENCY WORDS	Children answer 0–1 items correctly ...	...reteach tested skills using Section 3 of the Tier 2 Fluency Intervention Online PDFs
PHONEMIC AWARENESS	Children answer 0–3 items correctly ...	...reteach tested skills using the Tier 2 Phonemic Awareness Intervention Online PDFs
PHONICS	Children answer 0–3 items correctly ...	...reteach tested skills using the Tier 2 Phonics/Word Study Intervention Online PDFs and Section 2 and 4 of the Tier 2 Fluency Intervention Online PDFs
CATEGORY WORDS	Children answer 0–1 items correctly ...	...reteach tested skills using the Tier 2 Vocabulary Intervention Online PDFs

Response to Intervention

Use the appropriate sections of the Placement and Diagnostic Assessment and children's assessment results to designate children requiring:

 **Tier 2 Intervention Online PDFs**

WonderWorks Intervention Program

- Phonological and Phonemic Awareness
- Phonics
- Vocabulary
- Comprehension
- Fluency

Program Information

 Go Digital **For Additional Resources**

Unit Bibliography

Word Lists

Literature and Informational Text Charts

Web Sites

Resources

www.connected.mcgraw-hill.com

 **SCOPE & SEQUENCE**

	K	1	2	3	4	5	6
READING PROCESS							
Concepts About Print/Print Awareness							
Recognize own name							
Understand directionality (top to bottom; tracking print from left to right; return sweep, page by page)	✔						
Locate printed word on page	✔						
Develop print awareness (concept of letter, word, sentence)	✔						
Identify separate sounds in a spoken sentence	✔						
Understand that written words are represented in written language by a specific sequence of letters	✔						
Distinguish between letters, words, and sentences	✔						
Identify and distinguish paragraphs							
Match print to speech (one-to-one correspondence)	✔						
Name uppercase and lowercase letters	✔						
Understand book handling (holding a book right-side-up, turning its pages)	✔						
Identify parts of a book (front cover, back cover, title page, table of contents); recognize that parts of a book contain information	✔						
Phonological Awareness							
Recognize and understand alliteration							
Segment sentences into correct number of words							
Identify, blend, segment syllables in words		✔					
Recognize and generate rhyming words	✔	✔					
Identify, blend, segment onset and rime	✔	✔					
Phonemic Awareness							
Count phonemes	✔	✔					
Isolate initial, medial, and final sounds	✔	✔					
Blend spoken phonemes to form words	✔	✔					
Segment spoken words into phonemes	✔	✔					
Distinguish between long- and short-vowel sounds	✔	✔					
Manipulate phonemes (addition, deletion, substitution)	✔	✔					
Phonics and Decoding /Word Recognition							
Understand the alphabetic principle	✔	✔					
Sound/letter correspondence	✔	✔	✔	✔			
Blend sounds into words, including VC, CVC, CVCe, CVVC words	✔	✔	✔	✔			
Blend common word families	✔	✔	✔	✔			

KEY	✔ = Assessed Skill Tinted panels show skills, strategies, and other teaching opportunities.

	K	1	2	3	4	5	6
Initial consonant blends		✔	✔	✔			
Final consonant blends		✔	✔	✔			
Initial and medial short vowels	✔	✔	✔	✔	✔	✔	✔
Decode one-syllable words in isolation and in context	✔	✔	✔	✔			
Decode multisyllabic words in isolation and in context using common syllabication patterns		✔	✔	✔	✔	✔	✔
Distinguish between similarly spelled words	✔	✔	✔	✔	✔	✔	✔
Monitor accuracy of decoding							
Identify and read common high-frequency words, irregularly spelled words	✔	✔	✔	✔			
Identify and read compound words, contractions		✔	✔	✔	✔	✔	✔
Use knowledge of spelling patterns to identify syllables		✔	✔	✔	✔	✔	✔
Regular and irregular plurals	✔	✔	✔	✔	✔	✔	✔
Long vowels (silent e, vowel teams)	✔	✔	✔	✔	✔	✔	✔
Vowel digraphs (variant vowels)		✔	✔	✔	✔	✔	✔
r-Controlled vowels		✔	✔	✔	✔	✔	✔
Hard/soft consonants		✔	✔	✔	✔	✔	✔
Initial consonant digraphs		✔	✔	✔	✔	✔	
Medial and final consonant digraphs		✔	✔	✔	✔	✔	
Vowel diphthongs		✔	✔	✔	✔	✔	✔
Identify and distinguish letter-sounds (initial, medial, final)	✔	✔	✔				
Silent letters		✔	✔	✔	✔	✔	✔
Schwa words				✔	✔	✔	✔
Inflectional endings		✔	✔	✔	✔	✔	✔
Triple-consonant clusters		✔	✔	✔	✔	✔	
Unfamiliar and complex word families				✔	✔	✔	✔
Structural Analysis/Word Analysis							
Common spelling patterns (word families)		✔	✔	✔	✔	✔	✔
Common syllable patterns		✔	✔	✔	✔	✔	✔
Inflectional endings		✔	✔	✔	✔	✔	✔
Contractions		✔	✔	✔	✔	✔	✔
Compound words		✔	✔	✔	✔	✔	✔
Prefixes and suffixes		✔	✔	✔	✔	✔	✔
Root or base words			✔	✔	✔	✔	✔
Comparatives and superlatives			✔	✔	✔	✔	✔
Greek and Latin roots			✔	✔	✔	✔	✔
Fluency							
Apply letter/sound knowledge to decode phonetically regular words accurately	✔	✔	✔	✔	✔	✔	✔
Recognize high-frequency and familiar words	✔	✔	✔	✔	✔	✔	✔
Read regularly on independent and instructional levels							
Read orally with fluency from familiar texts (choral, echo, partner, Reader's Theater)							
Use appropriate rate, expression, intonation, and phrasing		✔	✔	✔	✔	✔	✔
Read with automaticity (accurately and effortlessly)		✔	✔	✔	✔	✔	✔
Use punctuation cues in reading		✔	✔	✔	✔	✔	✔

	K	1	2	3	4	5	6
Adjust reading rate to purpose, text difficulty, form, and style							
Repeated readings							
Timed readings		✔	✔	✔	✔	✔	✔
Read with purpose and understanding		✔	✔	✔	✔	✔	✔
Read orally with accuracy		✔	✔	✔	✔	✔	✔
Use context to confirm or self-correct word recognition		✔	✔	✔	✔	✔	✔

READING LITERATURE

Comprehension Strategies and Skills

	K	1	2	3	4	5	6
Read literature from a broad range of genres, cultures, and periods		✔	✔	✔	✔	✔	✔
Access complex text		✔	✔	✔	✔	✔	✔
Build background							
Preview and predict							
Establish and adjust purpose for reading							
Evaluate citing evidence from the text							
Ask and answer questions	✔	✔	✔	✔	✔	✔	✔
Inferences and conclusions, citing evidence from the text	✔	✔	✔	✔	✔	✔	✔
Monitor/adjust comprehension including reread, reading rate, paraphrase							
Recount/Retell	✔	✔					
Summarize		✔	✔	✔	✔	✔	✔
Story structure (beginning, middle, end)	✔	✔	✔	✔	✔	✔	✔
Visualize							
Make connections between and across texts		✔	✔	✔	✔	✔	✔
Point of view		✔	✔	✔	✔	✔	✔
Author's purpose							
Cause and effect	✔	✔	✔	✔	✔	✔	✔
Compare and contrast (including character, setting, plot, topics)	✔	✔	✔	✔	✔	✔	✔
Classify and categorize		✔	✔				
Literature vs informational text	✔	✔	✔				
Illustrations, using	✔	✔	✔	✔			
Theme, central message, moral, lesson		✔	✔	✔	✔	✔	✔
Predictions, making/confirming	✔	✔	✔				
Problem and solution (problem/resolution)		✔	✔	✔	✔	✔	✔
Sequence of events	✔	✔	✔	✔	✔	✔	✔

Literary Elements

	K	1	2	3	4	5	6
Character	✔	✔	✔	✔	✔	✔	✔
Plot development/Events	✔	✔	✔	✔	✔	✔	✔
Setting	✔	✔	✔	✔	✔	✔	✔
Stanza				✔	✔	✔	✔
Alliteration						✔	✔
Assonance						✔	✔
Dialogue							
Foreshadowing						✔	✔

	K	1	2	3	4	5	6
Flashback						✔	✔
Descriptive and figurative language		✔	✔	✔	✔	✔	✔
Imagery					✔	✔	✔
Meter					✔	✔	✔
Onomatopoeia							
Repetition		✔	✔	✔	✔	✔	✔
Rhyme/rhyme schemes		✔	✔	✔	✔	✔	✔
Rhythm		✔	✔				
Sensory language							
Symbolism							

Write About Reading/Literary Response Discussions

	K	1	2	3	4	5	6
Reflect and respond to text citing text evidence		✔	✔	✔	✔	✔	✔
Connect and compare text characters, events, ideas to self, to other texts, to world							
Connect literary texts to other curriculum areas							
Identify cultural and historical elements of text							
Evaluate author's techniques, craft							
Analytical writing							
Interpret text ideas through writing, discussion, media, research							
Book report or review							
Locate, use, explain information from text features		✔	✔	✔	✔	✔	✔
Organize information to show understanding of main idea through charts, mapping							
Cite text evidence	✔	✔	✔	✔	✔	✔	✔
Author's purpose/ Illustrator's purpose							

READING INFORMATIONAL TEXT

Comprehension Strategies and Skills

	K	1	2	3	4	5	6
Read informational text from a broad range of topics and cultures	✔	✔	✔	✔	✔	✔	✔
Access complex text		✔	✔	✔	✔	✔	✔
Build background							
Preview and predict	✔	✔	✔				
Establish and adjust purpose for reading							
Evaluate citing evidence from the text							
Ask and answer questions	✔	✔	✔	✔	✔	✔	✔
Inferences and conclusions, citing evidence from the text	✔	✔	✔	✔	✔	✔	✔
Monitor and adjust comprehension including reread, adjust reading rate, paraphrase							
Recount/Retell	✔	✔					
Summarize			✔	✔	✔	✔	✔
Text structure	✔	✔	✔	✔	✔	✔	✔
Identify text features		✔	✔	✔	✔	✔	✔
Make connections between and across texts	✔	✔	✔	✔	✔	✔	✔
Author's point of view				✔	✔	✔	✔
Author's purpose		✔	✔				

	K	1	2	3	4	5	6
Cause and effect	✔	✔	✔	✔	✔	✔	✔
Compare and contrast	✔	✔	✔	✔	✔	✔	✔
Classify and categorize		✔	✔				
Illustrations and photographs, using	✔	✔	✔	✔			
Instructions/directions (written and oral)		✔	✔	✔	✔	✔	✔
Main idea and key details	✔	✔	✔	✔	✔	✔	✔
Persuasion, reasons and evidence to support points/persuasive techniques						✔	✔
Predictions, making/confirming	✔	✔					
Problem and solution		✔	✔	✔	✔	✔	✔
Sequence, chronological order of events, time order, steps in a process	✔	✔	✔	✔	✔	✔	✔

Writing About Reading/Expository Critique Discussions

	K	1	2	3	4	5	6
Reflect and respond to text citing text evidence		✔	✔	✔	✔	✔	✔
Connect and compare text characters, events, ideas to self, to other texts, to world							
Connect texts to other curriculum areas							
Identify cultural and historical elements of text							
Evaluate author's techniques, craft							
Analytical writing							
Read to understand and perform tasks and activities							
Interpret text ideas through writing, discussion, media, research							
Locate, use, explain information from text features		✔	✔	✔	✔	✔	✔
Organize information to show understanding of main idea through charts, mapping							
Cite text evidence		✔	✔	✔	✔	✔	✔
Author's purpose/Illustrator's purpose							

Text Features

	K	1	2	3	4	5	6
Recognize and identify text and organizational features of nonfiction texts		✔	✔	✔	✔	✔	✔
Captions and labels, headings, subheadings, endnotes, key words, bold print	✔	✔	✔	✔	✔	✔	✔
Graphics, including photographs, illustrations, maps, charts, diagrams, graphs, time lines	✔	✔	✔	✔	✔	✔	✔

Self-Selected Reading/Independent Reading

	K	1	2	3	4	5	6
Use personal criteria to choose own reading including favorite authors, genres, recommendations from others; set up a reading log							
Read a range of literature and informational text for tasks as well as for enjoyment; participate in literature circles							
Produce evidence of reading by retelling, summarizing, or paraphrasing							

Media Literacy

	K	1	2	3	4	5	6
Summarize the message or content from media message, citing text evidence							
Use graphics, illustrations to analyze and interpret information	✔	✔	✔	✔	✔	✔	✔
Identify structural features of popular media and use the features to obtain information, including digital sources				✔	✔	✔	✔
Identify reasons and evidence in visuals and media message							
Analyze media source: recognize effects of media in one's mood and emotion							

KEY ✔ = Assessed Skill
Tinted panels show skills, strategies, and other teaching opportunities.

	K	1	2	3	4	5	6
Make informed judgments about print and digital media							
Critique persuasive techniques							

WRITING

Writing Process

	K	1	2	3	4	5	6
Plan/prewrite							
Draft							
Revise							
Edit/proofread							
Publish and present including using technology							
Teacher and peer feedback							

Writing Traits

	K	1	2	3	4	5	6
Conventions		✔	✔	✔	✔	✔	✔
Ideas		✔	✔	✔	✔	✔	✔
Organization		✔	✔	✔	✔	✔	✔
Sentence fluency		✔	✔	✔	✔	✔	✔
Voice		✔	✔	✔	✔	✔	✔
Word choice		✔	✔	✔	✔	✔	✔

Writer's Craft

	K	1	2	3	4	5	6
Good topic, focus on and develop topic, topic sentence			✔	✔	✔	✔	✔
Paragraph(s); sentence structure			✔	✔	✔	✔	✔
Main idea and supporting key details			✔	✔	✔	✔	✔
Unimportant details							
Relevant supporting evidence			✔	✔	✔	✔	✔
Strong opening, strong conclusion			✔	✔	✔	✔	✔
Beginning, middle, end; sequence		✔	✔	✔	✔	✔	✔
Precise words, strong words, vary words			✔	✔	✔	✔	✔
Figurative and sensory language, descriptive details							
Informal/formal language							
Mood/style/tone							
Dialogue				✔	✔	✔	✔
Transition words, transitions to multiple paragraphs				✔	✔	✔	✔
Select focus and organization			✔	✔	✔	✔	✔
Points and counterpoints/Opposing claims and counterarguments							
Use reference materials (online and print dictionary, thesaurus, encyclopedia)							

Writing Applications

	K	1	2	3	4	5	6
Writing about text	✔	✔	✔	✔	✔	✔	✔
Personal and fictional narrative (also biographical and autobiographical)	✔	✔	✔	✔	✔	✔	✔
Variety of expressive forms including poetry	✔	✔	✔	✔	✔	✔	✔
Informative/explanatory texts	✔	✔	✔	✔	✔	✔	✔
Description	✔	✔	✔	✔			
Procedural texts		✔	✔	✔	✔	✔	✔
Opinion pieces or arguments	✔	✔	✔	✔	✔	✔	✔

	K	1	2	3	4	5	6
Communications including technical documents		✔	✔	✔	✔	✔	✔
Research report	✔	✔	✔	✔	✔	✔	✔
Responses to literature/reflection				✔	✔	✔	✔
Analytical writing							
Letters		✔	✔	✔	✔	✔	✔
Write daily and over short and extended time frames; set up writer's notebooks							

Penmanship/Handwriting

	K	1	2	3	4	5	6
Write legibly in manuscript using correct formation, directionality, and spacing							
Write legibly in cursive using correct formation, directionality, and spacing							

SPEAKING AND LISTENING

Speaking

	K	1	2	3	4	5	6
Use repetition, rhyme, and rhythm in oral texts							
Participate in classroom activities and discussions							
Collaborative conversation with peers and adults in small and large groups using formal English when appropriate							
Differentiate between formal and informal English							
Follow agreed upon rules for discussion							
Build on others' talk in conversation, adding new ideas							
Come to discussion prepared							
Describe familiar people, places, and things and add drawings as desired							
Paraphrase portions of text read alone or information presented							
Apply comprehension strategies and skills in speaking activities							
Use literal and nonliteral meanings							
Ask and answer questions about text read aloud and about media							
Stay on topic when speaking							
Use language appropriate to situation, purpose, and audience							
Use nonverbal communications such as eye contact, gestures, and props							
Use verbal communication in effective ways and improve expression in conventional language							
Retell a story, presentation, or spoken message by summarizing							
Oral presentations: focus, organizational structure, audience, purpose							
Give and follow directions							
Consider audience when speaking or preparing a presentation							
Recite poems, rhymes, songs							
Use complete, coherent sentences							
Organize presentations							
Deliver presentations (narrative, summaries, research, persuasive); add visuals							
Speak audibly (accuracy, expression, volume, pitch, rate, phrasing, modulation, enunciation)							
Create audio recordings of poems, stories, presentations							

Listening

	K	1	2	3	4	5	6
Identify musical elements in language							
Determine the purpose for listening							

KEY	✔ = Assessed Skill Tinted panels show skills, strategies, and other teaching opportunities.

	K	1	2	3	4	5	6
Understand, follow, restate, and give oral directions							
Develop oral language and concepts							
Listen openly, responsively, attentively, and critically							
Listen to identify the points a speaker makes							
Listen responsively to oral presentations (determine main idea and key details)							
Ask and answer relevant questions (for clarification to follow-up on ideas)							
Identify reasons and evidence presented by speaker							
Recall and interpret speakers' verbal/nonverbal messages, purposes, perspectives							

LANGUAGE

Vocabulary Acquisition and Use

	K	1	2	3	4	5	6
Develop oral vocabulary and choose words for effect							
Use academic language		✔	✔	✔	✔	✔	✔
Identify persons, places, things, actions		✔	✔	✔			
Classify, sort, and categorize words	✔	✔	✔	✔	✔	✔	✔
Determine or clarify the meaning of unknown words; use word walls		✔	✔	✔	✔	✔	✔
Synonyms, antonyms, and opposites		✔	✔	✔	✔	✔	✔
Use context clues such as word, sentence, paragraph, definition, example, restatement, description, comparison, cause and effect		✔	✔	✔	✔	✔	✔
Use word identification strategies		✔	✔	✔	✔	✔	✔
Unfamiliar words		✔	✔	✔	✔	✔	✔
Multiple-meaning words		✔	✔	✔	✔	✔	✔
Use print and online dictionary to locate meanings, pronunciation, derivatives, parts of speech		✔	✔	✔	✔	✔	✔
Compound words		✔	✔	✔	✔	✔	✔
Words ending in -er and -est		✔	✔	✔	✔	✔	
Root words (base words)		✔	✔	✔	✔	✔	✔
Prefixes and suffixes		✔	✔	✔	✔	✔	✔
Greek and Latin affixes and roots			✔	✔	✔	✔	✔
Denotation and connotation					✔	✔	✔
Word families		✔	✔	✔	✔	✔	✔
Inflectional endings		✔	✔	✔	✔	✔	✔
Use a print and online thesaurus			✔	✔	✔	✔	✔
Use print and online reference sources for word meaning (dictionary, glossaries)		✔	✔	✔	✔	✔	✔
Homographs					✔	✔	✔
Homophones			✔	✔	✔	✔	✔
Contractions		✔	✔	✔			
Figurative language such as metaphors, similes, personification			✔	✔	✔	✔	✔
Idioms, adages, proverbs, literal and nonliteral language			✔	✔	✔	✔	✔
Analogies							
Listen to, read, discuss familiar and unfamiliar challenging text							
Identify real-life connections between words and their use							
Use acquired words and phrases to convey precise ideas							
Use vocabulary to express spatial and temporal relationships							

	K	1	2	3	4	5	6
Identify shades of meaning in related words	✔	✔	✔	✔	✔	✔	✔
Word origins				✔	✔	✔	✔
Morphology				✔	✔	✔	✔
Knowledge of Language							
Choose words, phrases, and sentences for effect							
Choose punctuation effectively							
Formal and informal language for style and tone including dialects							
Conventions of Standard English/Grammar, Mechanics, and Usage							
Sentence concepts: statements, questions, exclamations, commands		✔	✔	✔	✔	✔	✔
Complete and incomplete sentences; sentence fragments; word order		✔	✔	✔	✔	✔	✔
Compound sentences, complex sentences				✔	✔	✔	✔
Combining sentences		✔	✔	✔	✔	✔	✔
Nouns including common, proper, singular, plural, irregular plurals, possessives, abstract, concrete, collective		✔	✔	✔	✔	✔	✔
Verbs including action, helping, linking, irregular		✔	✔	✔	✔	✔	✔
Verb tenses including past, present, future, perfect, and progressive		✔	✔	✔	✔	✔	✔
Pronouns including possessive, subject and object, pronoun-verb agreement, indefinite, intensive, reciprocal; correct unclear pronouns		✔	✔	✔	✔	✔	✔
Adjectives including articles, demonstrative, proper adjectives that compare		✔	✔	✔	✔	✔	✔
Adverbs including telling how, when, where, comparative, superlative, irregular		✔	✔	✔	✔	✔	✔
Subject, predicate; subject-verb agreement		✔	✔	✔	✔	✔	✔
Contractions		✔	✔	✔	✔	✔	✔
Conjunctions				✔	✔	✔	✔
Commas			✔	✔	✔	✔	✔
Colons, semicolons, dashes, hyphens						✔	✔
Question words							
Quotation marks			✔	✔	✔	✔	✔
Prepositions and prepositional phrases, appositives		✔	✔	✔	✔	✔	✔
Independent and dependent clauses						✔	✔
Italics/underlining for emphasis and titles							
Negatives, correcting double negatives					✔	✔	✔
Abbreviations			✔	✔	✔	✔	✔
Use correct capitalization in sentences, proper nouns, titles, abbreviations		✔	✔	✔	✔	✔	✔
Use correct punctuation		✔	✔	✔	✔	✔	✔
Antecedents				✔	✔	✔	✔
Homophones and words often confused			✔	✔	✔	✔	✔
Apostrophes				✔	✔	✔	✔
Spelling							
Write irregular, high-frequency words	✔	✔	✔				
ABC order	✔	✔					
Write letters	✔	✔					
Words with short vowels	✔	✔	✔	✔	✔	✔	✔
Words with long vowels	✔	✔	✔	✔	✔	✔	✔

KEY	✔ = Assessed Skill
	Tinted panels show skills, strategies, and other teaching opportunities.

BM8

	K	1	2	3	4	5	6
Words with digraphs, blends, consonant clusters, double consonants		✔	✔	✔	✔	✔	✔
Words with vowel digraphs and ambiguous vowels		✔	✔	✔	✔	✔	✔
Words with diphthongs		✔	✔	✔	✔	✔	✔
Words with r-controlled vowels		✔	✔	✔	✔	✔	✔
Use conventional spelling		✔	✔	✔	✔	✔	✔
Schwa words				✔	✔	✔	✔
Words with silent letters			✔	✔	✔	✔	✔
Words with hard and soft letters			✔	✔	✔	✔	✔
Inflectional endings including plural, past tense, drop final e and double consonant when adding -ed and -ing, changing y to i		✔	✔	✔	✔	✔	✔
Compound words		✔	✔	✔	✔	✔	✔
Homonyms/homophones			✔	✔	✔	✔	✔
Prefixes and suffixes		✔	✔	✔	✔	✔	✔
Root and base words (also spell derivatives)				✔	✔	✔	✔
Syllables: patterns, rules, accented, stressed, closed, open				✔	✔	✔	✔
Words with Greek and Latin roots						✔	✔
Words from mythology						✔	✔
Words with spelling patterns, word families		✔	✔	✔	✔	✔	✔

RESEARCH AND INQUIRY

Study Skills

	K	1	2	3	4	5	6
Directions: read, write, give, follow (includes technical directions)			✔	✔	✔	✔	✔
Evaluate directions for sequence and completeness				✔	✔	✔	✔
Use library/media center							
Use parts of a book to locate information							
Interpret information from graphic aids		✔	✔	✔	✔	✔	✔
Use graphic organizers to organize information and comprehend text		✔	✔	✔	✔	✔	✔
Use functional, everyday documents				✔	✔	✔	✔
Apply study strategies: skimming and scanning, note-taking, outlining							

Research Process

	K	1	2	3	4	5	6
Generate and revise topics and questions for research				✔	✔	✔	✔
Narrow focus of research, set research goals				✔	✔	✔	✔
Find and locate information using print and digital resources		✔	✔	✔	✔	✔	✔
Record information systematically (note-taking, outlining, using technology)				✔	✔	✔	✔
Develop a systematic research plan				✔	✔	✔	✔
Evaluate reliability, credibility, usefulness of sources and information						✔	✔
Use primary sources to obtain information					✔	✔	✔
Organize, synthesize, evaluate, and draw conclusions from information							
Cite and list sources of information (record basic bibliographic data)					✔	✔	✔
Demonstrate basic keyboarding skills							
Participate in and present shared research							

Technology

	K	1	2	3	4	5	6
Use computer, Internet, and other technology resources to access information							
Use text and organizational features of electronic resources such as search engines, keywords, e-mail, hyperlinks, URLs, Web pages, databases, graphics							
Use digital tools to present and publish in a variety of media formats							

INDEX

A

ABC Big Book, read, **1**:S7

Animals in the Park, **1**:S31, S55

Academic language, **1**:S13, S18, S22, S24, S27, S28, S32, S37, S38, S42, S46, S48, S52, S56, S62, S66, S69, S70, S72, S75, S76, T12, T16, T18, T20, T30, T32, T34, T38, T40, T44, T50, T52, T58, T94, T98, T100, T102, T104, T112, T114, T116, T120, T122, T126, T132, T134, T140, T176, T180, T184, T194, T196, T204, T208, T214, T222, **2**:T12, T18, T20, T30, T32, T34, T38, T40, T44, T52, T58, T94, T100, T102, T104, T112, T114, T116, T120, T122, T126, T132, T140, T176, T182, T184, T194, T196, T198, T202, T204, T208, T214, T222, **3**:T12, T14, T16, T18, T20, T22, T30, T32, T34, T38, T40, T44, T50, T58, T94, T98, T100, T102, T104, T112, T114, T116, T120, T122, T126, T132, T134, T140, T176, T182, T184, T186, T194, T196, T198, T202, T204, T208, T214, T216, T222, **4**:T12, T16, T18, T20, T30, T32, T34, T38, T40, T44, T58, T94, T98, T100, T102, T104, T112, T114, T116, T120, T122, T126, T132, T134, T140, T176, T182, T184, T186, T192, T194, T196, T198, T202, T204, T208, T214, T222, **5**:T12, T16, T18, T20, T30, T32, T34, T38, T40, T44, T50, T94, T98, T100, T102, T104, T112, T114, T116, T120, T122, T126, T132, T134, T140, T176, T182, T184, T186, T194, T196, T202, T204, T208, T214, T222, **6**:T12, T16, T18, T20, T22, T30, T32, T34, T38, T40, T44, T50, T52, T58, T94, T98, T100, T102, T104, T112, T114, T116, T120, T122, T126, T132, T134, T140, T176, T180, T182, T184, T186, T194, T196, T198, T202, T204, T208, T214, T216, T222, T248, **7**:T12, T16, T18, T20, T22, T30, T32, T34, T38, T40, T44, T50, T52, T58, T94, T98, T100, T102, T104, T112, T114, T116, T120, T122, T126, T132, T134, T140, T176, T180, T182, T184, T186, T194, T196, T198, T202, T204, T208, **8**:T12, T18, T20, T22, T30, T32, T34, T38, T40, T44, T52, T58, T94, T100, T102, T104, T112, T114, T116, T120, T122, T126, T132, T140, T176, T182, T184, T186, T194, T196, T198, T202, T204, T208, T214, T216, T222, T248, **9**:T12, T18, T20, T22, T30, T32, T34, T38, T40, T44, T50, T52, T54, T94, T98, T100, T102, T104, T112, T114, T116, T120, T122, T126, T132, T134, T136, T140, T176, T180, T182, T184, T194, T196, T198, T204, T214, T222, T248, **10**:T12, T18, T20, T32, T34, T36, T40, T42, T46, T52, T54, T60, T96, T100, T102, T104, T114, T116, T118, T120, T122, T124, T134, T136, T142, T184, T196, T198, T204, T210, T216, T224

Access complex text

connection of ideas, **2**:T22, T104, **3**:T22, T104, **4**:T22, **10**:T22, T106, T188

genre, **8**:T104

organization, **1**:T22, T104, T186, **3**:T22, **5**:T104, **6**:T22, **7**:T104, **8**:T22, **9**:T22, T104

prior knowledge, **6**:T104, **7**:T22

purpose, **5**:T22, **7**:T186

sentence structure, **3**:T186, **4**:T104, **5**:T186, **6**:T186, **8**:T186

specific vocabulary, **2**:T186, **4**:T186, **9**:T186

Adjectives. *See* **Grammar**.

Alliteration, **2**:T20, T42, T62, **6**:T184, T206, T226, **7**:T44, **10**:T186, T208, T228

Alphabet

letter recognition, **1**:S8, S13, S18, S23, S28, S32, S37, S42, S47, S52, S56, S61, S66, S71, S76

uppercase/lowercase letter formation, **1**:T16, T98, T180, **2**:T16, T98, **3**:T16, T98, T180, **4**:T16, T98, **5**:T16, T98, **6**:T16, T98, **7**:T16, T98, **8**:T16, T98, **9**:T16

See also **Fluency: sound/spelling; Phonics/Word analysis: letter-sound association.**

Antonyms, **10**:T105, T127

Approaching Level Options

comprehension, **1**:T67, T149, T231, **2**:T67, T149, **3**:T67, T149, T231, **4**:T67, T149, T231, **5**:T67, T149, T231, **6**:T67, T149, T231, **7**:T67, T149, T231, **8**:T67, T149, T231, **9**:T67, T149, T231, **10**:T69, T151, T233

fluency, **1**:T65, T147, T148, T229, T230, **2**:T65, T66, T147, T148, T229, T230, **3**:T65, T66, T146, T147, T148, T229, T230, **4**:T65, T147, T229, **5**:T65, T147, T229, **6**:T65, T147, T229, **7**:T65, T147, T229, **8**:T65, T147, T229, **9**:T65, T147, T229

high-frequency words, **1**:T66, T148, T230, **2**:T66, T148, T230, **3**:T66, T148, T230, **4**:T66, T148, T230, **5**:T66, T148, T230, **6**:T66, T148, T230, **7**:T66, T148, T230, **8**:T66, T148, T230, **9**:T66, T148, T230, **10**:T68, T150, T232

Leveled Reader lessons, **1**:T60–T61, T142–T143, T224–T225, **2**:T60–T61, T142–T143, T224–T225, **3**:T60–T61, T142–T143, T224–T225, **4**:T60–T61, T142–T143, T224–T225, **5**:T60–T61, T142–T143, T224–T225, **6**:T60–T61, T142–T143, T224–T225, **7**:T60–T61, T142–T143, T224–T225, **8**:T60–T61, T142–T143, T224–T225, **9**:T60–T61, T142–T143, T224–T225, **10**:T62–T63, T144–T145, T226–T227

oral vocabulary, **1**:T67, T149, T231, **2**:T67, T149, T231, **3**:T67, T149, T231, **5**:T67, T149, T231, **6**:T67, T149, T231, **7**:T67, T149, T231, **8**:T67, T149, **9**:T67, T149, T231, **10**:T69, T151, T233

phonemic awareness, **1**:T62–T63, T144–T145, T226–T227, **2**:T62–T63, T144–T145, T226–T227, **3**:T62–T63, T144–T145, T226–T227, **4**:T62–T63, T144–T145, T226–T227, **5**:T62–T63, T144–T145, T226–T227, **6**:T62–T63, T144–T145, T226–T227, **7**:T62–T63, T144–T145, T226–T227, **8**:T62–T63, T144–T145, T226–T227, **9**:T62–T63, T144–T145, T226–T227, **10**:T64–T65, T146–T147, T228–T229

phonics, **1**:T64–T65, T146–T147, T228–T229, **2**:T64–T65, T146–T147, T227–T228, **3**:T64–T65, T146–T147, T228–T229, **4**:T64–T65, T146–T147, T228–T229, **5**:T64–T65, T146–T147, T228–T229, **6**:T64–T65, T146–T147, T228–T229, **7**:T64–T65, T146–T147, T228–T229, **8**:T64–T65, T146–T147, T227–T228, **9**:T64–T65, T146–T147, T228–T229, **10**:T66–T67, T148–T149, T229–T230

phonological awareness, **1**:T62, T144, T226, **2**:T62, T144, T226, **2**:T62, T144, T226, **3**:T62, T144, T226, **4**:T62, T144, T226, **5**:T62,

C

G

speaking activities, **1**:T33, T115, T197, **2**:T33, T115, T197, **3**:T33, T115, T197, **4**:T33, T115, T197, **5**:T33, T115, T197, **6**:T33, T115, T197, **7**:T33, T115, T197, **8**:T33, T115, T197, **9**:T33, T115, T197, **10**:T35, T117, T199

verbs (action words), **2**:T19, T32, T33, T41, T50, T51, T59, T83, T101, T114, T115, T123, T132, T133, T141, T165, T183, T196, T197, T205, T214, T215, T223, T247, **7**:T19, T33, T41, T51, T59, T83, T101, T115, T123, T133, T141, T165, T183, T197, T205, T215, T223, T247

Graphic organizers

charts, **1**:S74, **2**:T18, T100, **3**:T100, **4**:T32, **6**:T27, T191, **7**:T191, **8**:T27, T109, T191, **9**:T109, **10**:T29

lists, **1**:T18, T100, **8**:T100, T182, **9**:T182, **10**:T18, T184

Venn diagram, **7**:T27

webs, **1**:S16, S20, S26, S40, S44, S50, S64, S68, T182, **2**:T182, **6**:T100, **7**:T18, **8**:T18, **10**:T136

Guided retelling. *See* Retell.

H

Handwriting. *See* Penmanship.

High-frequency words

a, **2**:T17, T23, T26, T29, T39, T47, T57, T60, T66, T68, T72, T81, T181, T193, T203, T211, T221, T236, T245, **3**:T72, **4**:T148, T230, T240, **5**:T148, T230, **7**:T230, **8**:T66, T148, **9**:T66, **10**:T68

and, **3**:T99, T107, T111, T121, T129, T139, T142, T148, T150, T154, T163, **4**:T148, T181, T188, T193, T203, T211, T221, T230, T237, T240, T245, **5**:T148, T230, **7**:T230, **8**:T66, **9**:T66, **10**:T68

are, **5**:T99, T108, T111, T121, T129, T139, T142, T148, T150, T155, T163, T230, **6**:T181, T193, T203, T211, T221, T230, T237, T245, **7**:T230, **8**:T66, T148, **9**:T66, **10**:T68

can, **1**:S33, S39, S43, S49, S53, S57, S63, S67, S77, **2**:T236, **3**:T72, **4**:T148, T230, T240, **5**:T148, T230, **7**:T230, **8**:T66, **9**:T66, **10**:T68

do, **4**:T99, T105, T107, T111, T121, T129, T139, T142, T148, T150, T155, T163, T181, T193, T203, T209, T211, T221, T230, T237, T240, T245,

5:T148, T230, **7**:T230, **8**:T66, **9**:T66, **10**:T68

for, **7**:T17, T24, T29, T39, T47, T57, T66, T73, T81, T230, **8**:T66, T148, T181, T193, T203, T211, T221, T237, T245, **9**:T66

go, **3**:T181, T193, T203, T209, T211, T221, T224, T230, T236, T245, **4**:T148, T181, T193, T203, T211, T221, T230, T237, T245, **5**:T148, T230, **7**:T230, **8**:T66, **9**:T66, **10**:T68

good, **10**:T17, T31, T41, T59, T68, T75, T83

have, **7**:T17, T25, T29, T37, T39, T47, T57, T60, T66, T68, T73, T81, T230, **8**:T66, T148, T181, T187, T193, T203, T211, T221, T237, T245, **9**:T66

he, **5**:T181, T190, T193, T203, T211, T221, T224, T230, T232, T237, T245, **6**:T181, T193, T203, T221, T230, T237, T245, **7**:T230, **8**:T66, T148, **9**:T66, **10**:T68

help, **9**:T17, T29, T39, T47, T57, T66, T73, T81

here, **8**:T17, T29, T39, T47, T57, T66, T73, T181, T193, T203, T211, T221, T230, T237, T245

I, **1**:S9, S15, S19, S25, S29, S57, S62, S67, S73, S77, **2**:T236, T245, **3**:T72, **4**:T148, T230, T240, **5**:T148, T230, **7**:T230, **8**:T66, T148, **9**:T66, **10**:T68

is, **6**:T17, T23, T29, T39, T47, T57, T60, T66, T73, T81, T181, T193, T221, T230, T237, T245, **7**:T230, **8**:T66, T148, **9**:T66, **10**:T68

like, **2**:T99, T111, T121, T129, T139, T142, T148, T150, T154, T163, T181, T193, T203, T209, T211, T221, T236, T245, **3**:T72, **4**:T148, T230, **5**:T148, T230, **7**:T230, **9**:T66, **10**:T68

little, **6**:T17, T23, T29, T39, T47, T57, T66, T68, T73, T81, T181, T193, T203, T221, T230, T237, T245, **7**:T230, **8**:T66, T148, **9**:T66, **10**:T68

me, **8**:T17, T29, T39, T47, T57, T66, T73, T181, T193, T203, T211, T221, T230, T237, T245

my, **5**:T17, T24, T29, T39, T47, T57, T60, T66, T68, T73, T81, T148, T230, **6**:T181, T193, T203, T221, T230, T237, T245, **7**:T230, T237, T245, **8**:T66, T148, **9**:T66, **10**:T68

of, **7**:T99, T111, T121, T129, T139, T148, T155, T163, **8**:T81, T181, T193, T203, T211, T221, T230, T237, T245

said, **8**: T181, T193, T203, T211, T221, T230, T237, T245

see, **1**:T181, T187, T190, T193, T203, T211, T221, T224, T230, T232, T236, T240, T245, **2**:T181, T193, T203, T211, T221, T232, T236, T245, **3**:T72, **4**:T148, T230, **5**:T148, T230, **7**:T230, **8**:T66, T148, **9**:T66, **10**:T68

she, **6**:T99, T105, T111, T121, T129, T139, T148, T155, T163, T181, T193, T203, T221, T224, T230, T232, T237, T245, **7**:T230, **8**:T66, T148, **9**:T66, **10**:T68

the, **1**:T17, T29, T39, T45, T47, T57, T60, T66, T72, T81, T163, **2**:T181, T193, T203, T211, T221, T224, T236, T245, **3**:T72, **4**:T148, T230, T240, **5**:T148, T230, **7**:T230, **8**:T66, T148, **9**:T29, T66, T76, **10**:T68

they, **7**:T99, T111, T121, T129, T139, T148, T155, T163, **8**:T181, T193, T203, T211, T221, T230, T237, T245

this, **8**: T99, T111, T121, T129, T139, T148, T155, T181, T193, T203, T211, T221, T230, T237, T245

to, **3**:T17, T23, T29, T39, T47, T57, T66, T68, T72, T81, **4**:T148, T181, T188, T193, T203, T209, T211, T221, T230, T237, T240, T245, **5**:T148, T230, **7**:T230, **8**:T66, T148, **9**:T66, **10**:T68

too, **9**:T17, T29, T39, T47, T57, T66, T73, T81

want, **8**:T181, T193, T203, T221, T230, T237, T245

was, **6**:T99, T108, T111, T121, T129, T139, T142, T148, T150, T155, T163, T181, T193, T203, T221, T230, T237, T245, **7**:T230, **8**:T66, T148, **9**:T66, **10**:T68

we, **1**:T99, T111, T121, T129, T139, T148, T150, T154, T163, **2**:T181, T193, T203, T211, T221, T245, **3**:T72, **4**:T148, T230, **5**:T148, T230, **7**:T230, **8**:T66, T148, **9**:T66, **10**:T68

what, **8**:T99, T111, T121, T129, T139, T148, T155, T181, T193, T203, T211, T221, T230, T237, T245

who, **10**:T17, T31, T41, T59, T68, T75, T83

with, **5**:T181, T188, T193, T203, T211, T221, T230, T237, T245, **6**:T181, T190, T193, T203, T221, T230, T237, T245, **7**:T230, **8**:T66, T148, **9**:T66, **10**:T68

M

N

O

Key **X** = Unit X

Q

R

S

Key **X** = Unit X

T

U

Uppercase/lowercase letters

  letter recognition, **1**:S8, S13, S18, S23, S28, S32, S37, S42, S47, S52, S56, S61, S66, S71, S76

  penmanship, **1**:T16, T98, T180, **2**:T16, T98, **3**:T16, T98, T180, **4**:T16, T98, **5**:T16, T98, **6**:T16, T98, **7**:T16, T98, **8**:T16, T98, **9**:T16

V

Visualize. *See* **Comprehension strategies**.

Visual Vocabulary Cards, **1**:T11, T20, T34, T80, T81, T93, T102, T116, T162, T184, T198, T244, **2**:T20, T34, T47, T80, T93, T102, T116, T129, T163, T175, T198, **3**:T11, T34, T124, T162, T184, T198, **4**:T11, T20, T34, T80, T93, T102, T116, T175, T184, T198, **5**:T11, T20, T34, T80, T93, T102, T116, T175, T184, T198, **6**:T11, T20, T34, T75, T93, T102, T116, T124, T162, T175, T184, T198, **7**:T11, T20, T34, T93, T102, T116, T124, T162, T175, T184, T198, T206, **8**:T20, T34, T47, T80, T102, T116, T124, T129, T163, T175, T184, T198, **9**:T20, T34, T80, T81, T93, T102, T116, T162, T175, T198, T244, **10**:T11, T20, T36, T49, T82, T95, T104, T164, T177, T186, T200, T246

Vocabulary acquisition

  category words

    action words, **3**:T21, T43, T81

    animal homes, **7**:T185, T207, T245

    animal parts, **7**:T21, T43, T81

    baby animals, **10**:T187, T209, T247

    colors, **2**:T21, T43, T81

    days of the week, **1**:S59, S69

    family words, **1**:T103, T125, T163

    farm animals, **9**:T103, T125, T163

    feeling words, **1**:T21, T43, T81

    food words, **4**:T103, T125, T163, **5**:T185, T207, T245, **9**:T185, T207, T245

    household furniture, **9**:T21, T43, T81

    job words, **4**:T21, T43, T81

    movement words, **2**:T185, T207, T245

  names, **1**:S11, S21

  numbers, **1**:S35, S45

  opposites, **8**:T185, T207, T245, **10**:T105, T127, T165

  ordinal numbers, **8**:T103, T125, T163

  pets, **7**:T103, T125, T163

  position words, **4**:T185, T207, T245

  question words, **6**:T185, T207, T245, **10**:T21, T45, T83

  seasons, **6**:T21, T43, T81

  sensory words, **1**:T185, T207, T245

  sequence words, **3**:T185, T207, T245

  shape words, **2**:T103, T125, T163

  size words, **5**:T21, T43, T81

  sound words, **3**:T103, T125, T163

  tree parts, **5**:T103, T125, T163

  vehicles, **8**:T21, T43, T81

  weather words, **6**:T103, T125, T163

cognates, **1**:T81, T163, T245, **2**:T81, T163, T245, **3**:T81, T163, T245, **4**:T81, T163, T245, **5**:T81, T163, T245, **6**:T81, T163, T245, **7**:T81, T163, T245, **8**:T81, T163, T245, **9**:T81, T163, T245, **10**:T83, T165, T247

computer-related, **6**:T248, **7**:T248, **8**:T248, **9**:T248, **10**:T248

domain-specific, **1**:T103, T125, T163, **4**:T21, T43, T81, T103, T125, T163, **5**:T103, T125, T163, T185, T207, T245, **6**:T21, T43, T81, T103, T125, T163, **7**:T21, T43, T81, T103, T125, T163, T185, T207, T245, **8**:T21, T43, T81, **9**:T21, T43, T81, T103, T125, T163, T185, T207, T245, **10**:T187, T209, T247

function words and phrases. *See* **English Language Learners: high-frequency words, vocabulary**.

general academic, **1**:S14, S62, S69, T38, T52, T134, T176, T216, **2**:T52, T122, T126, T132, T134, T140

oral vocabulary, **1**:S16, S20, S26, S40, S44, S50, S64, S68, S74, T10–T11, T20, T34, T42, T67, T77, T80, T92–T93, T102, T116, T124, T149, T159, T162, T174–T175, T184, T198, T206, T231, T241, T244, **2**:T10–T11, T20, T34, T42, T67, T77, T80, T92–T93, T116, T124, T149, T159, T162, T174–T175, T184, T198, T206, T231, T241, T244, **3**:T10–T11, T20, T34, T42, T67, T77, T80, T92–T93, T102, T116, T124, T149, T159, T162, T174–T175, T184, T198, T206, T231, T241, T244, **4**:T10–T11, T20, T34, T42, T77, T80, T92–T93, T102, T116, T124, T149, T159, T162, T174–T175, T184, T198, T206, T231, T241, T244, **5**:T10–T11, T20, T34, T42, T77, T80, T92–T93, T102, T116, T124, T149, T159, T162, T174–T175, T184, T198, T206, T231, T241, T244, **6**:T10–T11, T20, T34, T42, T67, T77, T80, T92–T93, T102, T116, T124, T149, T159, T162, T174–T175, T184, T198, T206, T231, T241, T244, **7**:T10–T11, T20, T34, T42–T43, T67, T77, T80, T92–T93, T102, T116, T124, T149, T159, T162, T174–T175, T184, T198, T206, T231, T241, T244, **8**:T10–T11, T20–T21, T34, T42, T67, T77, T80, T92–T93, T102, T116, T124, T149, T159, T162, T174–T175, T184, T198, T206, T231, T241, T244, **9**:T10–T11, T20, T34, T42, T67, T77, T80, T92–T93, T102, T116, T124, T149, T159, T162, T174–T175, T184, T198, T206, T231, T241, T244, **10**:T10–T11, T20, T36, T44, T69, T79, T82, T94–T95, T104, T118, T126, T151, T161, T164, T176–T177, T186, T200, T208, T233, T243, T246

selection words, **2**:T12, T94, **4**:T12, T176, **7**:T12, **9**:T176, **10**:T178

story words, **1**:T12, T94, T176, **2**:T176, **3**:T12, T94, T176, **4**:T94, **5**:T12, T94, T176, **6**:T12, T94, T176, **7**:T94, T176, **8**:T12, T94, T176, **9**:T12, **10**:T12, T96

word walls, **1**:S33. *See also* **High-frequency words**.

word webs, **1**:S16, S20, S26, S40, S44, S64, S68, T182, **2**:T182, **6**:T100, **7**:T18, **8**:T18, **10**:T136

See also **Academic language; High-frequency words; Oral language**.

Vocabulary strategies

  ask and answer questions, **10**:T97

  compound words, **7**:T21, T43

  context clues, sentence clues, **5**:T207, **6**:T21, T43, **8**:T43, **9**:T185, T207, **10**:T21, T45

  figurative language, **6**:T103, T125, **7**:T185, T207

  inflectional endings, **5**:T103, T125

  plurals, **5**:T21, T43

  shades of meaning, **6**:T103, T125, **7**:T185, T207

Common Core State Standards Correlations

English Language Arts

College and Career Readiness Anchor Standards for **READING**

The K–5 standards on the following pages define what students should understand and be able to do by the end of each grade. They correspond to the College and Career Readiness (CCR) anchor standards below by number. The CCR and grade-specific standards are necessary complements—the former providing broad standards, the latter providing additional specificity—that together define the skills and understandings that all students must demonstrate.

Key Ideas and Details

1. Read closely to determine what the text says explicitly and to make logical inferences from it; cite specific textual evidence when writing or speaking to support conclusions drawn from the text.

2. Determine central ideas or themes of a text and analyze their development; summarize the key supporting details and ideas.

3. Analyze how and why individuals, events, and ideas develop and interact over the course of a text.

Craft and Structure

4. Interpret words and phrases as they are used in a text, including determining technical, connotative, and figurative meanings, and analyze how specific word choices shape meaning or tone.

5. Analyze the structure of texts, including how specific sentences, paragraphs, and larger portions of the text (e.g., a section, chapter, scene, or stanza) relate to each other and the whole.

6. Assess how point of view or purpose shapes the content and style of a text.

Integration of Knowledge and Ideas

7. Integrate and evaluate content presented in diverse media and formats, including visually and quantitatively, as well as in words.

8. Delineate and evaluate the argument and specific claims in a text, including the validity of the reasoning as well as the relevance and sufficiency of the evidence.

9. Analyze how two or more texts address similar themes or topics in order to build knowledge or to compare the approaches the authors take.

Range of Reading and Level of Text Complexity

10. Read and comprehend complex literary and informational texts independently and proficiently.

English Language Arts

Grade K

Each standard is coded in the following manner:

Strand	Grade Level	Standard
RL	K	1

Reading Standards for Literature

Key Ideas and Details		*McGraw-Hill Reading Wonders*
RL.K.1	With prompting and support, ask and answer questions about key details in a text.	**READING WRITING WORKSHOP BIG BOOK:** Unit 1, Week 3: 44-49 **LEVELED READERS:** Unit 1, Week 2: *Hop!* (A), *We Hop!* (O), *We Can Move!* (B) **Unit 2, Week 3:** *We Like Bugs!* (A), *The Bugs Run* (O), *I See a Bug!* (B) **Unit 3, Week 1:** *We Run* (A), *Go, Nat!* (O) **Unit 3, Week 2:** *A Noisy Night* (B) **Unit 4, Week 2:** *My Neighbors* (A), *Neighborhood Party* (O), *Parade Day* (B) **Unit 5, Week 1:** *My Garden* (A), *My Garden Grows* (O) **Unit 6, Week 2:** *The Rain* (A), *Weather Is Fun* (O), *Kate and Tuck* (B) **Unit 7, Week 3:** *We Want Water* (A), *A New Home* (O), *Bird's New Home* (B) **Unit 8, Week 3:** *Going Up* (A), *In the Clouds* (O), *How Sun and Moon Found Home* (B) **Unit 9, Week 1:** *Let Me Help You* (A), *How Can Jane Help?* (O), *I Used to Help Too* (B) **Unit 10, Week 1:** *Animal Band* (A), *We Want Honey* (O), *A Good Idea* (B) **YOUR TURN PRACTICE BOOK:** 29, 37, 45, 234 **READING WORKSTATION ACTIVITY CARDS:** 1, 2 **TEACHER'S EDITION:** Unit 1: T23, T106, T189 **Unit 2:** T177, T186-191 **Unit 3:** T25, T104-109 **Unit 4:** T35, T104-108, T142-143, T150-151, T186-191, T224-225, T232-233, T238-239 **Unit 5:** T61, T69, T238-239 **Unit 6:** T23-26, T61, T69, T75, T105-108, T143, T151, T186-191 **Unit 7:** T45, T107 **Unit 8:** T61, T69, T75, T105-108, T186-191 **Unit 9:** T22-26, T61, T69, T75, T104-109 **Unit 10:** T106-110, T145, T153, T159 **LITERATURE BIG BOOKS:** Unit 1, Week 1: *What About Bear?* **Unit 2 Week 3:** *I Love Bugs!* **Unit 3, Week 1:** *How Do Dinosaurs Go to School?* **Unit 4, Week 2:** *What Can You Do With a Paleta?* **Unit 6, Week 1:** *Mama, Is It Summer Yet?* **Unit 6, Week 2:** *Rain* **Unit 7, Week 2:** *The Birthday Pet* **Unit 7, Week 3:** *Bear Snores On* **Unit 8, Week 1:** *When Daddy's Truck Picks Me Up* **Unit 9, Week 2:** *Hen Hears Gossip* **Unit 10, Week 2:** *All Kinds of Families* **INTERACTIVE READ-ALOUD CARDS:** SS: "The Ugly Duckling", "Tikki Tikki Tembo" **Unit 1, Week 1:** "The Lion and the Mouse" **Unit 1, Week 2:** "The Tortoise and the Hare" **Unit 2, Week 1:** "Timimoto" **Unit 4, Week 1:** "Little Juan and the Cooking Pot" **Unit 4, Week 3:** "A Bundle of Sticks"
RL.K.2	With prompting and support, retell familiar stories, including key details.	**LEVELED READERS:** Unit 1, Week 2: *Hop!* (A), *We Hop!* (O, ELL), *We Can Move!* (B) **Unit 2, Week 3:** *I See a Bug!* (B) **Unit 3, Week 1:** *We Run* (A), *Go, Nat!* (O, ELL), *The Birdhouse* (B) **Unit 3, Week 2:** *City Sounds* (A), *Farm Sounds* (O, ELL), *A Noisy Night* (B) **Unit 4, Week 3:** *We Clean!* (A), *Can You Fix It?* (O, ELL), *Helping Mom* (B) **Unit 5, Week 1:** *The Mystery Seeds* (B) **Unit 6, Week 1:** *It Is Hot!* (A), *Little Bear* (O, ELL), *Ant and Grasshopper* (B) **Unit 6, Week 2:** *The Rain* (A), *Weather Is Fun* (O, ELL), *Kate and Tuck* (B) **Unit 8, Week 1:** *I Go Places* (A), *Run, Quinn!* (O, ELL), *Going to Gran's House* (B) **Unit 10, Week 2:** *My Box* (A), *Let's Make a Band* (O, ELL), *Going Camping* (B) **READING WORKSTATION ACTIVITY CARDS:** 5 **YOUR TURN PRACTICE BOOK:** 157, 167 **TEACHER'S EDITION:** Unit 1: T27, T109, T191 **Unit 2:** T75, T109, T143, T151, T157, T161, T186-191 **Unit 3:** T27, T109, T191 **Unit 4:** T109, T143, T151, T157, T225, T233, T239 **Unit 5:** T61, T69, T75, T79, T109, T143, T151, T157, T191, T225, T233, T239 **Unit 6:** T27, T61, T109, T191, T225 **Unit 7:** T109, T143, T144, T151, T157, T158, T191, T225, T233, T239 **Unit 8:** T61, T69, T75, T143, T151, T157, T191, T225, T233, T239 **Unit 9:** T27, T61, T69, T75, T79, T109, T143, T151, T159, T225, T233, T239 **Unit 10:** T29, T63, T71, T77, T81, T111, T145, T153, T157, T191, T227, T235, T241 **LITERATURE BIG BOOKS:** Unit 1, Week 1: *What About Bear?* **Unit 1, Week 2:** *Pouch!* **Unit 3, Week 1:** *How Do Dinosaurs Go to School?* **Unit 3, Week 2:** *Clang! Clang! Beep! Beep! Listen to the City* **Unit 6, Week 1:** *Mama, Is It Summer Yet?* **Unit 7, Week 2:** *The Birthday Pet*

Reading Standards for Literature

Key Ideas and Details		McGraw-Hill Reading Wonders
RL.K.3	With prompting and support, identify characters, settings, and major events in a story.	**LEVELED READERS:** Unit 1, Week 2: *Hop!* (A), *We Hop!* (O), *We Can Move!* (B) **Unit 2, Week 3:** *The Bugs Run* (O) **Unit 3, Week 2:** *A Noisy Night* (B) **Unit 3, Week 3:** *We Can Go* (A), *Going by Cab* (O), *Cal's Busy Week* (B) **Unit 4, Week 2:** *My Neighbors* (A), *Neighborhood Party* (O) **Unit 5, Week 1:** *My Garden* (A), *My Garden Grows* (O), *The Mystery Seeds* (B) **Unit 7, Week 2:** *My Cats* (A), *Their Pets* (O), *Will's Pet* (B) **Unit 8, Week 1:** *I Go Places* (A), *Run, Quinn!* (O), *Going to Gran's House* (B) **Unit 9, Week 2:** *Mike Helps Out* (A), *Clive and His Friend* (O), *Farmer White's Best Friend* **YOUR TURN PRACTICE BOOK:** 129, 217, 234 **READING WORKSTATION ACTIVITY CARDS:** 3, 4, 6, 7, 10, 11 **TEACHER'S EDITION: Unit 1:** T75, T108 **Unit 3:** T156-157, T186-191, T224-225 **Unit 4:** T104-109, T142-143, T150-151 **Unit 5:** T22-27, T60-61, T68-69, T74-75 **Unit 7:** T104-109, T142-143, T150-151, T156-157, T186-191, T224-225, T232-233, T238-239 **Unit 8:** T22-27, T60-61, T68-69, T75, T186-191 **Unit 9:** T22-29, T60-61, T68-69, T74-75, T104-109, T117, T142-143, T150-151, T156-157 **Unit 10:** T22-29, T62-63, T70-71, T76-77 **LITERATURE BIG BOOKS: Unit 3, Week 3:** *Please Take Me for a Walk* **Unit 4, Week 2:** *What Can You Do with a Paleta?* **Unit 7, Week 3:** *Bear Snores On* **Unit 8, Week 3:** *Bringing Down the Moon* **Unit 9, Week 1:** *Peter's Chair* **Unit 9, Week 2:** *Hen Hears Gossip* **Unit 10, Week 1:** *What's the Big Idea, Molly?* **INTERACTIVE READ-ALOUD CARDS: SS:** "The Ugly Duckling", "Tikki Tikki Tembo" **Unit 1, Week 1:** "The Lion and the Mouse" **Unit 1, Week 2:** "The Tortoise and the Hare" **Unit 3, Week 1:** "The Boy Who Cried Wolf" **Unit 4, Week 1:** "Little Juan and the Cooking Pot" **Unit 7, Week 3:** "Anansi: An African Tale" **Unit 9, Week 2:** "The Little Red Hen"

Craft and Structure		McGraw-Hill Reading Wonders
RL.K.4	Ask and answer questions about unknown words in a text.	**READING/WRITING WORKSHOP BIG BOOK: Unit 1, Week 2:** 32-37 **Unit 2, Week 1:** 8-13 **LEVELED READERS: Unit 4, Week 3:** *We Clean!* (A), *Can You Fix It?* (O, ELL), *Helping Mom* (B) **TEACHER'S EDITION: Unit 1:** T74 **Unit 4:** T127, T225, T238 **Unit 6:** T23, T189 **Unit 7:** T45 **Unit 9:** T45 **Unit 10:** T47
RL.K.5	Recognize common types of texts (e.g., storybooks, poems).	**LEVELED READERS: Unit 6, Week 1:** *Ant and Grasshopper* (B) **TEACHER'S EDITION: Unit 1:** T25, T208, T218 **Unit 4:** T126-127 **Unit 5:** T44-45, T54-55 **Unit 6:** T44, T74-75, T186 **Unit 7:** T44-45 **Unit 9:** T44-45, T126 **Unit 10:** T46 **LITERATURE BIG BOOK: Unit 1, Week 3:** *I Smell Springtime* **Unit 5, Week 1:** *Tommy* **Unit 6, Week 1:** *Covers* **Unit 7, Week 1:** *Kitty Caught a Caterpillar* **INTERACTIVE READ-ALOUD CARDS: SS:** "The Ugly Duckling", "Tikki Tikki Tembo" **Unit 1, Week 1:** "The Lion and the Mouse" **Unit 1, Week 2:** "The Tortoise and the Hare" **Unit 2, Week 1:** "Timimoto" **Unit 3, Week 1:** "The Boy Who Cried Wolf" **Unit 4, Week 3:** "A Bundle of Sticks" **Unit 5, Week 2:** "The Pine Tree" **Unit 6, Week 2:** "The Frog and the Locust" **Unit 6, Week 3:** "Rainbow Crow" **Unit 7, Week 3:** "Anansi: An African Tale" **Unit 8, Week 1:** "The King of the Winds" **Unit 9, Week 2:** "The Little Red Hen" **Unit 9, Week 3:** "Spider Woman Teaches the Navajo" **Unit 10, Week 1:** "The Elves and the Shoemakers"
RL.K.6	With prompting and support, name the author and illustrator of a story and define the role of each in telling the story.	**LEVELED READERS: Unit 2, Week 3:** *I See a Bug!* (B) **Unit 4, Week 2:** *Parade Day* (B), *Helping Mom* (B) **Unit 10, Week 1:** *A Good Idea* (B) **TEACHER'S EDITION: Unit 1:** T68, T94, T142 **Unit 2:** T176, T238-239 **Unit 3:** T12, T94, T176 **Unit 4:** T94, T156, T238 **Unit 5:** T12 **Unit 6:** T12, T94, T176 **Unit 7:** T94, T176 **Unit 8:** T12, T176 **Unit 9:** T12, T94-95 **Unit 10:** T12, T76, T96 **LITERATURE BIG BOOKS: Unit 1, Week 1:** *What About Bear?* **Unit 1, Week 2:** *Pouch!* **Unit 2, Week 3:** *I Love Bugs!* **Unit 3, Week 1:** *How Do Dinosaurs Go to School?* **Unit 5, Week 1:** *My Garden* **Unit 6, Week 2:** *Rain* **Unit 7, Week 2:** *The Birthday Pet* **Unit 8, Week 1:** *When Daddy's Truck Picks Me Up* **Unit 9, Week 2:** *Hen Hears Gossip* **Unit 10, Week 1:** *What's the Big Idea, Molly?* **READING WORKSTATION ACTIVITY CARDS:** 6

Reading Standards for Literature

Integration of Knowledge and Ideas		*McGraw-Hill Reading Wonders*
RL.K.7	With prompting and support, describe the relationship between illustrations and the story in which they appear (e.g., what moment in a story an illustration depicts).	**LEVELED READERS:** Unit 5, Week 1: *My Garden Grows* (O, ELL) **Unit 5, Week 3:** *Farm Fresh Finn* (B) **Unit 6, Week 1:** *It Is Hot!* **Unit 7, Week 3:** *Bird's New Home* (B) **READING WORKSTATION ACTIVITY CARDS:** 1, 4, 11 **TEACHER'S EDITION: Unit 1:** T25, T60-61, T108 **Unit 3:** T24, T60-T61, T68-T69 **Unit 5:** T22-27, T68-69, T238-239 **Unit 6:** T25, T60-61, T105, T188 **Unit 7:** T238-239 **Unit 8:** T25 **Unit 10:** T46-47 **LITERATURE BIG BOOKS: Unit 1, Week 1:** *What About Bear?* **Unit 2, Week 3:** *I Love Bugs!* **Unit 3, Week 1:** *How Do Dinosaurs Go to School?* **Unit 3, Week 2:** *Clang! Clang! Beep! Beep! Listen to the City* **Unit 5, Week 1:** *My Garden* **Unit 6, Week 3:** *Waiting Out the Storm* **Unit 8, Week 1:** *When Daddy's Truck Picks Me Up* **Unit 9, Week 1:** *The Clean Up!* **Unit 10, Week 1:** *The Variety Show* **Unit 10, Week 2:** *All Kinds of Families!* **INTERACTIVE READ-ALOUD CARDS: Unit 5, Week 2:** "The Pine Tree" **Unit 6, Week 2:** "The Frog and the Locust" **Unit 6, Week 3:** "Rainbow Crow"
RL.K.8	(Not applicable to literature.)	
RL.K.9	With prompting and support, compare and contrast the adventures and experiences of characters in familiar stories.	**LEVELED READERS: Unit 3, Week 1:** *Go, Nat!* (O, ELL) **READING WORKSTATION ACTIVITY CARD:** 15 **TEACHER'S EDITION: Unit 1:** S27, S51, S75, T35, T117, T136 **Unit 2:** T218-219 **Unit 3:** T35, T136, T218-219 **Unit 4:** T136-137 **Unit 6:** T54, T117, T136, T199, T218 **Unit 7:** T136-137, T199, T218 **Unit 8:** T35, T54, T218 **Unit 9:** T54, T117, T136 **Unit 10:** T37, T56, T138 **LITERATURE BIG BOOKS: Unit 1, Week 1:** *What About Bear?* **Unit 1, Week 2:** *Pouch!, Baby Animals on the Move* **INTERACTIVE READ-ALOUD CARDS: Unit 1, Week 1:** "The Lion and the Mouse" **Unit 1, Week 2:** "The Tortoise and the Hare" **Unit 2, Week 1:** "Timimoto" **Unit 7, Week 3:** "Anansi: An African Tale" **Unit 8, Week 1:** "The King of the Winds" **Unit 10, Week 1:** "The Elves and the Shoemakers"
Range of Reading and Level of Text Complexity		*McGraw-Hill Reading Wonders*
RL.K.10	Actively engage in group reading activities with purpose and understanding.	**READING/WRITING WORKSHOP BIG BOOKS: SS:** 36-41 **Unit 1:** 34-39, 46-51 **Unit 2:** 10-15, 28-33, 34-39 **Unit 3:** 10-15, 28-33, 46-51 **Unit 4:** 24-31, 38-45 **Unit 5:** 10-17, 38-45 **Unit 6:** 24-31, 38-45 **Unit 7:** 24-31, 38-45 **Unit 8:** 10-17, 24-31 **Unit 9:** 10-17, 24-31 **Unit 10:** 10-17, 24-31 **LEVELED READERS: Unit 5, Week 1:** *My Garden Grows* (ELL) **Unit 7, Week 2:** *Their Pets* (ELL) **Unit 7, Week 3:** *A New Home* (ELL) **TEACHER'S EDITION: Unit 1:** S12, S14, S17, S22, S24, S31, S36, S38, S41, S46, S48, S55, S62, S65, S70, S72, T22-27, T126-127 **Unit 2:** T30-31, T112-113, T130-131 **Unit 3:** T34-35, T94-95, T212-213 **Unit 4:** T112-113, T126-127, T130-131, T194-195, T199 **Unit 5:** T12-13, T48-49, T78-79, T117, T194-195 **Unit 6:** T12-13, T22-26, T94-95, T104-108, T117, T130-131, T176-177, T186-190, T194-195, T199 **Unit 7:** T112-113, T130-131, T160-161, T176-177, T194-195, T199, T212-213, T242-243 **Unit 8:** T12-13, T30-31, T34-35, T48-49, T112-113, T176-177, T212-213 **Unit 9:** T12-13, T30-31, T48-49, T94-95, T112-113, T117, T199, T212-213 **Unit 10:** T12-13, T32-33, T50-51, T96-97, T132-133 **INTERACTIVE READ-ALOUD CARDS: SS:** "The Ugly Duckling", "Tikki Tikki Tembo" **Unit 1, Week 1:** "The Lion and the Mouse" **Unit 1, Week 2:** "The Tortoise and the Hare" **Unit 3, Week 2:** "The Turtle and the Flute" **Unit 4, Week 1:** "Little Juan and the Cooking Pot" **Unit 4, Week 3:** "A Bundle of Sticks" **Unit 5, Week 2:** "The Pine Tree" **Unit 6, Week 2:** "The Frog and the Locust" **Unit 6, Week 3:** "Rainbow Crow" **Unit 7, Week 3:** "Anansi: An African Tale" **Unit 8, Week 1:** "The King of the Winds" **Unit 9, Week 2:** "The Little Red Hen" **Unit 9, Week 3:** "Spider Woman Teaches the Navajo" **Unit 10, Week 1:** "The Elves and the Shoemakers"

Reading Standards for Informational Text

Key Ideas and Details		McGraw-Hill Reading Wonders
RI.K.1	With prompting and support, ask and answer questions about key details in a text.	**READING/WRITING WORKSHOP BIG BOOKS:** Unit 2: 14-19 **LEVELED READERS:** Unit 1, Week 3: *The Beach* (A), *At School* (O), *See It Grow!* (B) **Unit 2, Week 1:** *We Need Tools* (A), *A Trip* (O), *What Can You See?* (B) **Unit 2, Week 2:** *Shapes!* (A), *Play with Shapes!* (O), *Use a Shape!* (B) **Unit 4, Week 1:** *You Cook* (A), *On the Job* (O), *The Neighborhood* (B) **Unit 8, Week 2:** *See This!* (A), *Places to See* (O), *My Trip to Yellowstone* (B) **Unit 9, Week 3:** *Look Where It Is From* (A), *What's for Breakfast?* (O), *Nature at the Craft Fair* (B) **Unit 10, Week 3:** *Help Clean Up* (A), *Let's Save Earth* (O), *Babysitters for Seals* (B) **YOUR TURN PRACTICE BOOK:** 53, 147 **READING WORKSTATION ACTIVITY CARDS:** 1 **TEACHER'S EDITION:** Unit 1: T126-127, T186-191, T225, Unit 2: T22-27, T44-45, T107 Unit 4: T22-27, T44-45, T61, T69, T75, T186-191, T208-209 Unit 5: T104-109, T151, T157, T186-191, T209 Unit 6: T23-26, T105-108, T187-188 Unit 7: T23, T25 Unit 8: T104-109, T126-127, T142-143, T151, T157, T209 Unit 9: T35, T127, T186-191 Unit 10: T188-193, T227, T241 **LITERATURE BIG BOOKS:** Unit 1, Week 2: *Baby Animals on the Move* Unit 1, Week 3: *Senses at the Seashore* Unit 2, Week 1: *The Handiest Things in the World, Discover with Tools* Unit 4, Week 1: *Whose Shoes?"A Shoe for Every Job"* Unit 4, Week 3: *Roadwork* Unit 5, Week 2: *A Grand Old Tree* Unit 5, Week 3: *An Orange in January* Unit 7, Week 1: *ZooBorns!* Unit 9, Week 3: *Bread Comes to Life* Unit 10, Week 3: *Panda Kindergarten* **INTERACTIVE READ-ALOUD CARDS:** SS: "Kindergarteners Can!" Unit 1, Week 3: "A Feast of the Senses" Unit 2, Week 3: "From Caterpillar to Butterfly" Unit 4, Week 2: "Cultural Festivals" Unit 9, Week 1: "Helping Out at Home" Unit 10, Week 2: "The Perfect Color"
RI.K.2	With prompting and support, identify the main topic and retell key details of a text.	**LEVELED READERS:** Unit 1, Week 3: *The Beach* (A), *At School* (O, ELL), *See It Grow!* (B) **Unit 2, Week 1:** *We Need Tools* (A), *A Trip* (O, ELL), *What Can You See?* (B) **Unit 5, Week 2:** *The Tree* (A), *Many Trees* (O, ELL), *Our Apple Tree* (B) **Unit 5, Week 3:** *The Farmers' Market* (A), *Let's Make a Salad!* (O, ELL) **Unit 9, Week 3:** *Look Where It Is From* (A) **READING WORKSTATION ACTIVITY CARDS:** 5 **TEACHER'S EDITION:** Unit 4: T191 Unit 5: T104-109, T126-127, T142-143, T150-151, T156-157, T186-190, T208-209, T224-225 Unit 8: T104-109, T127, T160-161, T248-249 Unit 9: T127, T186-191, T224-225, T232-233, T248-249 Unit 10: T188-193, T211, T226-227, T240-241, T250-251 **LITERATURE BIG BOOKS:** Unit 1, Week 3: *Senses on the Seashore* Unit 5, Week 2: *A Grand Old Tree,* "From a Seed to a Tree" Unit 5, Week 3: *An Orange in January* Unit 8, Week 2: *Ana Goes to Washington, D.C.* Unit 9, Week 3: *Bread Comes to Life* Unit 10, Week 3: *Panda Kindergarten* **INTERACTIVE READ-ALOUD CARDS:** Unit 1, Week 3: "A Feast of the Senses" Unit 2, Week 3: "From Caterpillar to Butterfly" Unit 4, Week 2: "Cultural Festivals" Unit 9, Week 1: "Helping Out at Home" Unit 10, Week 2: "The Perfect Color"
RI.K.3	With prompting and support, describe the connection between two individuals, events, ideas, or pieces of information in a text.	**LEVELED READERS:** Unit 7: *Two Cubs* (A), *Animal Bodies* (O, ELL), *Two Kinds of Bears* (B); **Unit 9:** *Look Where It is From* (A), *What's for Breakfast?* (O, ELL) **READING WORKSTATION ACTIVITY CARDS:** 8, 9 **TEACHER'S EDITION:** Unit 6: T24, T25, T106 Unit 7: T22-26, T60-61, T68-69, T74-75, T208-209 Unit 8: T44-45, T95 **LITERATURE BIG BOOKS:** Unit 2, Week 2: *Shapes All Around* Unit 7, Week 1: *ZooBorns!* Unit 7, Week 3: "Animal Homes" Unit 8, Week 1: *Getting from Here to There* Unit 8, Week 2: *Ana Goes to Washington, D.C.* Unit 9, Week 3: *Bread Comes to Life* **INTERACTIVE READ-ALOUD CARDS:** Unit 2, Week 3: "From Caterpillar to Butterfly" Unit 6, Week 1: "A Tour of the Seasons" Unit 8, Week 2: "The Best of the West" Unit 9, Week 1: "Helping Out at Home" Unit 10, Week 3: "Protect the Environment"
Craft and Structure		*McGraw-Hill Reading Wonders*
RI.K.4	With prompting and support, ask and answer questions about unknown words in a text.	**LEVELED READERS:** Unit 1, Week 3: *At School* (O, ELL), *See It Grow!* (B) **Unit 2, Week 1:** *A Trip* (O, ELL) **Unit 4, Week 1:** *You Cook* (A), *On the Job* (O, ELL) **Unit 5, Week 2:** *The Tree* (A) **Unit 5, Week 3:** *The Farmers' Market* (A) **Unit 7, Week 1:** *Animal Bodies* (O, ELL) **Unit 9, Week 3:** *Nature at the Craft Fair* (B) **Unit 10, Week 3:** *Let's Save Earth* (O, ELL), *Babysitters for Seals* (B) **TEACHER'S EDITION:** Unit 4: T127 Unit 5: T107 Unit 7: T209 Unit 8: T127, T209 Unit 10: T234
RI.K.5	Identify the front cover, back cover, and title page of a book.	**READING/WRITING WORKSHOP:** Unit 1: 8-13, 26-31, 44-49 Unit 2: 8-13, 26-31, 44-49 Unit 3: 8-13, 26-31, 44-49 Unit 4: 8-15, 22-29, 36-43 **LEVELED READERS:** Unit 10, Week 3: *Help Clean Up* (A) **TEACHER'S EDITION:** Unit 1: T30-31, T176 Unit 4: T12 Unit 5: T94, T176, T232 Unit 7: T12, T60, T68, T74, T94 Unit 8: T87, T94 Unit 9: T176 Unit 10: T178, T226 **LITERATURE BIG BOOKS:** Unit 1, Week 3: *Senses at the Seashore* Unit 2, Week 1: *The Handiest Things in the World* Unit 4, Week 1: *Whose Shoes? A Shoe for Every Job*

Reading Standards for Informational Text

Craft and Structure		McGraw-Hill Reading Wonders
RI.K.6	Name the author and illustrator of a text and define the role of each in presenting the ideas or information in a text.	**LEVELED READERS:** Unit 5, Week 3: *Let's Make a Salad!* (O, ELL), **Unit 7, Week 1:** *Two Cubs* (A), *Animal Bodies* (O, ELL), *Two Kinds of Bears* (B) **READING WORKSTATION ACTIVITY CARDS:** 12 **TEACHER'S EDITION: Unit 1:** T176 **Unit 2:** T12 **Unit 4:** T12 **Unit 5:** T94, T176, T232 **Unit 6:** T12, T94, T176 **Unit 7:** T12, T60, T68, T74, T94 **Unit 8:** T94 **Unit 9:** T176 **Unit 10:** T178 **LITERATURE BIG BOOKS: Unit 1, Week 3:** *Senses at the Seashore* **Unit 2, Week 1:** *The Handiest Things in the World* **Unit 2, Week 2:** *Shapes All Around* **Unit 8, Week 2:** *Ana Goes to Washington, D.C.* **Unit 9, Week 3:** *Bread Comes to Life*

Integration of Knowledge and Ideas		McGraw-Hill Reading Wonders
RI.K.7	With prompting and support, describe the relationship between illustrations and the text in which they appear (e.g., what person, place, thing, or idea in the text an illustration depicts).	**READING/WRITING WORKSHOP BIG BOOK: Unit 2, Week 1:** 14-19 **LEVELED READERS: Unit 1, Week 3:** *The Beach* (A) **Unit 2, Week 1:** *We Need Tools* (A) **Unit 2, Week 2:** *Shapes!* (A), *Play with Shapes!* (O, ELL), *Use a Shape!* (B) **Unit 9, Week 3:** *What's for Breakfast?* (O, ELL) **READING WORKSTATION ACTIVITY CARDS:** 1 **TEACHER'S EDITION: Unit 1:** T126-T127, T186-191, T224-225 **Unit 2:** T24, T60-61, T124-T127, 143 **Unit 3:** T45, 127, T208-209 **Unit 4:** T22-27 **Unit 6:** T126-127, T209 **Unit 9:** T208-209, T232-233 **Unit 10:** T190, T244-245 **LITERATURE BIG BOOKS: Unit 1, Week 3:** *Senses at the Seashore*, pp. 4-34 **Unit 2, Week 1:** *The Handiest Things in the World* **Unit 2, Week 2:** *Shapes All Around* **Unit 3, Week 2:** *Sounds Are Everywhere* **Unit 3, Week 3:** *A Neighborhood* **Unit 4, Week 1:** *Whose Shoes? A Shoe for Every Job* **Unit 6, Week 2:** *Cloud Watch* **Unit 9, Week 3:** *Nature's Artists* **INTERACTIVE READ-ALOUD CARDS: Unit 3, Week 3:** "Field Trips" **Unit 6, Week 1:** "A Tour of the Seasons" **Unit 9, Week 1:** "Helping Out at Home"
RI.K.8	With prompting and support, identify the reasons an author gives to support points in a text.	**READING WORKSTATION ACTIVITY CARDS:** 12 **TEACHER'S EDITION: Unit 2:** T26, T108 **Unit 4:** T26, T190 **Unit 5:** T108, T190 **Unit 8:** T108 **Unit 9:** T190 **Unit 10:** T210-211 **LITERATURE BIG BOOKS: Unit 1, Week 3:** *Senses at the Seashore* **Unit 2, Week 1:** *The Handiest Things in the World* **Unit 2, Week 2:** *Shapes All Around* **Unit 4, Week 1:** *Whose Shoes? A Shoe for Every Job* **Unit 4, Week 3:** *Roadwork* **Unit 5, Week 2:** *A Grand Old Tree* **Unit 5, Week 3:** *An Orange in January* **Unit 8, Week 2:** *Ana Goes to Washington, D.C.* **Unit 9, Week 3:** *Bread Comes to Life* **Unit 10, Week 3:** *Save Big Blue!*
RI.K.9	With prompting and support, identify basic similarities in and differences between two texts on the same topic (e.g., in illustrations, descriptions, or procedures).	**READING/WRITING WORKSHOP BIG BOOK: Unit 1, Week 3:** A Feast of the Senses **READING WORKSTATION ACTIVITY CARDS:** 16 **TEACHERS EDITION: Unit 1:** T199 **Unit 2:** T54-55, T117, T126-127 **Unit 4:** T116-117, T218-219 **Unit 5:** T136-137, T198-199, T208-209, T218-219 **Unit 7:** T35, T54, T117 **Unit 8:** T136 **Unit 9:** T218 **Unit 10:** T128-129, T201, T220 **LITERATURE BIG BOOKS: Unit 1, Week 3:** *Senses at the Seashore* **Unit 2, Week 1:** *The Handiest Things in the World* **Unit 2, Week 2:** *Shapes All Around*, "Find the Shapes" **Unit 5, Week 3:** *An Orange in January*, "Farmers' Market" **Unit 10, Week 2:** *Good For You* **INTERACTIVE READ-ALOUD CARDS: Unit 1, Week 3:** "A Feast of the Senses" **Unit 2, Week 2:** "Kites in Flight" **Unit 5, Week 3:** "Farms Around the World" **Unit 7, Week 1:** "Baby Farm Animals" **Unit 7, Week 2:** "The Family Pet" **Unit 10, Week 3:** "Protect the Environment!"

Range of Reading and Level of Text Complexity		McGraw-Hill Reading Wonders
RI.K.10	Actively engage in group reading activities with purpose and understanding.	**READING/WRITING WORKSHOP BIG BOOKS: Start Smart:** 18-23, 53-58 **Unit 1:** 10-15, 28-33, 52-57 **Unit 2:** 16-21, 52-57 **Unit 3:** 34-39, 52-57 **Unit 4:** 10-17 **Unit 5:** 24-31 **Unit 6:** 10-17 **Unit 7:** 10-17 **Unit 8:** 38-45 **Unit 9:** 38-45 **Unit 10:** 38-45 **LEVELED READERS: Unit 5, Week 2:** *Many Trees* (ELL) **TEACHER'S EDITION: Unit 1:** S60, T112-113, T126-127, T199 **Unit 2:** T22-27, T44-45, T74-75, T186-191 **Unit 3:** T126-127, T198-199, T212-213 **Unit 4:** T12-13, T30-31, T116-117, T176-177 **Unit 5:** T34-35, T92-95, T160-161, T174-177, T198-199 **Unit 6:** T35, T126-127, T208-209 **Unit 7:** T12-13, T22-27, T30-31, T34-35, T48-49, T116-117 **Unit 8:** T94-95, T116-117 **Unit 9:** T34-35, T176-177, T194-195, T208-209 **Unit 10:** T118-119, T178-179, T201 **INTERACTIVE READ-ALOUD CARDS: SS:** "Kindergarteners Can!" **Unit 1, Week 3:** "A Feast of the Senses" **Unit 2, Week 3:** "From Caterpillar to Butterfly" **Unit 3, Week 3:** "Field Trips" **Unit 4, Week 2:** "Cultural Festivals" **Unit 5, Week 1:** "Growing Plants" **Unit 5, Week 3:** "Farms Around the World" **Unit 6, Week 1:** "A Tour of the Seasons" **Unit 7, Week 1:** "Baby Farm Animals" **Unit 7, Week 2:** "The Family Pet" **Unit 8, Week 2:** "The Best of the West" **Unit 8, Week 3:** "A View from the Moon" **Unit 9, Week 1:** "Helping Out at Home" **Unit 10, Week 2:** "The Perfect Color" **Unit 10, Week 3:** "Protect the Environment"

Reading Standards for Foundational Skills

These standards are directed toward fostering students' understanding and working knowledge of concepts of print, the alphabetic principle, and other basic conventions of the English writing system. These foundational skills are not an end in and of themselves; rather, they are necessary and important components of an effective, comprehensive reading program designed to develop proficient readers with the capacity to comprehend texts across a range of types and disciplines. Instruction should be differentiated: good readers will need much less practice with these concepts than struggling readers will. The point is to teach students what they need to learn and not what they already know—to discern when particular children or activities warrant more or less attention.
Note: In Kidergarten, children are expected to demonstrate increasing awareness and competence in the areas that follow.

Print Concepts		*McGraw-Hill Reading Wonders*
RF.K.1	Demonstrate understanding of the organization and basic features of print.	**TEACHER'S EDITION: Unit 1:** S10, S18, S23, S28, S29, S32, S37, S39, S42, S43, S47, S52, S53, S56, S61, S62, S63, S66, S71, S77, T12, T15, T16, T60, T97, T98, T180, T189, T192 **Unit 2:** T12, T15, T30, T97, T112, T179, T180, T212, T224 **Unit 3:** T15, T26, T94, T97, T106, T112, T130, T142, T176, T179, T211, T232 **Unit 4:** T12, T15, T23, T30, T47, T48, T60, T68, T94, T97, T105, T108, T112, T129, T130, T142, T150, T179, T187, T194, T211, T212, T224 **Unit 5:** T12, T15, T30, T47, T48, T60, T68, T94, T97, T112, T129, T130, T142, T150, T176, T179, T211, T212, T224, T232 **Unit 6:** T12, T15, T29, T37, T47, T97, T129, T179, T211 **Unit 7:** T15, T16, T47, T94, T97, T98, T129, T150, T176, T179, T180, T211, T212, T232 **Unit 8:** T12, T15, T47, T48, T68, T94, T97, T129, T142, T179 **Unit 9:** T12, T15, T25, T47, T60, T94, T97, T129, T142, T176, T179, T211 **Unit 10:** T12, T15, T49, T62, T96, T97, T13, T144, T178, T179, T213
RF.K.1a	Follow words from left to right, top to bottom, and page by page.	**READING/WRITING WORKSHOP: Start Smart:** 4-5, 22-23, 40-41 **LITERATURE BIG BOOK: Start Smart, Week 3:** *ABC Big Book* **Unit 4, Week 2:** *What Can You Do With a Paleta?* **TEACHER'S EDITION: Unit 1:** S10, S62, T12, T60, T189 **Unit 2:** T30, T112, T224 **Unit 3:** T26, T94, T176 **Unit 4:** T12, T23, T30, T48, T60, T68, T94, T105, T108, T112, T130, T142, T150, T187, T194, T212, T224 **Unit 5:** T68, T94, T112, T130, T142, T150, T176, T212, T224, T232 **Unit 6:** T12 **Unit 7:** T94, T150 **Unit 8:** T12, T68, T94, T142 **Unit 9:** T12, T25, T60, T94, T142 **Unit 10:** T12, T62, T96, T144, T178
RF.K.1b	Recognize that spoken words are represented in written language by specific sequences of letters.	**TEACHER'S EDITION: Unit 1:** S39, S63 **Unit 2:** T212 **Unit 3:** T47-129, T211 **Unit 4:** T47, T129, T211 **Unit 5:** T47, T129, T211 **Unit 6:** T29, T37, T47, T129, T211 **Unit 7:** T47, T129, T176, T211, T212 **Unit 8:** T47, T48, T129, T211 **Unit 9:** T47, T129, T176, T211 **Unit 10:** T49, T131, T213
RF.K.1c	Understand that words are separated by spaces in print.	**TEACHER'S EDITION: Unit 1:** S29, S39, S43, S53, S63, S77 **Unit 2:** T12, T180 **Unit 3:** T94, T106, T112, T130, T142, T232 **Unit 5:** T12, T30, T48, T60, T94 **Unit 7:** T232
RF.K.1d	Recognize and name all upper- and lowercase letters of the alphabet.	**YOUR TURN PRACTICE BOOK:** 3, 7, 8, 11, 15, 16, 20, 24, 34, 42, 50, 58, 66, 84, 92, 100, 108, 116, 134, 142, 143-144, 162, 172, 192, 202, 212, 222, 232 **TEACHER'S EDITION: Unit 1:** S23, S18, S23, S28, S32, S37, S42, S47, S52, S56, S61, S66, S71, T15, T16, T97, T98, T180, T192 **Unit 2:** T15, T97, T179 **Unit 3:** T15, T97, T179 **Unit 4:** T15, T97, T179 **Unit 5:** T15, T97, T179 **Unit 6:** T15, T97, T179 **Unit 7:** T15, T16, T97, T98, T179, T180 **Unit 8:** T15, T97, T179 **Unit 9:** T15, T97, T179 **Unit 10:** T15, T97, T179

Phonological Awareness		*McGraw-Hill Reading Wonders*
RF.K.2	Demonstrate understanding of spoken words, syllables, and sounds (phonemes).	**TEACHER'S EDITION: Unit 1:** S13, S18, S23, S42, S47, S52, S56, S61, S66, S71, T14, T36, T102, T118, T124, T184, T206 **Unit 2:** T14, T20, T42, T70, T96, T102, T124, T144, T178, T184, T206, T210, T226 **Unit 3:** T20, T36, T42, T62, T96, T102, T118, T124, T144, T184, T206, T226 **Unit 4:** T20, T28, T42, T56, T62, T70, T102, T118, T128, T138, T145, T152, T184, T192, T200, T206, T210, T220, T226 **Unit 5:** T14, T20, T28, T36, T42, T62, T63, T72, T102, T110, T118, T124, T138, T144, T145, T152, T184, T192, T206, T210, T226, T227, T234 **Unit 6:** T20, T28, T36, T42, T46, T56, T62, T63, T70, T102, T124, T138, T144, T152, T154, T184, T192, T206, T210, T220, T227, T234 **Unit 7:** T20, T28, T36, T42, T46, T62, T102, T110, T118, T124, T128, T138, T144, T145, T178, T184, T206, T210, T220, T226, T234 **Unit 8:** T20, T28, T42, T46, T56, T62, T63, T102, T110, T118, T124, T128, T138, T144, T145, T152, T184, T200, T206, T226, T227, T234 **Unit 9:** T14, T20, T42, T62, T102, T124, T144, T184, T206, T210, T220, T226, T227, T234 **Unit 10:** T20, T44, T48, T58, T64, T72, T104, T126, T130, T140, T146, T147, T154, T212, T222, T229, T236
RF.K.2a	Recognize and produce rhyming words.	**LITERATURE BIG BOOKS: Start Smart, Weeks 1-3:** *Big Book of Rhymes* **TEACHER'S EDITION: Unit 1:** S23, S42, S47, S52, T102, T124 **Unit 2:** T210 **Unit 3:** T20, T42, T62 **Unit 4:** T184, T206, T226 **Unit 5:** T184, T206, T226 **Unit 6:** T102, T124, T144 **Unit 7:** T102, T124, T144 **Unit 8:** T102, T124, T144 **Unit 9:** T102, T124, T144
RF.K.2b	Count, pronounce, blend, and segment syllables in spoken words.	**LITERATURE BIG BOOK: Smart Start, Week 3:** *Big Book of Rhymes* **TEACHER'S EDITION: Unit 1:** S56, S61, S66, S71 **Unit 2:** T184, T206, T226 **Unit 3:** T184, T206, T226 **Unit 5:** T20, T42, T62 **Unit 9:** T20, T42, T62, T184, T206, T226 **Unit 10:** T20, T44, T64

Reading Standards for Foundational Skills

Phonological Awareness		McGraw-Hill Reading Wonders
RF.K.2c	Blend and segment onsets and rimes of single-syllable spoken words.	**YOUR TURN PRACTICE BOOK:** 88, 96, 104, 112, 124, 130, 138, 148, 158, 168, 182, 183, 188, 198, 208, 228, 242, 243, 248, 256, 264, 272, 280, 293 **TEACHER'S EDITION: Unit 1:** T184, T206 **Unit 2:** T102, T124, T144 **Unit 3:** T102, T124, T144 **Unit 4:** T20, T42, T62 **Unit 5:** T102, T124, T144 **Unit 6:** T20, T42, T62 **Unit 7:** T20, T42, T62, T184, T206, T226 **Unit 8:** T20, T42, T62, T184, T206, T226 **Unit 10:** T104, T126, T146
RF.K.2d	Isolate and pronounce the initial, medial vowel, and final sounds (phonemes) in in three-phoneme (consonant-vowel-consonant, or CVC) words. (This does not include CVCs ending with /l/, /r/, or /x/.)	**YOUR TURN PRACTICE BOOK:** 80, 193 **TEACHER'S EDITION: Unit 1:** T14, T36, T118 **Unit 2:** T14, T70, T96, T178 **Unit 3:** T36, T96, T118 **Unit 4:** T28, T70, T110, T118, T128, T138, T145, T152, T192, T200, T210, T220 **Unit 5:** T14, T28, T36, T63, T72, T110, T118, T138, T145, T152, T192 **Unit 6:** T28, T36, T46, T56, T62, T63, T70, T138, T152, T154, T184, T192, T206 **Unit 7:** T28, T36, T110, T118, T178 **Unit 8:** T28, T46, T56, T63, T110, T118, T145, T152
RF.K.2e	Add or substitute individual sounds (phonemes) in simple, one-syllable words to make new words.	**TEACHER'S EDITION: Unit 5:** T210, T220, T227, T234 **Unit 6:** T210, T220, T227, T234 **Unit 7:** T128, T138, T145, T152, T210, T220, T227, T234 **Unit 8:** T128, T138, T145, T152, T200, T227, T234 **Unit 9:** T210, T220, T227, T234 **Unit 10:** T48, T58, T72, T130, T140, T147, T154, T212, T222, T229, T236

Phonics and Word Recognition		McGraw-Hill Reading Wonders
RF.K.3	Know and apply grade-level phonics and word analysis skills in decoding words.	**TEACHER'S EDITION: Unit 1:** S19, S43, S67, T28, T29, T97, T105, T121, T179, T181, T210, T211, T220, T245 **Unit 2:** T15, T39, T46, T97, T128-129, T179, T203, T221 **Unit 3:** T15, T38, T39, T46, T56, T97, T110, T111, T128, T179, T181, T210 **Unit 4:** T15, T17, T28-29, T30-31, T37 , T39, T46, T47, T48-49, T57, T66, T73, T76, T81, T97, T99, T110, T111, T112-113, T121, T128, T129, T130-131, T139, T148, T155, T158, T163, T179, T181, T193, T194-195, T203, T210, T211, T212-213, T221, T230, T237, T240, T245 **Unit 5:** T14, T17, T28, T29, T30-31, T36, T39, T47, T48-49, T56, T57, T66, T73, T76, T81, T99, T110-111, T112-113, T118, T119, T121, T128, T129, T130-131, T138, T139, T146, T148, T153, T155, T158, T163, T181, T192, T193, T194-195, T200, T203, T210, T211, T212-213, T220, T221, T228, T230, T237, T240, T245 **Unit 6:** T15, T17, T29, T30-31, T39, T46, T47, T48-49, T57, T66, T73, T81, T97, T99, T111, T112-113, T121, T128, T129, T130-131, T139, T148, T155, T158, T163, T178, T179, T181, T193, T194-195, T201, T203, T210, T212-213, T221, T230, T237, T240, T245 **Unit 7:** T15, T17, T28-29, T30-31, T37, T46, T47, T48-49, T56, T57, T64, T65, T66, T73, T76, T81, T96, T97, T99, T110, T112-113, T119, T121, T128, T129, T130-131, T139, T146, T148, T155, T158, T163, T178, T179, T181, T192, T193, T194-195, T201, T203, T210, T211, T212-213, T220, T221, T230, T237, T240, T245 **Unit 8:** T15, T17, T29, T30-31, T39, T46, T47, T48-49, T57, T66, T73, T76, T81, T97, T99, T111, T112-113, T121, T128, T129, T130-131, T139, T148, T155, T158, T163, T179, T181, T193, T194-195, T201, T203, T210, T211, T212-213, T220, T221, T230, T237, T240, T245 **Unit 9:** T15, T17, T29, T30-31, T37, T39, T46, T47, T48-49, T56, T57, T64, T65, T66, T71, 72, T73, T76, T81, T97, T99, T110-111, T112-113, T119, T120, T121, T128, T129, T130-131, T138, T139, T146, T147, T148, T153, T154, T155, T158, T163, T179, T181, T192-193, T194-195, T201, T202, T203, T210, T211, T212-213, T220, T221, T228, T229, T230, T235, T236, T237, T240, T245 **Unit 10:** T15, T17, T30-31, T32-33, T39, T40, T41, T48, T49, T50-51, T58, T59, T66, T67, T68, T74, T75, T83, T97, T99, T101, T110, T112-113, T114-115, T121, T123, T130, T131, T140, T141, T148, T149, T150, T156, T157, T160, T165, T179, T181, T182, T183, T191, T194-195, T196-197, T203, T204, T205, T212-213, T222, T223, T230, T231, T232, T238, T239, T242, T247
RF.K.3a	Demonstrate basic knowledge of one-to-one letter-sound correspondences by producing the primary or many of the most frequent sounds for each consonant.	**PHONICS/WORD STUDY WORKSTATION ACTIVITY CARDS:** 1, 2, 3, 4, 5, 6, 7, 8, 9, 10, 11, 12, 13, 14, 15, 16, 17, 18, 19, 20, 21, 22, 23, 24 **TEACHER'S EDITION: Unit 1:** T28, T179, T210, T220 **Unit 2:** T15, T97, T179 **Unit 3:** T97, T110, T179 **Unit 4:** T97, T110, T179 **Unit 5:** T14, T28, T36, T56, T118, T138, T192, T200, T220, T228 **Unit 6:** T15, T97, T179 **Unit 7:** T56, T96, T97, T110, T146, T178, T179, T192, T220 **Unit 8:** T15, T97, T179 **Unit 10:** T97, T110, T179

Reading Standards for Foundational Skills

Phonics and Word Recognition		McGraw-Hill Reading Wonders
RF.K.3b	Associate the long and short sounds with the common spellings (graphemes) for the five major vowels.	**YOUR TURN PRACTICE BOOK:** 36, 62, 101-102, 135-136, 138, 246, 248, 254, 256, 262, 264, 270, 278 **PHONICS/WORD STUDY WORKSTATION ACTIVITY CARDS:** 2, 7, 10, 14, 19, 25, 26, 27, 28, 29, 30 **TEACHER'S EDITION:** Unit 1: T97, T105 Unit 2: T46, T128–T129, T221 Unit 3: T15, T38, T56 Unit 4: T15, T28-29, T37 Unit 5: T110-111, T119, T146, T153 Unit 6: T193, T201, T211 Unit 7: T15, T28-29, T37, T46, T64, T65, T119, T201 Unit 8: T201, T220 Unit 9: T15, T29, T37, T56, T64, T65, T71, 72, T76, T97, T110-111, T119, T120, T138, T146, T147, T153, T154, T179, T192-193, T201, T202, T220, T228, T229, T235, T236 Unit 10: T15, T30-31, T39, T40, T58, T66, T67, T74, T99, T112-113, T121, T140, T148, T149, T156, T181, T182, T191, T194-195, T203, T204, T222, T230, T231, T238

Phonological Awareness		McGraw-Hill Reading Wonders
RF.K.3c	Read common high-frequency words by sight (e.g., *the, of, to, you, she, my, is, are, do, does*).	**READING/WRITING WORKSHOP:** Start Smart: 9, 16-22, 27 Unit 1: 7-13, 14-19, 25-31 Unit 2: 7-13, 14-19, 25-31 Unit 3: 7-13, 25-31, 32-37 Unit 4: 7-15, 21-29, 35-43 Unit 5: 7-15, 21-29, 35-43 Unit 6: 7-15, 21-29, 35-43 Unit 7: 7-15, 21-29, 35-43 Unit 8: 7-15, 21-29, 35-43 Unit 9: 7-15, 21-29, 35-43 Unit 10: 7-15, 21-29, 35-43 **YOUR TURN PRACTICE BOOK:** 4, 9-10, 12, 17-18, 21, 25-26], 31-32, 39-40, 47-48, 55-56, 63-64, 71-72, 89-90, 97-98, 105-106, 113-114, 121-122, 131-132, 139-140, 149-150, 159-160, 169-170, 179-180, 189-190, 199-200, 209-210, 219-220, 229-230, 239-240, 249-250, 257-258, 265-266, 273-274, 281-282, 291-292 **TEACHER'S EDITION:** Unit 1: S19, S43, S67, T29, T121, T181, T211, T245 Unit 2: T39, T129, T203 Unit 3: T39, T111, T181 Unit 4: T17, T29, T30-31, T39, T47, T48-49, T57, T66, T73, T76, T81, T99, T111, T112-113, T121, T129, T130-131, T139, T148, T155, T158, T163, T181, T193, T194-195, T203, T211, T212-213, T221, T230, T237, T240, T245 Unit 5: T17, T29, T30-31, T39, T47, T48-49, T57, T66, T73, T76, T81, T99, T111, T112-113, T121, T129, T130-131, T139, T148, T155, T158, T163, T181, T193, T194-195, T203, T211, T212-213, T221, T230, T237, T240, T245 Unit 6: T17, T29, T30-31, T39, T47, T48-49, T57, T66, T73, T81, T99, T111, T112-113, T121, T129, T130-131, T139, T148, T155, T158, T163, T181, T193, T194-195, T203, T211, T212-213, T221, T230, T237, T240, T245 Unit 7: T17, T29, T30-31, T39, T47, T48-49, T57, T66, T73, T76, T81, T99, T111, T112-113, T121, T129, T130-131, T139, T148, T155, T158, T163, T181, T193, T194-195, T203, T211, T212-213, T221, T230, T237, T240, T245 Unit 8: T17, T29, T30-31, T39, T47, T48-49, T57, T66, T73, T76, T81, T99, T111, T112-113, T121, T129, T130-131, T139, T148, T155, T158, T163, T181, T193, T194-195, T203, T211, T212-213, T221, T230, T237, T240, T245 Unit 9: T17, T29, T30-31, T39, T47, T48-49, T57, T66, T73, T76, T81, T99, T111, T112-113, T121, T129, T130-131, T139, T148, T155, T158, T163, T181, T193, T194-195, T203, T211, T212-213, T221, T230, T237, T240, T245 Unit 10: T17, T31, T32-33, T41, T49, T50-51, T59, T68, T75, T78, T83, T101, T113, T114-115, T123, T131, T141, T150, T157, T160, T165, T183, T195, T196-197, T205, T212-213, T223, T232, T239, T242, T247
RF.K.3d	Distinguish between similarly spelled words by identifying the sounds of the letters that differ.	**TEACHER'S EDITION:** Unit 2: T46, T128 Unit 3: T46, T128, T210 Unit 4: T46, T128, T210 Unit 5: T128, T210 Unit 6: T46, T128, T210 Unit 7: T46, T128, T210 Unit 8: T46, T128, T210 Unit 9: T46, T128, T210 Unit 10: T48, T130, T212

Reading Standards for Foundational Skills

Fluency		McGraw-Hill Reading Wonders
RF.K.4	Read emergent-reader texts with purpose and understanding.	**READING/WRITING WORKSHOP:** Unit 1: 32-37, 44-49, 50-55 Unit 2: 32-37, 44-49, 50-55 Unit 3: 8-13, 32-37, 50-55 Unit 4: 8-15, 22-29, 36-43 Unit 5: 8-15, 22-29, 36-43 Unit 6: 8-15, 22-29, 36-43 Unit 7: 8-15, 22-29, 36-43 Unit 8: 8-15, 22-29, 36-43 Unit 9: 8-15, 22-29, 36-43 Unit 10: 8-15, 22-29, 36-43

LEVELED READERS: Unit 1, Week 1: *Soup!* (A), *Mouse and Monkey* (O, ELL), *Come and Play!* (B) Unit 1 Week 2: *Hop!* (A), *We Hop!* (O, ELL) *We Can Move!* (B) Unit 1, Week 3: *The Beach* (A), *At School* (O, ELL), *See It Grow!* (B) Unit 2, Week 1: *We Need Tools* (A), *A Trip* (O, ELL), *What Can You See?* (B) Unit 2, Week 2: *Shapes!* (A), *Play with Shapes!* (O, ELL), *Use a Shape!* (B) Unit 2, Week 3: *We Like Bugs!* (A), *The Bugs Run* (O, ELL), *I See a Bug!* (B) Unit 3, Week 1: *We Run* (A), *Go, Nat!* (O, ELL), *The Birdhouse* (B) Unit 3, Week 2: *City Sounds* (A), *Farm Sounds* (O, ELL), *A Noisy Night* (B) Unit 3, Week 3: *We Can Go* (A), *Going by Cab* (O, ELL), *Cal's Busy Week* (B) Unit 4, Week 1: *You Cook* (A), *On the Job* (O, ELL), *The Neighborhood* (B) Unit 4, Week 2: *My Neighbors* (A), *Neighborhood Party* (O, ELL), *Parade Day* (B) Unit 4, Week 3: *We Clean!* (A) *Can You Fix It?* (O, ELL), *Helping Mom* (B) Unit 5, Week 1: *My Garden* (A), *My Garden Grows* (O, ELL), *The Mystery Seeds* (B) Unit 5, Week 2: *The Tree* (A), *Many Trees* (O, ELL), *Our Apple Tree* (B) Unit 5, Week 3: *The Farmer* (A), *Let's Make a Salad!* (O, ELL), *Farm Fresh Finn* (B) Unit 6, Week 1: *It Is Hot!* (A), *Little Bear* (O, ELL), *Ant and Grasshopper* (B) Unit 6, Week 2: *The Rain* (A), *Weather Is Fun* (O, ELL), *Kate and Tuck* (B) Unit 6 Week 3: *Bad Weather* (A), *Getting Ready* (O, ELL), *The Storm* (B) Unit 7, Week 1: *Two Cubs* (A), *Animal Bodies* (O, ELL), *Two Kinds of Bears* (B) Unit 7, Week 2: *My Cats* (A), *Their Pets* (O, ELL), *Will's Pet* (B) Unit 7, Week 3: *We Want Water* (A) *A New Home* (O, ELL), *Bird's New Home* (B) Unit 8, Week 1: *I Go Places* (A), *Run, Quinn!* (O, ELL), *Going to Gran's House* (B) Unit 8, Week 2: *See This!* (A), *Places to See* (O, ELL), *My Trip to Yellowstone* (B) Unit 8, Week 3: *Going Up* (A), *In the Clouds* (O, ELL), *How Sun and Moon Found Home* (B) Unit 9, Week 1: *Let Me Help You* (A), *How Can Jane Help?* (O, ELL), *I Used to Help, Too* (B) Unit 9, Week 2: *Mike Helps Out* (A), *Clive and His Friend* (O, ELL), *Farmer White's Best Friend* (B) Unit 9, Week 3: *Look Where It Is From* (A), *What's for Breakfast?* (O, ELL), *Nature at the Craft Fair* (B) Unit 10, Week 1: *Animal Band* (A), *We Want Honey* (O, ELL), *A Good Idea* (B) Unit 10, Week 2: *My Box* (A), *Let's Make a Band* (O, ELL), *Going Camping* (B) Unit 10, Week 3: *Help Clean Up* (A), *Let's Save Earth* (O, ELL), *Babysitters for Seals* (B)

TEACHER'S EDITION: Unit 1: S14, S48, T48-49, T112-113, T150-151, T232-233 Unit 2: T48-49, T130-131, T224-225 Unit 3: T60-61, T130-131, T212-213 Unit 4: T30-31, T48-49, T60-61, T65, T68-69, T72, T74-75, T78-79, T112-113, T130-131, T142-143, T147, T150-151, T156-157, T160-161, T194-195, T212-213, T224-225, T229, T232-233, T236, T238-239, T242-243 Unit 5: T30-31, T48-49, T60-61, T65, T68-69, T72, T74-75, T78-79, T112-113, T130-131, T142-143, T147, T150-151, T156-157, T160-161, T194-195, T212-213, T224-225, T229, T232-233, T236, T238-239, T242-243 Unit 6: T30-31, T48-49, T60-61, T65, T68-69, T72, T74-75, T78-79, T112-113, T130-131, T142-143, T147, T150-151, T194-195, T212-213, T224-225, T229, T232-233, T236 Unit 7: T30-31, T48-49, T60-61, T65, T68-69, T72, T74-75, T78-79, T112-113, T130-131, T142-143, T147, T150-151, T156-157, T160-161, T194-195, T212-213, T224-225, T229, T232-233, T236, T238-239, T242-243 Unit 8: T30-31, T48-49, T60-61, T65, T68-69, T72, T74-75, T78-79, T112-113, T10-131, T142-143, T147, T150-151, T156-157, T160-161, T194-195, T212-213, T224-225, T229, T232-233, T236, T238-239, T242-243 Unit 9: T30-31, T48-49, T60-61, T65, T68-69, T72, T74-75, T78-79, T112-113, T130-131, T142-143, T147, T150-151, T156-157, T160-161, T194-195, T212-213, T224-225, T229, T232-233, T236, T238-239, T242-243 Unit 10: T32-33, T50-51, T62-63, T67, T70-71, T74, T76-77, T80-81, T114-115, T132-133, T144-145, T149, T152-153, T156, T158-159, T162-163, T196-197, T214-215, T226-227, T231, T234-235, T238, T240-241, T244-245

College and Career Readiness Anchor Standards for WRITING

The K–5 standards on the following pages define what students should understand and be able to do by the end of each grade. They correspond to the College and Career Readiness (CCR) anchor standards below by number. The CCR and grade-specific standards are necessary complements—the former providing broad standards, the latter providing additional specificity—that together define the skills and understandings that all students must demonstrate.

Text Types and Purposes

1. Write arguments to support claims in an analysis of substantive topics or texts, using valid reasoning and relevant and sufficient evidence.

2. Write informative/explanatory texts to examine and convey complex ideas and information clearly and accurately through the effective selection, organization, and analysis of content.

3. Write narratives to develop real or imagined experiences or events using effective technique, well-chosen details, and well-structured event sequences.

Production and Distribution of Writing

4. Produce clear and coherent writing in which the development, organization, and style are appropriate to task, purpose, and audience.

5. Develop and strengthen writing as needed by planning, revising, editing, rewriting, or trying a new approach.

6. Use technology, including the Internet, to produce and publish writing and to interact and collaborate with others.

Research to Build and Present Knowledge

7. Conduct short as well as more sustained research projects based on focused questions, demonstrating understanding of the subject under investigation.

8. Gather relevant information from multiple print and digital sources, assess the credibility and accuracy of each source, and integrate the information while avoiding plagiarism.

9. Draw evidence from literary or informational texts to support analysis, reflection, and research.

Range of Writing

10. Write routinely over extended time frames (time for research, reflection, and revision) and shorter time frames (a single sitting or a day or two) for a range of tasks, purposes, and audiences.

CCSS Common Core State Standards
English Language Arts

Grade K

Writing Standards

Text Types and Purposes		*McGraw-Hill Reading Wonders*
W.K.1	Use a combination of drawing, dictating, and writing to compose opinion pieces in which they tell a reader the topic or the name of the book they are writing about and state an opinion or preference about the topic or book (e.g., My favorite book is…).	**READING/WRITING WORKSHOP:** Unit 1: 38-39 Unit 3: 58 Unit 5: 32-33 Unit 6: 18-19 Unit 9: 18-19 Unit 10: 46-47 **TEACHER'S EDITION:** Unit 1: T87, T100, T114, T122 Unit 3: T196, T204, T214 Unit 5: T100, T114, T122-123, T132, T144 Unit 6: T32, T40, T41 Unit 9: T5, T18, T32, T40-41, T50 Unit 10: T17, T184, T198, T206, T216 **WRITING WORKSTATION ACTIVITY CARDS:** 5, 20
W.K.2	Use a combination of drawing, dictating, and writing to compose informative/explanatory texts in which they name what they are writing about and supply some information about the topic.	**READING/WRITING WORKSHOP:** Unit 2: 20-21 Unit 4: 44 Unit 5: 44-45 Unit 6: 44 Unit 7: 16-17, 44 Unit 8: 30-31 Unit 9: 44 **TEACHER'S EDITION:** Unit 1: S15, S33, S53, S67, S77, T182, T196, T204 Unit 2: T100, T122, T164 Unit 3: T18, T32, T40 Unit 4: T18, T32, T40, T114, T122, T196, T204 Unit 5: T182, T196, T204 Unit 6: T52-53, T135 Unit 7: T18, T32, T40, T100, T114, T122 Unit 8: T53, T100, T114, T122, T135 Unit 9: T182, T196, T204, T214 Unit 10: T18, T34, T42-43, T52 **WRITING WORKSTATION ACTIVITY CARDS:** 18, 23
W.K.3	Use a combination of drawing, dictating and writing to narrate a single event or several loosely linked events, tell about the events in the order in which they occurred, and provide a reaction to what happened.	**READING/WRITING WORKSHOP:** Unit 3: 38-39, 56 Unit 5: 44 Unit 6: 30 Unit 8: 16, 46-47 Unit 9: 30 Unit 10: 16 **TEACHER'S EDITION:** Unit 2: T196, T204, T246 Unit 3: T114, T122, T164 Unit 5: T32, T40, T82, T164, T246 Unit 6: T114, T123, T164, T246 Unit 8: T32, T40, T82, T196, T204 Unit 9: T82, T100, T114, T122-123, T132 Unit 10: T18, T34, T42, T43, T52, T84, T116, T166, T248 **WRITING WORKSTATION ACTIVITY CARDS:** 1, 4, 5, 7, 15

Writing Standards

Production and Distribution of Writing		McGraw-Hill Reading Wonders
W.K.4	(Begins in grade 3.)	
W.K.5	With guidance and support from adults, respond to questions and suggestions from peers and add details to strengthen writing as needed.	**TEACHER'S EDITION: Unit 1:** T32, T40 (Go Digital: Writing), T50, T58 (Go Digital: Writing), T122 (Go Digital: Writing), T132, T140 (Go Digital: Writing), T204 (Go Digital: Writing), T214, T222 (Go Digital: Writing) **Unit 2:** T40 (Go Digital: Writing), T50, T58 (Go Digital: Writing), T122 (Go Digital: Writing), T132, T140 (Go Digital: Writing), T204 (Go Digital: Writing), T214, T222 (Go Digital: Writing) **Unit 3:** T40 (Go Digital: Writing), T50, T58 (Go Digital: Writing), T122 (Go Digital: Writing), T132, T140 (Go Digital: Writing), T204 (Go Digital: Writing), T222 (Go Digital: Writing) **Unit 4:** T40 (Go Digital: Writing), T50, T58 (Go Digital: Writing), T122 (Go Digital: Writing), T132, T140 (Go Digital: Writing), T204 (Go Digital: Writing), T214, T222 (Go Digital: Writing) **Unit 5:** T40 (Go Digital: Writing), T50, T58 (Go Digital: Writing), T122 (Go Digital: Writing), T132, T140 (Go Digital: Writing), T204 (Go Digital: Writing), T214, T222 (Go Digital: Writing) **Unit 6:** T40 (Go Digital: Writing), T50, T58 (Go Digital: Writing), T122 (Go Digital: Writing), T132, T140 (Go Digital: Writing), T204 (Go Digital: Writing), T214, T222 (Go Digital: Writing) **Unit 7:** T40 (Go Digital: Writing), T58 (Go Digital: Writing), T122 (Go Digital: Writing), T140 (Go Digital: Writing), T164, T204 (Go Digital: Writing), T222 (Go Digital: Writing) T246 **Unit 8:** T40 (Go Digital: Writing), T50, T58 (Go Digital: Writing), T122 (Go Digital: Writing), T132, T140 (Go Digital: Writing), T164, T204 (Go Digital: Writing), T214, T222 (Go Digital: Writing), T246 **Unit 9:** T40 (Go Digital: Writing), T50, T58 (Go Digital: Writing), T122 (Go Digital: Writing), T132, T140 (Go Digital: Writing), T204 (Go Digital: Writing), T214, T222 (Go Digital: Writing) **Unit 10:** T42 (Go Digital: Writing), T52, T60 (Go Digital: Writing), T124 (Go Digital: Writing), T134, T142 (Go Digital: Writing), T166, T206 (Go Digital: Writing), T224 (Go Digital: Writing), T248 **WRITING WORKSTATION ACTIVITY CARDS:** 10, 11, 12, 13, 14, 16
W.K.6	With guidance and support from adults, explore a variety of digital tools to produce and publish writing, including in collaboration with peers.	**TEACHER'S EDITION: Unit 1:** T134 **Unit 2:** T216 **Unit 6:** T248-249 **Unit 7:** T52, T134, T216, T248-249 **Unit 8:** T52, T134, T216, T248-249 **Unit 9:** T216, T248-249 **Unit 10:** T218, T250-251 **ConnectED Digital Resources:** My Binder (My Work)
Research to Build and Present Knowledge		McGraw-Hill Reading Wonders
W.K.7	Participate in shared research and writing projects (e.g., explore a number of books by a favorite author and express opinions about them).	**TEACHER'S EDITION: Unit 1:** T52, T134, T216 **Unit 2:** T52, T134, T216 **Unit 3:** T52, T134, T216 **Unit 4:** T52, T134, T216 **Unit 5:** T52, T100, T114, T122-123 **Unit 6:** T52, T134, T216 **Unit 7:** T52, T134, T216, T248-249 **Unit 8:** T52, T134, T216 **Unit 9:** T52, T134, T216 **Unit 10:** T54, T136, T218 **WRITING WORKSTATION ACTIVITY CARDS:** 20, 23 **ConnectED Digital Resources:** Collaborate (Projects)
W.K.8	With guidance and support from adults, recall information from experiences or gather information from provided sources to answer a question.	**READING/WRITING WORKSHOP: Unit 7:** 44 **TEACHER'S EDITION: Unit 1:** T32, T40, T100 **Unit 2:** T52, T134, T216 **Unit 3:** T100, T214 **Unit 4:** T18, T52, T100, T134, T182, T216 **Unit 5:** T18, T52, T134, T216 **Unit 6:** T52, T100, T134, T216 **Unit 7:** T50, T52, T132, T134, T196, T204, T214, T216 **Unit 8:** T52, T134, T216 **Unit 9:** T52, T134, T216 **Unit 10:** T54, T102, T136, T218
W.K.9	(Begins in grade 4.)	
Range of Writing		McGraw-Hill Reading Wonders
W.K.10	(Begins in grade 3.)	

College and Career Readiness Anchor Standards for SPEAKING AND LISTENING

The K–5 standards on the following pages define what students should understand and be able to do by the end of each grade. They correspond to the College and Career Readiness (CCR) anchor standards below by number. The CCR and grade-specific standards are necessary complements—the former providing broad standards, the latter providing additional specificity—that together define the skills and understandings that all students must demonstrate.

Comprehension and Collaboration

1. Prepare for and participate effectively in a range of conversations and collaborations with diverse partners, building on others' ideas and expressing their own clearly and persuasively.

2. Integrate and evaluate information presented in diverse media and formats, including visually, quantitatively, and orally.

3. Evaluate a speaker's point of view, reasoning, and use of evidence and rhetoric.

Presentation of Knowledge and Ideas

4. Present information, findings, and supporting evidence such that listeners can follow the line of reasoning and the organization, development, and style are appropriate to task, purpose, and audience.

5. Make strategic use of digital media and visual displays of data to express information and enhance understanding of presentations.

6. Adapt speech to a variety of contexts and communicative tasks, demonstrating command of formal English when indicated or appropriate.

CCSS Common Core State Standards
English Language Arts
Grade K

Speaking and Listening Standards

Comprehension and Collaboration		McGraw-Hill Reading Wonders
SL.K.1	Participate in collaborative conversations with diverse partners about kindergarten topics and texts with peers and adults in small and larger groups.	**TEACHER'S EDITION:** Unit 1: S10-11, S44, S58, T11, T54-55, T117, T134, T136-137, T216 **Unit 2:** T34, T51, T52, T134, T222 **Unit 3:** T20, T33, T45, T175, T216 **Unit 4:** T11, T20, T52, T54, T58, T93, T134, T136, T140, T175, T216, T218 **Unit 5:** T11, T20, T52, T93, T120, T136, T174, T175, T216, T222 **Unit 6:** T11, T52, T54, T93, T136, T140, T216, T218 **Unit 7:** T10-11, T52, T54, T55, T93, T134, T136, T137, T175, T218, T219 **Unit 8:** T11, T54, T58, T80, T92, T93, T134, T136, T140, T175, T218, T222 **Unit 9:** T10-11, T52, T54, T93, T136, T140, T175, T218, T222 **Unit 10:** T11, T20, T56, T60, T95, T104, T136, T138, T142, T177, T186, T220, T224
SL.K.1a	Follow agreed-upon rules for discussions (e.g., listening to others and taking turns speaking about the topics and texts under discussion).	**READING/WRITING WORKSHOP:** Unit 1: 6-7, 24-25 **Unit 2:** 24-25 **Unit 3:** 6-7, 24-25, 42-43 **Unit 4:** 6-7, 20-21, 34-35 **Unit 5:** 6-7, 20-21, 34-35 **Unit 6:** 6-7, 20-21, 36-43 **Unit 7:** 6-7, 20-21, 34-35 **Unit 8:** 6-7, 20-21 **Unit 9:** 6-7, 8-15, 20-21, 34-35 **Unit 10:** 6-7, 20-21 **YOUR TURN PRACTICE BOOK:** 31-32, 45, 68, 70-71, 81-82, 93 **READING WORKSTATION ACTIVITY CARDS:** 1, 6, 18, 19 **WRITING WORKSTATION ACTIVITY CARDS:** 1, 11, 13, 21+D89 **TEACHER'S EDITION:** Unit 1: T11, T134, T216 **Unit 2:** T52, T134, T222 **Unit 3:** T175, T216 **Unit 4:** T11, T52, T58, T93, T134, T140, T216 **Unit 5:** T11, T52, T93, T175, T216 **Unit 6:** T11, T52, T93, T140, T216 **Unit 7:** T11, T52, T55, T93, T134, T137, T219 **Unit 8:** T11, T58, T93, T134, T140, T222 **Unit 9:** T11, T52, T93, T140, T175, T222 **Unit 10:** T11, T60, T95, T142, T224
SL.K.1b	Continue a conversation through multiple exchanges.	**READING/WRITING WORKSHOP:** Unit 1: SS4-SS5, SS22-SS23, SS40-SS41, 6-7, 24-25, 42-43 **Unit 2:** 6-7, 8, 14-19, 24, 25, 42-43, 46, 47, 48, 51, 54, 55, 58 **Unit 3:** 6-7, 14-19, 24-35, 42-43 **Unit 4:** 6-7, 20-21, 34-35 **Unit 5:** 6-7, 20-21, 34-35 **Unit 6:** 8-15 **Unit 7:** 6-7, 8-15, 20-21, 22-29, 34-35, 36-43 **Unit 8:** 6-7, 8-15, 20-21, 22-29, 34-35, 36-43 **Unit 9:** 6-7, 8-15, 20-21, 22-29, 34-35 **Unit 10:** 6-7, 8-15, 20-21, 22-29, 34-35, 36-43 **YOUR TURN PRACTICE BOOK:** 29, 45, 53, 61, 68 **READING WORKSTATION ACTIVITY CARDS:** 1, 6, 17, 18 **WRITING WORKSTATION ACTIVITY CARDS:** 1, 9, 11 **PHONICS/WORD STUDY WORKSTATION ACTIVITY CARDS:** W11, W12, R2, R3 **SCIENCE/SOCIAL STUDIES WORKSTATION ACTIVITY CARDS:** W4, W26, R10 **LITERATURE BIG BOOKS:** Smart Start: *Animals in the Park* **Unit 2, Week 1:** *The Handiest Things in the World* **Unit 2, Week 2:** *Shapes All Around* **Unit 3, Week 2:** *Clang! Clang! Beep! Beep! Listen to the City* **Unit 4, Week 1:** *Whose Shoes? A Shoe for Every Job* **Unit 4, Week 2:** *What Can You Do with a Paleta?* **Unit 4, Week 3:** *Roadwork* **Unit 5, Week 3:** *An Orange in January* **Unit 6, Week 1:** *Mama, Is It Summer Yet?* **Unit 6, Week 2:** *Rain* **Unit 7, Week 1:** *ZooBorns!* **Unit 7, Week 2:** *The Birthday Pet* **Unit 8, Week 1:** *When Daddy's Truck Picks Me Up* **Unit 8, Week 2:** *Ana Goes to Washington, D.C.* **Unit 9, Week 3:** *Bread Comes to Life* **Unit 10, Week 3:** *Panda Kindergarten* **TEACHER'S EDITION:** Unit 1: S10-S11, S21, S26-S27, S34-S35, S44-S45, S54, S58-S59, S64, S68-S69, S74-S75, T11, T34, T35, T52, T53, T54-55, T81, T84, T93, T101, T117, T123, T133, T134, T135, T136-137, T162, T175, T183, T197, T199, T215, T216, T217, T218 **Unit 2:** T11, T19, T33, T41, T51, T52, T64, T93, T134, T136, T137, T175, T204, T215, T216, T217, T218 **Unit 3:** T11, T19, T54-55, T58, T93, T117, T134, T135, T136-137, T175, T216, T217, T218 **Unit 4:** T11, T54, T93, T134, T136, T175, T216, T218 **Unit 5:** T11, T52, T54, T93, T136, T175, T216, T218 **Unit 6:** T11, T52, T54, T136, T218 **Unit 7:** T10-11, T52, T54, T93, T134, T136, T175, T218 **Unit 8:** T11, T54, T58, T80, T92, T93, T136, T140, T175, T218, T222 **Unit 9:** T10-11, T54, T93, T136, T140, T175, T218 **Unit 10:** T11, T56, T95, T136, T138, T177, T220 **INTERACTIVE READ-ALOUD CARDS:** Smart Start, Week 1: "The Ugly Duckling" **Smart Start, Week 2:** "Tikki Tikki Tembo" **Smart Start, Week 3:** "Kindergarteners Can!" **Unit 1, Week 1:** "The Lion and the Mouse" **Unit 1, Week 2:** "The Tortoise and the Hare" **Unit 1, Week 3:** "A Feast of the Senses" **Unit 2, Week 1:** "Timimoto" **Unit 2, Week 2:** "Kites in Flight" **Unit 2, Week 3:** "From Caterpillar to Butterfly" **Unit 3, Week 1:** "The Boy Who Cried Wolf" **Unit 3, Week 2:** "The Turtle and the Flute" **Unit 3, Week 3:** "Field Trips" **Unit 4, Week 1:** "Little Juan and the Cooking Pot" **Unit 4, Week 2:** "Cultural Festivals" **Unit 4, Week 3:** "The Bundle of Sticks" **Unit 5, Week 1:** "Growing Plants" **Unit 5, Week 2:** "The Pine Tree" **Unit 5, Week 3:** "Farmers Around the World" **Unit 6, Week 1:** "A Tour of the Seasons" **Unit 6, Week 1:** "The Frog and the Locust" **Unit 6, Week 3:** "Rainbow Crow" **Unit 7, Week 1:** "Baby Farm Animals" **Unit 7, Week 2:** "The Family Pet" **Unit 7, Week 3:** "Anansi, An African Tale" **Unit 8, Week 1:** "The King of the Winds" **Unit 8, Week 2:** "The Best of the West" **Unit 8, Week 3:** "A View From the Moon" **Unit 9, Week 1:** "Helping Out at Home" **Unit 9, Week 2:** "The Little Red Hen" **Unit 9, Week 3:** "Spider Woman Teaches the Navajo" **Unit 10, Week 1:** "The Elves and the Shoemakers" **Unit 10, Week 1:** "Good for You!" **Unit 10, Week 1:** "Help Save Big Blue!"

Speaking and Listening Standards

Comprehension and Collaboration		McGraw-Hill Reading Wonders
SL.K.2	Confirm understanding of a text read aloud or information presented orally or through other media by asking and answering questions about key details and requesting clarification if something is not understood.	**READING/WRITING WORKSHOP:** Unit 1: 6-7, 26-31, 33, 35, 37, 42-43, 45, 47, 49, 51, 53, 55 **Unit 2:** 6-7, 8, 9, 10, 13, 14-19, 24-25, 27, 28, 30, 33, 34, 35, 46, 47, 48, 51, 54, 55, 58 **Unit 3:** 6-7, 9, 12, 13, 16, 17, 19, 33, 34, 37, 42-43, 46, 47, 49, 51, 53, 55 **Unit 4:** 6-7, 9-15, 20-21, 23-25, 28-29, 34-43 **Unit 5:** 8-15, 23-28 **Unit 6:** 8-15, 22-29 **Unit 7:** 8-15, 18-19, 20-21, 22-29, 34-35, 36-43 **Unit 8:** 6-7, 8-15, 20-21, 22-29, 34-35, 36-43 **Unit 9:** 6-7, 8-15, 20-21, 22-29, 34-35, 36-43 **Unit 10:** 6-7, 8-15, 20-21, 22-29, 34-35, 36-43
		LEVELED READERS: Unit 1, Week 3: *The Beach* (A), *See It Grow!* (O, ELL), *At School* (B) **Unit 2, Week 1:** *We Need Tools* (A), *A Trip* (O, ELL), *What Can You See?* (B) **Unit 3, Week 1:** *We Run* (A), *Go, Nat!* (O, ELL), *The Birdhouse* (B) **Unit 4, Week 2:** *My Neighbors* (A), *Neighborhood Party* (O, ELL), *Parade Day* (B) **Unit 5, Week 1:** *My Garden* (A), *My Garden Grows* (O, ELL), *The Mystery Seeds* (B) **Unit 5, Week 3:** *The Farmer* (A), *Let's Make a Salad!* (O, ELL), *Farm Fresh Finn* (B) **Unit 6, Week 1:** *It Is Hot!* (A), *Little Bear* (O, ELL), *Ant and Grasshopper* (B) **Unit 7, Week 2:** *My Cats* (A), *Their Pets* (O, ELL), *Will's Pet* (B) **Unit 7, Week 3:** *We Want Water* (A), *A New Home* (O, ELL), *Bird's New Home* (B) **Unit 8, Week 2:** *See This!* (A), *Places to See* (O, ELL), *My Trip to Yellowstone* (B) **Unit 8, Week 3:** *Going Up* (A), *In the Clouds* (O, ELL) *How Sun and Moon Found Home* (B) **Unit 9, Week 2:** *Mike Helps Out* (A), *Clive and His Friend* (O, ELL), *Farmer White's Best Friend* (B) **Unit 9, Week 3:** *Look Where It Is From* (A), *What's for Breakfast?* (O, ELL), *Nature at the Craft Fair* (B) **Unit 10, Week 2:** *My Box* (A), *Let's Make a Band* (O, ELL), *Going Camping* (B) **Unit 10, Week 3:** *Help Clean Up* (A), *Let's Save Earth* (O, ELL) *Babysitters for Seals* (B)
		YOUR TURN PRACTICE BOOK: 29-30, 35-38, 45-46, 53, 59-61, 68, 79-80, 85-86, 93-94, 99, 101-103, 107, 109-111, 115, 118, 123, 127-128, 129, 137, 141, 143-144, 147, 153-154, 164-165, 174, 187, 207, 217, 221, 227, 231, 234
		READING WORKSTATION ACTIVITY CARDS: 7, 8, 16, 20
		WRITING WORKSTATION ACTIVITY CARDS: 4, 6, 9
		TEACHER'S EDITION: Unit 1: T11, T22-26, T186-191 **Unit 2:** T35, T186-191, T244 **Unit 3:** T104-108, T137, T175 **Unit 4:** T11, T55, T92, T137, T175, T219, T244 **Unit 5:** T11, T52, T93, T175, T186 **Unit 6:** T11, T20, T26, T93, T175 **Unit 7:** T11, T52, T55, T93, T137, T175, T219, T242 **Unit 8:** T11, T55, T78, T92-93 **Unit 9:** T11, T52, T55, T80, T93, T137, T162, T175, T219, T242 **Unit 10:** T11, T57, T80, T95, T139, T221, T244
		LITERATURE BIG BOOKS: Unit 1, Week 1: *What About Bear?* Unit 1, Week 2: *Pouch!* Unit 1, Week 3: *Senses at the Seashore* Unit 2, Week 1: *The Handiest Things in the World* Unit 2, Week 2: *Shapes All Around* Unit 3, Week 1: *How Do Dinosaurs Go to School?* Unit 3, Week 2: *Clang! Clang! Beep! Beep! Listen to the City* Unit 3, Week 3: *Please Take Me for a Walk* Unit 4, Week 1: *Whose Shoes? A Shoe for Every Job* Unit 4, Week 2: *What Can You Do with a Paleta?* Unit 4, Week 3: *Roadwork* Unit 5, Week 1: *My Garden* Unit 5, Week 2: *A Grand Old Tree* Unit 6, Week 3: *Waiting Out the Storm* Unit 7, Week 3: *Bear Snores On* Unit 8, Week 3: *Bringing Down the Moon* Unit 9, Week 1: *Peter's Chair* Unit 9, Week 2: *Hen Hears Gossip* Unit 10, Week 1: *What's the Big Idea, Molly?* Unit 10, Week 2: *All Kinds of Families*
		INTERACTIVE READ-ALOUD CARDS: Smart Start, Week 1: "The Ugly Duckling" **Smart Start, Week 2:** "Tikki Tikki Tembo" **Smart Start, Week 3:** "Kindergarteners Can!" **Unit 1, Week 1:** "The Lion and the Mouse" **Unit 1, Week 2:** "The Tortoise and the Hare" **Unit 1, Week 3:** "A Feast of the Senses" **Unit 2, Week 1:** "Timimoto" **Unit 2, Week 2:** "Kites in Flight" **Unit 2, Week 3:** "From Caterpillar to Butterfly" **Unit 4, Week 1:** "Little Juan and the Cooking Pot" **Unit 4, Week 2:** "Cultural Festivals" **Unit 4, Week 3:** "The Bundle of Sticks" **Unit 5, Week 1:** "Growing Plants" **Unit 5, Week 2:** "The Pine Tree" **Unit 6, Week 1:** "A Tour of the Seasons" **Unit 6, Week 2:** "The Frog and the Locust" **Unit 6, Week 3:** "Rainbow Crow" **Unit 8, Week 1:** "The King of the Winds" **Unit 8, Week 2:** "The Best of the West" **Unit 8, Week 3:** "A View From the Moon" **Unit 9, Week 1:** "Helping Out at Home" **Unit 9, Week 2:** "The Little Red Hen" **Unit 9, Week 3:** "Spider Woman Teaches the Navajo" **Unit 10, Week 1:** "Help Save Big Blue!"

Speaking and Listening Standards

Comprehension and Collaboration		McGraw-Hill Reading Wonders
SL.K.3	Ask and answer questions in order to seek help, get information, or clarify something that is not understood.	**READING/WRITING WORKSHOP:** Unit 1: 6-7, 26-31, 33, 36, 37, 42-43, 45, 47, 49, 51, 53, 55 **Unit 2:** 6, 7, 14-19 **Unit 3:** 8-13, 14-19, 42-43 **Unit 4:** 6-7, 9, 11, 14, 20-29, 34-43 **Unit 5:** 6-7, 9, 11, 14, 20-29, 34-43 **Unit 6:** 6-7, 9, 11, 14, 20-29, 34-43 **Unit 7:** 6-7, 20-21 **Unit 8:** 6-7, 20-21 **Unit 9:** 6-7, 20-21 **Unit 10:** 6-7 **LEVELED READERS: Unit 2, Week 1:** *We Need Tools* (A), *What Can You See?* (O, ELL), *A Trip* (B) **Unit 4, Week 1:** *You Cook* (A), *On the Job* (O, ELL), *The Neighborhood* (B) **Unit 4, Week 3:** *We Clean!* (A), *Can You Fix It?* (O, ELL), *Helping Mom* (B) **Unit 5, Week 1:** *My Garden* (A), *My Garden Grows* (O, ELL), *The Mystery Seeds* (B) **Unit 5, Week 3:** *The Farmer* (A), *Let's Make a Salad!* (O, ELL), *Farm Fresh Finn* (B) **Unit 6, Week 1:** *It Is Hot!* (A), *Little Bear* (O, ELL), *Ant and Grasshopper* (B) **Unit 6, Week 3:** *Bad Weather* (A), *Getting Ready* (O, ELL), *The Storm* (B) **Unit 7, Week 1:** *Two Cubs* (A), *Animal Bodies* (O, ELL), *Two Kinds of Bears* (B) **Unit 8, Week 2:** *See This!* (A), *Places to See* (O, ELL), *My Trip to Yellowstone* (B) **Unit 9, Week 1:** *Let Me Help You* (A) *How Can Jane Help?* (O, ELL), *I Used to Help Too* (B) **Unit 10, Week 1:** *Animal Band* (A), *We Want Honey* (O, ELL), *A Good Idea* (B) **Unit 10, Week 3:** *Help Clean Up* (A), *Let's Save Earth* (O, ELL) *Babysitters for Seals* (B) **READING WORKSTATION ACTIVITY CARDS:** 7, 16, 20 **WRITING WORKSTATION ACTIVITY CARDS:** 4, 6, 9 **TEACHER'S EDITION: Unit 1:** T13, T216, T233 **Unit 2:** T95, T131, T137 **Unit 3:** T31, T49 **Unit 4:** T11, T55, T93, T137, T216, T219 **Unit 5:** T11, T52, T134, T216 **Unit 6:** T11, T93 **Unit 7:** T52, T93, T134, T182, T196, T205 **Unit 8:** T11, T93, T175 **Unit 9:** T13, T22, T52, T55 **Unit 10:** T11, T95, T97 **LITERATURE BIG BOOKS: Unit 1, Week 1:** *What About Bear?* **Unit 1, Week 2:** *Pouch!* **Unit 1, Week 3:** *Senses at the Seashore* **Unit 2, Week 1:** *The Handiest Things in the World* **Unit 2, Week 2:** *Shapes All Around* **Unit 3, Week 1:** *How Do Dinosaurs Go to School?* **Unit 3, Week 2:** *Clang! Clang! Beep! Beep! Listen to the City* **Unit 3, Week 3:** *Please Take Me for a Walk* **Unit 4, Week 1:** *Whose Shoes? A Shoe for Every Job* **Unit 4, Week 2:** *What Can You Do with a Paleta?* **Unit 4, Week 3:** *Roadwork* **Unit 9, Week 1:** *Peter's Chair* **Unit 9, Week 2:** *Hen Hears Gossip* **Unit 10, Week 2:** *All Kinds of Families!* **Unit 10, Week 3:** *Panda Kindergarten* **INTERACTIVE READ-ALOUD CARDS: Unit 1, Week 1:** "The Lion and the Mouse" **Unit 1, Week 2:** "The Tortoise and the Hare" **Unit 1, Week 3:** "A Feast of the Senses" **Unit 2, Week 1:** "Timimoto" **Unit 2, Week 2:** "Kites in Flight" **Unit 2, Week 3:** "From Caterpillar to Butterfly" **Unit 3, Week 1:** "The Boy Who Cried Wolf" **Unit 3, Week 2:** "The Turtle and the Flute" **Unit 4, Week 1:** "Little Juan and the Cooking Pot" **Unit 4, Week 2:** "Cultural Festivals" **Unit 9, Week 2:** "The Little Red Hen"

Presentation of Knowledge and Ideas		McGraw-Hill Reading Wonders
SL.K.4	Describe familiar people, places, things, and events and, with prompting and support, provide additional detail.	**READING/WRITING WORKSHOP BIG BOOK: Unit 1:** 6-7, 42-43 **Unit 2:** 6-7, 24-25, 42-43 **Unit 3:** 6-7, 24-25, 42-43 **Unit 4:** 6-7, 20-21, 34-35 **Unit 5:** 6-7, 20-21, 34-35 **Unit 6:** 6-7, 20-21, 34-35 **Unit 7:** 6-7, 20-21, 34-35 **Unit 8:** 6-7, 20-21, 34-35 **Unit 9:** 6-7, 20-21, 34-35 **Unit 10:** 6-7, 20-21, 34-35 **YOUR TURN PRACTICE BOOK:** 27-28, 35-38, 51-52, 61, 67, 68, 83, 85-86, 93-94, 103, 107, 109-110, 115, 117, 118, 141, 157, 167, 174, 193, 221, 231 **READING WORKSTATION ACTIVITY CARDS:** 10, 12, 14, 16 **WRITING WORKSTATION ACTIVITY CARDS:** 1, 2, 8, 16, 19, 22 **TEACHER'S EDITION: Unit 1:** S58, S74-75, T19, T33, T134, T183, T197, T205 **Unit 2:** T175, T182 **Unit 3:** T11, T93, T175, T177 **Unit 4:** T10-11, T18-19, T92, T114-115, T132-133, T135, T175, T182-183, T197, T214-215 **Unit 5:** T54, T136, T175, T218 **Unit 6:** T11, T13, T52, T54, T136, T175, T218 **Unit 7:** T54, T136, T163, T175, T218 **Unit 8:** T54, T175, T216 **Unit 9:** T11, T93, T136, T175, T183 **Unit 10:** T102, T116, T136, T177 **LITERATURE BIG BOOKS: Smart Start:** *Animals in the Park* **Unit 1, Week 1:** *What About Bear?* **Unit 1, Week 2:** *Pouch!* **Unit 1, Week 3:** *Senses at the Seashore* **Unit 2, Week 1:** *I Love Bugs!* **Unit 4, Week 1:** *Whose Shoes? A Shoe for Every Job* **Unit 4, Week 2:** *What Can You Do with a Paleta?* **Unit 4, Week 3:** *Roadwork* **Unit 5, Week 1:** *My Garden* **Unit 5, Week 2:** *A Grand Old Tree* **Unit 5, Week 3:** *An Orange in January* **Unit 6, Week 1:** *Mama, Is It Summer Yet?* **Unit 6, Week 2:** *Rain* **Unit 7, Week 1:** *ZooBorns!* **Unit 7, Week 2:** *The Family Pet* **Unit 7, Week 3:** *Bear Snores On* **Unit 8, Week 1:** *When Daddy's Truck Picks Me Up* **Unit 8, Week 2:** *Ana Goes to Washington, D.C.* **Unit 9, Week 1:** *Peter's Chair* **Unit 9, Week 2:** *Hen Hears Gossip* **Unit 9, Week 3:** *Bread Comes to Life* **Unit 10, Week 1:** *What's the Big Idea, Molly?* **Unit 10, Week 2:** *All Kinds of Families!* **INTERACTIVE READ-ALOUD CARDS: Smart Start, Week 2:** "Tikki Tikki Tembo" **Smart Start, Week 3:** "Kindergarteners Can!" **Unit 1, Week 1:** "The Lion and the Mouse" **Unit 1, Week 2:** "The Tortoise and the Hare" **Unit 1, Week 3:** "A Feast of the Senses" **Unit 2, Week 1:** "Timimoto" **Unit 2, Week 2:** "Kites in Flight" **Unit 2, Week 3:** "From Caterpillar to Butterfly" **Unit 3, Week 1:** "The Boy Who Cried Wolf" **Unit 3, Week 2:** "The Turtle and the Flute" **Unit 4, Week 3:** "The Bundle of Sticks" **Unit 5, Week 3:** "Farms Around the World" **Unit 6, Week 3:** "Rainbow Crow" **Unit 7, Week 3:** "Anansi: An African Tale" **Unit 8, Week 3:** "A View From the Moon" **Unit 9, Week 3:** "Spider Woman Teaches the Navajo" **Unit 10, Week 1:** "The Elves and the Shoemakers" **Unit 10, Week 1:** "Good for You!"

Speaking and Listening Standards

Presentation of Knowledge and Ideas		McGraw-Hill Reading Wonders
SL.K.5	Add drawings or other visual displays to descriptions as desired to provide additional detail.	**YOUR TURN PRACTICE BOOK:** 27-28, 30-32, 35-38, 43-46, 51-53, 59-60, 61, 62, 67-70, 77-80, 83, 85-86, 88, 93-94, 99, 101-102, 103-104, 107, 109-112, 115, 117-118, 123, 127-128, 129, 130, 133, 135-136, 137, 138, 141, 143-144, 147, 148, 151, 153-154, 157, 158, 164-165, 167, 168, 174, 187, 193, 207, 217, 221, 227, 231, 234 **READINGWORK STATION ACTIVITY CARDS:** 1, 6, 12, 15, 16, 20 **WRITING WORKSTATION ACTIVITY CARDS:** 1, 2, 4, 9, 17, 20, 23 **TEACHER'S EDITION: Unit 1:** T32, T41, T123, T214 **Unit 2:** T40-41, T123, T132 **Unit 3:** T41, T134, T217 **Unit 4:** T32, T41, T52, T123, T134, T205 **Unit 5:** T53, T134, T217 **Unit 6:** T53, T122-123, T135, T140, T163, T197, T205, T222 **Unit 7:** T33, T41, T114, T123 **Unit 8:** T53, T132, T134, T216 **Unit 9:** T41, T53, T123, T205, T214, T241 **Unit 10:** T43, T137, T216
SL.K.6	Speak audibly and express thoughts, feelings, and ideas clearly.	**READING/WRITING WORKSHOP: Unit 1:** 6-7, 8-13, 14-19, 24-25, 26-31, 42-43 **Unit 2:** 6-7, 8, 9, 10, 13, 14-19, 24-25, 33, 34, 35, 42-43, 46, 47, 48, 51, 54, 55, 58 **Unit 3:** 6-7, 13, 26, 27, 30, 31, 42-43, 44-49 **Unit 4:** 6-8, 22-29, 34-35 **Unit 5:** 6-7 **Unit 6:** 6-7 8-15, 22-29 **Unit 7:** 6-7 **Unit 8:** 20-21, 34-35 **LEVELED READERS: Unit 1, Week 2:** *Hop!* (A), *We Hop!* (O, ELL), *We Can Move!* (B) **Unit 2, Week 3:** *We Like Bugs!* (A), *The Bugs Run* (O, ELL), *I See a Bug* (B) **Unit 3, Week 1:** *We Run* (A), *Go, Nat!* (O, ELL), *The Birdhouse* (B) **Unit 5, Week 3:** *The Farmer* (A), *Let's Make a Salad!* (O, ELL), *Farm Fresh Finn* (B) **Unit 6, Week 1:** *It Is Hot!* (A), *Little Bear* (O, ELL), *Ant and Grasshopper* (B) **Unit 6, Week 2:** *The Rain* (A), *Weather Is Fun* (O, ELL), *Kate and Tuck* (B) **YOUR TURN PRACTICE BOOK:** 29, 37, 39-40, 43-44, 45, 47-48, 53, 61, 68, 71-72, 81-82, 83, 89-90, 97-98, 103, 105-106, 107, 113-114, 115, 121-122, 129, 131-132, 137, 141, 147, 149-150, 151, 187, 221, 227, 231 **READING WORKSTATION ACTIVITY CARDS:** 1, 3, 12, 17 **WRITING WORKSTATION ACTIVITY CARDS:** 1, 2, 6, 20, 25 **TEACHER'S EDITION: Unit 1:** T134, T175, T222 **Unit 2:** T58, T175, T222 **Unit 3:** T58, T140, T222 **Unit 4:** T58, T140, T175, T222 **Unit 5:** T11, T58, T140, T222 **Unit 6:** T11, T58, T140, T175, T222 **Unit 7:** T52, T58, T140, T175, T222 **Unit 8:** T11, T58, T93, T40, T175, T222 **Unit 9:** T11, T52, T58, T140, T222, T245 **Unit 10:** T11, T95, T142, T177, T224 **LITERATURE BIG BOOKS: Unit 1, Week 1:** *What About Bear?* **Unit 1, Week 2:** *Pouch!* **Unit 1, Week 3:** *Senses at the Seashore* **Unit 2, Week 1:** *The Handiest Things in the World* **Unit 2, Week 2:** *Shapes All Around* **Unit 2, Week 3:** *I Love Bugs!* **Unit 3, Week 2:** *A Grand Old Tree* **Unit 3, Week 3:** *An Orange in January* **Unit 5, Week 1:** *My Garden* **Unit 6, Week 1:** *Mama, Is It Summer Yet?* **Unit 8, Week 2:** *Ana Goes to Washington, D.C.* **INTERACTIVE READ-ALOUD CARDS: Unit 1, Week 1:** "The Lion and the Mouse" **Unit 1, Week 2:** "The Tortoise and the Hare" **Unit 1, Week 3:** "A Feast of the Senses" **Unit 2, Week 1:** "Timimoto" **Unit 2, Week 2:** "Kites in Flight" **Unit 2, Week 3:** "From Caterpillar to Butterfly" **Unit 3, Week 1:** "The Boy Who Cried Wolf" **Unit 3, Week 2:** "The Turtle and the Flute" **Unit 3, Week 3:** "Field Trips" **Unit 4, Week 1:** "Little Juan and the Cooking Pot" **Unit 4, Week 2:** "Cultural Festivals" **Unit 4, Week 3:** "The Bundle of Sticks" **Unit 5, Week 1:** "Growing Plants" **Unit 7, Week 2:** "The Family Pet"

College and Career Readiness Anchor Standards for LANGUAGE

The K–5 standards on the following pages define what students should understand and be able to do by the end of each grade. They correspond to the College and Career Readiness (CCR) anchor standards below by number. The CCR and grade-specific standards are necessary complements—the former providing broad standards, the latter providing additional specificity—that together define the skills and understandings that all students must demonstrate.

Conventions of Standard English

1. Demonstrate command of the conventions of standard English grammar and usage when writing or speaking.

2. Demonstrate command of the conventions of standard English capitalization, punctuation, and spelling when writing.

Knowledge of Language

3. Apply knowledge of language to understand how language functions in different contexts, to make effective choices for meaning or style, and to comprehend more fully when reading or listening.

Vocabulary Acquisition and Use

4. Determine or clarify the meaning of unknown and multiple-meaning words and phrases by using context clues, analyzing meaningful word parts, and consulting general and specialized reference materials, as appropriate.

5. Demonstrate understanding of figurative language, word relationships, and nuances in word meanings.

6. Acquire and use accurately a range of general academic and domain-specific words and phrases sufficient for reading, writing, speaking, and listening at the college and career readiness level; demonstrate independence in gathering vocabulary knowledge when encountering an unknown term important to comprehension or expression.

CCSS Common Core State Standards
English Language Arts

Grade K

Language Standards

Conventions of Standard English		McGraw-Hill Reading Wonders
L.K.1	Demonstrate command of the conventions of standard English grammar and usage when writing or speaking.	**TEACHER'S EDITION: Unit 1:** T16, T19, T32-33, T41, T36, T98, T101, T114-115, T122-123, T125, T133, T141, T165, T180, T183, T197, T205, T214-215, T223, T247 **Unit 2:** T16, T18-19, T32-33, T40-41, T50-51, T59, T83, T98, T101, T115, T123, T133, T141, T165, T180, T183, T185, T197, T205, T215, T223 **Unit 3:** T16, T98, T180, T183, T197, T215 **Unit 4:** T16, T18-19, T32-33, T40-41, T47, T51, T59, T98, T101, T114-115, T122-123, T129, T133, T139, T141, T180, T182-183, T196-197, T204-205, T211, T215, T221, T223 **Unit 5:** T16, T21, T43, T83, T98, T103, T180, T196, T247 **Unit 6:** T16, T19, T33, T41, T44, T47, T51, T53, T59, T83, T98, T101, T114, T115, T123, T129, T133, T141, T180, T183, T185, T197, T205, T207, T211, T215, T223, T247 **Unit 7:** T16, T19, T33, T41, T47, T51, T83, T98, T114-115, T123, T129, T133, T139, T141, T165, T180, T182, T183, T196, T197, T204-205, T211, T215, T223, T247 **Unit 8:** T16, T19, T21, T33, T41, T47, T50-51, T83, T98, T101, T115, T123, T129, T133, T141, T180, T182-183, T196-197, T205, T211, T215, T223 **Unit 9:** T16, T19, T21, T32-33, T41, T47, T51, T59, T83, T98, T101, T103, T114-115, T123, T133, T141, T165, T129, T180, T183, T185, T197, T205, T211, T215, T223, T247 **Unit 10:** T16, T21, T34, T42, T49, T85, T100, T131, T182, T187, T198, T213, T249
L.K.1a	Print many upper- and lowercase letters.	**TEACHER'S EDITION: Unit 1:** T16, T98, T180 **Unit 2:** T16, T98, T180 **Unit 3:** T16, T98, T180 **Unit 4:** T16, T47, T98, T129, T139, T180, T211, T221 **Unit 5:** T16, T98, T180 **Unit 6:** T16, T47, T98, T129, T180, T211 **Unit 7:** T16, T47, T98, T129, T139, T180, T211 **Unit 8:** T16, T47, T98, T129, T180, T211 **Unit 9:** T16, T47, T98, T129, T180, T211 **Unit 10:** T16, T49, T100, T131, T182, T213 **YOUR TURN PRACTICE BOOK:** 34, 42, 50, 58, 66, 76, 84, 92, 100, 108, 116, 126, 134, 142, 152, 162, 172, 184, 192, 202, 212, 222, 232, 244, 252, 260, 268, 276, 284
L.K.1b	Use frequently occurring nouns and verbs.	**TEACHER'S EDITION: Unit 1:** T19, T32-33, T41, T36, T101, T114-115, T122-123, T125, T133, T141, T165, T183, T197, T205, T214-215, T223, T247 **Unit 2:** T18-19, T32-33, T40-41, T50-51, T59, T83, T101, T115, T123, T133, T141, T165, T183, T185, T197, T205, T215, T223 **Unit 5:** T103 **Unit 6:** T19, T33, T44, T51, T53, T83, T114, T223, T247 **Unit 7:** T19, T33, T41, T51, T83, T114-115, T123, T133, T141, T165, T183, T197, T205, T215, T223, T247 **Unit 8:** T10, T18, T114, T115 **Unit 9:** T21, T103, T185 **Unit 10:** T187 **YOUR TURN PRACTICE BOOK:** 23, 41, 65, 73, 83, 107, 115, 141, 151, 161, 191, 201, 211, 221, 241, 251, 259, 267, 295
L.K.1c	Form regular plural nouns orally by adding /s/ or /es/ (e.g., *dog, dogs; wish, wishes*).	**TEACHER'S EDITION: Unit 5:** T21, T43 **Unit 6:** T33, T41, T51, T59, T101, T115, T123, T133, T141, T183, T197, T205, T215
L.K.1d	Understand and use question words (interrogatives) (e.g., *who, what, where, when, why, how*).	**TEACHER'S EDITION: Unit 3:** T183, T197, T215 **Unit 6:** T185, T207 **Unit 7:** T182, T196, T204-205 **Unit 9:** T103, T125 **Unit 10:** T21
L.K.1e	Use the most frequently occurring prepositions (e.g., *to, from, in, out, on, off, for, of, by, with*).	**TEACHER'S EDITION: Unit 3:** T29, T47 **Unit 5:** T193, T211 **Unit 7:** T29, T47 **Unit 8:** T19, T33, T41, T50-51, T83, T101, T115, T123, T133, T141, T183, T197, T205, T223
L.K.1f	Produce and expand complete sentences in shared language activities.	**TEACHER'S EDITION: Unit 4:** T18-19, T32-33, T40-41, T51, T59, T101, T114-115, T122-123, T133, T141, T182-183, T196-197, T204-205, T215, T223 **Unit 5:** T83, T196, T247 **Unit 8:** T182-183, T196-197, T215, T223; **Unit 9:** T19, T32-33, T41, T51, T59, T83, T101, T114-115, T123, T133, T141, T165, T183, T197, T205, T215, T223, T247 **Unit 10:** T34, T42, T85, T198, T249

Language Standards

Conventions of Standard English		McGraw-Hill Reading Wonders
L.K.2	Demonstrate command of the conventions of standard English capitalization, punctuation, and spelling when writing.	**TEACHER'S EDITION:** Unit 1: T16, T72, T129, T211, T221 Unit 2: T47, T57, T129, T139, T211, T221 Unit 3: T19, T47, T50-51, T53, T57, T59, T83, T101, T115, T120, T123, T132-133, T139, T141, T183, T196-197, T205, T211, T214-215, T221, T223, T247 Unit 4: T16, T47, T57, T98, T129, T139, T211, T221 Unit 5: T16, T47, T57, T98, T101, T115, T123, T139, T180, T211, T221 Unit 6: T12, T16, T47, T57, T98, T129, T139, T176, T211, T221 Unit 7: T16, T47, T57, T98, T129, T139, T180, T211, T214, T221 Unit 8: T16, T32, T47, T98, T101, T114, T129, T132, T164, T211, T221 Unit 9: T47, T129, T211 Unit 10: T49, T53, T103, T116, T131, T213, T216
L.K.2a	Capitalize the first word in a sentence and the pronoun *I*.	**TEACHER'S EDITION:** Unit 3: T19, T50-51, T53, T59, T83, T115, T123, T132-133, T197, T223 Unit 5: T101, T115, T123 Unit 8: T32, T101, T114, T132 Unit 10: T53, T103, T116, T216
L.K.2b	Recognize and name end punctuation.	**TEACHER'S EDITION:** Unit 3: T101, T115, T123, T132-133, T141, T183, T196-197, T205, T214-215, T223, T247 Unit 6: T12, T176 Unit 7: T214 Unit 8: T32, T101, T114, T132, T164
L.K.2c	Write a letter or letters for most consonant and short-vowel sounds (phonemes).	**TEACHER'S EDITION:** Unit 1: T16, T72, T129, T211 Unit 2: T47, T129, T211 Unit 3: T47, T120, T211 Unit 4: T16, T47, T98, T129, T139, T211, T221 Unit 5: T16, T47, T98, T180, T211 Unit 6: T16, T47, T98, T129, T211 Unit 7: T16, T47, T57, T98, T129, T139, T180, T211 Unit 8: T16, T47, T98, T129, T211 Unit 9: T47, T129, T211 Unit 10: T49, T131, T213 **YOUR TURN PRACTICE BOOK:** 34, 42, 50, 58, 51-52, 62, 66, 76, 84, 85, 86, 88, 92, 100, 104, 108, 116, 126, 130, 134, 138, 142, 148, 158, 162, 164-165, 168, 172, 192, 202, 212, 222, 232 **PHONICS AND WORD STUDY WORKSTATION ACTIVITY CARDS:** 1, 2, 3, 4, 5, 6, 7, 8, 9, 10, 11, 12, 13, 14, 15, 16, 17, 18, 19, 20, 21, 22, 23, 24
L.K.2d	Spell simple words phonetically, drawing on knowledge of sound-letter relationships.	**TEACHER'S EDITION:** Unit 1: T221 Unit 2: T57, T139, T221 Unit 3: T57, T139, T221 Unit 4: T47, T57, T129, T139, T211, T221 Unit 5: T57, T139, T221 Unit 6: T57, T139, T221 Unit 7: T47, T57, T129, T139, T211, T221 Unit 8: T47, T129, T139, T211, T221 **YOUR TURN PRACTICE BOOK:** 30, 38, 46, 54, 62, 74, 75, 80, 88, 96, 104, 112, 124, 125, 130, 138, 148, 158, 168, 182, 183, 188, 198, 208, 228, 242, 243, 256, 264, 272, 280, 293, 294
Knowledge of Language		**McGraw-Hill Reading Wonders**
L.K.3	(Begins in grade 2.)	
Vocabulary Acquisition and Use		**McGraw-Hill Reading Wonders**
L.K.4	Determine or clarify the meaning of unknown and multiple-meaning words and phrases based on *kindergarten reading and content*.	**TEACHER'S EDITION:** Unit 4: T127 Unit 5: T45, T46, T108, T187 Unit 6: T21, T23, T33, T41 Unit 7: T24, T45, T189, T209 Unit 9: T21, T24, T25, T43, T185, T189, T207 Unit 10: T25, T187, T209
L.K.4a	Identify new meanings for familiar words and apply them accurately (e.g., knowing *duck* is a bird and learning the verb to *duck*).	**TEACHER'S EDITION:** Unit 5: T108, T185, T187 T207 Unit 6: T21, T189 Unit 7: T24, T45, T189 Unit 8: T21 Unit 9: T25, T45, T185, T207 Unit 10: T25, T47
L.K.4b	Use the most frequently occurring inflections and affixes (e.g., *-ed, -s, re-, un-, pre-, -ful, -less*) as a clue to the meaning of an unknown word.	**TEACHER'S EDITION:** Unit 5: T45, T46, T187 Unit 6: T23, T33, T41 Unit 9: T21, T24, T43, T189 Unit 10: T187, T209

Vocabulary Acquisition and Use		McGraw-Hill Reading Wonders
L.K.5	With guidance and support from adults, explore word relationships and nuances in word meanings.	**TEACHER'S EDITION: Unit 1:** T10-11, T34, T43 **Unit 2:** T10, T43, T103, T116, T125, T135, T175, T185, T207, T245 **Unit 3:** T10, T116, T175 **Unit 4:** T10-11, T12-13, T21, T34, T43, T44-45, T54, T67, T80, T81, T83, T92-93, T94-95, T103, T116, T125, T126-127, T133, T136, T141, T149, T165, T174-175, T176-177, T183, T185, T188, T198, T207, T208-209, T218, T231, T245, T247 **Unit 5:** T10-11, T12-13, T21, T34, T43, T54, T67, T80, T81, T92-93, T94-95, T116, T149, T174-175, T185, T195, T207, T218, T245 **Unit 6:** T10-11, T20, T34, T35, T42, T43, T44, T67, T81, T92-93, T103, T108, T116, T125, T126-127, T136, T149, T163, T174-175, T176-177, T185, T198, T208-209, T218, T231, T245 **Unit 7:** T10-11, T12-13, T21, T25, T34, T43, T54, T67, T81, T92-93, T94-95, T103, T116, T126-127, T136, T149, T163, T174-175, T185, T190, T207, T208-209, T218, T231, T245 **Unit 8:** T10-11, T12-13, T21, T23, T34, T43, T44-45, T54, T67, T81, T92-93, T94-95, T103, T116, T125, T126-127, T136, T149, T163, T174-175, T185, T198, T207, T208-209, T218, T231, T245 **Unit 9:** T10-11, T12-13, T34, T44-45, T54, T67, T81, T92-93, T103, T116, T126-127, T136, T149, T163, T174-175, T176-177, T185, T198, T207, T208-209, T218, T231, T245 **Unit 10:** T10-11, T25, T36, T46-47, T56, T69, T83, T94-95, T96-97, T105, T106-111, T118, T127, T128-129, T136-137, T138, T151, T165, T176-177, T178-179, T187, T189, T190, T200, T209, T210-211, T220, T233, T247
L.K.5a	Sort common objects into categories (e.g., shapes, foods) to gain a sense of the concepts the categories represent.	**TEACHER'S EDITION: Unit 2:** T43, T103, T125, T135 **Unit 4:** T103, T183 **Unit 5:** T21, T185, T207 **Unit 6:** T43 **Unit 8:** T43 **Unit 10:** T127, T129, T136-137
L.K.5b	Demonstrate understanding of frequently occurring verbs and adjectives by relating them to their opposites (antonyms).	**YOUR TURN PRACTICE BOOK:** 241, 283 **TEACHER'S EDITION: Unit 6:** T44 **Unit 7:** T25 **Unit 8:** T23, T185, T207 **Unit 9:** T189 **Unit 10:** T25, T105, T127, T189, T190
L.K.5c	Identify real-life connections between words and their use (e.g., note places at school that are colorful).	**READING/WRITING WORKSHOP: Unit 1:** Smart Start: 4-5, 22-23, 40-41; 6-7, 24-25, 42-43 **Unit 2:** 6-7, 24-25, 42-43 **Unit 3:** 6-7, 24-25, 42-43 **Unit 4:** 6-7, 20-21, 34-35 **Unit 5:** 6-7, 20-21, 34-35 **Unit 6:** 6-7, 20-21, 34-35 **Unit 7:** 6-7, 20-21, 34-35 **Unit 8:** 6-7, 20-21, 34-35 **Unit 9:** 6-7, 20-21, 34-35 **Unit 10:** 6-7, 20-21, 34-35 **YOUR TURN PRACTICE BOOK:** 23, 33, 41, 49, 57, 65, 73, 83, 107, 115, 133, 141, 151, 161, 171, 191, 201, 211, 221, 241, 251, 259, 267, 275, 283, 295 **TEACHER'S EDITION: Unit 1:** T10-11, T34, T43 **Unit 2:** T10, T116, T175 **Unit 3:** T10, T116, T175 **Unit 4:** T10-11, T12-13, T21, T34, T43, T44-45, T54, T67, T80, T81, T83, T92-93, T94-95, T103, T116, T125, T126-127, T133, T136, T141, T149, T165, T174-175, T176-177, T183, T185, T198, T207, T208-209, T218, T231, T245, T247 **Unit 5:** T10-11, T12-13, T21, T34, T43, T54, T67, T80, T81, T92-93, T94-95, T116, T149, T174-175, T185, T198, T218, T245 **Unit 6:** T10-11, T20, T34, T35, T42, T67, T81, T92-93, T103, T116, T125, T126-127, T136, T149, T163, T174-175, T176-177, T185, T198, T208-209, T218, T231, T245 **Unit 7:** T10-11, T12-13, T21, T25, T34, T43, T54, T67, T81, T92-93, T94-95, T103, T116, T126-127, T136, T149, T163, T174-175, T185, T207, T208-209, T218, T231, T245 **Unit 8:** T10-11, T34, T81, T92-93, T102, T116, T124, T136, T149, T163, T174-175, T185, T198, T207, T208-209, T218, T231, T245 **Unit 9:** T10-11, T12-13, T20, T34, T42-43, T54, T67, T92-93, T103, T116-117, T124-125, T136, T149, T174-175, T176-177, T185, T198, T206-207, T218, T231 **Unit 10:** T10-11, T25, T36, T46-47, T56, T69, T83, T94-95, T96-97, T106-111, T118, T128-129, T138, T151, T165, T176-177, T178-179, T187, T190, T200, T209, T210-211, T220, T233, T247 **INTERACTIVE READ-ALOUD CARDS: SS:** "The Ugly Duckling", "Kindergarteners Can!", "Tikki Tikki Tembo" **Unit 1, Week 1:** "The Lion and the Mouse" **Unit 1, Week 2:** "The Tortoise and the Hare" **Unit 2, Week 3:** "From Caterpillar to Butterfly" **Unit 3, Week 2:** "The Turtle and the Flute" **Unit 4, Week 1:** "Little Juan and the Cooking Pot" **Unit 4, Week 2:** "Cultural Festivals" **Unit 4, Week 3:** "A Bundle of Sticks" **Unit 6, Week 3:** "Rainbow Crow" **Unit 7, Week 3:** "Anansi: An African Tale" **Unit 9, Week 2:** "The Little Red Hen" **Unit 9, Week 3:** "Spider Woman Teaches the Navajo" **Unit 10, Week 1:** "The Elves and the Shoemakers" **ConnectED Digital Resources:** Visual Glossary

Language Standards

Vocabulary Acquisition and Use		*McGraw-Hill Reading Wonders*
L.K.5d	Distinguish shades of meaning among verbs describing the same general action (e.g., *walk, march, strut, prance*) by acting out the meanings.	**TEACHER'S EDITION:** Unit 2: T185, T207, T245 **Unit 4:** T188 **Unit 6:** T35, T108 **Unit 7:** T185, T190, T207
L.K.6	Use words and phrases acquired through conversations, reading and being read to, and responding to texts.	**READING/WRITING WORKSHOP:** Smart Start: 4-5, 22-23, 40-41 **Unit 1:** 6-7, 24-25, 42-43 **Unit 2:** 6-7, 24-25, 42-43 **Unit 3:** 6-7, 24-25, 42-43 **Unit 4:** 6-7, 20-21, 34-35 **Unit 5:** 6-7, 20-21, 34-35 **Unit 6:** 6-7, 20-21, 34-35 **Unit 7:** 6-7, 20-21, 34-35 **Unit 8:** 6-7, 20-21, 34-35 **Unit 9:** 6-7, 20-21, 34-35 **Unit 10:** 6-7, 20-21, 34-35 **TEACHER'S EDITION: Unit 1:** S26, S34, S44 **Unit 2:** T20-21, T93, T198 **Unit 3:** T20, T93, T198 **Unit 4:** T10-11, T12-13, T20-21, T22-27, T34, T42-43, T44-45, T54-55, T67, T80, T81, T92-93, T94-95, T176-177, T184-185, T186-191, T198, T205, T206-207, T208-209, T215, T218-219, T223, T218-219, T231, T244, T245 **Unit 5:** T10-11, T12-13, T20-21, T22-27, T34, T42-43, T44-45, T54-55 , T117, T162-163, T174-175, T176-177, T184-185, T186-191, T198, T199, T206-207, T208-209, T218-219, T231, T244-245 **Unit 6:** T10-11, T20-21, T34-35, T42-43, T44-45, T54-55, T67, T80, T81, T92-93, T94-95, T102-103, T104-109, T116, T124-125, T126-127, T136-137, T149, T231, T244 **Unit 7:** T10-11, T12-13, T20-21, T22-27, T34-35, T42-43, T44-45, T54-55, T67, T80, T81, T92-93, T94-95, T102-103, T104-109, T116, T124-125, T126-127, T136-137, T149, T231, T244, T245 **Unit 8:** T10-11, T12-13, T20-21, T22-27, T34-35, T42-43, T44-45, T54-55, T67, T80, T81, T92-93, T94-95, T102-103, T104-109, T116, T124-125, T126-127, T136-137, T149, T231, T244, T245 **Unit 9:** T10-11, T12-13, T20-21, T22-27, T34-35, T42-43, T44-45, T54-55, T162, T163, T174-175, T176-177, T184-185, T186-191, T198, T199, T206-207, T208-209, T218-219, T231, T244, T245 **Unit 10:** T10-11, T12-13, T20-21, T22-29, T36, T44-45, T46-47, T56-57, T69, T82, T83, T94-95, T96-97, T104-105, T106-111, T118, T126-127, T128-129, T138-139, T151, T179, T233, T246, T247 **LITERATURE BIG BOOKS: Unit 1, Week 2:** *Pouch!* **Unit 2, Week 2:** *Shapes All Around* **Unit 2, Week 3:** *I Love Bugs!* **Unit 3, Week 1:** *How Do Dinosaurs Go to School?* **Unit 4, Week 1:** *Whose Shoes? A Shoe for Every Job* **Unit 4, Week 2:** *What Can You Do with a Paleta?* **Unit 5, Week 2:** *A Grand Old Tree* **Unit 5, Week 3:** *An Orange in January* **Unit 6, Week 1:** *Mama, Is It Summer Yet?* **Unit 7, Week 1:** *ZooBorns!* **Unit 7, Week 2:** *The Birthday Pet* **Unit 8, Week 2:** *Ana Goes to Washington, D.C.* **Unit 8, Week 3:** *Bringing Down the Moon* **Unit 9, Week 3:** *Bread Comes to Life* **Unit 10, Week 1:** *What's the Big Idea, Molly?* **Unit 10, Week 2:** *All Kinds of Families!* **INTERACTIVE READ-ALOUD CARDS: SS:** "The Ugly Duckling", "Kindergarteners Can!", "Tikki Tikki Tembo" **Unit 1, Week 1:** "The Lion and the Mouse" **Unit 1, Week 2:** "The Tortoise and the Hare" **Unit 2, Week 3:** "From Caterpillar to Butterfly" **Unit 3, Week 2:** "The Turtle and the Flute" **Unit 4, Week 1:** "Little Juan and the Cooking Pot" **Unit 4, Week 2:** "Cultural Festivals" **Unit 4, Week 3:** "A Bundle of Sticks" **Unit 6, Week 3:** "Rainbow Crow" **Unit 7, Week 3:** "Anansi: An African Tale" **Unit 9, Week 2:** "The Little Red Hen" **Unit 9, Week 3:** "Spider Woman Teaches the Navajo" **Unit 10, Week 1:** "The Elves and the Shoemakers"